52/-

PA 8-67

BARRIERS
to NEW COMPETITION

BARRIERS
to NEW COMPETITION

*Their Character and Consequences
in Manufacturing Industries*

JOE S. BAIN

HARVARD UNIVERSITY PRESS · CAMBRIDGE

1965

Distributed in Great Britain by
Oxford University Press, London

Library of Congress Catalog Card Number 56–11278

Printed in the United States of America

PREFACE

For about twenty years students of business competition have been trying to answer an important question: to what extent is the market performance of firms determined by the market structures of their industries? For example, are dimensions of performance like profit rates and relative efficiency in production systematically linked with dimensions of market structure like the degree of seller concentration and the extent of product differentiation within an industry?

The questions posed in such inquiry have in the main not been the postulates of free-lance empiricists, but rather certain hypotheses stated or suggested by economic theory — particularly Chamberlinian and post-Chamberlinian price theory. In a sense, therefore, this empirical work has been devoted to testing the predictions of a systematic *a priori* theory. In another sense more has been involved, since before conducting an experiment, the student in general has first had to elaborate or develop the received *a priori* theory, which has often been rudimentary or inchoate, and to state the hypotheses expressed or implied in the theory in a form which would make them practically susceptible to empirical test. Thus, the "designing of experiments" is a crucial step in such empirical research.

A particular sort of experimental design is represented in the testing for associations between market structure and performance. One group of the predictions of price theory is singled out, elaborated, and stated in a form suitable for confrontation with available evidence. The search for these structure-performance links, stimulated in very important part by the early insights of Edward S. Mason, seems worth continuing not only because the testing of theory with objective empirical data is here actually possible, but also because a knowledge of these links is useful in formulating public policies toward monopoly and competition in business.

The present work reports on a modest effort in the continuing endeavor to ascertain the extent and character of the association of industrial market structures to market performance. It concerns the nature and the effects of one potentially strategic dimension of market structure — the "condition of entry," or the relative ease or difficulty of entry of new competitors to an industry. In other terms, it seeks to measure the varying force among industries of "potential" competition, or threatened new entry, and to inquire whether and in what way variations in this force influence the market performance of established firms. Such novelty as the work possesses is largely in its extended emphasis on this particular aspect of market structure; although in earlier studies the degrees of seller and of buyer concentration have received considerable attention as potential determinants of market performance, up to now we have lacked any detailed empirical inquiry into the character and consequences of conditions of entry to our industries.

As in comparable endeavors of this sort, it was necessary before beginning empirical study to develop and elaborate an *a priori* theory which had been received in extremely rudimentary form. The condition of entry had to be given a more complete and general definition, and an adequate set of hypotheses had to be deduced concerning its effects on performance. I had sketched out such a theory in a paper for the Talloires conference of the International Economic Association in 1951, and in the first chapter here I present a simplified summary of that theory.

Thereafter, the procedure was straightforward and empirical, involving attempts first to measure the condition of entry for a selected sample of industries and second to ascertain the extent of the association of the condition of entry to market performance. It has been possible for the moment to pursue the first task further than the second. The character and relative importance of various impediments to entry have been examined in some detail, as have been the heights of the aggregate barriers to entry to the various industries. But as to the associations of the condition of entry to performance, it has been feasible in the main only to conduct some rather rudimentary tests involving profit margins and efficiency of market organization as aspects of market performance. Findings on structure-performance links are thus incomplete and quite tentative, and much more needs to be done both in analyzing larger samples of industries and in developing further data on performance.

The method of empirical analysis employed might be characterized as cross-sectional; that is, a substantial sample of industries has been examined with respect largely to a single dimension of market structure and a few dimensions of market performance. So far as empirical confirmation or disconfirmation of theoretical hypotheses is sought, this approach is evidently superior to that of the intensive study of all aspects of structure and performance in an individual industry. For no matter how firmly one may believe that market structure determines performance, he can never really demonstrate that this is true from a single instance (or a very few); given the character of the data and the essential lack of laboratory conditions for their control, a basically statistical analysis and comparison of numerous cases is required. However, a true multivariate cross-sectional analysis — involving numerous dimensions of both

structure and performance — would be more satisfactory than what we
have been able to develop here. Some crude cross-classification tests involving both seller concentration and the condition of entry as determinants of performance are about as much as the currently available data
have permitted.

Because it has been impossible to carry tests for the association of
the condition of entry to performance very far, the major contribution
to economic information contained below may well be that of developing
data on the character of the condition of entry and its determinants, with
particular reference to manufacturing industries. Drawing both on various
documentary material and on information secured from numerous firms,
I have attempted to develop measures both of the height of barriers to
entry to such industries and of the absolute and relative importance of
specific sorts of barrier, such as economies of large-scale production,
product differentiation, and "absolute" impediments like patents and
resource ownership. These data are tabulated and briefly summarized in
Chapters 3 through 6. Intensive students of industrial organization will
probably wish to refer to supporting materials concerning individual
industries, contained in Appendixes B, C, and D. Those interested in
the problem of scale economies *per se* should refer especially to Chapter 3
and Appendixes B and C.

Concerning all empirical findings on the condition of entry, it may be
said first that they rest heavily on various estimates obtained from business
executives in response to questions concerning relevant conditions and
phenomena in their industries. (Techniques of interrogation and the
character of responses are discussed in Chapter 2.) Generally, these
estimates refer to the period around 1951 or 1952, when they were obtained. They are supported by data from documents and other published
sources, and these refer usually to the 1940's, although occasionally to
somewhat earlier periods. Drawing upon all data, the writer has endeavored to characterize the condition of entry to each industry as it
was approximately at the beginning of the 1950's, and no systematic attempt has been made to bring findings up to date as of 1956. Various
possibly relevant changes have occurred in some industries since 1951 or
1952. But conditions of entry seem from observation to be stable enough
so that our findings concerning them, at least in their broad and strategic
aspects, are in general reasonably applicable to market situations of the
present and near future.

Acknowledgements of specific sources of data are contained in the text
and appendixes that follow, although direct industry sources are not
acknowledged because in most cases they supplied information with the
understanding that the source would not be revealed. This necessary
omission in no way reflects any deficiency in gratitude for the indis-

pensable assistance rendered, or in admiration for the excellent analyses of relevant matters offered by many who cooperated. As to summarizations of data in this volume, from both acknowledged and unacknowledged sources, what appears as "findings" frequently reflects not only the raw data received but also my processing and interpretation of these data; thus, I frequently share responsibility for the factual accuracy of the findings. Those who cooperated by supplying data have not been requested to validate the conclusions drawn from them.

I would like to express my gratitude for the generous support of this study by the Merrill Foundation, provided through the grant to the Research Group on Monopoly Policy at Harvard University, as directed by Dean Edward S. Mason. As members of the group, both Dean Mason and Professor Carl Kaysen were sources of valued advice and counsel as the study progressed, and made numerous helpful suggestions for revision of the initial draft of the study. I am, however, solely responsible for the design of the study, the interpretation of all data, and the views expressed.

Joe S. Bain

Berkeley, California
April, 1956

CONTENTS

1 THE IMPORTANCE OF THE CONDITION OF ENTRY   1

2 THE CONTENT AND ORGANIZATION of the Study   42

3 ECONOMIES OF LARGE SCALE as Barriers to Entry   53

4 PRODUCT DIFFERENTIATION ADVANTAGES of Established Firms as Barriers to Entry   114

5 ABSOLUTE COST ADVANTAGES of Established Firms as Barriers to Entry   144

6 THE OVER-ALL BARRIERS TO ENTRY, and Theory as to their Consequences   167

7 EMPIRICAL EVIDENCE OF THE MARKET PER-FORMANCE in Industries under Various Conditions of Entry   182

8 THE CONDITION OF ENTRY AND THE PUBLIC POLICY Designed to Secure Workable Competition   205

APPENDICES

A Examples of Individual-Industry Questionnaires   223
B Economies of Large Plants: Supplementary Data   227
C Economies of Large Firms: Supplementary Data   250
D Product-Differentiation Barriers to Entry in Individual Industries   263

WORKS CITED   319

INDEX   323

TABLES

I. Composition of the Sample of 20 Manufacturing Industries, and Some Significant Characteristics of Each — 45

II. Classification of 18 Census Industries According to Percentages of Industry Values Added, Supplied by the Largest Plants, 1947 — 70

III. Proportions of National Industry Capacity Contained in Single Plants of Most Efficient Scale, for 20 Industries, per Engineering Estimates, Circa 1951 — 72

IV. Classification of 20 Industries According to Percentages of National Industry Capacities Contained in Single Plants of Most Efficient Scale — 73

V. Proportion of National Industry Capacity and of Specified Submarket Capacities Contained in Single Plants of Most Efficient Scale, for 12 Industries Affected by Market Segmentation, per Estimates Circa 1951 — 76

VI. Classification of 20 Industries by Percentages of Individual Market Capacities Contained in a Single Plant of Most Efficient Scale — 77

VII. Relationship of Relative Unit Costs to Plant Scale in 7 Manufacturing Industries — 80

VIII. Actual Sizes of Firms and Minimum Optimal Sizes of Plants, Expressed as Percentages of the National Industry Capacity or Output, in 20 Manufacturing Industries — 84

IX. The Extent of Estimated Economies of Multiplant Firms in 20 Manufacturing Industries — 86

X. Classification of 20 Industries According to the Influence of Product Differentiation on Intra-Industry Competition — 123

XI. Classification of 20 Industries According to Height of Barrier to Entry Created by Product Differentiation — 127

XII. Classification of Industries According to the Estimated Incidence of Economies of Sales Promotion to the Multiplant Firm — 137

XIII. Classification of Industries According to Capital Requirements for a Single Optimal Plant, and Related Information — 158

XIV. Summary of Relative Heights of Specific Entry Barriers in 20 Industries — 169

XV. Ranking of 20 Manufacturing Industries According to the Estimated Height of the Aggregate Barrier to Entry — 170

XVI. Profit Rates on Equity (after Income Taxes) for Dominant Firms in 20 Industries, 1936–40 and 1947–51 — 192

XVII. Number of Industries of "High" and of "Moderate to Low" Concentration Which Have Industry Average Profit Rates on Equity of Specified Sizes, 1936–40 and 1947–51 — 197

XVIII. Number of Industries with "Very High," "Substantial," and "Moderate to Low" Barriers to Entry Which Have Industry Average Profit Rates on Equity of Specified Sizes — 1936–40 and 1947–51 — 198

XIX. Number of Industries, All of High Seller Concentration, with "Very High," "Substantial," and "Moderate to Low" Barriers to Entry, Which Have Industry Average Profit Rates on Equity of Specified Sizes — 1936–40 and 1947–51 — 200

BARRIERS
to NEW COMPETITION

1

THE IMPORTANCE
OF THE CONDITION OF ENTRY

This book analyzes the character and significance of the "condition of entry" to manufacturing industries; it is based on an investigation of the force of latent competition from potential new sellers in twenty such industries in the United States.

The investigation was made because of two beliefs: (1) that most analyses of how business competition works and what makes it work have given little emphasis to the force of the potential or threatened competition of possible new competitors, placing a disproportionate emphasis on competition among firms already established in any industry; (2) that so far as economists have recognized the *possible* importance of this "condition of entry," they have no very good idea of how important it actually is.

If these are reasonable beliefs, it seems important to do two things — to develop systematic theory concerning the potential importance of the condition of entry as an influence on business conduct and performance, and to assess, in those ways that are open, the extent and nature of its actual importance. These are the main tasks of this book. In addition, we may read from our tentative findings some directions for the formulation of public policy toward business monopoly and competition. First, however, let us survey the facts and concepts which we are about to explore.

Actual competition versus the threat of entry

When competition is named as a regulator of enterprise outputs and prices, it is usually the competition among the firms already established in this or that industry which is emphasized. On the level of market conduct, detailed attention is given to whether the price-calculating policies of established firms are formulated independently or in the light of a "recognized interdependence" with each other, whether or not there is collusion among these firms, and the extent to which collusion, if found, is imperfect. On the level of market structure, much emphasis is placed on those characteristics of the industry that presumably influence competitive conduct as among established rivals, and particularly on the number and size distribution of these rival sellers and on the manner in which their products are differentiated from one another. The immediate competition among established firms gets most of the attention.

This is true both of abstract economic theory and of the empirical investigations which implement, test, or apply it. When conventional price theory treats the working of business competition, it devotes nearly all of its detailed analysis to the consequences of rivalry within various alternative conformations of established sellers, so much so that the effects of the actual or threatened entry of new sellers are generally mentioned, if at all, cryptically and almost as an afterthought. Similarly, empirical studies of market structure commonly center on seller concentration within established groups, product differentiation within these groups, and other determinants of the character of competition among established sellers. Most studies of individual industries refer, when discussing competition, almost entirely to rivalry among established firms.

Correspondingly, the condition of entry has generally received only nominal attention as a regulator of market conduct and performance. Typical versions of abstract price theory do recognize the long-run impact of an assumed "free" or "easy" entry of new firms to industries with many small sellers. But when they turn to the very important category of oligopolistic industries, they ordinarily fail to distinguish numerous possible alternative situations with respect to the condition of entry, and to identify and develop appropriate assumptions relative to the structural determinants of the condition of entry. They thus fail to offer any systematic predictions concerning the effect of variations in the condition of entry on the market conduct of established sellers and on industry performance in the long term. The theory of pricing in non-atomistic markets is generally too oversimplified to identify or distinguish potentially large and significant variations of behavior within the oligopolistic sector of industries.

Much empirical investigation of business structure and competition has followed the lead of abstract theory, and has been hindered by the fact that abstract theory provided few leads in the area of the condition of entry. Although investigations of the extent of existing seller concentration in various industries have become widespread in government agencies and elsewhere, measurement of the height and nature of barriers to entry has never been systematically undertaken. Studies of competitive conduct and performance have paid much attention to such matters as the role of the price leader in eliminating or canalizing competition among established sellers and in influencing the ultimate relation of price to cost in his industry, but ordinarily they have given much less attention to the extent to which established firms shape price policies in the light of their anticipation of new entry, by deciding whether or not to try to forestall it. In brief, neither the theoretically possible nor the actual significance of variations in the condition of entry has received much attention from economists.

A strong emphasis on actual competition among existing sellers is of course appropriate. Such competition, with its determinants, is most probably of first importance as a regulator of business activity. But the substantial neglect of the condition of entry is definitely unfortunate, since there is considerable evidence of the importance of the condition of entry as a co-regulator of business conduct and performance.

Let us understand the term "condition of entry" to an industry to mean something equivalent to the "state of potential competition" from possible new sellers. Let us view it moreover as evaluated roughly *by the advantages of established sellers in an industry over potential entrant sellers, these advantages being reflected in the extent to which established sellers can persistently raise their prices above a competitive level without attracting new firms to enter the industry.* As such, the "condition of entry" is then primarily a structural condition, determining in any industry the intra-industry adjustments which will and will not induce entry. Its reference to market conduct is primarily to potential rather than actual conduct, since basically it describes only the circumstances in which the potentiality of competition from new firms will or will not become actual. If we understand the condition of entry in this way, its possible importance as a determinant of competitive behavior is clear.

Conventional price theory has been quite explicit concerning the effects of one type of condition of entry — *free* or *easy* entry. It has deduced from reasonable premises the valid conclusion that in markets with many small sellers, easy entry in the long run will force price to equality with minimal average costs and will bring output to a level sufficient for supplying all demands at this price. When price theory has turned to markets with few sellers and to conditions of entry other than easy, it has ordinarily been inexplicit, cryptic, or silent. But relatively elementary elaborations of received theory make it clear that variations in the condition of entry as it departs from the "easy" pole may have a substantial influence on the performance of established firms in any industry.

Even in atomistically organized industries, barriers to entry may, under certain conditions, result in a long-term elevation of prices and profits and a restriction of output; if established firms are restricted in number and encounter diseconomies of scale, entry will operate to limit prices only after they exceed a certain super-competitive level. In oligopolistic industries, something additional is generally true. Each of the few large established sellers — whether they act collectively or singly — will appraise the condition of entry and, anticipating that entry may occur if price exceeds a given level, will regulate his price policies accordingly. There will thus be a sort of "recognized interdependence" of actions not only among established sellers but between established sellers and potential entrants. In this event, variations in the condition of entry may be expected to have substantial effects on the behavior of established sellers, *even though over long intervals actual entry seldom or never takes place*. Elementary extensions of the deductive logic of conventional price theory thus suggest an important role of the condition of entry, and emphasize the desirability of finding how much in fact it does vary from industry to industry.

Empirical observation reinforces the impression that the condition of entry may be an important determinant of market behavior, especially in the case of oligopolistic industries. Examination of any considerable number of concentrated industries reveals great differences in market conduct and performance among them, in spite of the fact that in each a recognized interdependence among established sellers definitely appears to be present. Variations in the degree of seller concentration or of product differentiation among oligopolies may explain a part of these differences in behavior, but not all of them. The other most evident structural variation among oligopolies is that of the condition of entry, and from casual observation this variation seems to be at least loosely associated with variations in behavior. A more systematic empirical study of the importance of the condition of entry is thus indicated.

The meaning of the condition of entry

As suggested above, the condition of entry is a structural concept. Like some other aspects of market structure, it may be viewed as potentially subject to quantitative evaluation in terms of a continuous variable. This variable is the percentage by which established firms can raise price above a specified competitive level without attracting new entry — a percentage which may vary continuously from zero to a very high figure, with entry becoming "more difficult" by small gradations as it does so. As the difficulty of entry (thus understood and evaluated) increases, some systematic variations in the behavior of established firms may be anticipated.

The preceding description is obviously unspecific in numerous details. On the ground that this is primarily an empirical study dealing with available data, and that we do not wish to fashion a precision instrument for use in ditch-digging, it does not seem profitable here to develop a very polished and detailed definition of the condition of entry. (The writer has taken some steps in that direction in an earlier article,[1] and even the moderate degree of detail and precision attempted there seems out of place in the present setting.) Nevertheless, it seems useful to be somewhat more explicit by simply stating, without a detailed theoretical discussion, what is to be understood by various terms and notions expressed or implied in the definition so far presented.

As stated, the condition of entry may be evaluated by the extent to which established sellers can persistently raise their prices above a competitive level without attracting new firms to enter the industry. The first term needing consideration is "attracting new firms to enter the industry." This implies some specific definition of the concept of *entry*, involving both the notion of the "new firm" and of the meaning of the verb "to enter." As a first approximation, entry of a new firm may be taken to mean here the combination of two events: (1) the establishment of an independent legal entity, new to the industry, as a producer therein; and (2) the concurrent building or introduction by the new firm of physical production capacity that was not used for production in the industry prior to the establishment of the new firm. An addition to industry capacity already in use, plus emergence of a firm new to the industry, are thus required.

This definition excludes two related events from the concept of "entry." The first is the acquisition of existing producing capacity by a new legal entity, whether by purchase from a preëxisting firm, by reorganization involving a change of corporate name and structure, or through other means. Simple change of ownership or control of existing operating capacity is not considered as entry. The second exclusion is the expansion of capacity by an established firm. If, for example, a small established firm doubles its capacity, this is to be considered as a phase of competition among established firms rather than an act of entry. Growth of an already established rival firm in an industry is thus not considered as entry to that industry. Both of these exclusions are in some degree arbitrary, since the introduction of a new owner of old capacity may constitute a distinct change in a competitive situation, and since expansion of an established competitor may, from the standpoint of another established firm, have about the same significance as entry of a new firm with new capacity. Nevertheless, present purposes call for distinguishing competition among established competitors from the entry of new competitors, and we thus draw the lines indicated. As we proceed, we will have occasion to refer to the significance of events closely related to entry as defined.

Given these exclusions, a firm new to the industry may enter that industry by building new capacity to produce, by converting for use in

---

[1] See J. S. Bain, "Conditions of Entry and the Emergence of Monopoly," *Monopoly and Competition and Their Regulation,* edited by E. H. Chamberlin (London, 1954), pp. 215–241.

this industry plants previously used in another industry, or by reactivating capacity that has been previously used in the instant industry but is currently idle. Any of these acts by a new firm, singly or in combination, will constitute entry, according to the definition, and will continue to do so, even though the new firm also acquires operating capacity from an already established firm. Acquisition of a going concern by a new firm, together with expansion of the facilities of the going concern, thus constitutes entry to the extent of the expansion. Detailed implementation of this definition would require further specifications, such as the duration of the idleness required to distinguish "idle" plant from "operating" plant, but from the preceding the general intent of our definition should be clear.

Thus we see that the condition of entry may be evaluated by the degree to which established firms can raise their prices above a competitive level without inducing new firms to bring added capacity into use in the industry. How many new firms or how big? For the moment we may say "one or more" new firms and "any size," although we will treat the subject directly when we consider the difference between the *immediate* and the *general* condition of entry.

The second crucial concept is the "competitive level of prices," which, by definition, established firms may exceed more and more *without attracting entry* as the condition of entry becomes progressively more difficult. The "competitive level of prices" is defined here as the minimum attainable average cost of production, distribution, and selling for the good in question, such cost being measured to include a normal interest return on investment in the enterprise.

In effect, this is equivalent to the level of price hypothetically attributed to long-run equilibrium in pure competition. If equilibrium were of the stationary sort frequently described in theory textbooks, in which each firm produced regularly and uninterruptedly at its most efficient output, then this competitive price would equal the minimum attainable average cost (interest returns included) for the most efficient scale of firm when its capacity is always utilized at the optimal rate. In actual situations, where demand is unstable and uncertain and equilibrium is necessarily an adjustment to an average of varying situations over time, the competitive level of price and cost is elevated sufficiently to cover, for the most efficient scale of firm, the added costs of resulting periodic deviations from an optimal rate of utilization, and those coming from unavoidable errors in estimates of future demands, costs, and the like.[2]

---

[2] Minimal costs as defined presuppose the use of optimal available production techniques. Where product differentiation and sales promotion are encountered, such costs also include sales-promotion costs as incurred according to profit-maximizing criteria. The distinction between the lowest attainable average cost for the firm (supposedly attained in purely competitive long-run equilibrium) and the close approximation to that lowest cost supposedly attained in equilibrium in monopolistic

This competitive or minimum-cost level of price is a useful reference point for evaluating the condition of entry. Completely easy or unimpeded entry involves the inability of established firms to raise price above this level at all — persistently or on the average through time — without attracting new entry. If price may persistently exceed this level at all without inducing entry, then entry is somewhat impeded. The greater the persistent percentage excess attainable without inducing entry, the more difficult entry may be said to be.

It will be noted that this measure of the condition of entry refers to an independently defined standard of cost and not necessarily to the actual costs of firms established in the industry. It thus is a measure not simply of the profit margins they are able to establish without inducing entry, but rather of the margin between an entry-inducing price and minimal competitive costs as defined. There will tend to be a direct relationship between the two margins. But it is quite possible, for example, that in an industry where price could be substantially elevated above a competitive level without inducing entry, profits could nevertheless be absent because established firms were built to inefficient sizes.

A third term that must be considered is "persistently." We refer for our measure to the height of price which can be *persistently* attained by established sellers without inducing entry. This condition is inserted deliberately to give a long-run and structural aspect to our definition of the condition of entry, rather than to make it merely reflect transitory and varying short-term conditions from year to year. By a persistent elevation of price relative to a competitive level, therefore, we mean one maintained on the average over a substantial period of time, long enough to encompass a typical range of varying conditions of demand, factor prices, and the like. Such a period might normally be thought of as five or ten years. The definition thus refers, in brief, to the average relationship of the actual with a competitive price that can be maintained over a number of years without attracting entry. The relationship to entry of the short-run level of price — set only for a few months or year, for example — is deliberately neglected as erratic and without much significance in most industries.

We turn now to a very necessary elaboration of our definition of the condition of entry, designed to take into account (1) differences among established firms in an industry, and (2) differences among potential entrant firms. So far, we have referred to all established firms in an industry as an aggregate, and to entrant firms without reference to their number

---

competition will be neglected in defining minimal cost throughout the following discussion. Hypothetically, the basic minimal cost level from which the condition of entry is measured should refer alternatively to the two levels, depending upon whether or not product differentiation is present.

or identity. In so doing, we have spoken as if generally all established firms in an industry would charge a single price and have a single common competitive level of price or of minimum cost. Also, we have not recognized the existence or consequences of possible cost and other differences among potential entrant firms. Although both suppositions could be adopted for purposes of simplified theorizing, neither will be supported by fact, and thus it is necessary to elaborate the definition.

With respect to established firms, the complications are two. There may be a type of differentiation among their products which supports some system of differentials among their prices, so that actually they will at no time charge a single common price but rather maintain a certain regimen of different prices. And they may have somewhat different minimal costs to be used in defining the "competitive" level of price, since there may be quality differences among their products or differential advantages in cost. In view of these cost and price differences, then, how do we define the maximum excess of price over competitive cost at which entry may be forestalled?

There is no simple answer, since existence of the sort of cost and price differences noted actually means that the condition of entry to an industry has become intrinsically a more complicated concept and cannot be fully measured by any single firm's difference between an actual and a competitive price. It could be measured fully only through an array of individual differences for all individual firms — i.e., margins of actual prices above minimal costs — which would be encountered when all firms had concurrently raised their prices just short of the point that would induce new entry. Since this theoretically satisfactory procedure of complex measurement is not practically useful, an arbitrary simplification is required.

We will tentatively suggest that, where interfirm differences exist within the industry, the condition of entry may be conveniently evaluated in the following terms. First, the relevant gap between price and minimal cost (just short of that sufficient to induce entry) will be the one encountered when all established firms elevate their prices concurrently by similar amounts or proportions, maintaining any customary competitive price differentials. (It will not refer to gaps associated with isolated hypothetical price increases by one or a few firms, since these would be relatively uninteresting.) Second, the condition of entry may then be measured specifically as the maximum gap between price and minimal cost at which entry may be forestalled, for the most favored established firm or firms in the industry, supposing concurrent price elevations by all established firms. (The "most favored firm" may be identified as that with the largest price-minimal cost gap.) This single measure may be elaborated by any information revealing a significantly different gap for other established firms. Closer or more elaborate approximations seem unlikely to be implemented with data that are or can be made available.

Our next problem concerns differences among potential entrant firms. The condition of entry is measured by the long-run gap between minimal cost and price which the most favored firms can reach without attracting entry — but whose entry and how much? Do we assume that all entrants are alike and that there will be an unlimited and perfectly elastic supply of entrant firms if the entry-inducing gap is exceeded? If not, what do we assume about the number and size of entrants attracted as an entry-inducing gap is reached?

It is not realistic to assume that all potential entrants are alike either in their capacity to enter or with respect to the gap which will just induce them to enter. Nor can we assume that established firms are confronted by an indefinitely large supply of entrant firms if they exceed some critical price-to-minimal-cost gap. The more plausible assumptions are (1) that potential entrant firms may differ as to the gap which will induce them to enter, conceivably to the point where every potential entrant differs from every other in this respect; and (2) that any specific entry-inducing gap may induce only the entry of a finite number of firms. Then for any industry the condition of entry is fully measured only by a succession, within any range conceivably relevant to market behavior, of successively higher entry-inducing price-minimal cost gaps that will attract successive firms or groups of firms to enter the industry.

We may therefore establish two complementary concepts: *the immediate condition of entry* and *the general condition of entry*. The *immediate condition of entry* refers to the impediments to entry by the firm or firms that can most easily or readily be induced to enter the industry in a given situation. This immediate condition is evaluated by the long-run price-minimal cost gap (for the most favored established firms) which is just short of sufficient (just sufficient at the margin) to induce the entry of what we may call the most favored potential entrant or entrants. At any stage in its development, each industry has some immediate condition of entry thus defined and evaluated, although the number of potential entrant firms referred to by the measure could vary greatly from industry to industry.

The *general condition of entry* then refers to the succession of values of the immediate condition of entry as entry to the industry occurs — to the distribution of price-minimal cost gaps just necessary to induce successively less favored firms or groups of firms to enter an industry consecutively, beginning with the most favored firm. At any stage in its development, each industry has a general condition of entry in prospect (as well as one past, or one faced by various established firms before entering the industry), reflecting the succession of entry-inducing long-run price-minimal cost gaps at which successive increments to entry are expected to occur. At one extreme, this condition might be represented in the sustained repetition of a single value of the immediate condition of entry, reflecting in effect a perfectly elastic supply of entry. At the other, it might be represented in a series of different values each of which referred to the entry of only a single firm. In most cases, the general condition of entry to an industry should be expected *a priori* to lie between these two extremes.

If the condition of entry refers to the conditions for the inducement to entry of successive finite numbers of firms, it should also logically refer to the *size* of each entry, viewed either as realized *ex post* or anticipated *ex ante*. That is, a full measure of each *immediate* condition of entry (successions of which define the *general* condition) must include not only a measure of the long-run price-minimal cost gap for principal established firms necessary to induce some increment to entry, but also a measure of the long-run scale (attained *ex post* or expected to be attained *ex ante*) of the firms included in that increment. Such a measure of scale might be expressed as a percentage of total industry output. If the scale to be attained by entrants is a range of alternative values depending on the choice alternative policies open to established sellers, then the condition of entry is measured in part by such a range of values.

The last elaboration on the measure of the condition of entry represents a refinement of an order not very useful for application to actual data. Nevertheless, it may be possible in evaluating various conditions of entry to make some general appraisal of the comparative scales likely to be attained by potential entrants if they enter, and of the circumstances, if any, that would limit their sizes.

The preceding elaborations and definitions of terms should make the general meaning of the condition of entry to an industry sufficiently explicit for our purposes here. It refers to advantages which established firms in an industry have over potential entrant firms; it is evaluated in general by measures of the heights of entry-inducing prices relative to defined competitive levels. One major matter that has not received attention in this definition, however, concerns the "lags of entry," or time intervals consumed by entrants in making their entries effective.

Given any particular immediate condition of entry, as evaluated by some entry-inducing excess of price over a competitive level, there is still room for variation in the length of time an entrant firm requires to make its entry effective. For purposes of a first approximation we may say that entry is initiated when a new firm has taken more or less irrevocable steps to establish and use new capacity in an industry, and is completed when the firm has established and "broken in" all production and other facilities necessary to permit it to produce in routine fashion at its planned rate of output. The "lag period," then, is the time interval between these two dates, and may vary greatly from industry to industry. In the women's garment industry it might be only a few months; in the cement industry it might be a year or two; in the distilled liquor industry, more than four years would be required to develop aged stocks of whiskey.

The longer the lag period in question, the less influence any given threat of entry will be likely to have on established sellers. The fact that establishing a price at some given level may induce three new firms to enter the industry is more likely to deter established firms from setting so high a price if the entry will be made effective in six months than if it will be made effective in six years. The *effect* of any given condition of entry on market behavior will therefore be likely to vary with the length of the entry lags which accompany it.

Whether the "value" of the condition of entry should be modified to reflect the length of entry lags seems principally a semantic issue. Because there is logically no unique method of combining measures of an entry-inducing price gap and an entry lag, we will follow the convention here of defining or evaluating the condition of entry to any industry without reference to entry lags — i.e., in terms of the excess of an entry-inducing price over a competitive level, whatever the lag. We will, however, consider data on entry lags as supplementary information useful in predicting the consequences of the condition of entry as defined. This procedure seems to place entry lags in their proper role in analysis.

The determinants of the condition of entry

Once the condition of entry has been so defined and measured, the next question is what *determines* the condition of entry to any industry. What is the nature of the advantages that established firms may possess, and what technological or institutional circumstances give rise to these advantages?

The identity of the immediate determinants of the condition of entry is suggested by considering the characteristics ordinarily attributed to a situation of theoretical "easy entry." In modern price theory, "easy entry" is ordinarily conceived as a situation in which there is no impediment to the entry of new firms, in which established firms possess no advantages over potential entrant firms, or in which, more precisely, established firms cannot persistently elevate price by any amount above the competitive minimal-cost level without attracting sufficient new entry to bring price back to that level. The condition of entry, as we have seen, can be measured by the percentage by which the prices of established firms can exceed the competitive level without attracting entry. Then with easy entry, the immediate condition of entry has a value of *zero* at every point in any possible sequence of entry (each added entrant firm has no disadvantage relative to those already established), and the general condition of entry is correspondingly represented by a single zero value. Entry, of course, ceases to be easy and becomes more difficult as values of the condition of entry progressively in excess of zero are encountered, or as at one point or another in the progression of entry established firms can receive super-competitive prices without inducing entry.

The essential characteristics of the situation in which easy entry prevails should furnish a direct clue to the determinants of the condition of entry in general. For easy entry, three conditions must in general be simultaneously fulfilled. At any stage in the relevant progression of entry (1) *established firms have no absolute cost advantages* over potential entrant firms; (2) *established firms have no product differentiation advantages* over potential entrant firms; and (3) *economies of large-scale firm are negligible*, in the sense that the output of a firm of optimal (lowest-cost) scale is an insignificant fraction of total industry output. Let us see briefly what each of these conditions means and why it is important.

The condition that with easy entry established firms should have no absolute cost advantages means that, for a given product, potential entrant firms should be able to secure just as low a minimal average cost of production after their entry as established firms had prior to this entry. This in turn implies (a) that established firms should have no price or other advantages over entrants in purchasing or securing any productive factor (including investible funds); (b) that the entry of an added firm should have no perceptible effect on the going level of any factor price; and (c) that established firms have no preferred access to productive techniques. If these conditions are fulfilled, then established firms, if they should wish to elevate price above the competitive level without attracting entry, have no ability to do so by virtue of the fact that the *level* of their costs is any lower than potential entrant firms will be able to secure. Established firms (before entry) and the entrant (after entry) have costs on the same level for any given product. If product differentiation exists, the equivalent of this condition must be fulfilled.

The condition that with easy entry there should be no product differentiation advantage to established firms means either that there must be no product differentiation or that, if product differentiation is present, potential entrant firms should be able to secure a relationship of price to cost just as favorable as that enjoyed by established firms. Generally, if the possibility of differences in products, production costs, and selling costs is recognized, the potential entrant firm should always be able to secure as favorable a relation of price to unit production plus selling cost as established firms, so that established firms can never make a profit when an entrant could not, or break even when entrant would lose money. For this to be true, there must be no net price or selling cost advantage accruing to established firms by reason of buyer preferences for their products, and also no price advantages in securing factors of production. The condition of lack of product differentiation advantages is obviously essential to easy entry, since otherwise established firms could raise their prices somewhat above the competitive level without creating a situation in which potential entrants could sell profitably.

The condition that there should be no significant economies to the large scale firm means of course that an entrant firm, even if it enters at an optimal or lowest-cost scale, will add so little to industry output that its entry will have no perceptible effect on going prices in the industry. In order to avail itself of the lowest costs available to established firms, the entrant need not augment industry output enough to make the industry price less attractive; thus, the pursuit of economies of scale to the ultimate is possible and provides no deterrent to entry. The importance of this condition is evident when we consider the opposite possibility.

If, in order to enter at optimal scale, a firm must add a significant fraction to industry output, several possibilities are open. If established firms maintain their going outputs, entry at such a scale will tend in general to bring about a reduction of industry price. If they maintain or increase their prices, the obtainable market share for the entrant may very well be insufficient to permit optimal scale operations. Furthermore, retaliatory pricing by established firms may be engendered, and entry at a scale small enough not to disturb the market will require suboptimal scale and higher costs.

In one way or another, entry tends to be deterred sufficiently so that established firms are probably enabled to elevate price at least somewhat above the lowest-cost level without inducing entry. The potential entrant, if he enters at significantly large scales himself, will probably expect or fear either an industry price after entry which is somewhat below that which prevails before entry, or a market share involving costs above those of optimal scale.[3] Thus he will probably not be induced to enter by a somewhat super-competitive industry price. If he considers entry at insignificant scales, he will have costs above the competitive level and thus again will not be induced to enter by a somewhat supercompetitive price. Significant economies of scale thus tend to impede entry, and their absence is generally essential to easy entry.

The three conditions just described are both necessary and sufficient

[3] Instances are logically conceivable in which a market share permitting lowest-cost scale could be secured by an entrant — e.g. where established firms were generally of super-optimal scale before entry, so that sellers in general would not be forced to suboptimal scales by sharing the market among more of them. But that this, plus the absence of some retaliation in price by established firms, should be found seems unlikely.

for easy entry to exist. If this is true, it is clear that we have by implication identified the sources of departure from easy entry and the immediate determinants of the condition of entry as defined.

Departures of the condition of entry from the "zero pole" of easy entry must be attributable to one or more of the following: (1) absolute cost advantages of established firms; (2) product differentiation advantages of established firms; and (3) significant economies of large-scale firms. Correspondingly, the heights of barriers to entry, or the "values" of the condition of entry (expressed as the percentages by which established firms can set prices above a competitive level while forestalling entry), will clearly depend on the degree of these absolute cost and product differentiation advantages and on the extent of scale economies to large firms. The specific nature of these determinants of the condition of entry are presumably more or less obvious, but a brief summary of their character will serve to suggest the character of the institutional and other conditions from which they arise.

Absolute cost advantages to established firms will in general arise from one of three things: (1) the entry of a single firm may perceptibly elevate one or more factor prices paid by both established firms and the entrant firm, thus raising the level of costs; (2) established firms may be able to secure the use of factors of production, including investible funds, at lower prices than potential entrants can; (3) established firms may have access to more economical techniques of production than potential entrants, thus enabling them to secure lower costs. Such absolute cost advantages tend to give established firms a lower level of costs than the potential entrant, and thus enable them to set prices above a competitive level while still forestalling entry.

Product differentiation advantages of established firms result, of course, from the preferences of buyers for established as compared to new entrant products. What will constitute an effective product differentiation advantage will depend on the importance of economies of scale in production and selling in the industry. If there are no economies of scale, so that unit production plus selling costs are not increased by restricting output to very small amounts, a potential entrant firm may be said to be without disadvantage if he can receive as high a price relative to unit cost as established firms *at some output*, even though he is able to do so only at a much smaller output than established firms. (Existence of a large number of such potential entrants — even though each was restricted in sales volume — would provide easy entry.) Conversely, possession of an advantage by established firms in the case of no scale economies requires their ability to secure at some output a higher price or lower selling cost — or generally a higher ratio of price to production plus selling cost — than the most favored potential entrants can secure at any output.[4] Existence of such product differentiation advantages is possible and would confer on established firms the ability to elevate price above a competitive level while forestalling entry.

If there are some systematic economies of scale to the firm, so that unit costs of production plus selling decline relative to price over some range of outputs, absence of advantage to established sellers requires the ability of entrants in general to attain not only comparable prices but also to obtain them at comparable sales volumes and thus to secure comparable costs as well. Conversely, the possession of advantage by established firms would require only that they be able to sell at a higher price than potential entrants can at approximately optimal scales, even though potential entrants could gain a price parity at small and inefficient scales. In effect, entrants, in order to lack disadvantage, must not only get parity in price, but must get it at economically large sales volumes.

Not much more need be said of the nature of advantages to established firms that are inherent in substantial economies to the large-scale firm. The fact that an entrant must add significantly to industry output to attain lowest costs, and would have perceptibly higher costs at smaller outputs, bestows on established firms the ability to elevate price somewhat above the competitive level without attracting entry. The economies in question may be either those of large-scale production and distribution, or, as suggested in the preceding footnote, those of large-scale sales promotion. Clearly, the advantage of established firms is increased and the condition of entry becomes more difficult both as the optimal scale of the firm becomes larger relative to the market, and as the rise of costs at smaller scales becomes steeper.

A question related to these immediate determinants of the condition of entry as we have defined it concerns the identity of the basic institutional and technological circumstances that give rise to the various immediate deterrents to entry. No exhaustive treatment is required here, but the following tabulation suggests the sorts of circumstances which typically give rise to impeded entry and which may logically be the subject of an investigation bearing generally upon the condition of entry:

I. *Typical circumstances giving rise to an absolute cost advantage to established firms.*

    A. Control of production techniques by established firms, via either patents or secrecy. (Such control may permit exclusion of entrants

---

[4] A variant of this is that the potential entrants could, in the absence of scale economies *other than* price or selling-cost advantages of large-scale sales promotion, secure an equivalent price relative to unit costs, but only at an output constituting a significant fraction of the market. In this event the established firms would also enjoy some net advantage, although it would be attributable in some sense to the significance of scale economies *per se*.

from access to optimal techniques, or alternatively the levying of a discriminatory royalty charge for their use.)

B. Imperfections in the markets for hired factors of production (e.g. labor, materials, etc.) which allow lower buying prices to established firms; alternatively ownership or control of strategic factor supplies (e.g. resources) by established firms, which permits either exclusion of entrants from such supplies, driving entrants to use inferior supplies, or discriminatory pricing of supplies to them.

C. Significant limitations of the supplies of productive factors in specific markets or submarkets for them, relative to the demands of an efficient entrant firm. Then an increment to entry will perceptibly increase factor prices.

D. Money-market conditions imposing higher interest rates upon potential entrants than upon established firms. (These conditions are apparently more likely to be effective as a source of advantage to established firms as the absolute capital requirement for an efficient entrant increases.)

II. *Typical circumstances giving rise to a product differentiation advantage to established firms.*

A. The accumulative preference of buyers for established brand names and company reputations, either generally or except for small minorities of buyers.

B. Control of superior product designs by established firms through patents, permitting either exclusion of entrants from them or the levying of discriminatory royalty charges.

C. Ownership or contractual control by established firms of favored distributive outlets, in situations where the supply of further outlets is other than perfectly elastic.

III. *Typical circumstances discouraging entry by sustaining significant economies of the large-scale firm.*

A. Real economies (i.e. in terms of quantities of factors used per unit of output) of large-scale production and distribution such that an optimal firm will supply a significant share of the market.

B. Strictly pecuniary economies (i.e. monetary economies only, such as those due to the greater bargaining power of large buyers) of large-scale production, having a similar effect.

C. Real or strictly pecuniary economies of large-scale advertising or other sales promotion, having a similar effect.

These circumstances are in a sense the ultimate determinants of the condition of entry to an industry. We have emphasized throughout that the condition of entry is a structural concept, and that it is evaluated by the extent to which established firms can, on the average over a long period, elevate price above a long-run competitive level while still forestalling entry. Consistently, the ultimate determinants of the condition of entry either reflect or refer directly to long-run structural characteristics of markets, and it is these which determine the condition of entry as we have defined it here.

If these are the determinants of the condition of entry, we should be equally clear about the things that are *not* its determinants. The true determinants are the things that determine for established firms the possible price-cost relations which would and would not induce entry; they are not those things determining whether or not actual entry takes place at a particular time. Thus, although the persistent product-differentiation advantage of established firms is a true determinant of the condition of entry, the current and transitory relation of industry demand to capacity is not.

It is true, of course, that if an industry is currently plagued with heavy excess capacity (caused, for example, by a secular decline in demand against long-lived plants) prices may average below costs and no entry may take place for many years. But this does not necessarily mean that the condition of entry is therefore difficult, for it does not remove the fact that a persistent slight excess of price above minimal long-run average costs (perhaps unlikely to occur in this situation) could be sufficient to induce entry. We must thus in general reject current secular or cyclical movements of demand, capacity, and cost as determinants of the condition of entry to an industry, just as we reject the current record of accomplished entry as direct or conclusive evidence of what the condition of entry is. Such things as the relationship of demand to capacity in an industry would affect the condition of entry as defined only so far as they persisted in a given state for some time, and so far as, in addition, they affected the manner in which potential entrants would react to given persistent differences between the actual price and a competitive price.[5]

We have by now frequently noted that the condition of entry to an industry is a structural and long-term condition. But that does not mean it is necessarily permanent and immutable. The basic structural characteristics of a market can change, and the condition of entry may then change in response. Thus the discovery of new deposits of a given natural

[5] The principal possible exception would occur if monotonic long-term secular movements in demand or cost, followed by lagging adjustments of industry capacity, caused potential entrants to react differently to given persistent differences between the prices of established firms and their minimal costs. That the reaction of potential entrants might be affected in this way seems entirely possible.

resource might undercut the absolute cost advantage held by established processing firms which had controlled all previously known deposits; the development of a new product design by an outsider might reduce the product-differentiation advantages of established sellers of similar products; technological changes might either increase or decrease the economies of large-scale production in any line at any time. When such changes take place, the condition of entry to any industry will tend to be altered.

This raises the question whether the condition of entry and its determinants are sufficiently stable through time so that they may be viewed provisionally as quasi-independent long-run determinants of market behavior. If the condition of entry and its determinants change slowly through time and are not easily subject to deliberate alteration by the action of potential entrants, and if they thus represent primarily a structural framework for market behavior rather than a result of this behavior, this is a legitimate view. On the other hand, of course, is the possibility that the condition of entry is a sort of unstable will-o'-the-wisp rapidly changing through time, or that it is readily altered by the action of potential entrants. In this event, it should hardly be studied as a long-run structural determinant of market behavior.

It is definitely posited for purposes of the present study — on the basis of extensive empirical observation — that the condition of entry as defined and its ultimate determinants are usually stable and slowly changing through time, and are not generally susceptible to alteration by prospective entrants to various markets. Thus the condition of entry and the various specific advantages of established firms which fix its value may in general be viewed as long-run structural determinants of enterprise action.

This generalization, like many others about economic affairs, is, of course, true only subject to exceptions, or as a representation of a general tendency. Certainly the condition of entry has shifted fairly rapidly over time in a few industries, and certainly potential entrants periodically have succeeded in changing it to their advantage in some cases. Nevertheless, these exceptions seem infrequent and unusual enough to justify our proceeding on the basis of our assumption.

Only one specific exception may deserve special attention as we study various industries. In some industries (though definitely not in a majority of them), the ability of potential entrants to make effective product innovations has periodically broken down the product advantages of established firms and effectively eased entry to the markets in question. Here, the role of existing product preferences as structural determinants of action can be questioned. It will be interesting to see if we can identify some more fundamental determinants of the condition of entry in this area, in the shape of those things which determine whether or not potential entrants are likely to be in a position to make effective product innovations.

Theory concerning effects of the condition of entry

Our reason for paying so much attention to the condition of entry is our belief in its substantial influence on market behavior or performance in various industries. The force of potential competition, that is, may be viewed as a regulator of prices and outputs of an importance comparable to that of actual competition. But in what ways? What impact may the condition of entry be expected to have on market performance in an industry, and how will variation in the condition of entry from one industry to another cause market performance to differ between them?

These questions may be approached in two ways — through theorizing or deductive logic, and through empirical testing. Later we will attempt a few empirical tests for the effect of the condition of entry, so far as available data permit. Unfortunately, these data as yet do not permit very much, so that no comprehensive or conclusive empirical testing is possible. We are thus forced at this time to rely on *a priori* theory as the primary source for our knowledge of the consequences of the condition of entry.

If we approach the prediction of the consequences of the condition of entry as a full-dress problem in formal theory, a very complicated and elaborate system of hypotheses may emerge through simple extensions of received doctrine. The condition of entry is intrinsically a very complex idea and can assume a wide range of significantly different "values" with significantly different probable effects; in addition the consequences of the condition of entry will vary with variations in the structure of any market as among established sellers. Thus a very considerable variety of formal theoretical models could be constructed in order to distinguish (1) a large number of variant patterns of the "general condition of entry"; (2) different sources of impediments to entry, so far as these differences are significant; and (3) different structural situations as among established sellers.

Some beginnings in this direction were made in an earlier article.[6] It does not seem desirable here to reproduce or to extend the full theoretical arguments or the relatively elaborate range of theoretical hypotheses developed there. Such hypotheses are too detailed for even tentative testing and verification with data now on hand or likely to be available in the near future. It does seem desirable, however, to set down as a tentative guide to our investigations some simplified and compressed hypotheses concerning the effects of the condition of entry.

Three things seem to be of primary importance in determining the

[6] Bain, "Conditions of Entry and the Emergence of Monopoly."

probable effect of the condition of entry. The first is the *value* of the condition of entry, as measured by the percentage by which established firms may set price above a competitive level while forestalling entry.[7] This "value" may be construed as a single value for the immediate condition of entry when calculated with reference to the most favored potential entrant or entrants, or as a series of successive values for the general condition of entry when calculated with reference to successive potential entrants or groups thereof of a progressively less favored status. The second thing is the degree of concentration among sellers already established in the market, the corresponding existence or nonexistence of a recognized interdependence or of express or tacit collusion among them, and the corresponding *degree* of interdependence among them or degree of imperfection of their express or tacit collusion. The third thing is the source of the departure from easy entry, and in particular whether or not the departure involves the existence of significant economies to the large-scale firm.

The interaction of the three determinants mentioned should, hypothetically, determine the effect of the condition of entry. A fourth potential determinant, neglected here, is whether or not established firms will ever encounter *diseconomies* of large scale; i.e. rising unit costs because the firm exceeds a certain size. We neglect this possibility as improbable, and will assume approximately constant unit costs as firm size exceeds the minimum necessary for lowest costs.

The "value" of the condition of entry — and we will refer here primarily to the succession of individual values encompassed in the general condition of entry — is obviously important because it potentially places a limit on the level that prices in an industry can maintain in the long run. In this connection, two distinctions among different general conditions of entry may be drawn.

The first distinction refers to differences among various potential entrants. First, there is potentially the general condition of entry in which, in a given situation or after a given stage in the development of an industry has been reached, all potential entrant firms are in the same status or have the same disadvantage relative to established firms, and will moreover continue in this status regardless of how many of them enter the industry. In effect, there is then a perfectly elastic supply of entry at a given entry-inducing price-to-minimal-cost gap; the immediate condition of entry will remain at the same value for each successive entrant in turn; and the general condition of entry will thus be represented by a single value of the immediate condition of entry (representing the excess of industry price over a given level of competitive price) regardless of how

---

[7] For purposes of theorizing, the percentage may be identified as that for the most favored established firm.

much entry occurs. Such a situation might occur, for example, if established firms selling a given product had a ten per cent advantage in production cost over all potential entrants by virtue of patent rights (economies of scale being negligible), and if an indefinitely large number of new firms could enter only with this ten per cent cost disadvantage.

Second, there is the general condition of entry reflecting differential advantages among successive potential entrants, such that the disadvantage of potential entrants, as registered by the entry-inducing gap, is successively greater or becomes so as one after another actually enters the industry. Thus, by individuals or by groups, the potential entrants are classified, and as we proceed through the classes the percentage by which actual prices may exceed a given competitive level without inducing entry becomes greater. This may result either because the potential entrants have differential disadvantages *ab initio*, or because the actual further entry of one or more makes the condition of entry more difficult for remaining potential entrants.

The second distinction refers to the height of the barrier to entry. This distinction should be made separately in the cases of the "constant" general condition of entry, where all potential entrants are and remain in the same state of disadvantage relative to established firms, and the "progressive" general condition of entry, where successive potential entrants suffer progressively greater disadvantages.

Suppose there is a constant general condition of entry to an industry, represented by a single value of the immediate condition of entry. Then, after the industry reaches a given stage, there is a single percentage by which industry prices may persistently exceed a given competitive level while forestalling entry, regardless of how many new firms actually enter the industry; if the percentage excess becomes and remains greater, all potential entrants (to an indefinitely large number) will be ready to enter the industry. A given core of established firms thus has a more or less mutable advantage over any and all potential entrants. (As we will see below, a constant condition of entry can occur only where economies of large scale firm are absent or negligible, so that established and potential entrant firms' costs will not be perceptibly elevated by the reduction of their market shares as entry ensues.[8]) In this situation, the condition of entry may assume any of four sorts of values, each designated by a special term hereafter used only with the special meaning about to be set forth.

(1) *There may be "easy" entry*, so that price in the long-run cannot at all exceed the competitive cost level of all established firms without attracting entry.

(2) The value of the condition of entry may be positive (as measured

---

[8] The reader will remember the assumption of no diseconomies of large scale.

with reference to the most favored established firms) but so low that certain consequences ensue. That is, there may be what we will refer to as *"ineffectively impeded"* entry in the following sense: The most favored established firms could raise their prices (prices of other firms in the industry moving concurrently) somewhat above the competitive level without attracting entry, but they could make greater long-run profits by setting their prices above the entry-forestalling level and attracting further entrants to some point than they could make by setting prices low enough to forestall entry. This implies that the entry-forestalling price permits these firms only a rather small profit and similarly small percentage excess of price over minimal cost. It implies further that if entry is induced by higher prices, it will take place with sufficient lags to permit these established firms more attractive profits during an interval in which entrants are becoming established. This situation is appropriately characterized as having an *ineffectively impeded* entry.[9]

(3) The value of the condition of entry may be positive and there may be *"effectively impeded"* entry in the following sense: The most favored established firms could raise their prices (other prices in the industry moving concurrently) enough above their competitive level without attracting entry to make their long-run profits at the best entry-forestalling price greater than if they charged higher prices and induced entry (thus sharing the market with further sellers). At the same time, the best entry-forestalling price *is below that which would maximize their profits if there were no threat of entry.* This implies that the entry-forestalling price is moderately above costs, but not as high as a "monopolistic" price would be in the absence of any threat of entry.

(4) The value of the condition of entry may be positive and *entry may be effectively "blockaded"* — in the sense that the entry-forestalling level of industry prices is above that which would maximize the profits of the most-favored firms in the absence of any entry threat. They therefore have no virtual incentive to raise prices high enough to induce entry.

The preceding refers to four sorts of value of the condition of entry if the value is always at a single level for any number of successive entrants. So far as such a constant general entry condition is encountered, the sort of value may obviously influence market performance within an industry. Before exploring these influences, let us consider the possible values of the condition of entry when there is a "progressive" general condition of entry.

---

[9] It is clear that the longer the lags encountered in inducing entry the greater an excess of entry-forestalling price over cost will be considered as ineffectively impeding entry.

In this instance, there is a differential advantage among successive potential entrants — either *ab initio* or developing as further entry occurs — so that the immediate condition of entry, as measured with reference to the initial minimal costs of the most favored established firms, becomes higher as successive firms or groups thereof enter the industry. Then if the percentage by which industry price may exceed that designated competitive level, while just forestalling the entry of the most favored potential entrant or entrants, is at a certain value, the percentage excess attainable while forestalling the entry of the next most favored potential entrant is larger, and so forth. The general condition of entry is represented by some succession of values of the immediate condition of entry referring to successively less favored entrants.

There are generally two possible sources of a "progressive" condition of entry. First, different potential entrant firms may have differential advantages in absolute cost or from product differentiation. These may be either advantages which exist initially before any firms enter, or advantages which develop as entry occurs — for example, the entrants who are "first in" the industry thereby secure advantages over the remainder. In either event, some potential entrants will tend to be able to secure higher prices or lower costs than others, thus leading to a progression in the value of the immediate condition of entry as entry occurs.

Second, there may be significant economies of scale, in the sense that an optimal-sized firm will slupply a significant fraction of the total market and that unit costs for a firm will become progressively larger at progressively smaller scales. In this event, a progression in the absolute value of the condition of entry is more or less inevitable as further entry occurs, even though all established and potential entrant firms might have precisely the same cost conditions. This is because successive entry will successively tend to force all established firms to significantly smaller market shares and significantly higher costs, and to confront all remaining potential entrants with the prospect of smaller market shares and higher costs. Therefore, higher and higher prices (relative to minimal attainable costs) will be required to attract further entry as additional entry raises the going level of costs by forcing more and more uneconomical sizes on firms entered in the industry. Thus, where there are significant scale economies, a progressive condition of entry is more or less automatically encountered.

What of the possible values of the progressive general condition of entry? It is at this point that theorizing becomes especially difficult, since an indefinitely large number of different patterns of the condition of entry is logically possible. For purposes of initial rough generalization, however, it may be sufficient to distinguish a few general patterns. These are briefly listed, in each case with the supposition that the immediate condition of entry is measured with reference to the minimal costs of the most favored established firms:

(5) *The immediate condition of entry is initially at a small absolute value; with successive entry assumes only slightly larger absolute values; and at every step in a relevant sequence of entry is ineffectively impeded from the standpoint of the most favored established firms.* In other words, the condition of entry is always low enough so that a higher entry-inducing price would be more profitable to established firms in the long run than the best entry-forestalling price.

(6) *The immediate condition of entry is initially at a small absolute value and progresses to successively larger absolute values with successive entry; but in the course of increasing it progresses from ineffectively impeded to effectively impeded from the standpoint of the most favored established firms* (and possibly later to a *blockaded* value). That is, entry becomes effectively impeded in the sense that the highest entry-forestalling price would in the long run be more profitable to them than a higher price which would induce entry.

(7) *The immediate condition of entry is initially at a value regarded as effectively impeded by established firms;* in increasing with progressive entry it either remains *effectively impeded* or becomes *blockaded.*

(8) *The immediate condition of entry is initially at a blockaded value* — that is, the highest entry-forestalling price exceeds that which would maximize the profits of established firms.

(9) *The immediate condition of entry is at a relatively small absolute value initially, but with successive entry steadily progresses to substantially larger absolute values. Nevertheless, the condition of entry continues through a sequence of entry to be regarded as ineffectively impeded by established firms and never reaches an effectively impeded value.* This is because with successive entry the rise of the entry-forestalling price relative to minimal costs is matched by a rise in their actual costs, so that higher and higher entry-forestalling prices do not offer adequate profits. (This pattern should be found only where there are substantial economies of scale. In this instance, established firms in a long sequence of entry never find it most profitable to set price low enough to exclude entry.) [10] The sequence of ineffectively impeded values would tend to be followed ultimately in the progression of entry by a blockaded value at the point where the most profitable price only permits established firms to break even and will not attract entry.

[10] When they do, the scale-economies case would fall under 6, 7, or 8 above.

We have thus listed five main sorts of the "progressive" general condition of entry, in addition to four sorts of "constant" condition. The total list may be shortened, however, by combining cases of which the predicted effects will not differ significantly. In effect, case 5 above, in which the value of the condition of entry will remain small and be regarded as ineffectively impeded indefinitely does not differ significantly from case 2. Similarly, case 7 involving progressions from an initial effectively impeded condition of entry, merges with case 3, representing a constant effectively impeded condition of entry, without important loss of detail in analysis; case 8 similarly merges with case 4. Thus only cases 6 and 9 need to be added to our initial list of four. The combined list may now be renumbered to read as follows:

I. Constantly *easy* entry.

II. Continual *ineffectively impeded* entry, either at a single constant small absolute value of the condition of entry or at a succession of small but increasing absolute values.

III. Initial *effectively impeded* entry, followed in a progression of entry by either *effectively impeded* or *blockaded* entry. (The absolute value of the immediate condition of entry may remain constant or increase with progressive entry.)

IV. Initial *ineffectively impeded* entry, at small absolute values of the condition of entry, progressing to somewhat higher absolute values and to *effectively impeded* entry.

V. Initial *ineffectively impeded* entry at small absolute values of the condition of entry, followed by substantially higher absolute values as entry ensues, but with the condition of entry nevertheless regarded as *ineffectively impeded* throughout a substantial progression of entry — and never reaching an *effectively impeded* value.

VI. Continually *blockaded* entry, either at a single absolute constant value of the condition of entry or at a succession of increasing absolute values.

So much for the classification of entry conditions *per se*. As indicated above, the effects of the condition of entry should depend upon two more things: the degree of concentration among established sellers in any market, and the presence or absence of significant economies to the large-scale firm.

The degree of seller concentration is essentially important because it may be expected to determine whether or not, or to what extent, the established sellers in a market will in effect act collectively in determining their prices. "Collective" market-policy determination or pricing action may, in the sense we use the term here, result from express collusion or consensus of established sellers, from a tacit understanding based on the past experience of rival firms with each other's policies, or from a recognized interdependence such that each seller alters his price significantly or makes other significant alterations of policy only in the expectancy of some more or less predictable concurrent action or reaction of his rivals.

However it may result, collective action means in general that the principal sellers in an industry will change price concurrently, and in addition that every principal seller will change his price significantly only to match rival changes or with the anticipation that there will be, in response to his change, concurrent and similar changes of other prices in the industry. Therefore, the consequences to him of his own major price changes will become the consequences of a similar general change in the level of industry prices, including his own. The emergence of "collective action" patterns generally requires that the principal sellers in the market control substantial individual shares of the market, so that the price adjustments of any one will clearly affect the others and produce the requisite interdependence and the recognition of it. From this it follows that as seller concentration increases, and thus the shares of the market controlled by individual sellers, collective action among sellers becomes more probable.

The pattern of market conduct opposite to collective action is strictly independent action. In this case the individual seller will act, in pricing and other market activities, non-collusively and with substantial neglect of the possible reactions of his competitors. He will not necessarily follow his rivals, nor anticipate that his rivals will follow him or match his policies. This is typically because his own actions will have no perceptible effect on his rivals (or theirs on his), and in turn that is because the individual seller supplies a negligible fraction of the market. We thus see the converse of our last proposition, namely that collective action becomes less probable as seller concentration decreases.

The presence or absence of what we have called "collective action" has long been recognized in economic theory as strategic to the character of competition among established sellers. Markets in which there is a significant concentration of sellers have been designated as *oligopolistic*, as distinguished from the atomistic markets in which sellers are many and individually small. It has been argued in general that in oligopolistic industries there is a definite tendency (via express or tacit collusion or recognized interdependence) for sellers to act "collectively" or in unison in establishing prices and outputs, whereas in atomistic industries any attempted collusion will fail and every seller will act independently in adjusting himself to a market price and output which he feels to be outside of his influence of control. Correspondingly, it has been argued that the "collective action" pattern of conduct in oligopoly tends to lead in the direction of monopolistic or quasi-monopolistic price and output results, although these may be tempered or poorly approximated so far as collusion is imperfect, as express or tacit agreements cannot be reached, or as forays of independent action are undertaken. The "independent" pattern of conduct in atomistic markets, on the other hand, tends to lead to results that feature lower industry prices and larger industry outputs, and that are designated as "competitive."

The additional question posed here concerns what influence, if any, the presence or absence of "collective action" has upon the way in which the condition of entry to an industry affects market performance in that industry. In effect, will the established sellers in an industry behave any differently in the face of a given condition of entry if they are few and have developed a conduct-pattern of collective action than if they are many and pursue a conduct-pattern of independent action?

The presence or absence of a collective-action pattern of conduct should have one major influence in this regard. Suppose that all sellers, or at any rate the principal sellers, in an industry act collectively, in the sense that each views his own price changes as equivalent to similar changes by the whole industry. Then each will regard the effect of his own price changes on entry (whether he is leading others or following others and thus validating their leadership) as similar to the effect of a concurrent industry-wide price change on entry. And if this is so, two things follow. First, the individual seller will always calculate, in considering his own price adjustments, as if his own price adjustment had a definite (and in a sense maximum) effect on entry, since his own adjustment is effectively equivalent to an industry-wide price adjustment of similar magnitude. He will be led to consider that his own price adjustments can alternatively forestall or induce entry to the industry. Second, the seller will be led, in making his own price adjustments, to consider the effect upon industry profits, via entry, of an industry-wide price adjustment equivalent to his own, and upon his share of these profits.

In consequence, he will be led to consider the alternatives of forestalling or attracting entry through his own price adjustments, and this primarily in terms of the anticipated effect of industry-wide price adjustments on entry and of such entry upon industry profits and his share of them. This should be true, as a general tendency, whether the seller is operating as a member of a cartel trying to agree on price, or as an independent seller in an oligopoly, operating subject to tacit collusion or a strong recognized interdependence with rivals. Finally, industry price adjustments will tend to be made only in the full recognition of their effects in inducing entry, and of such entry on industry profits and on the individual seller's share of them.

Suppose alternatively that every seller in the industry acts independently, on the supposition that his own price and output adjustments will not and cannot perceptibly influence his established rivals. That is, any first seller supposes that each of his competitors will do whatever he would have done otherwise (whether to hold to his going price or to make some adjustment) regardless of what he, the first seller, does. (He thus effectively accepts market-price movements as data belond his control.) This sort of attitude will generally result from the fact that each seller controls a negligible fraction of the total market in which he sells. *If this is so, it will also be true in general that no seller will take account of the possible influence of his price adjustments on entry, since he will correctly believe such an influence to be negligible.* Thus the entry-forestalling or entry-inducing effects of individual price adjustments will not be taken into account by those making them. It will therefore also be true that the effect upon industry profits of the inducement of or discouragement to entry attributable to individual price adjustments will not be considered by any seller or by sellers in general. Industry-wide price movements — the result of many individual and independent movements — will therefore emerge without regard to their effects on entry and thus on industry profits, since no price-determining unit will take account of these effects. This will be true even though all the many individual prices in an industry will in fact generally move concurrently (though independently) in response to broad economic determinants.

We thus have two general types of situations. In the first, the effects of industry-wide price adjustments on entry and of entry on industry profits are taken into account by sellers individually or collectively. In the second, these effects are not taken into account and do not influence pricing decisions, because of independence of action and the fact that each seller is a negligible factor in the market.

These are of course typical or polar situations, and between them many variant or modified situations may exist. Thus we have collective action tempered by sporadic independent action in pricing, so that sellers usually but not always act as if their own price changes were more or less equivalent to industry-wide changes. Or we may have independent action tempered by some slight recognition of interdependence. For purposes of predicting very roughly the general effects of the condition of entry, however, it should be enough to distinguish the two general patterns of conduct so far mentioned — collective action and independent action. Correspondingly, we may distinguish (a) seller concentration sufficiently high to implement or lead to collective-action patterns of conduct; and (b) seller concentration low enough to lead to substantial independence of action by individual sellers. A more detailed classification, recognizing modified and in-between cases, may be neglected for present purposes.

The third general determinant of the effect of the condition of entry is whether or not significant economies of the large-scale firm are found in an industry. As already noted above, the primary significance of the existence of significant scale economies (such that a firm of optimal scale will supply an appreciable fraction of industry output and that smaller firms will have distinctly higher costs) is that it tends to lead more or less automatically to a progressively higher barrier to entry as progressive entry occurs. It leads, that is, to a specific and especially troubling type of pattern of the general condition of entry — troubling both because the impediment to further entry tends to be increased by entry itself and because the source of the impediment (advantages of size inherent in techniques of production or commerce) is not easily attacked or modified by policy measures when the impediment to entry is undesirable. Barriers to entry resting on product differentiation or absolute cost considerations, on the other hand, do not *per se* or necessarily result in the progressive heightening of barriers to entry as further entry occurs, or in steeply "progressive" patterns of the general condition of entry.

A second significance of the existence of significant scale economies is that this will ordinarily tend to be associated with moderate to high concentration among established sellers — a phenomenon the possible significance of which has been suggested in preceding paragraphs. In predicting the effects of the condition of entry, therefore, it is useful to make a definite distinction between cases where significant economies of scale are and are not present.

Given the three major determinants of the effect of the condition of entry on market performance — i.e., the value of the condition of entry, the degree of seller concentration, and the source of the departure from easy entry — we may now turn directly to these effects, at least so far as they are predictable by *a priori* economic theory. Through elaborations of this theory, certain deductions may be drawn concerning the probable effect of the condition of entry on the price policies and on other aspects of the market conduct of established sellers, and thereby on their ultimate market performance so far as that is reflected in such things as the degree of monopolistic output restriction attained within the industry, the excess of prices over actual costs (as measured by the size of profits), the efficiency of production, and the size of selling costs. Although we will not attempt any full or formal development of the relevant theoretical arguments here, it is useful to state and explain briefly the general content of available theoretical predictions concerning such effects of the condition of entry.

In doing so, a primary distinction must be drawn between industries of high and low seller concentration. If there is an atomistic structure in an industry, no seller will presume that he can influence the course of entry to the industry by his own market adjustments; he can himself neither attract nor forestall entry thereby. The condition of entry (reflecting the relation of an entry-forestalling industry-wide level of price to minimal costs) will tend to be neglected by sellers in an atomistic industry; their market policies will be uninfluenced by it. Industry-wide price movements will occur without regard to whether or not they will induce entry. The condition of entry then will serve in atomistic industries only as a sort of automatic regulator of market performance, setting limits to long-run movements of the industry-wide relation of price to cost by imposing the corrective effect of entry if the movements exceed these limits.

Given this general rule, it is not difficult to perceive the effects of the six sorts of general condition of entry (listed on page 25) on the market performance of atomistic industries. If there were constantly easy entry to an industry, so that any number of firms could enter at no price or cost disadvantage as compared to previously established firms, price could never in the long run exceed the common minimal costs of production for all established firms. (As we have seen, differential advantages among established firms are not consistent with completely easy entry.) Any tendency for price to rise higher would induce sufficient new entry to bring it back to the competitive level. Correspondingly, there could never persist in the long run any monopolistic output restriction, any profits in excess of a normal interest return on investment, and none other than "competitive" selling costs (arrived at through a multitude of independent selling policies).

A more interesting question is whether, with atomistic market structures, conditions of entry that involve some advantages of established over potential entrant firms can lead in the long run to prices higher than are encountered with easy entry. Elementary price analysis suggests that in an atomistic market structure, and *in the absence of diseconomies of large scale to the firm*, the competition of established firms will tend to bring about a competitive level of prices regardless of barriers to entry, as they increase their outputs relative to market demand and reduce their prices until their marginal and average costs are equal to their selling prices.[11] Entry is not requisite to a full competitive adjustment, since the ability of all firms to expand indefinitely without exceeding minimal costs (or incurring equivalent disadvantages), plus the independent pricing attributable to atomism, lead to the result even without entry. In this

---

[11] With product differentiation, it should do so to a close approximation. The difference between this case and that without product differentiation will be neglected here as relatively insignificant.

case, therefore, it may be argued that the existence of various degrees and types of impediment to entry (numbers II through VI, page 25) will not make the long-run industry performance significantly different than it would be under completely easy entry.

We have just said that in the atomistic situations outlined, and with no diseconomies to large-scale firms, competition should in the long run bring price to a minimal cost level with or without entry. But whose minimal cost level, if there are significant differential advantages among established firms? Formally, this is an inappropriate question, since the significant differential advantages among established firms which it supposes to exist could not survive with atomistic competition in the long run if there were no diseconomies or equivalent disadvantages of large-scale firms. Instead, competition would force prices to the level of minimal average costs for a group of most-advantaged firms and drive all other firms from the industry through losses. Then all surviving firms would enjoy substantially equivalent minimal cost levels, and prices would equal these cost levels for all firms simultaneously. It follows from this that the coexistence of (a) atomism, (b) no disadvantages of large scale of firm, and (c) significant differential advantages as among established firms connotes an unstable market structure. With or without entry this structure will evolve toward elimination of differential advantages among surviving firms, and possibly toward the elimination of the atomistic structure. In the latter event, the predictions developed here for atomistic structures with impeded entry would of course no longer apply.

Atomistic market structures, within which differential advantages among established firms exist, should, if they are not unstable and in transition to something else, be attributable to the existence of diseconomies to or other disadvantages of large-scale firms. We have argued that such diseconomies are unlikely to be important and may be in general assumed away for a simplified theoretical argument. But if significant diseconomies to the expansion of established firms are encountered in atomistic markets, then a competitive course of market conduct involving independent adjustments by each seller may lead to results somewhat different from those just predicted. Each individual firm is then unable to extend its output indefinitely at minimal costs, and encounters progressively rising average and marginal costs as output extends beyond an "optimal" scale. As soon as the demand for industry output at prices equal to the minimal costs of the most favored established firms exceeds the sum of the optimal outputs for these firms, this excess will lead to a competitive extension of their outputs with rising average and marginal costs and prices. Such a price rise will be accompanied, according to the condition of entry, by the entry of further sellers as the prices rise high enough to induce them to enter in spite of their disadvantages. The increase of output by entry and enlargement of the output of established firms will proceed until a competitively determined supply is equal to demand at a price in excess of the minimal average costs of the most favored sellers, and perhaps also of other sellers. In this situation, the more favored sellers will tend to make excess profits and to operate at scales in excess of the optimum. The amount of these excesses will tend to become greater as their advantages over other established firms and potential entrants is greater, or as the general condition of entry proceeds more quickly in a progression of entry to a high value. On the other hand, the long-run price finally arrived at will not in general exceed the minimal average cost of the most favored excluded entrant. Whether the condition of entry would be regarded as blockaded, effectively impeded, or ineffectively impeded is not relevant, since individual sellers in any event disregard the condition of entry. But the progression of absolute values of the immediate condition of entry represented in the general condition of entry will be strategic to the final price-cost adjustment.

Too much emphasis, however, could be given to the logical possibilities just described. Observation suggests that the existence of atomistic market structures is closely related to the existence of relatively easy entry, and that atomistic structures do not commonly emerge mainly because of diseconomies of scale and in spite of substantial entry barriers. If this is so, variations in the condition of entry are likely to be relatively unimportant as influences on market performance in industries of atomistic structure.[12]

[12] Two further questions concerning the condition of entry to atomistic markets may be mentioned briefly. First, need distinctions be drawn as to source of barriers to entry? Generally no, because significant economies of scale will not persistently be found in conjunction with atomistic market structures. Except for unstable market structures in transition, only product differentiation advantages or absolute cost advantages of established firms will constitute barriers to entry in atomistic markets. And there are no important theoretical distinctions to draw between the effects of product differentiation and of absolute cost advantages as entry barriers.

Second, will the condition of entry have any influence on the *short-run* behavior of atomistic markets — that is, upon the way in which they adapt to fluctuations or secular movements in demand, technology, and so forth? The predictions discussed above refer entirely to long-run "equilibrium" tendencies in atomistic markets, or to the destination or ultimate resting point which industry market adjustments seek relative to any given set of governing economic conditions. We have argued that variations in the condition of entry from one atomistic market to another should not *a priori* be expected to be important determinants of variations in such long-run tendencies among atomistic industries. It has frequently been held, however, that very easy entry to atomistic industries is a primary source of recurring and even chronic difficulties in adapting to changes in demand, cost, and the like over time. The general tenor of the argument is that such easy entry permits a large and excessive number of small enterprises to crowd into such industries in times of peak demand and general prosperity, failing to anticipate subsequent declines in demand, increases in productivity, and so forth, and that thereafter changes of this sort make for redundant capacity and destructive competition, which is not eliminated easily because of the long lives of fixed plants and the reluctance of firms to exit from the industry.

That periodic or chronic maladjustments have been encountered in atomistic

Conversely, the condition of entry will tend to have its major effect in concentrated or oligopolistic industries. In these, (1) collusion or interdependent pricing tends to permit deliberate elevation of prices to the extent allowed by the condition of entry, the height of which thus becomes strategic; (2) firms individually and collectively will calculate the effects of their policies in inducing or forestalling entry; and (3) concentration may, unlike atomism, be expected to be accompanied by numerous alternative patterns of the condition of entry.

Given these tendencies, the condition of entry may have a major influence on market conduct and performance in oligopolistic industries, although detailed and precise predictions of its effects are hazardous for a number of reasons. One of these is that oligopolistic collusion of either the express or tacit variety may be imperfect in various degrees, especially because of secret defections from agreed-upon or common prices or because of disagreement on the most desirable price. A second is that there may be differential advantages among established sellers or differences in their views of strategic market variables which lead them to different opinions concerning the desirability of attracting or forestalling entry via pricing, or concerning what prices will and will not forestall entry. There must thus be some allowance for uncertainty in theories that concern the policy established settlers will follow and whether or not it will succeed. Nevertheless, predictions of general tendencies inherent in oligopolistic situations may be developed by adopting certain simplifying assumptions.

To this end, we will generally assume that there is effective concurrence of market action by established sellers in establishing some approximation to a joint-profit-maximizing price, referring to the effects of possible imperfections of express or tacit collusion parenthetically. We will also assume that, so far as there are differential advantages among established firms and as these lead to differences in opinion regarding the desirability of attracting or forestalling entry, the largest or principal firms will effectively determine the industry policy. We will presume, moreover, that they will in general be the most favored established firms. We will assume finally that the dominant established firms are in general correct in their appraisals of what will attract and forestall entry, and thus do not inadvertently do one thing when the other is intended. Exceptions to this rule may be recognized parenthetically. At this point we

---

industries with easy entry and historically declining demands is well known. And it is conceivable that more substantial barriers to entry — almost never found in such atomistic industries — would have some retarding influence on the periodic development of overcapacity. Unless we wish to fashion a special theory to rationalize certain observed events, however, it is not readily deduced that variations in the condition of entry are primarily accountable for variations in the performance of atomistic industries in this regard. We will therefore leave the issue open for the time being.

may also reiterate the earlier assumption that diseconomies of large-scale firms are generally negligible or absent.

Given these assumptions, let us consider the effect in oligopolistic industries of the six sorts of entry conditions listed on page 25, in each case recognizing any significant distinctions which depend on the source of the barrier to entry.

With constantly *easy* entry (I), with which no established firms can ever enjoy any long-run advantage over potential entrants, price will in the long run not tend persistently to exceed the minimal-cost level of established firms. The pressure of entry will always drive price back toward this level. But several complications require note.

First, the attainment of oligopolistic seller concentration is nevertheless possible — for example, by merger. Second, the development of concentration may seem advantageous to established sellers if there are entry lags which will permit them to elevate prices and earn supernormal profits during a period before the entry, attracted by such prices, takes place. Third, if such industries become concentrated they may then tend to experience periods of pricing at super-competitive levels, followed by the attraction of entry, by a resulting approach to atomistic structure, and thus by pricing at the competitive level. The instability of market structure which is thus implicit in the conjoining of oligopolistic concentration and very easy entry may recur in cycles (though not necessarily); it will, for example, if the atomism produced by attracting entry is later remedied by new mergers.

Fourth, if structural instability of the market is induced by monopolistic pricing over short intervals, there will be not only higher prices at times, but also excess capacity from redundant plant, the latter persisting even with a return to competitive pricing until some plants wear out. If plants are long-lived, the concentrated industry with easy entry may be chronically plagued with the "short-run" excess capacity which is attracted and reattracted by recurring episodes of monopolistic pricing. Severe social wastes may then result. This may be true even though, as is necessarily true with easy entry, there are no significant long-run economies of large-scale firms.

Fifth, approximately the same tendencies may be inherent in governmentally imposed or sponsored cartels, like those frequently found in agriculture. The major difference is that a government agency may have the power (where a private agreement does not) to elevate price and attract redundant capacity indefinitely, or to blockade entry arbitrarily in order to preserve the working of the cartel. Finally, large sellers in concentrated markets faced with easy entry will of course try to erect barriers to entry in various ways, for instance by attempting to establish product differentiation. It is difficult to predict how frequently seller concentration will actually be conjoined with completely easy entry, but the logical possibility is clearly open, and especially so if entry lags are long.

A closely related condition of entry (II) appears where, in any relevant progression of potential entry, there is always a small absolute value of the immediate condition of entry and where entry is always "ineffectively impeded." Price can exceed the minimal costs of the most favored established firms a little but never very much without attracting some further entry,[13] and these firms continually, through any sequence of entry, will anticipate greater long-run profits from setting a high entry-inducing price, reaping extra profits during a lag period, and attracting further entry, than from setting a lower entry-forestalling price. This is presumably because lags encountered in inducing entry are appreciable and because the long-run profit margin at the best entry-forestalling price is not large.

This condition of entry is effectively confined to cases where economies of the large-scale firm are absent or negligible, since otherwise the progressive attraction of entry would force a progressive and ultimately substantial rise in the absolute barrier to entry as firms had to operate at distinctly uneconomical small scales. The only important barriers to entry are therefore those of the absolute cost advantages or product differentiation advantages of established over potential entrant firms. But product differentiation is not reflected, for example, in significant economies of large-scale advertising.[14]

[13] The absolute value may or may not increase a little with further entry.

[14] It may be noted that large-scale economies must be insignificant in category II in the usual sense but not in another sense. That is, the output of a firm of optimal or lowest-cost scale must be a small or negligible fraction of total industry output (even though the firm may experience higher unit costs at still smaller scales), so that the attraction of a unit of entry will not significantly affect the market shares or unit costs of established and further potential entrant firms. (If it did, the barrier to entry would become progressively and significantly larger as each successive unit of entry was attracted.)

But scale economies may be significant in the following sense and still permit of a condition of entry which remains at a small absolute value (potentially even a constant value) through a progression of entry. In effect, we may have the situation where (1) although the output of a firm of optimal scale is a negligible fraction of total industry output, there are substantial economies of scale (declining costs) as the firm's output increases up to this optimum; and (2) *over the same output range the potential entrant's absolute cost or product differentiation disadvantage increases.* Then in order to avoid or minimize his absolute cost or product differentiation disadvantage, the entrant would have to enter at a suboptimal scale where costs were elevated because of small size, whereas in order to avoid diseconomies of unduly small scale he would have to suffer a magnified absolute cost or product differentiation disadvantage. In this case economies of scale on the one hand and product differentiation or absolute cost disadvantages *which are related to scale* on the other combine to fix a minimum inescapable disadvantage, even though optimal scale itself might be a negligible or relatively unimportant consideration. This case can properly fall under entry cases II, III, IV, or VI, in none of which scale economies need be significant in the usual sense.

The prospect for market conduct and performance is much the same as if entry were easy. Price cannot in the long run persistently exceed the minimal costs of the most favored firms by very much, although it can do so by a relatively small absolute percentage, and possibly by one that increases somewhat as the inducement of entry progresses. But since the possibility of forestalling entry by relatively low prices will in general be less attractive to the most favored and other established firms than that of reaping larger temporary profits at higher prices (which will induce entry), concentrated markets in this category will tend to be afflicted, like those in the first category, with the periodic emergence of prices substantially above the competitive level, with consequent structural instability tending toward atomism, and with periodic or chronic excess plant capacity.

As in the first case, the attraction of entry may ultimately lead to stability with an atomistic structure and competitive pricing. But any induced atomism is just as likely to be followed by a regrouping of structure through mergers or otherwise, and by the beginning of another cycle of high pricing and excessive entry. The latter possibility is perhaps stronger in this second case, since here relatively few established firms may have small differential advantages of absolute cost or product differentiation over all others. Then the emergence of competitive pricing following the attraction of entry will tend to result in their regaining a dominance of the market, reinstating high concentration, and thereafter setting off another cycle of high, entry-inducing pricing.

The major possible escape from these tendencies is that at some point the market will reach, through induced entry, a low enough concentration so that independence of pricing or imperfection of collusion will keep price below the entry-inducing level, while at the same time (1) the differential advantages of the firms now established are small enough that a stable structure will persist, and (2) the propensity of these established firms to reconcentrate through merger is checked by failure to agree or by law.

The third sort of condition of entry to be considered is that in which, with a concentrated market, the condition of entry is initially "effectively impeded" (and thereafter the same or "blockaded") at moderate absolute values. In this case, the most favored established firms can set a price that is moderately above the competitive level but below the industry joint-profit-maximizing level and that will forestall further entry to the industry. Moreover, by not exceeding the best entry-forestalling price and thus restricting the number of competitors, these firms expect greater long-run profits than they could get by establishing a higher price and ultimately attracting further entrants to share their market. This is evidently because long-run profits, while forestalling entry, are appreciable as compared to the temporary higher profits which entry lags would permit at higher prices.

The predicted course of action here is distinctly different from that for the cases of easy entry and of ineffectively impeded entry. Further entry, that is, will not tend to be attracted, since prices will be kept low enough to discourage it. There will thus be a relatively stable market structure except for possible shifts in market shares among established sellers. Price will tend appreciably to exceed the minimal level of costs unless imperfections of collusion or neglect of interdependence in pricing keep it lower, but it will nevertheless be only moderately above the competitive level and clearly lower than that of a monopolist protected from entry. It is quite conceivable, for example, that few dominant established firms might be willing to forestall entry at a price only a very few percentage points above cost if entry lags were short and if a substantial quantity of entry might be attracted by higher prices.

So much for tendencies relative to structural stability and the relationship of prices to minimal costs. What of accompanying tendencies in efficiency, in profits, and in selling costs? In predicting such performance in this category, distinctions must be drawn between barriers to entry that do and do not involve significant economies of the large-scale firm.

If significant scale economies are absent or negligible, so that the effectively impeded entry results solely from the product differentiation or absolute cost advantages of established firms, established firms can in general attain minimal costs at any of a wide range of scales. Two things then tend to follow. When such firms have settled into the position of pricing to forestall entry, all in general will operate at scales consistent with minimal costs. And the excess of price over minimal costs attained in the entry-forestalling equilibrium will be the same as the excess of price over actual costs, or the profit margin. Therefore excess profits equivalent per unit to the price-to-minimal-cost gap will be earned in the long run. Since there will in this instance be no periodic inducement of excessive entry, as there might be in cases I and II, there will be no corresponding tendency toward periodic or chronic losses from excess plant capacity.

If the preferences of buyers for the products of established as compared to new entrant firms are the primary bases of the "effectively impeded" entry — as may well be the case in numerous concentrated consumer-goods industries — then substantial advertising and other selling costs will ordinarily be incurred in sustaining the preferred product positions of established sellers. This tendency may also be present in similar industries under case II when the impediment to entry inheres in product differentiation, but the incentive to maintenance of barriers through continued advertising and sales promotion seems likely to be greater when the barriers offer a more valuable protection, as in the present case.

If the barrier to entry rests on the absolute cost advantages of established firms, such as result from resource control, and patent control of techniques, no similar tendency toward excessive selling costs is noted, although there might be a parallel stimulus toward enlarged expenditures on industrial research and technological development.

If significant economies of scale are present as a source of impediment to entry, structural stability with pricing to forestall entry is still to be expected, and a moderate excess of price over minimal costs will tend to persist if collusion is effective or interdependence strong. But conclusions with respect to efficiency and to profits are potentially different. The number of firms which can operate with maximal efficiency is distinctly limited. Thus if an efficient firm will supply at least one-fourth of the total market at prices likely to be charged, no more than four firms can operate with optimal efficiency of scale. If entry is attracted to increase the number of firms beyond this limit, some or all firms will operate at suboptimal scales and with higher actual costs. Generally this will in turn elevate the barrier to further entry a bit (further potential entrants anticipating higher actual costs), but in any event efficiency among established firms will be impaired.

Given this, the question in point is what the degree of seller concentration or number of sellers will be, relative to the efficiency ideal, when established sellers come to regard the immediate condition of entry as "effectively impeded." Will the number of firms be optimal, thus permitting lowest-cost operations, or will it be excessive, thus elevating the general level of costs through the inefficiencies of insufficient scale? Either may be the case. The structure of the industry may accidentally be such that established firms are generally of optimal scale, and the barrier to entry may then be large enough to encourage them to forestall further entry at a price moderately above minimal cost. In this event efficiency of scale will be optimal, and also the profit margin will be the same as the excess of price above minimal cost. Or the structure of the industry may initially be such that firms are smaller than is most economical, either "by accident" or because entry was deliberately attracted by high prices when firms were fewer. In this event, given a presently effectively impeded entry, actual costs will persistently remain above the minimal level and the profit margin will be smaller than the excess of price over minimal costs. However, some excess profits will presumably still be earned if the entry-forestalling price is to be regarded as attractive. In this latter case, larger absolute gaps between price and minimal cost may be required to provide effectively impeded entry, and fairly serious departures from optimal scale are theoretically possible. Elimination of these inefficiencies will not come through entry (which would worsen matters if it were attracted), and will not necessarily come about through a "rationalization" by mergers or other devices aimed at reducing the number of firms. A secularly growing industry demand would, of course, be a welcome corrective.

The exploration of case III has enabled us to discover two tendencies in price and market behavior which could be found extensively in concentrated markets. First, with the barriers to entry at some moderate level such that established firms can forestall entry at a price which allows some excess profit but is well below a theoretical monopoly level, long-run price policies designed to forestall entry may emerge, with a resultant structural stability of the market, only moderately super-competitive prices, and moderate excess profits. The second tendency, associated with the existence of significant economies of the large-scale firm, is that it is *possible* for oligopolistic responses to the conditon of entry, when it includes barriers resulting from scale economies, to lead toward a stable market structure in which further entry is forestalled and in which some inefficiencies of insufficient scale are chronic. On the other hand, it is at least equally possible that entry will be forestalled at a point where established firms are in general at efficient scales. The tendencies just described carry over into the remaining cases (IV, V, and VI), which may be analyzed much more quickly, by simple extensions of the arguments so far developed.

Suppose (case IV) that in concentrated markets there is initially "ineffectively impeded" entry as calculated with reference to the prices that will induce one or a few firms to enter the industry. But suppose also that after one or a few units of entry have been brought in, the barrier to entry becomes absolutely higher for further entrants and is effectively impeded from the standpoint of the most favored established firms. Then the market structures will be initially unstable, as entry will be attracted through prices above the entry-forestalling level. But the attraction of a finite and limited number of entrants will result, together with an increase in the price which will just forestall further entry, so that it will stand enough above minimal and actual costs to make it profitable to forestall further entry. At this point the structure of the market will become stable and the results will be similar to those predicted for case III above, with the same distinctions according to the sources of impediment to entry applying unchanged. Development of "case IV" into "case III" industries through structural change will fail only if imperfection of collusion or similar phenomena preclude the attraction of entry which will initially be desired by established firms.

Case V is that in which the entry-forestalling price rises higher and higher above minimal costs as entry occurs but never exceeds an "ineffectively impeded" value — that is, it never exceeds actual costs by enough to make the forestalling of entry attractive — until finally a point is reached in the progression of entry where the most profitable price only allows established firms to break even, and thus precludes further inducement of entry. This can occur only where there are significant scale economies (which elevate actual costs as entry progresses), and where in addition the relation of cost to scale is such as to give rise to a peculiar succession of values of the immediate condition of entry. Predicted behavior in this case leads obviously to the progressive attraction of a great excess of entry, terminating at or near a point where price is far above minimal cost but equal to actual cost for established firms, and where great diseconomies of small scale (or of an excessive number of firms) are encountered. In general this seems, from both observation and logic, to be an extreme, limiting, and unlikely case, although it illustrates the pole toward which the tendency observed in case IV may lead when economies of scale are important. It deserves special mention perhaps in order to emphasize that it illustrates a somewhat bizarre case, rather than a tendency for much of oligopoly, as Professor Chamberlin might have had it.[15]

In the sixth case established firms are at the outset and thereafter protected by blockaded entry conditions, in the sense that the level of industry prices which would maximize their profits if they were completely protected from entry is lower than that which will attract further entry. Established firms may pursue a joint-profit-maximizing policy while entirely neglecting the possibility of induced entry. In this case, we tend to get (1) a stable market structure, and (2) a large excess of price over minimal cost. If significant economies of scale are absent we also tend to get maximal efficiency in scale of firms and high excess profits. If significant scale economies are present, the same efficiency and profit results may ensue, or it is equally possible that inefficiencies of insufficient scale and reduced profits may be encountered. If product differentiation advantages of established firms are strategic in impeding entry, large selling costs to maintain these advantages may in general be anticipated.

In markets where there is an oligopolistic concentration of sellers, the condition of entry should thus be expected to have a distinct impact upon the market conduct of established sellers and upon the ultimate market performance which emerge. A primary distinction may be drawn among three sorts of cases: (A) those where barriers to entry are absent or where entry is ineffectively impeded through any relevant progression of entry (I and II); (B) those where entry is effectively impeded or becomes so after the attraction of a limited amount of entry (III and IV); and (C) those where entry is either blockaded initially or approaches a

[15] E. H. Chamberlin, *Theory of Monopolistic Competition*, 1st edition (Cambridge, Mass., 1933), pp. 92 ff.

blockaded limit through an unbroken succession of ineffectively impeded values (V and VI).

In situation A, oligopolistic pricing is likely to lead to a chronic instability of market structure, wastes of periodic or chronic excess capacity, and periodic monopolistic pricing episodes interspersed with returns of price toward a competitive level. Stability at reasonably competitive prices will occur only if oligopolistic collusion or the recognition of interdependence by sellers is quite imperfect, or if the attraction of entry brings about an atomistic structure which remains. The emergence of oligopoly in these cases (which do not admit of important scale economies) is potentially unfortunate from a social standpoint, but by no means unlikely to occur.

In situation B, the prospect is for a stable market structure with entry forestalled, initially or after a certain progression of entry; and also for a long-run price moderately in excess of a competitive level, but lower than monopolistic prices would be in the absence of a threat of entry, and for moderate excess profits. If significant economies of large-scale firm are not involved, long-run efficiency at optimal scales and an absence of wasteful excess capacity are in prospect. If such scale economies are involved, slight to moderate departures from optimal efficiency, due to suboptimal scales, either may or may not emerge, depending on the character of the general condition of entry.

In situation C, extreme monopolistic excesses of price over minimal cost, with a stable market structure, are generally in prospect. If scale economies are not significant, similarly high excess profits and optimal efficiency in scale will result. If they are, it is possible though not necessarily probable that moderate to severe wastes of insufficient scale may be encountered, together with the reduction or elimination of excess profits.

To this is may be added that the existence of barriers to entry resting on the preference of buyers for the products of established sellers may be expected frequently to be accompanied by excesses of selling expenditures by established firms, aimed at maintaining these barriers to entry. On the other hand, variations in the condition of entry seem unlikely *a priori* to be major determinants of variations in behavior in unconcentrated or atomistic markets, although this is in part because relatively easy entry is generally common to such markets.

This prediction, and the more complex prediction concerning the effects of the condition of entry in oligopoly, deserve some testing or verification from available empirical data. Even if they cannot be fully tested at present, the framework of hypotheses provides a rationale for investigating what the actual conditions of entry are in our industries.

Let us now turn to the empirical findings of our study.

2

THE CONTENT AND ORGANIZATION
of the Study

We have now defined the condition of entry, identified its determinants, and summarized theoretical predictions concerning its influence on business performance. The condition of entry to industries appears as a potentially significant dimension of market structure, with a substantial influence on the market behavior of business enterprises.

The predictions presented are "theoretical" in that they are logical deductions concerning what the importance of the condition of entry should be; they are also highly general, in that they predict the consequences of various logically possible sorts of condition of entry rather than of specifically known sorts of condition of entry found in actual industries. Since a theoretical approach to the topic does have these limitations, in an empirical study of the condition of entry it would be desirable:

(1) To ascertain in detail, for each of a large and representative sample of industries, the value of the condition of entry and the identity and relative importance of its various determinants;

(2) To develop empirical generalizations concerning the extent and pattern of the differences in the condition of entry among industries, and concerning the relative and absolute importance as barriers to entry of economies of scale, product differentiation, and absolute cost differentials;

(3) To test for associations of the condition of entry to market performance, and thus accept or reject various predictions concerning probable associations.

As is usual in economic investigations, our reach exceeds our grasp. Limitations of time and of data restrict the sample of industries studied; information on the character and determinants of the condition of entry in these industries is not entirely adequate; available performance data permit only a rather fragmentary testing for the association of the condition of entry to market performance. Thus restrained, we have been able in this study to analyze the condition of entry and its determinants for a sample of twenty American manufacturing industries, assembling relevant data already on hand and developing a considerable body of new data; to frame some inductive generalizations concerning the importance of various barriers to entry to the twenty industries; to assemble available data measuring certain aspects of market performance in these industries; and to make a few preliminary and partial tests for predicted associations of the condition of entry to market performance.

Although our findings are thus tentative, based on less than completely adequate data, and limited to a relatively small sample of industries, they seem to develop enough new information to justify presentation and discussion.

The organization of this volume

The information developed in this study could be presented in many ways. A temptation is to begin as the research work itself began, with twenty synoptic industry studies, and then to draw various generalizations from these studies. This would be a lengthy procedure, however, and perhaps inappropriate in a volume intended mainly to emphasize a cross-sectional analysis of structure and behavior in many industries. We will therefore proceed in the following fashion.

In the next three chapters, we shall summarize in turn the relative and absolute importance as barriers to entry within our twenty industries of economies of large-scale plants and firms (Chapter 3), of product differentiation advantages of established firms (Chapter 4), and of absolute cost advantages of established firms (Chapter 5). The emphasis in these chapters will be entirely on the determinants of the condition of entry and on the extent to which and the way in which each sort of determinant creates barriers to entry.

In Chapter 6, we will draw together certain findings concerning different types of barriers to entry and attempt to estimate in summary the overall resultant condition of entry to each of the twenty industries of our sample. The emphasis will be on the range of different values or patterns of the condition of entry encountered as among a selected group of American manufacturing industries. We will also draw upon theory to predict the implications of existing entry conditions in our sample of industries.

In Chapter 7, we will present the results of certain tests of predicted associations of the condition of entry to market performance. As suggested, these tests are unfortunately incomplete and somewhat inconclusive. Finally, in Chapter 8, we will discuss the apparent application of our empirical findings to problems of public policy.

Composition of the sample of industries

The twenty industries selected for study are not a random sample of industries in the United States. They were pre-selected in the light of various aims of the study and of the availability of data, and reflect in consequence a number of deliberately introduced "biases" as well as some unavoidable ones.

First, the sample includes only manufacturing industries. This restriction was imposed because of the supposition that industries from different sectors of the economy constitute a non-homogeneous universe with respect to conditions of entry, so that generalizations drawn from a small sample including industries from several sectors would be of doubtful meaning. Given the practical limitation of the study to twenty industries, it seemed best to sample fairly intensively in a single sector of the economy. The manufacturing sector was the most attractive, particularly since it is generally thought to be the one in which significant barriers to entry are most frequently encountered. In any event, far more data are available on manufacturing industries than on those in other sectors.

Second, the sample refers in the main to *large* industries — to those with unusually large outputs or value products. The greater public interest in such industries and their greater impact on the general welfare would recommend introduction of this bias, although interest in a strict analysis of conditions of entry would not. Actually, this emphasis is practically determined by the fact that the bulk of extensive studies, useful governmental documents, and adequate statistical and other data refer to large industries. Hence a potential bias in our findings should be recognized, since there is no *a priori* warrant for supposing that conditions of entry will be unassociated with the size of the industry.

The extent of this bias is indicated by these facts: [1]

(1) Although the 20 industries chosen represented in 1947 only a little over 4 per cent of the total of 452 industries recognized in the *Census of Manufactures*, they accounted for about 20 per cent of the total value product of these 452 industries;

(2) They included 8 of the 18 manufacturing industries with 1947 value products in excess of one and a half billion dollars apiece, 10 of 38 industries with 1947 value products in excess of one billion dollars apiece, 5 of 51 industries with 1947 value products between one-half billion and one billion apiece, and only 5 of the 363 manufacturing industries with value products below a half-billion dollars apiece. Data on the 1947 value products of the 20 industries of the sample are listed in Column 1 in Table I below.

[1] For a summary of the relevant Census data, see 81st Congress, 1st Session, H. R., Committee on Judiciary, Subcommittee on Study of Monopoly Power, *Hearings*, Serial No. 14, Part 2–B, pp. 1436–1456.

TABLE I

Composition of the Sample of 20 Manufacturing Industries, and Some Significant Characteristics of Each [a]

Industry	Value product in 1947 (in millions of dollars)	Percentage of industry value product supplied by 4 largest firms in 1947	Consumers' or producers' good	Durability in use (predominant tendency)
Passenger automobiles	n.a.[b]	90 [c]	Consumer	Durable
Meat packing	n.a.[d]	41 [e]	Consumer	Non-durable
Steel	n.a.[f]	45 [g]	Producer	Durable
Petroleum refining	6,624	37	Both	Non-durable
Flour milling	2,512	29	Both	Non-durable
Shoes	1,717	28	Consumer	Semi-durable
Canned fruits and vegetables	1,641	27	Consumer	Non-durable
Tires and tubes	1,547	77	Both	Semi-durable
Cigarettes	1,132	90	Consumer	Non-durable
Soap and glycerin	1,086	79	Consumer	Non-durable
Tractors	891	67	Producer	Durable
Farm machinery, except tractors	889	36	Producer	Durable
Distilled liquors	870	75	Consumer	Non-durable
Rayon	705 [h]	78 [h]	Producer	Semi-durable
Metal containers	680	78	Producer	Non-durable
Copper	n.a.[i]	92 [j]	Producer	Durable
Cement	409	30	Producer	Durable
Typewriters	154	79	Producer	Durable
Fountain pens	147	57	Consumer	Semi-durable
Gypsum products	128	85	Producer	Durable

[a] Numerical data are from the 1947 *Census of Manufactures*, unless otherwise noted.
[b] Not available. Value added of *motor vehicles and parts* in 1947 was 3.58 billion dollars.
[c] Refers to 1951 national passenger car registrations.
[d] Not available. Value added of wholesale fresh meat packing in 1947 was 0.98 billion dollars, and of prepared meats was an additional 0.24 billion. Value added here is a small fraction of value product.
[e] Refers to value added for wholesale fresh meat packing only. Inclusion of retail slaughter and farm slaughter would reduce the figure perceptibly.
[f] Not available. Value added in 1947 for steel works and rolling mills was 2.28 billion dollars.
[g] Refers to value-added figures.
[h] Includes all synthetic fibres.
[i] Not available. Value added of primary copper only in 1947 was 135 million dollars.
[j] Refers to the control of copper refining capacity in the U. S. in 1947.

(3) The sample is weighted in the direction of industries with high seller concentration. Data from the 1947 *Census of Manufactures* show four classes of manufacturing industries defined according to seller concentration: I, industries in which the first four firms supply 75 to 100 per cent of industry value product; II, those in which the first four supply 50 to 75 per cent; III, those in which the first four supply 25 to 50 per

cent; IV, those in which the first four supply less than 25 per cent.[2] The numbers of industries in the four concentration classes, in descending order of concentration, are 47, 103, 164, and 138. The corresponding proportions of the total number of industries are (I) 10.4 per cent, (II) 23.8 per cent, (III) 36.3 per cent, and (IV) 30.5 per cent. This applies to the total population of manufacturing industries. In our sample of 20 industries, the corresponding numbers in the four concentration classes, in descending order of concentration, are 9, 3, 8, and 0, and the corresponding proportions of the 20 industries are (I) 45 per cent, (II) 15 per cent, (III) 40 per cent, and (IV) 0 per cent.

Industries in which from 25 per cent to 75 per cent of value product was supplied by four sellers (those with moderate to moderately low seller concentration) have about the same importance in the sample of 20 industries as they do in the total population. Industries in which more than 75 per cent of value product was supplied by four sellers are grossly over-represented in the sample, whereas industries of quite low concentration (less than 25 per cent of value product supplied by four sellers) are totally unrepresented, even though there are 138 of them and though they supplied over 35 per cent of total manufacturing-industry value product in 1947.

Some such bias could well have been introduced deliberately, on the ground that the condition of entry is expected *a priori* to be a more important aspect of market structure in relatively concentrated industries. Actually, the bias is the result of the character of available data, which tend to feature not only large but also more or less concentrated industries. We will be able to say relatively little about the influence of the condition of entry in manufacturing industries of very low concentration, but a good deal of the condition of entry in more or less oligopolistic industries, since our sample includes industries supplying about one-third of the total value-product of all manufacturing industries in which four sellers supply over 25 per cent of individual-industry value product.

With respect to other potentially significant aspects of market structure, it has been possible to secure a reasonably representative cross-section of manufacturing industries. Table I reveals, for example, that the sample contains 9 industries whose outputs are dominantly producers' goods, 8 whose outputs which are primarily consumers' goods, and 3 in which substantial shares of the outputs go to both producers and consumers. Also, 8 industries have outputs classed as non-durable in use (foods, fuels, cigarettes, soap, etc.); 4 produce goods classified as semi-durable in use (with some durability but normally not for more than two years); 8 supply outputs normally quite durable in use. As to type of

---

[2] Value added rather than value product figures are used in 12 of the 452 industries, and 4 of those 12 are in our sample.

productive technique, 5 industries are classified as processing farm products and 4 as processing minerals; 3 are primarily or in significant part chemical industries; 5 manufacture or assemble mechanical devices; and the remaining 3 (shoes, tires and tubes, metal containers) fall primarily in a "miscellaneous fabrication" category. In some other potentially significant respects also, such as the pattern of growth or change of demand in recent decades and the relative stability or variability of techniques and of products, there is evidently a similar diversity among the industries of the sample. The sorts of diversity achieved not only impart a certain representative character to the sample, but also complicate the analytical task by introducing more "random variables" of a structural sort, to be considered in determining the net effects on performance of the condition of entry.

One further characteristic of the sample of industries deserves notice. It is drawn from a group of industries pre-selected according to the criteria that there should be a roughly corresponding industry group recognized in the *Census of Manufactures*, that Census data on seller concentration should be available, and that the composition of the Census industry should be such in each case that the concentration data reflected seller concentration within the "theoretical industry" or individual theoretical industries which the Census industry contained.[3]

[3] A "theoretical industry" means a group of sellers offering a group of products which are close substitutes for each other to a common group of buyers. A "Census industry" may obviously contain a single theoretical industry, as when it includes only a single sort of product sold to a national market — or even just part of such an industry, as when it excludes some close-substitute products. It more frequently contains a group of theoretical industries, as when it includes several non-substitute products or several regional or local outputs which are not offered to a single common group of buyers.

The seller concentration computed for a Census industry will generally correspond to concentration in the corresponding theoretical industry or component theoretical industries if the Census industry is not under-inclusive (does not exclude outputs of closely competitive products), and if one of two further things is true. One of these is that the Census industry should include only a single group of products all of which are close substitutes for each other and all of which are sold to a single national market. The alternative is that if the Census industry is essentially fragmented into several groups of products which are not close substitutes or into several separate geographical market areas, all principal sellers in the industry should be diversified among areas or products so that their relative importance in each major product line or area is about the same. If the required conditions are fulfilled, then the over-all seller concentration figures for the Census industry will represent concentration for either the corresponding theoretical industry or for each of the component theoretical industries (i.e., product markets or area markets). If not — for example if the Census industry is under-inclusive or if there is specialization by sellers among component regions or products — then the Census industry-concentration data will have no such theoretical reference and will be apparently without analytical significance. (For a further discussion of this matter see J. S. Bain, "Relation of Profit Rate to Industry Concentration," *Quarterly Journal of Economics*, 65: 297–304, August 1951.) As indicated, the sample of industries used in this study was drawn from a list pre-selected

A final and fairly obvious comment on the sample concerns the number of items. It is clear from a statistical standpoint that with 20 of 452 manufacturing industries drawn for study, neither the absolute number of items nor the proportion of all items sampled is sufficient to guarantee the reliability of conclusions inductively derived from a study of the sample. Tentative indications are the most that can be hoped for. Two things, however, may be said in defense of so small a sample. First, in trying to measure industrial structure in a dimension like the condition of entry, we have no secondary source in the form of a statistical or other compilation applying to numerous industries, as we do' for example in the case of seller concentration in manufacturing industries. As a result, the required data must be painstakingly compiled or manufactured — one industry at a time — through a series of intensive investigations. An impossible amount of time and effort would be required to develop such data for a large number of industries. Second, unsatisfactorily small as the number twenty may be with reference to industries included, it is far more satisfactory than the one, two, or three industries that have constituted the apparent empirical reference of numerous past generalizations in the area under study. We thus hope for some improvement in scientific procedure.

Methods employed in assembling and analyzing data

Most of the work on this study has consisted of assembling, developing, and organizing old and new data bearing on the condition of entry to the twenty industries in question, and in interpreting these data within the general theoretical framework described in Chapter I. Some comment on the methods of developing, assembling, and organizing data is in order.

For data on the condition of entry and its determinants and on market performance the study has made use of three major sources of information. First, for each of the 20 industries, a comprehensive canvass was made of the published materials available and relevant to the issues at hand. These materials included volume-length economic studies of individual industries (available in good quality for 5 of the industries), similarly oriented articles and monographs, reports of governmental agencies, governmental documents, popular books and periodical articles,

---

to fulfill, to a reasonable approximation, the criterion of the theoretical relevance of the Census concentration data applying to them. In making this pre-selection, the classification employed in the 1935 *Census of Manufactures* was referred to. Census data for 1947 are now available, and some relevant revisions in the Census classification of industries have been made. For all but a couple of industries used here, however, the criterion in question is roughly met by the 1947 Census concentration data as well. Automobiles and copper constitute two significant exceptions, and for them other sources of concentration data have been used.

trade journals, general business journals, and standard sources of financial and other statistical information. Important sources of this type will be cited individually in the course of the presentation of findings. From this canvass emerged an initial digest for each industry of relevant published information, as well as a synoptic general "background" analysis. For at least two-thirds of the industries sampled, the data available from published sources were insufficient to support the type of analysis projected, although fairly adequate general data were found in nearly all cases.

Second, some important information was acquired by securing access to unpublished manuscripts (including doctoral dissertations) and by consultation with persons engaged in making studies of certain industries. These will be cited when relevant in subsequent discussions, but especial mention should be made of the invaluable assistance supplied by the unpublished manuscripts of Professor Richard Heflebower (rubber tires) and Dr. Frederick Moore (copper), and by the consultation of Mr. Bruce Cheek (shoes) and Professor Leonard Doyle (canned goods).

Finally, it was found essential to develop primary data bearing on the condition of entry in each of the twenty industries. This was done in general by extensive questioning of executives in various firms in these industries. This questioning involved neither the use of familiar shot-gun questionnaire or survey methods, nor to any significant extent the extemporaneous arm-chair quiz. The essential steps involved were as follows. First, a lengthy preliminary survey was made of each industry, to provide the author with an orientation in its characteristics and a knowledge of the conspicuous blanks in existing information. Second, a detailed set of questions was designed for each industry in turn, to elicit information bearing on the condition of entry therein. Each industry was favored with a separate and special list of questions, and no general-purpose questionnaire was used. The questions generally involved some detailed reference to the specific characteristics of individual industries, and were grouped to refer separately to economies of scale, product-differentiation advantages of established firms, and their absolute cost advantages. (Examples of the questions are included in Appendix A.) Third, communication was established with the executives of companies in each industry, explaining the nature and purpose of the project. Either specific or tentative offers of cooperation were secured from executives of about a hundred firms. Fourth, the questions were submitted in writing only to those offering cooperation, and answers were subsequently received in most cases. The typical replies were in written form, although oral conferences were substituted in some cases and were used as a follow-up in others.

An essential question concerns the quality and reliability of such information. No single characterization would apply to all the replies received, but they may be described in a general way. In most cases, direct and explicit answers to some or all of the questions were secured. Failures to reply involved a small percentage who withdrew initial offers of cooperation after realizing the magnitude and complexity of the task involved, plus a very few who made perfunctory replies essentially not addressed to the questions. In perhaps a third of the remaining cases, there was an avoidance of a part but not all of the questions, on grounds such as difficulties of estimation and lack of knowledge. So far as questions were answered — as they were in the majority of cases — two types of replies were received. The first were in general lengthy and detailed, running for example from 5,000 to 10,000 or more words; frequently they included essays on relevant characteristics of the productive processes or markets of the industries in question and revealed the use of careful estimating procedures and reference to systematically analyzed data and experience. The second included brief and occasionally cryptic replies — though ordinarily very direct ones — which were usually characterized by the respondents as arm-chair guesses. It may be added that the persons doing the guessing were ordinarily well qualified by long experience in their industries to make meaningful guesses.

As regards the reliability of the information submitted in the replies, there is perhaps some natural tendency on the part of the academician to place considerable trust in lengthy and well documented replies and somewhat less in quick and admittedly "guess-estimating" answers. Checks for reliability, however, have suggested that as a whole the body of information assembled from all replies is fairly accurate and reliable. Where independent sources of information were available — from industry studies, governmental reports, analyses of industry financial data, and so forth — the information received in the replies has ordinarily been consistent with that in other sources. Comparisons of different and independent replies concerning the same industry have typically revealed consistency rather than disparity of viewpoint, thus suggesting the existence of a common and systematic factual basis for the replies. And replies have on the whole not revealed much, if any, "slanting" in line with the self-interest of the firm or industry, as might be revealed in replies tending to justify the *status quo* or the size, organization, or market policy of the particular firm, or tending to minimize impediments to competition. To be sure, sources disagree to some extent and there are occasional evidences of bias or of an *ex parte* representation of facts, but by and large the replies seem fairly reliable, and the sorts of disagreement encountered could generally be the result of a predictable dispersion of careful estimates concerning various situations or quantities. We have thus felt justified in regarding the information assembled from these replies as in general probably reliable, with the exception of some information where reliability is impeached by several other sources or which on equivalent grounds seems capricious in character.

So far as these data are reliable, then, they add importantly to the empirical findings on which this study is based. This is obviously true as regards their addition to the other data available, since they supply information on many points in many industries where previously there was none. It is also true as regards their contribution to the qualitative character of available data. Much of the relevant material previously available on the industries under study has consisted of the analysis and interpretation, after the fact and by "outsiders," of available records of market conduct, costs and prices, and the like. On the other hand, the replies to the questions submitted in connection with this study represent in general what might be called "engineering estimates" of numerous situations and quantitative relationships, viewed analytically and in abstraction from the influence of the random disturbances that always influence and obscure the meaning of records of past experience. From the standpoint of economic analysis, this sort of data (if reliable) is better suited to use in analysis than most other sorts.

The general time reference of all the estimates contained in the replies is "circa 1951," with a maximum range from 1949 to 1952. The number of replies received per industry ranged from two to five. Strict confidence about the source of replies was explicitly accepted in most cases, and waived in only a very few. As a consequence we make no specific acknowledgements at all, although a blanket expression of gratitude for friendly cooperation is due to the numerous firms and more numerous executives who contributed their time to supplying requested information.

It would not be a great overstatement to say that this study rests — as far as substantive findings on the condition of entry are concerned — in very large part on replies to questionnaires, with supplementary and supporting reference to other available sources. (This is not true, however, of the origin of very essential background materials on the economics of particular industries and of data on market performance.) In presenting our findings, we will draw on all sources, collating and combining findings as appropriate. Data on market performance have not been accumulated in any comprehensive fashion. We have relied largely on various sources of financial and other statistical data to supply certain data bearing on profits, selling costs, and productive efficiency in the industries of our sample. Such data are incomplete and frequently somewhat unsatisfactory, but the prodigious task of developing *de novo* more adequate performance data had to be eschewed at this time.

A final issue concerns methods of analyzing data on the condition of entry and on performance to test for hypothetically predicted associations of market structure to performance. By and large, the data found available or developed are not sufficiently elaborate to support the use of multiple correlation or other similarly complex statistical techniques applicable to this sort of testing. We have been confined to the use of extremely simple and crude methods of discerning possible or probable associations of the condition of entry to market performance.

3

ECONOMIES OF LARGE SCALE
as Barriers to Entry

The presence of significant economies of the large-scale plant and firm tends, as we have seen in Chapter 1, to provide a certain deterrent to entry.

Economies of the large plant or firm are reflected in a decline of the production and distribution costs per unit of output as the plant or firm is increased in designed productive capacity and if at the same time it actually produces at the successively larger designed capacities. The decline in unit costs with increases in the scale of plant or firm will ordinarily tend to be encountered over a certain limited range of increasing scales of plant or firm, and then cease to be encountered if the scales of plant or firm are increased still further. The scales of plant or firm (as measured in designed rates of output) at which the lowest attainable unit costs are attained are referred to as *optimal scales.* There may be a range of alternative optimal scales for a plant or firm in a particular industry if, after a critical size necessary for lowest costs has been reached, further increases in size will neither increase nor decrease unit costs. The smallest scale at which a plant or firm may achieve the lowest attainable unit cost may be referred to as the *minimum optimal scale* of the plant or firm.

In these terms, *significant* economies of scale to the plant or firm exist if its minimum optimal scale is a significant fraction of the total scale or capacity of the industry, and if, in addition, unit costs are significantly elevated at much smaller than minimum optimal scales. This fraction should be considered significant if its addition to going industry output (or the addition of a fraction at which costs are not significantly higher) will result in a reduction of industry selling prices which is notable to established sellers in the sense of being distinguishable from the effects of small random variations in market conditions, which is identifiable as the result of the output increment in question, and which is large enough to be felt. (What is "notable" in this sense will obviously depend somewhat on the relative stability or instability of demand and cost conditions in the market of a particular industry; the greater the general instability of the market, the larger the effect of an incursion of new output which may go unidentified and virtually unnoticed.)

Alternatively, the criterion of whether or not the fraction of industry output supplied by a plant or firm of minimum optimal scale (or a close equivalent) is significant may be whether, if established plants or firms shared a fixed total market with one additional plant or firm of minimum optimal scale, their own outputs would be notably reduced. The two criteria (based on either the price effects or the market-share effects of the entry to an industry of one more plant or firm of minimum optimal scale) come to about the same thing. For purposes of a rough approximation, we might guess that in most manufactured-goods markets a five per cent or larger reduction in price or in market shares (attributable very roughly to the entry of a minimum-optimal-scale plant or firm supplying one-twentieth of the total market) would be "notable" in the sense described, whereas a one per cent or two per cent reduction probably would not be notable. Circumstances will alter cases, however — particularly the circumstance of the relative stability or instability of the market.

Why does the presence of significant scale economies of plant or firm (in the sense defined) tend to provide a deterrent to entry? As we have argued in Chapter 1, the circumstance that an entrant would have to add a significant fraction to the output of the industry in order to attain lowest unit costs or a close approximation thereto will under most circumstances have one of four effects (or some combination of two or more of them). First, the entrant may enter at a small enough scale so that his entry will tend to have no perceptible effect on the prices or outputs of established firms (thus inducing no retaliation), but in this case the entrant will be of suboptimal scale and have higher than the lowest costs which are attainable at the minimum optimal scale. Second, he may enter at larger scales — at or near the minimum optimal scale — thus necessarily influencing either prices or outputs in the industry, and encounter a situation in which established firms lower their prices rather than reducing their outputs enough to allow the entrant a market share at going prices. In this case, entry in effect reduces industry prices, resulting in post-entry prices for both established firms and the entrant which are lower than the pre-entry price for established firms. Third, with entry at or near the minimum optimal scale, established firms may restrict output enough to allow the entrant a significant market share with unchanged prices. But in this case, it is not unlikely that the sharing of the market with another plant or multiplant firm of significant size will force sellers generally toward suboptimal scales, and thus elevate the costs of some or all established firms and of the entrant firm above the minimum attainable. (This will tend to be the result except in the event that the entrant firm can take sufficient business away from established firms to attain optimal scale, while at the same time not inducing a price reaction — a possibility which might be enhanced if established firms in general were operating at well beyond minimum optimal scales.) Fourth, the established firms may retaliate against the entrant by lowering prices to prevent him from becoming established in the market.

Thus, in summary, the entrant in those industries where the minimum optimal scale of plant or firm is significantly large may ordinarily or probably anticipate either higher than minimum attainable costs (due to suboptimal scale), or a lower selling price than that prevailing in the industry before his entry, or both. If this is so, it seems likely that established firms will in general be able to elevate their prices at least somewhat above their minimum attainable average costs without attracting entry. The extent of the gap between the best prices at which entry may be forestalled and the minimum attainable average costs of production and distribution is then (in the absence of other barriers to entry) a measure of the extent of the deterrent to entry which is provided by scale economies. We will have occasion at the end of the chapter to consider in more detail the nature of the association between scale economies and the relative ease of entry. For the moment, it may be observed that the deterrent to entry will tend to increase as both (a) the minimal optimal scale becomes a larger proportion of total industry output, and (b) the rise of unit costs becomes steeper as scale is reduced below the minimum optimal scale.

Actually, the effect just described of scale economies on the condition of entry is only one of two distinct effects. This first effect, reflecting as it does the importance of the proportion of industry output supplied by an optimal plant or firm, may be called the *percentage effect* of scale economies on the condition of entry. But scale economies may be important to entry not only because the supply of a significant fraction of industry output is required for efficiency, but also because large absolute amounts of capital investment are required for efficiency. That is, absolute capital requirements may be so large that relatively few individuals or groups could secure the needed capital, or that entrants could secure it only at interest rates and other terms which placed them at a net cost disadvantage to established sellers.

This *absolute-capital-requirement effect* is not the same as the percentage effect, and it may be important without the percentage effect being so, just as the percentage effect may be important without any important absolute-capital-requirement effect being found. This of course is because the percentage effect depends on the ratio of the absolute size of the optimal plant or firm to the absolute size of the total market of the industry, and not on the absolute plant or firm size alone.

The two effects of scale economies are not only clearly distinguishable, but the second — the absolute-capital-requirement effect — is appropriately considered under the heading of absolute cost advantages of established firms. We will return to it in Chapter V, and confine ourselves in this chapter to a consideration of the percentage effect of scale economies on the condition of entry.

Given our general hypotheses concerning the possible importance of scale economies in deterring entry (via the percentage effect), the major purposes of this chapter are two. First, we wish to appraise, for our sample of twenty manufacturing industries, the extent and the character of economies of large-scale plant and of large-scale multiplant firm. This will involve, in the cases successively of plants and firms, appraisal both of the minimum optimal scale and of the shape of the relation of unit costs to scale at smaller scales — in both cases where plant or firm scales are expressed as percentages of the total scale or capacity of the industry in question. Second, we wish to interpret these findings in order to get an idea of the apparent consequences for the condition of entry of existing scale economies in manufacture, as far as these consequences are those of the percentage effect.

A general view of economies of scale

It is a matter of common observation, and has also become well established in the literature of both pure and applied economic theory, that there is in any industry some systematic relationship between the scale of a plant or firm and its unit costs of production and distribution. This relationship is generally expressed in the following way.

Let scale be measured as the rate of output per unit of time which a plant or firm is designed best to produce (precisely, the rate of output which it can produce more economically than any other size of plant or firm). Let us suppose further that any plant or firm is operated at just its best rate of output. Producing at that rate of output, it will have a certain cost per unit of output for production, or for production plus distribution. Plants or firms of larger and smaller scales in a given industry will each in turn, according to the same principle, have given costs per unit of output. As we proceed from smaller-scale to larger-scale plants or firms, will unit costs change, and if so in what pattern? Will larger plants or firms have lower unit costs than smaller ones and if so to what extent? If they will, is a point reached where further increases in scale will not reduce unit costs further? If the latter is so, what is the minimum optimal scale of plant or firm, or smallest scale at which the lowest attainable unit costs are reached, when this scale is expressed either in absolute terms or in terms of proportions of market output?

The general answers commonly given to these questions are the following. First, if in any industry we begin by considering the smallest feasible scale of plant or firm, and then consider successively larger ones over a range including all relevant or practically conceivable scales, we will find that increases in the scale of plant or firm generally result in lower unit costs up to some point. Whereas a plant or firm designed to produce x units per day will have costs of $8 per unit, a plant or firm designed to produce and producing 3x units per day will have costs of $7 per unit.

What is the explanation for such *economies* of increasing the scale of the plant or firm? First, increasing scale permits a greater specialization of factors or agencies of production — a specialization impossible at smaller scales because of indivisibilities or "lumpiness" in particular forms of these factors or agencies, so that they can be acquired or used only in certain finite sizes. This specialization permits *real economies* in quantities of material and effort used to produce a unit of output, and corresponding savings in monetary costs. Second, increasing scale may permit the plant or firm to secure lower monetary prices for what it purchases or uses — as through the increased bargaining power which may be associated with large-scale buying — even though there is no lessening its real costs. Thus, *strictly pecuniary economies* (not matched by real economies) may also be associated with large scale.

The usual explanations of *economies of large-scale plant* emphasize the real savings of the use of specialized machinery, and of specialization of labor and of management functions, within the single factory or technical productive unit. Strictly pecuniary economies are not emphasized, perhaps because of the belief that a single plant will not ordinarily be large enough to take advantage of these economies. The common explanations of *economies of the large-scale firm* (which is larger than a single plant and thus in essence *the multiplant firm*) mention possible real economies of specialization of management, but emphasize strictly pecuniary economies such as those of large-scale buying. Also mentioned are savings in shipping cost for a multiplant operation in those cases where nation-wide distribution is for other reasons a prerequisite.[1] For some purposes, the distinction between real and strictly pecuniary economies is quite relevant, since the social benefits of the latter are often questioned, but from the standpoint of appraising the effect of scale economies on entry, all economies which result in systematic money savings are on a single footing.

---

[1] There are other terms also used in explaining real economies of scale — "principle of multiples," "principle of massed reserves," the "0.6 principle" as applied to containers, and so forth. These serve to point up interesting technological details of industrial processes, but the basic principles described are generally subsumed under those of "specialization" and "indivisibilities," provided we recognize that a single sort of factor or agency of production may occur in a variety of forms or designs, some superior to others if no restriction is placed on plant or firm scale, with different degrees of indivisibility or lumpiness as among different forms.

The second question is whether, with progressive increases in scale, a point is generally reached where further increases will not reduce unit costs further. The usual answer to this question is "generally yes." That is, the opportunities offered for cost reduction through specialization or through massive buying power are ultimately exhausted as the plant or firm increases in scale, until a point is reached in the range of possible scales beyond which further increases in scale will not bring about further reductions in cost. At some finite scale, therefore, there will be reached a point beyond which a larger plant or firm will not have lower unit costs. (From the foregoing example, a plant or firm producing 4x units of output per day might have costs per unit of $7, the same as those of a plant or firm producing 3x.)

This follows from the logic of the theoretical arguments supporting the idea of declining costs with increasing scale; that is, the indivisibilities of specialized factors or agencies which favor large size will finally all be overcome with a certain finite increase in size, and similarly the advantages of massed buying power tend to be exhausted at a finite scale of firm. Experience seems more or less to bear out the argument. As stated so far, however, the argument says only that there is some finite scale of plant or firm in any industry at which lowest unit costs are reached; it does not state how big this scale is, or what proportion of industry output will be supplied by an optimal plant or firm. This is actually about as far as deductive logic based on a few very elementary premises can safely take the theorist, but it leaves us with an embarrassing lack of information on a crucial matter.

A third question concerns the *pattern* of decline of unit costs as scale increases toward the optimum. Do unit costs decline steeply or gradually as plant or firm size is increased up to the lowest-cost scale? Also, do they decline more and more gradually with successively increased scale, more and more steeply, or at a constant rate of decrease? The answers ordinarily given here are two. First the initial rate of decrease of costs with increasing scale of plant or firm is not predictable on the basis of available knowledge; it may be large, medium, or small, depending on the techniques and buying markets of the industry. Second, with progressive increases in scale, unit costs will decline at progressively lower rates of decrease until a point is reached where they will not decline at all. This makes a convenient but not necessary corollary to the observation that unit costs cease declining in response to increases in scale at some finite scale.[2]

The fourth question relates to the minimum optimal scales of plant

[2] Not necessary unless the spreading of the fixed costs of indivisible units of equipment over larger outputs is involved, and this is not evidently the main force in economies of large scale.

and of firm, especially when these are expressed as percentages of the total scale or capacity of the industry. Actually, *a priori* theorizing from any reasonably reliable empirical generalization about technology and the like will not permit a general answer to this question, and available empirical data on particular cost-scale relations have been too scanty and unreliable to support inductive generalizations. Thus, most of the information on this point comes from free-hand guessing (often influenced by dubious general theories of technology or of technological development), although such pontifical findings are frequently intertwined with other theorizing in a manner which makes it difficult to distinguish valid deduction from vigorous but unsupported assertion.

Several "schools of thought" exist among the guess-estimators on this point. The dominant opinion among economists in the United Kingdom, expressed by such writers as E. A. G. Robinson,[3] P. Sargent Florence,[4] and J. Steindl,[5] seems to be that economies of scale are either frequently or generally quite important — enough to justify high degrees of seller concentration and to provide substantial deterrents to entry. Writers of the school would not be surprised if a firm of minimum optimal scale in manufacturing would normally supply a sizeable percentage of industry output. This line of emphasis may reflect the fact that there is in the United Kingdom no strong popular anti-monopoly bias of the sort found in the United States. It may also reflect the fact that the technical reorganization and concentration of British industry are felt by Britishers to have proceeded less far than in the United States, and with an adverse effect in the comparative efficiency of English industry.

Thus the British writings are generally consistent with pro-concentration, pro-merger, pro-cartel policy proposals, whatever may be the accuracy of the underlying factual observations and whatever the logic of the policy proposals thus developed. These British writers are much more likely to be concerned with explaining the failure of firms in unconcentrated industries to take advantage of the allegedly manifest advantages of very large-scale operations (citing deficiencies of capital markets and the like) than with documenting their assertions relative to the supposed advantages of large scale.

A part of the British position in question is that economies of the large-scale, multiplant firms are quite important. This is essential to a sophisticated development of the position, since it is fairly apparent that economies of large plants will not justify a proposal for a more or less across-the-board "rationalization" movement to develop higher concentration and

[3] *The Structure of Competitive Industry* (New York, 1932).
[4] *The Logic of Industrial Organisation* (London, 1933).
[5] *Small and Big Business — Economic Problems of the Size of Firms* (Oxford, 1945).

correspondingly reduce the number of firms. Thus the Britishers hold that there are numerous and important economies of large firms (other than large-plant economies) and that these are in an important degree real economies, potentially conferring real social benefits.

What we have described as the British view has been shared to a certain degree by some American writers, either native or émigré, although generally with caution if at all and frequently with qualifications.[6] The more typically American school, however, reflects the popular anti-monopoly or "antitrust" bias of this country, and is consistent in general with a policy position that high concentration is not necessary for efficiency and that much of American industry is substantially more concentrated than necessary. This orientation is evidently in some cases alloyed with a kind of Simons-Knight tradition stemming from the University of Chicago, which (1) admires competition for various reasons, and (2) seeks for facts, or an interpretation of facts, that will support the thesis that atomistic competition is compatible with efficiency in the American economy. A further ingredient of the alloy is of course the views of the institutionalist or quasi-institutionalist interpreters of the American merger movement and of market conduct in American industry, such as Frank Fetter, for example.

The major ingredients of this American position[7] are (1) that real economies of large plants do exist, but are insufficient to justify much concentration, and (2) that economies of large multiplant firms either are nonexistent or are only of a strictly pecuniary character, thus conferring no social benefits. As to the extent of economies of large plants, no analysis of the relevant facts is generally developed. Thus the members of this school are inclined simply to grant the existence of economies to plants as large as now exist (but not larger), and at the same time hold (rightly or wrongly) that full exploitation of such economies would generally be consistent with roughly atomistic market structures. As to economies of large firms, it is argued that increase in concentration resulting from the development of multiplant firms is unjustified by any real economies, although some writers admit that there are strictly pecuniary economies of unspecified size. All of this is consistent with an attack on any degree of concentration greater than that required for one efficient plant per firm, which is generally a moderate or low concentration. This American literature on scale economies, like the British, reads more as if it had been developed to rationalize a policy proposal or a preformed judgment than as if it reflected inductive generalizations based on any extensive investi-

---

[6] See, e.g., A. R. Burns, *The Decline of Competition* (New York, 1936), Ch. 1.

[7] See *TNEC Monograph No. 13, Relative Efficiency of Large, Medium-Sized, and Small Business*, pp. 95–139; also George J. Stigler, "Monopoly and Oligopoly by Merger," *American Economic Review* (May 1950), pp. 23–34.

gation of the relevant facts. In some versions, the general position is further defended by equating the efficiency of plants and firms with their survival-ability (which of course depends on much besides the level of production and distribution costs), and by adducing the survival of many small business units in concentrated "industries" as proof of the "efficiency" of these units.

On the matter of the sizes of minimum-optimal plants and firms relative to the sizes of their markets, therefore, we find very little actual information in the literature. Both major schools of thought rely upon qualitative and substantially untested generalizations about productive and commercial techniques which supposedly determine the response of costs to variations in the scale of plant and of firm. The important thing at this point is to recognize that this assortment of opinions does not constitute information, and to set out to find some.

Concerning ideas on the general relation of production and distribution costs to scale of plant or firm, three added matters also deserve emphasis.

The first concerns possible *diseconomies of large scale*. Does the growth of plants or firms beyond some critical size typically result in an increase in unit costs of production and distribution? We have seen that in the general literature it is held that the decline in unit costs with increasing scale becomes more and more gradual as scale increases, until a "minimum optimal" scale is reached beyond which unit costs will decline no further. This is held to apply generally to both plants and multiplant firms. Now if scale is increased progressively beyond this minimum-optimal level, will it finally become so big as to be less efficient than smaller scales, so that, for example, a "medium-sized" or "large" plant or firm is actually more efficient than a "giant" one?

There is a lack of specific information on this point. The *a priori* literature in general expresses three views. First, if diseconomies of large plants are encountered, they can in general be avoided by duplicating optimal-scale plants, so that larger-than-optimum plant outputs could elevate costs only because of discontinuities in plant sizes.[8] Second, *if* diseconomies of large multiplant firms are encountered, they are due to what is variously described as (a) red tape in large organizations; (b) imperfect expansibility of the management factor (it is less efficient in its larger forms, just as some types of machinery are more efficient if bigger); or (c) the fact that "management" or "the firm" is really a fixed factor (or like one) against which diminishing returns take place. Third, such dis-

---

[8] This generally takes care of possible diseconomies of outshipment freight costs from the individual plant, imposed by the need of reaching more distant buyers as plant output increases. The most efficient size of a single plant may be limited by such diseconomies; the efficient size of a firm is not.

economies *either are or are not* actually encountered as the essential consequences of large scale.

The "either there are or there aren't" character of opinions on the last point deserves emphasis, since there seems to be no one generally accepted set of beliefs about diseconomies of scale, and precious little evidence to bulwark various individual beliefs. It can be said that significant findings have not emerged to the effect that the largest firms actually found in various industries generally tend to be less efficient than somewhat smaller firms, and from this many have concluded that at least within observed ranges significant net diseconomies of big firms have not been encountered. Actually, what we have is a lack of any convincing substantiation of the notion that such diseconomies do exist, although in the present state of empirical research on this subject it could hardly be said that the thesis is disproved.

For purposes of making theoretical predictions of the effect of the condition of entry on market performance, I have been ready to assume,[9] wherever such assumption was needed, that significant diseconomies of large-scale firm will not be encountered in practice. This assumption has been made on the ground that, except perhaps with reference to extremely large and unlikely scales, the allegation that diseconomies of large firms will be encountered rests not only on unsubstantial evidence, but also on *a priori* arguments proceeding from unconvincing casual assumptions. Much more information would of course be useful. Unfortunately, the investigations upon which the present study is based reveal relatively little new evidence on diseconomies of scale to the firm, although what has been found is generally consistent with the thesis that such diseconomies have not normally been encountered in American manufacturing operations.

The second matter concerns the assumptions made concerning attained output rate in defining the relation of unit cost to scale. In its simplest form, appropriate under the assumption of a stationary long-run equilibrium in any industry, the scale-cost relation, as represented in the so-called "long-run unit cost curve," refers to the effect of scale on unit cost, assuming that every alternative scale of plant or firm will be regularly and steadily operated at its best rate of output. Such "best rate" is in effect that particular rate of output at which that scale of plant or firm is more efficient than any other scale. The unit costs corresponding to the alternative scales that are being compared are those costs resulting from regular operation of each plant or firm at this "best rate."

In a non-stationary economy in which no industry, firm, or plant will succeed in operating at even an approximately steady rate for very long, the scale-cost relation thus defined is not directly relevant to an appraisal

---

[9] See pp. 20 and 34 above.

of actual efficiency. The plant or firm will have a somewhat fluctuating output over time, and at a given scale will thus operate at a number of somewhat different output rates. Correspondingly, it will have a certain "load factor" reflecting the ratio of average actual rate of use to the capacity or best rate of use, and this load factor will generally be smaller than one. In this circumstance, the relevant relationship of unit cost to scale is that which prevails when it is assumed that each alternative scale of plant or firm is operated subject to prevailing or anticipated market fluctuations, and is thus subject to a resultant typical load factor on its capacity. The long-run average unit cost of each alternative scale should be calculated on this assumption, and conclusions as to minimum optimal scales and shapes of such curves should be derived accordingly.

This is only a practical and necessary adaptation of simplified conventional price theory to fit actual conditions of the scale-cost relation. Businessmen will normally think of the scale-cost relation in these terms unless otherwise requested not to, and we have made no such request in our investigations. Why is the adaptation worth emphasizing? It would not be if the general shape of the cost-scale relationship and the locus of the minimum optimal scale were generally unaffected by varying utilization, with effects only on the level of unit costs. But in fact there are reasons to believe that the incidence of varying utilization may at times alter the relation of long-run average unit costs to scale.

Perhaps the principal reasons are the following: (1) that smaller-scale operations may frequently be "less capitalistic," in the sense of using a smaller proportion of long-lived equipment (or other "fixed" factors) and a larger proportion of labor and materials, than larger-scale operations; (2) that larger-scale operations thus realize their maximum advantage under conditions of steady operations at planned capacity, wherein a 100 per cent load factor on long-lived equipment permits minimal depreciation and interest costs and wherein there is no premium on having a high proportion of costs variable and thus adjustable to current output rates; and (3) that therefore a reduction of the load factor at any scale through fluctuating output rates, plus the corresponding introduction of the opportunity to adapt variable costs to current outputs, gives a comparative advantage to smaller-scale operations. Thus the optimal size of plant or firm and the shape of the scale-cost relation may be altered by market instability, in this instance in the direction of reducing optimal scales. Market instability might have other effects for other reasons. All that we need say as prefatory to investigation is that the net relation of cost to scale under prevailing or anticipated conditions of market instability is the relevant one.

The third added matter concerns what might be called "economies or advantages of large-scale sales promotion." The economies of large-scale plant or firm so far referred to are economies in the costs of producing goods (as at the factory in the case of manufacturing) and of distributing them, in the sense of performing certain functions of physical distribution. Such functions normally include transportation, assembly, storage, and so forth, *but do not include* sales promotion expenses like advertising and personal promotional representation. In calculating the relation of scale to production-plus-distribution expense for a firm with either one plant or multiple plants, distribution expenses will be included only to the extent that they are either directly paid or indirectly absorbed (totally or in regard to increments above a certain level) by the firm in question. The shape of the scale-cost relation in a manufacturing industry could thus be somewhat influenced by the degree of forward integration of the manufacturers into distribution, though not necessarily so. In any event, nothing further than expenses of production plus those of physical distribution has entered into the cost-scale relationship so far described, whereas advertising and related sales-promotion expenses have been neglected.

In following this line, we have honored tradition in the field of theoretical cost analysis, which typically segregates sales-promotion costs from other costs. The reasons for doing so are partly historical, since the initial formal recognition of separate sales-promotion costs in theoretical literature [10] did not come about until a cost-scale analysis referring essentially to production-distribution costs alone was already rather fully developed. But it was also based in logic. For although there appears to be some "unique" and "reversible" general relationship between the unit costs of production plus distribution and the scale or long-run rate of output of plant or firm, there is some question as to whether such a unique and reversible general relationship holds in the same sense between unit sales promotion costs and the long-run rate of output and sales of the plant or firm.

Even if it did, of course, it would be of a different form. The traditional scale-cost relation refers to the relation of the amounts produced by various scales of plants or firms to the unit costs of producing and distributing them; the parallel sales-promotion-cost relationship would refer, for example, to the relationship of sales promotion costs (translated into an average per unit of sales) to the amount which can be sold at a given price. Thus the identity of the independent variable changes in passing from the production-cost to the sales-promotion-cost relationship (it changes from output to cost). Also, the output variables in the two cases are not identical (one is the amount produced and the other the amount sold), but only tend to become equal in a process of market adjustment. There is thus ample warrant, either with or without a unique relation of

[10] See Chamberlin, *Theory of Monopolistic Competition*, Chs. 6, 7.

sales-promotion cost to sales, for treating the two cost-scale relationships separately for purposes of a formal theory of market action, and for a corresponding distinction for purposes of our investigations.

This of course does not remove the fact that in addition to gaining through reduced production and distribution costs, plants or firms, in increasing their size, may also be realizing advantages in sales promotion. Nor does it remove the fact that such advantages should be considered along with scale economies in the narrower sense in determining the aggregate advantage attained with scale, the most advantageous scale (with all things considered), and the effect of advantages of scale upon entry.

The idea that there may be something describable as "economies (advantages) of large-scale sales promotion" evidently stems from the observation of the apparently preferred promotional positions of very large firms in some industries. It has been rationalized by suggestions such as the one that advertising may often be most effectively done through the "national media" (principally nationwide television or radio networks and magazines of national circulation); that a firm has to be big and have a big advertising budget in order to take advantage of these media; and that if it does it will somehow get a better relation of price to selling cost than smaller firms could.

If such a relationship did exist, it would be reflected, for example, in the ability of a firm with larger aggregate selling costs to expand physical sales volume more than proportionally to selling costs while holding price constant, thus getting a lower unit selling cost at the same price, or alternatively in its ability to expand physical sales volume proportionally to selling costs (thus not increasing unit selling costs) and at the same time to get a higher price per unit. There are obviously numerous possible variants of these phenomena which are theoretically equivalent. If such a relationship existed, it would be generally of a *ceteris paribus* variety, reflecting the responses of the firm's sales volume or price to its promotional outlay, which would occur if variations in this outlay did not induce reactions in the promotional outlays of competitor firms.[11] The question may thus be posed, as indeed it has been in our investigation, whether such a relationship exists in various industries, and if so what its characteristics are.

The main difficulty in proceeding very far with this line of analysis and investigation is that there is substantial doubt whether in any industry any unique general relationship between sales promotion costs and either sales volumes or selling price really exists — that is, whether it exists in the sense that sales volume or price responds systematically (and in

[11] In oligopolistic industries, this proviso is very important, and qualifies the meaning of "large-scale promotional economies" in an essential sense.

the same way for any firm) to an increase in sales promotion costs, and also whether it would respond in reverse direction in the same pattern to a reduction in such costs.

Some alternatives to the idea of a unique and reversible relationship seem equally attractive in logic and generally fit at least as well with observations. One of these alternatives is that *advantages to firms having large sales volumes* have been previously attained and are now being enjoyed, but that as of the current time such volumes cannot be reached on equal terms, via the route of large sales-promotion expenses, by those not currently enjoying them.

For example, an established firm, A, may, for one historical reason or another, have secured a very large sales volume — perhaps a half of the total market — and having done so, may be able currently to protect this market share at a lower advertising cost per unit of physical sales volume than another established firm, B (which has a tenth of the market), needs to protect that share. This may be because the saturation of media with very large aggregate advertising outlays pays off more than in proportion to the aggregate outlay, if the aim is to defend an already established market position. Thus one cent per unit on a volume of 10 billion units ($100,000,000 total) may hold the line against a rival's two cents per unit on 2 billion units ($40,000,000). Further, to continue our example, *either firm B or a new entrant firm C might be quite unable, by spending $100,000,000 a year on advertising, to get a volume as large as the 10 billion units which firm A enjoys, even though firm A made no retaliatory increase in its advertising budget.* Then A's advantage would not be one which inhered in the size of advertising budget alone, and which could thus be bought on equal terms. The fact of "being there first" may have given A an absolute advantage, even though this advantage may be in some sense the result of large sales.

The formalization of one possibility under this heading would be that small or new entrant firms might enjoy some economies of large-scale sales promotion, but on an inferior level as compared to large established firms — so that unit promotional costs for the former would be higher for any attained sales volume than promotional costs for the latter, even though they declined with increased promotional outlay. Another possibility would be that although the established firms in some senses were enjoying economies of large-scale promotion, small firms or entrants would nevertheless find no economies or diseconomies if they attempted to expand sales via promotion. Either possibility would be consistent with the notion that historical promotional outlays of established firms have altered consumer preference patterns in such wise that current promotional efforts meet an altered terrain.

A second alternative, which may be nearly but not exactly the same as the first, is that the basic advantage is simply one of general product preferences that favor certain firms: *they have become big because of these preferences rather than getting preferred positions by virtue of size or large advertising budgets.* In this case the idea of selling-cost economies or advantages of large scale may drop out, and the essential phenomenon may be recognized simply as one of product-differentiation advantages of some firms over others, basically unconnected with scale.

Whether we go this far or not, there is substantial doubt that in any industry a uniformly applicable and unique selling cost-sales volume relationship exists, applying to big established firms, little established firms, and new entrant firms alike. Each category of firms might face a quite different sales cost-volume relationship of this order. If this is so, it would be a Procrustean procedure to consider selling-cost advantages of large firms as simply a phase of advantages of scale parallel to the production-distribution cost advantages described. It seems more proper to treat them as a part of an elaborated analysis of product differentiation advantages. We will follow this procedure here, thus delaying consideration of the issue just discussed until Chapter 4.

The findings discussed in this chapter

As indicated above, this chapter is mainly concerned with findings on the relationship of the scale of plant or firm to the unit costs of production and distribution — first with reporting on them and then with appraising their relevance to the condition of entry. The primary source of findings relative to both plants and firms is found in the replies to the questionnaires described in the preceding chapter. We will also draw upon certain data from the *Census of Manufactures* on plant sizes, as well as upon certain available fragments of data bearing on the relation of cost to plant and firm size.

The remainder of this chapter accordingly falls into three main sections. The first of these will concern the economies of large plants in the twenty manufacturing industries under study, and will fall into two subsections, the first reporting on *Census of Manufactures* data bearing on the actual sizes of plants in 1947, and the second summarizing our questionnaire findings relative to the minimum optimal sizes of plants and to the shapes of cost-scale relationships for plants. We include in Appendix B a summary of other data bearing on plant size and cost, for comparison with questionnaire findings.

The second main section of this chapter will deal with the economies of large firms in the twenty manufacturing industries in question. The text summarizes questionnaire findings on minimum optimal firm sizes and on the cost-scale relationship for firms, while parallel findings from other sources are reviewed in Appendix C.

The third main section will deal with an interpretation of the findings on economies of large plants and large firms. The larger part of this interpretation will be given over to analyzing what impact the economies ascertained are likely to have — via the so-called *percentage effect* — on the condition of entry to the industries in question. But we will also comment on the extent to which economies of large plants and firms as ascertained favor seller concentration within these twenty industries, and on the extent to which they supply a justification for existing degrees of plant and firm concentration.

Economies of large plants: Census data

The primary questions in regard to economies of large-scale plants are (1) what is the minimum optimal plant scale when expressed as a percentage of the total scale or capacity supplying a single market; and (2) what is the shape of the scale-to-cost relationship at smaller scales? For purposes of these questions, "costs" refer either to production costs alone or to production plus distribution costs.

An initial notion of the sizes of plants requisite for efficiency in our twenty industries may be supplied by data on the actual sizes of plants built in these industries. In any of them, a wide range of plant sizes is found. This of course does not mean that all are equally efficient; various forces may keep many plants at sizes smaller than the optimum, while at the same time the firms operating them may for various reasons be able to survive. Conversely, it cannot be argued effectively that only the very largest plants are big enough for maximum efficiency. A plant is generally counted as the aggregate of production facilities at a single location, and it is quite possible that a large firm may have built two or more plants (or collections of plant facilities) of optimal technical size on a single location, without incurring any cost disadvantage but also without any significant cost advantage over a single plant of minimum optimal size. In fact, much evidence and testimony suggests that this is the case with the very largest plants in a number of the twenty industries. Correspondingly, there is no obvious way, from reading statistics on plant sizes, to determine just what is the minimum optimal scale.

The following arguments, however, may be advanced: that the firms operating the largest plants are generally multiplant firms, with plants in a number of different locations; that in building any principal plant they were thus not forestalled from building it to at least optimal size, since they could do that before adding another plant at a second location, and in general would do so; and that, therefore, the largest plants are likely to be at least as large as required for maximum efficiency. This argument is of course subject to qualification; for example, that the rational adjustment of plant scales posited may be slow in coming in a firm which has acquired a number of existing plants by purchase or merger, or that some plants serving small and distant corners of the market may have their scale primarily determined by the size of the local or special market. Nevertheless, it seems useful in a first approximation to regard the largest plant sizes in various industries as effective maximum estimates of minimum optimal plant scales.

Data giving some notion of the actual sizes of the largest plants in the twenty industries are available in the 1947 *Census of Manufactures*, though individual plant sizes are not shown. But plants are grouped into size-classes (size as measured by the number of employees), and for each size-class of plants there is shown (1) the number of plants, and (2) the proportion of total Census industry employment and of total Census industry "value added" supplied by each size-class of plants. Taking either employment or value added as an approximate measure of scale, certain inferences may then be drawn about the scales of plants in the largest size-class in each industry.[12]

Two alternative estimates of the sizes of the largest plants, both expressed as percentages of Census industry value added, have been drawn from these data. The first estimate is the average size of all plants in the largest size-class in each industry. This is undoubtedly a low estimate of the size of the *largest* plant in an industry, but will generally tend to lie above the size of the median plant in the largest size group. The second estimate is the maximum possible average size of the largest four plants in each industry — computed in general by attributing to all the plants in the largest size-class *other than the first four* the minimum possible market share (i.e., the mean market share of plants in the second size class) and by averaging all the rest of the total market share in the largest size-class over four plants. This estimate is of course generally higher than the first; it will be whenever the number of plants in the top class exceeds four, and will diverge further from the first estimate as the population of the top size-class increases. It tends to give a better approximation to the size of the largest actual plant, but the accuracy of the approximation varies, of course, with the population of the size-class. No attempt has been made to develop a more precise estimate, since the data will not bear too much weight in any event.

For the industries in question, the following general estimates were developed. With the automobile and copper industries eliminated for this purpose because of gross deficiencies in Census data, the number of plants in the largest size-class lay between 3 and 15 in all but 3 of the

[12] The data in question were used by the Federal Trade Commission for its study *The Divergence Between Plant and Company Concentration*, 1947. The staff of the Commission made available to me its tabulated calculations of plant concentration as developed from the Census data.

18 industries examined; for those 3, the number was large enough to make any simple estimating procedure quite hazardous. The average share of Census industry value added supplied by all plants in the largest size-class ranged from 20.1 per cent (typewriters) to 0.7 per cent (shoes), with the median percentage for the 18 industries at 3.8. For the second estimate, the maximum possible average market share of the largest four plants in the industry ranged from 19.1 per cent (cigarettes) to 1.7 per cent (shoes) with the median percentage at 7.9.

The data are more fully reviewed in Table II. The first frequency column (f_1) classifies industries according to the market-share interval within which the average size of all plants in the largest size-class of plants fell, market share being measured by the percentage of the Census industry value added supplied by a plant. The second frequency column (f_2) shows the same information when the plant size referred to in each industry is the maximum possible average market share of the largest four plants.

TABLE II

Classification of 18 Census Industries According to Percentages of Industry Values Added, Supplied by the Largest Plants, 1947 [a]

Percentage of Census industry value added supplied by the average of the largest plants	Number of industries with the largest plant size in the specified percentage interval	
	When "largest plant size" refers to average size of plants in largest size class of plants (f_1)	When "largest plant size" refers to the maximum possible average size of the largest 4 plants in industry (f_2)
0– 2.4	6	2
2.5– 4.9	5	4
5.0– 7.4	2	3
7.5– 9.9	3	2
10.0–14.9	1	3
15.0–24.9 [b]	1	4
Total	18	18

[a] Compiled from data from the 1947 *Census of Manufactures*. The composition of the sample is described in Chapter 2.
[b] The highest value in this class was 20.1 per cent.

This table shows that in from 2 to 6 industries the value added of some average of largest plants was below 2.5 per cent of total industry value added, and that in 6 to 11 industries it was below 5 per cent. It would perhaps not be amiss, therefore, to observe that in at least a third of the industries the minimum plant scale requisite for lowest costs probably did not exceed 5 per cent of total Census industry capacity and may not have exceeded 2.5 per cent of that amount. In from 5 to 9 industries, on the other hand, the value added of some average of largest plants exceeded 7.5 per cent of the industry total. Thus in perhaps another third of the industries the most efficient plant size per maximum estimates runs above 7.5 per cent of total industry capacity. In the "in-between" third of the industries examined, the maximum estimates of optimal plant size will run generally between 2.5 per cent and 7.5 per cent of industry capacity, depending on the method of estimation.

Interpretation of these findings as they bear on the condition of entry is not yet in order. The estimates are more or less top-limit estimates of plant sizes required for maximum efficiency, and since the largest plants identified in the Census may consist of multiples of optimal technical units on single locations, these may frequently be overestimates. Further, value added in a single year is a rather unsatisfactory measure of "scale" as that term is ordinarily understood, both because of the uncertain relation of value added to output and because varying rates of utilization of plants as well as scales of plants affect current value figures. Also, the data in question express the output of the plant as a percentage of the total national value added within the Census industry, whereas in fact the theoretical industry or separate market which a plant supplies may be somewhat smaller. We will thus delay any interpretation until further data have been presented.

Economies of large plants: questionnaire data

The second and major source of data on plant economies was found in replies to the questionnaires described above. These data, as summarized in succeeding tables, were generally secured in the answers to questions concerning (1) the minimum physical production capacity of plant required for lowest unit costs; and (2) the percentage by which total unit costs would be higher at various smaller plant capacities. By comparing the data relative to physical capacities with total capacity and output figures for each industry, these estimates were reduced throughout to a form that showed in each industry the relationship of unit cost to the proportion of national industry capacity supplied by the plant. Scale or capacity was thus measured throughout in "percentage-of-the-market" terms.

In general, the scale-to-cost relationship in question refers to production plus distribution costs. Production costs alone are generally referred to in those cases where outshipment and other distribution costs have no significant general effect on the net economies of large plants or the choice of plant sizes, but outshipment and other distribution costs are included in the calculation of plant-scale economies in those cases where they have a significant effect on the net advantages of increasing the size of plant. Costs of sales promotion are not taken into account in these estimates.

The first issue concerns the estimated minimum optimal scale of plant in each of our 20 industries. With scale expressed as a percentage of national industry capacity, the results from our "enginering estimates" are shown in Table III.[13] It shows a wide diversity among industries in this respect, the extent of which is suggested by summarizing the findings of Table III in a frequency distribution in Table IV. The latter table classifies industries according to the percentage of the national industry market which would be supplied by a single plant of minimum optimal scale, when this market share is measured by the mean of extreme estimates shown in Table III.

TABLE III

Proportions of National Industry Capacity Contained in Single Plants of Most Efficient Scale, for 20 Industries, per Engineering Estimates, Circa 1951

Industry	Percentage of national industry capacity contained in one plant of minimum efficient scale	Industry	Percentage of national industry capacity contained in one plant of minimum efficient scale
Flour milling	1/10 to 1/2	Rubber tires and tubes [g]	1 3/8 to 2 3/4
Shoes [a]	1/7 to 1/2	Gypsum products [h]	2 to 3
Canned fruits and vegetables	1/4 to 1/2	Rayon [i]	4 to 6
Cement	4/5 to 1	Soap [j]	4 to 6
Distilled liquors [b]	1 1/4 to 1 3/4	Cigarettes	5 to 6
Farm machines, except tractors [c]	1 to 1 1/2	Automobiles [k]	5 to 10
Petroleum refining [d]	1 3/4	Fountain pens [l]	5 to 10
Steel [e]	1 to 2 1/2	Copper [m]	10
Metal containers	1/3 to 2	Tractors	10 to 15
Meat packing: [f]			
fresh	1/50 to 1/5		
diversified	2 to 2 1/2	Typewriters	10 to 30

[a] Refers to shoes other than rubber.
[b] Capacity refers to total excluding brandy. Costs refer explicitly to 4-year whiskey, packaged.
[c] Refers primarily to complex farm machines.
[d] Optimal balanced integration of successive processes assumed. Inshipment and outshipment largely by water assumed; optimal scale may be smaller with scattered market and land shipment.
[e] Refers to fully integrated operation producing flat rolled products. Percentage figures are based on capacity circa 1950; subsequent growth of national capacity would lead to slightly lower percentages today.
[f] Percentages are of total non-farm slaughter; diversified operation includes curing, processing, etc.
[g] Purchase of materials at a constant price assumed; production of a wide variety of sizes assumed.
[h] Combined plasterboard and plaster production assumed.
[i] Refers to plant producing both yarn and fibre.
[j] Includes household detergents.
[k] Plant includes integrated facilities for production of components as economical. Final assembly alone — 1 to 3 per cent.
[l] Total includes conventional pens and ballpoints, but plant specialization by price class assumed.
[m] Assumes electrolytic refining.

[13] In this table, the inclusion of two limiting percentages for an industry — e.g. 0.5 per cent to 2.5 per cent — defines the range within which engineering estimates

In 11 of the 20 industries, a minimum optimal plant would account for a rather small fraction of national capacity, or under 2.5 per cent. In 5 others the fraction would run above 7.5 per cent, and the rest lie in between. In general, the industries with slight economies of scale of plant are engaged in the processing of agricultural or mineral materials, whereas greater plant economies are frequently encountered in industries making mechanical devices. These engineering estimates of the importance of economies of large plant present an over-all picture not greatly different from that derived by approximating optimal scales as the average of actual plant sizes in the largest plant-size intervals in the Census (column f_1 of Table II). But they clearly ascribe less importance to such economies than the estimates of optimal scales as the maximum possible average sizes of the largest 4 actual plants in each of these industries (column f_2 of Table II). This finding seems consistent with our observation that the largest actual plants in an industry frequently represent a duplication of optimal-scale facilities on a single site.

The findings of Tables III and IV, however, reflect the percentages

TABLE IV

Classification of 20 Industries According to Percentages of National Industry Capacities Contained in Single Plants of Most Efficient Scale (from Table III)

Percentage of national industry capacity contained in a plant of optimal scale	Number of industries with optimal scale plant (per mean estimate) in the specified percentage interval (f_3)
0–2.4	11
2.5– 4.9	1
5.0– 7.4	3
7.5– 9.9	2
10.0–14.9	2
15.0–24.9	1
Total	20

fell. In studying Table III, the reader interested in detail should pay especial attention to its footnotes, most of which either supply explicit definitions of industry categories covered or state assumptions concerning the type of plant or operation described. Important examples of this are the following. The petroleum refining estimate assumes fully diversified refinery equipment and also assumes only the limitations on plant scale imposed by tanker transport of products to a large and densely populated market; overland transport to typical inland markets imposes severer limitations. The automobile figure does not refer to assembly alone, but to a balanced complex of plants including components-producing plants of the sort typically integrated by assemblers; this would normally involve the use of several assembly plants of optimal size. The rayon plant in question would be one producing both yarn and fibre, and these two materials were aggregated in computing the percentages shown. In general, we have tried to select the optimal technique, product-mix, and so forth as the frame of reference for plant-scale calculations.

of national Census industry capacities supplied by single plants. As
such, they can hardly be taken at face value so long as the suspicion
remains that many Census industries may be broken into several separate
and largely noncompeting regional submarkets or product submarkets,
and that plants in such industries ordinarily specialize in only one such
submarket. In these cases the relevant measure of the scale of a minimum
optimal plant should be the proportion of the industry capacity supplying
a single submarket provided by such a plant. This proportion will of
course tend to be larger than the proportion of national capacity provided by the same plant.

It appears that in 12 of the 20 industries the national industry is
divided into distinct submarkets, with plant specialization among such
submarkets. A significant geographical segmentation of the national
market is found in 7 industries — flour, cement, petroleum refining, steel,
metal containers, meat packing, and gypsum products; national markets
are broken into regions and a single plant will mainly supply one region.
A significant division of the market by product lines, with a single plant
typically specializing in one or a few lines, is found in 5 industries —
shoes, canned fruits and vegetables, farm machinery, automobiles, and
fountain pens.[14] In the case of both geographical and product segmentation, the relevant measure of minimum optimal plant scale is the percentage of a specific regional or product submarket which such a plant
will supply.[15] In the remaining 8 industries — distilled liquors, rubber
tires and tubes, rayon, soap, cigarettes, copper, tractors, and typewriters
— either separate product and regional submarkets do not exist in important degree, or if they do there is typically no specialization by plants
among submarkets.

The industries of our sample in which market segmentation is important are predominantly those for which the percentages of national industry capacities represented by single plants of minimum optimal scale
are quite small. In 9 of the first 10 industries arrayed in order of increasing proportions of national Census industry capacity supplied by a plant
in Table III, significant market segmentation is found; only two industries
in which such segmentation is found — automobiles and fountain pens —
lie in the range of great economies of large plants as measured by percentages of the national Census industry capacity. Where technology does
not give some importance to plant economies in industries of our sample,

[14] In addition, the metal container industry, which shows distinct regional segmentation, also shows product segmentation as between packers' and general-line cans,
and considerable plant specialization by product line.
[15] In many of the segmented markets, of course, there is some competition across
the boundaries of the segments. This does not appear to have any systematically important impact on the percentage effect of plant scale economies within segments,
and we have neglected it in our calculations.

geography and product specialization by plants apparently do. Correspondingly, revised plant-size data showing percentages of individual submarket capacities supplied by minimum optimal plants will differ markedly from those in Tables III and IV.

To make the revision required, we have restated the minimum optimal plant capacity for each of the 12 industries involved; first, as a percentage of the capacity supplying the largest regional or product submarket identified in the industry; and second, as a percentage of capacity supplying the smallest of the major submarkets identified. For example, 4 major regional markets were identified in the petroleum refining industry. The proportion of national capacity supplied by a single minimum optimal refinery had been estimated in Table III at 1.75 per cent; the corresponding percentages for the largest and smallest of the four major regional markets were 4.3 per cent and 11.5 per cent. In the fountain pen industry the proportion of aggregate national capacity supplied by a minimum optimal plant was estimated at from 5 to 10 per cent. Dividing the market into high-priced or gift pens and low-priced pens including ballpoints (and recognizing differences in techniques for producing the two lines) the corresponding percentages become 25 to 33.3 per cent and 10 to 15 per cent.

Subjective judgments have inescapably influenced the identifications of submarkets used in calculations, particularly in the identification of regions, in the decision as to what is a "major" region or product line, and in the decision as to whether market segmentation is significant. We have tried to follow available information and industry practice systematically. If there is a bias, it is probably in the direction of defining areas and product lines rather broadly and of recognizing segmentation only if there is strong supporting evidence.

The revisions of market-share data recognizing segmentation for the 12 industries affected are described in Table V, which shows in successive columns the proportion supplied by a minimum optimal plant (a) of national Census industry capacity, from Table III; (b) of the capacity supplying the largest regional or product submarket; and (c) of the capacity supplying the smallest major submarket. When these revisions have been made and the results combined with the unrevised data for the remaining eight industries, we can present in Table VI two frequency distributions parallel to that in Table IV. These classify industries according to the percentage of market capacity provided by a minimum optimal plant, in the first case (column f_4 of Table VI) when the capacities of optimal plants in the twelve revised industries are expressed as percentages of the total capacities supplying the largest submarkets in their industries, and in the second (column f_5) when these capacities are expressed as percentages of the total capacities supplying the smallest

TABLE V

Proportion of National Industry Capacity and of Specified Submarket Capacities Contained in Single Plants of Most Efficient Scale, for 12 Industries Affected by Market Segmentation, per Estimates Circa 1951 [a]

Industry	Percentage of national industry capacity contained in one plant of minimum efficient scale (from Table III)	Percentage of capacity supplying largest submarket contained in one plant of minimum efficient scale	Percentage of capacity supplying smallest major submarket contained in one plant of minimum efficient scale
Flour milling	$\frac{1}{10}$ to $\frac{1}{2}$	$\frac{1}{3}$ to $1\frac{1}{2}$	$1\frac{1}{2}$ to 7
Shoes	$\frac{1}{7}$ to $\frac{1}{2}$	$\frac{3}{5}$ to $1\frac{1}{5}$	8 to 10
Canned fruits and vegetables	$\frac{1}{4}$ to $\frac{1}{2}$	$2\frac{1}{2}$ to 5	10 to 20
Cement	$\frac{4}{5}$ to 1	4 to 5	27 to $33\frac{1}{3}$
Farm machines, except tractors	1 to $1\frac{1}{2}$	4 to 6	4 to 6
Petroleum refining	$1\frac{3}{4}$	$4\frac{1}{3}$	$11\frac{1}{2}$
Steel	1 to $2\frac{1}{2}$	$2\frac{1}{2}$ to $6\frac{1}{4}$	20 to 50
Metal containers	$\frac{1}{3}$ to 2	2 to 12	$8\frac{1}{2}$ to 50
Meat packing: fresh	$\frac{1}{50}$ to $\frac{1}{5}$	$\frac{1}{10}$ to 1	$\frac{1}{4}$ to $2\frac{1}{4}$
diversified	2 to $2\frac{1}{2}$	8 to 10	24 to 30
Gypsum products	2 to 3	8 to 12	20 to 30
Automobiles	5 to 10	10 to 20	30 to 60
Fountain pens	5 to 10	10 to 15	25 to $33\frac{1}{3}$

[a] See relevant footnotes in Table III.

major submarkets identified. The last column in Table VI repeats column f_3 from Table IV, for purposes of comparison.

The revised data in Table VI suggest several interesting things about the size of minimal optimal plants in our twenty industries. If the reference is jointly to largest submarkets of industries with segmented markets and to the national markets of those with unsegmented markets (f_4 in Table VI) then in 5 of the 20 cases an optimal plant would supply less than 2.5 per cent of its market, in 8 less than 5 per cent and in 14 cases less than 7.5 per cent. If this is true and if, further, it should be true that the plant-scale curve were fairly flat for most of a range of suboptimal scales back to, let us say, a half of optimum, then in from 8 to 14 of the 20 cases, the scale requirements for a reasonably efficient plant should not be such as to require the addition of a very important fraction to market output. A firm constructing an efficient plant probably would not induce serious repercussions from established firms in its market. If unit costs were markedly increased with moderate reductions of scale, of course, the preceding would be true of fewer industries.

On the other hand, in 6 cases — gypsum products, automobiles, type-

TABLE VI

Classification of 20 Industries [a] by Percentages of Individual Market Capacities Contained in a Single Plant of Most Efficient Scale

	Number of industries with optimal plant-scale in the specified percentage interval		
Percentage of individual market capacity contained in a plant of optimal scale	Where percentage is that of the total capacity supplying the largest recognized submarket (f_4)	Where percentage is that of the total capacity supplying the smallest recognized submarket (f_5)	Where percentage is that of the total capacity supplying the national market (f_3 from Table IV)
0– 2.4	5	3	11
2.5– 4.9	3	1	1
5.0– 7.4	6	4	3
7.5– 9.9	0	1	2
10.0–14.9	4	3	2
15.0–19.9	1	1	0
20.0–24.9	1	1	1
25.0–29.9	0	3	0
30.0–34.9	0	1	0
35.0–39.9	0	1	0
40.0–49.9	0	1	0
Total	20	20	20

[a] The meat packing industry is considered for purposes of this table as involving only so-called *fresh* meat packing.

writers, fountain pens, tractors, and copper — the proportion of the total capacity supplying either the unsegmented national market or the largest submarket provided by a single optimal plant runs from 10 to 25 per cent. If unit costs are significantly raised at suboptimal scales of, let us say, half of optimum, then in these cases a reasonably efficient plant would have to supply a more significant percentage of the markets it entered, and might expect to induce some repercussions from established firms.

The picture changes markedly if our attention shifts in the case of the 12 segmented industries from the largest to the smallest major submarkets (f_5 in Table VI). Now we find that in 11 of the 20 cases (rather than 6) the proportion of the relevant market capacity supplied by a minimum optimal plant exceeds 10 per cent, and in 6 cases it exceeds 25 per cent. Plant economies are sufficient to require supplying an important fraction of the market in order to be efficient in half or more of the cases. The importance of plant economies thus potentially bulks large indeed in the smaller regional submarkets and smaller product lines, whereas it is evidently less in the major submarkets, as it frequently is also in the industries with relatively unsegmented national markets.

The preceding all refers to the estimated minimum optimal scales of plants, and moreover simply reports findings without interpreting them; interpretation of findings is reserved for the last part of this chapter.

Evaluation of the extent and importance of economies of large plants can be much more complete and satisfactory if it rests also on a knowledge of how unit costs are related to plant scale at scales smaller than the minimum optimal scale — of the shape of the so-called plant-scale curve in each of the industries in question.

Unfortunately, only relatively fragmentary information has been developed from questionnaires concerning the shapes of these plant-scale curves. What has been found may be summarized as follows. First, there are 13 industries for which detailed quantitative data on the shapes of plant-scale curves were not received, although for most of these some qualitative judgments on the matter were obtained. These may be summarized as follows:

Industry	Percentage of capacity supplying largest recognized submarket which is supplied by a single optimal plant	Judgment as to relative unit costs at smaller scales
Typewriters	10 to 30	*Substantially higher* at from 7.5 to 5 per cent of national market.
Automobiles	10 to 20	*Moderately higher* at 5 per cent of largest submarket; *steeply higher* at 2 per cent of largest submarket; *uneconomic* at still smaller scales.
Tractors	10 to15	*Slightly higher* back to 5 per cent of national market; *moderately higher* at between 1 and 2.5 per cent.
Farm machinery, ex tractors	4 to 6	*Moderately higher* at 2.5 per cent of largest submarket.
Steel	2.5 to 6.25	*Up by 5 per cent or more of costs* at scales at or below 1.25 to 3 per cent of largest submarket.
Meat packing: fresh	0.1 to 1	*Only slightly higher at smaller scales.*
diversified	8 to 10	*Only slightly higher* back to 1 per cent or less of largest regional market.
Canned fruits and vegetables	2.5 to 5	*Up 2 to 5 per cent of costs* at smaller scales.
Shoes	0.6 to 1.2	*Up from 1 to 10 per cent of costs* at scales substantially smaller than 0.6 per cent of largest submarket.
Fountain pens	10 to 15	*Higher but no definite estimate.*

Gypsum products	8 to 12	*Higher but no definite estimate.*
Copper	10	*Higher but no definite estimate.*
Metal containers	2 to 12	*Higher but no definite estimate.*
Flour	0.3 to 1.5	*Higher but no definite estimate.*

Though no single simple picture emerges, certain conclusions stand out. For 5 industries, including 4 in which the estimated scale of a minimum optimal plant is a sizeable proportion of the capacity supplying the largest submarket, not even a qualitative judgment of the effect of reduced scale on unit cost was received. In 4 other industries (typewriters, automobiles, farm machines, steel) in which minimum optimal scale was fairly large, halving the minimum optimal scale would raise unit costs "moderately," whereas in tractors and diversified meat packing only a slight cost increase would result from a half-optimal scale. There were 4 industries in this group for which minimum optimal scales were so small, as proportions of principal submarket capacities, that the shape of the scale curve at smaller scales is of minor interest. (These were canned fruits and vegetables, shoes, fresh meat packing, and flour.)

Somewhat more specific information on the shapes of scale curves is available from questionnaire replies for the remaining 7 industries — cement, rayon, soap, petroleum refining, cigarettes, tires and tubes, and liquor. Before presenting these data, however, two explanatory comments should be made. First, all but 1 of these 7 industries fall in a category in which the estimated size of a minimum optimal plant, when measured as a percentage of capacity supplying either an unsegmented national market or the largest recognized submarket, is in the next to highest range. None of the industries is in the top quartile in Table III, where industries are arrayed by size of optimal scale expressed as percentage of the capacity supplying the national market. But 4 of them (tires, rayon, soap, and cigarettes) are in the third or next to highest quartile, and 2 others (petroleum refining and cement) fall in roughly the same class when the measure of scale is revised to refer to a percentage of the largest submarket. Thus only in the liquor industry is the estimated size of minimum optimal plant in the lower ranges.

Second, the costs included are generally total costs at the factory gate, plus shipping and distribution costs paid or absorbed by the manufacturer where these are significant. Thus raw material costs are definitely included in addition to processing costs, as are packaging costs — and, especially for cigarettes and liquor, excise taxes. It is notable *that the virtual advantages of large-scale plants with respect to processing costs only, which virtual advantages are frequently large, are greatly diluted by the incursion by all sizes of plants of relatively constant costs per unit for raw materials, packaging, excise-tax stamps, and the like.* This dilution proceeds to the point of substantially reducing (often almost to the vanishing point) the net advantages to larger plants. The observation applies in full force to the soap, petroleum refining, cigarette, tire and tube, and liquor industries.

Third, the market percentages used refer in the cases of the cement and petroleum refining industries to the largest recognized geographical submarkets. The apparent importance of economies of large plants would loom a good deal larger in the smaller submarkets in these industries. In the other 5 industries represented, significant market segmentation was not found.

The data on the shapes of plant-scale curves in these industries are shown in Table VII, by representing the relationship of relative costs (costs at minimum optimal scale are registered as 100) to the percentages of the unsegmented national market or largest submarket supplied by various alternative sizes of plants at the minimum optimal and smaller scales. Interpolation between or extrapolation beyond actual specific estimates has not been undertaken in this table.

TABLE VII

Relationship of Relative Unit Costs to Plant Scale in 7 Manufacturing Industries

	Relative unit costs of production at plant scales corresponding to specified market percentages of either the unsegmented national market or the largest recognized submarket (optimal costs = 100) [a]								
	5	4	3.5	3	2	1.5	1	0.5	0.25
Cement	100	..	105	..	115	..	135	..	..
Rayon	..	100	..	..	108	..	125	..	..
Soap	..	100	..	..	103	..	105	..	..
Petroleum refining [b]	..	100	100.5	101	102	103	105	108	115
Cigarettes	100	..	..	..	101	..	102	..	..
Tires and tubes	..	..	..	..	100	101	..	104.5	105.5
Liquor	..	..	..	..	..	100	100.5	101	102

[a] The unsegmented national market is referred to in all cases except cement and petroleum refining.
[b] Refers to seaboard refinery operation using water transport.

Two findings stand out. First, 5 of the 7 industries find their minimum optimal scales, by low estimate, at either 4 or 5 per cent of the unsegmented national market or largest regional submarket. This places them, as noted, in the next to highest quartile of industries as arrayed in order of size of optimal plant, and in a category where plant scale as judged by optimal scale alone might be considered an important factor. It is only for 2 of these 5 industries, however, that costs apparently rise steeply enough at suboptimal scales so that reasonably good efficiency would require supplying a significant share of the market. Examination of the 2-per-cent column in Table VII reveals that at a scale required to supply 2 per cent of the market, cement and rayon costs would be seriously elevated. But for the cigarette, petroleum refining, and soap industries they would be up only 1, 2, and 3 per cent at the equivalent scale, and only 2, 5, and 5 per cent at scales sufficient to supply 1 per cent each of the respective markets. The importance of plant scale economies suggested by minimum-optimal-scale data alone thus tends to diminish significantly in the light of scale curve data in three of the five cases just discussed. It is sustained, however, in the other two.

Second, the relative flatness of the plant-scale curve at scales back to a fourth or less of optimal scale — noted already for soap, petroleum refining, and cigarettes — is found also for tires and tubes and liquor. If we were to hazard a generalization from this scanty sample, it would be that there is a substantial share of manufacturing industries in which operation at one-half of the designated optimal plant scale imposes very slight total unit cost disadvantages, whereas operation at one-fourth of optimal scale may in the same cases impose unit cost disadvantages of five per cent or less. On the other hand, there appears to be at least a minority of industries in which movement back to one-half of minimum optimal scale imposes a moderate and perhaps quite significant cost disadvantage, and in which operation at a quarter of optimal scale imposes a severe cost disadvantage.

The qualitative findings listed earlier are in general consistent with this thesis. If we put together those findings with the data of Table VII, the following tentative and very rough classification of industries emerges:

(1) *Industries with very important plant scale economies*, in the sense that the proportion of market capacity (unsegmented national market or largest submarket) in an optimal scale plant is quite large (10 per cent and up), and that the rise of unit costs is at least moderately great at half-optimal scales:

> Automobiles
> Typewriters

(2) *Industries with moderately important plant scale economies*, in the sense that 4 or 5 per cent of market capacity (unsegmented national market or largest submarket) would be supplied by an optimal plant and that costs would be up at least moderately at half-optimal scales:

> Cement
> Farm machinery
> Rayon

Steel

(Tractors) [16]

(3) *Industries with relatively unimportant plant scale economies,* because either of small optimal scales, or of flat plant-scale curves, or of both:

Canned fruits and vegetables

Cigarettes

Flour

Liquor

Meat packing (both fresh and diversified)

Petroleum refining

Soap

Shoes

Tires and tubes

(4) *Industries for which available data do not permit classification* (although minimum optimal scales are generally large):

Copper

Gypsum products

Fountain pens

Metal containers

The preceding classification serves as a summary of our findings from questionnaire data. The measure of scale mainly used, of course, refers to the percentage of either the unsegmented national market or of the largest recognized submarket. For the industries with segmented markets (as listed in Table V above) plant-scale economies will generally be substantially more important in the smaller submarkets than is indicated above. This observation might apply with especial force to shoes (see, e.g., men's high-price dress shoes), petroleum refining (see, e.g., the markets of the Rocky Mountain and interior Southwest areas), and steel (in all except two or three central areas).

Since the preceding refers entirely to data from questionnaire replies, an examination of data from other sources is indicated. The findings of such an examination are summarized in Appendix B. In general and subject to minor exceptions of detail noted, the supplementary evidence on plant economies tends to be consistent with the questionnaire estimates previously referred to, although of course this evidence is seldom sufficient to provide anything like substantial verification of those estimates. Therefore, no revised summary of our general conclusion relative to the economies of large plants is necessary at this point.

[16] Tractors fit category 2 except that the minimum optimal scale is larger and the scale curve apparently flatter.

Economies of large firms: questionnaire data

The extent to which economies of large scale are realized if firms grow beyond the size of a single optimal-scale plant has been a subject of controversy among economists. If a distinction is drawn between "production and distribution cost" and other advantages of scale — so that sales promotion, price-raising, and similar advantages of big firms are properly excluded from cost-savings in production and distribution — there is no general agreement among economists as to whether or to what extent the multiplant firm is more economical. If thus may come as no surprise that business executives questioned on the same matter with regard to our sample of industries revealed similar diversity of mind. Very distinct differences of opinion about the existence and importance of economies of multiplant firms were frequently encountered in the same industry, and in a pattern not satisfactorily explicable by the hypothesis that the individual would generally claim maximum economies for his own size of firm. The estimates of economies of large-scale firm based on questionnaire data should thus be viewed as extremely tentative.

Whatever the ostensible importance of economies of the multiplant firms, exploitation of them will not necessarily but may require the multiplant firm to control a larger proportion of any individual submarket than is needed for one optimal plant. In those instances, that is, where national markets are segmented regionally or by product lines, the multiplant firm may be able to realize its economies while operating only one plant in each submarket. Then concentration by firms in individual submarkets should not be further encouraged and entry should not be further impeded by economies of the multiplant firm. On the other hand there may be economies of multiplant firms which can be realized *only* through operating two or more optimal-size plants either in a single submarket or in a single unsegmented national market. This will encourage a concentration by firms in the relevant submarket or national market greater than that encouraged by plant economies alone, and will further impede entry. The distinction thus drawn is relevant to any appraisal of the impact of economies of the multiplant firm on entry and on concentration within submarkets.

Let us first examine some statistics on actual firm sizes in our 20 industries. The first column of numbers in Table VIII shows the *average size* of the first 4 firms in each industry, where size is measured generally as the share of total national market output supplied in 1947. This measure is a synthetic number, and of course will be smaller than the market share of the largest firm, larger than that of the fourth largest firm, and so forth.

Although in treating plant size we ascribed some potential importance

TABLE VIII

Actual Sizes of Firms and Minimum Optimal Sizes of Plants, Expressed as Percentages
of the National Industry Capacity or Output, in 20 Manufacturing Industries

Industry	Average market share of first 4 firms in 1947 [a]	Mean estimate of percentage of national industry capacity in one optimal plant [b] (approximate)	Ratio of actual average firm size to estimated optimal plant size
Copper	23.1 [c]	10	2.3
Cigarettes	22.6	5½	4.1
Automobiles	22.5 [d]	7½	3.0
Gypsum products	21.2	2½	8.5
Typewriters	19.9	20	1.0
Soap	19.8	5	4.0
Rayon	19.6	5	3.9
Metal containers	19.5	1⅙	16.7
Tires and tubes	19.2	2¹⁄₁₆	9.3
Distilled liquor	18.7	1½	12.5
Tractors	16.8	12½	1.3
Fountain pens	14.4	7½	1.9
Steel	11.2 [e]	1¾	6.4
Meat packing (diversified)	10.3 [f]	2¼	4.6
Petroleum refining	9.3	1¾	5.3
Farm machinery	9.0	1¼	7.2
Cement	7.4	⁹⁄₁₀	8.2
Flour	7.3	³⁄₁₀	24.3
Shoes	7.0	⁹⁄₂₈	21.8
Canned fruits and vegetables	6.6	⅜	17.6

[a] Percentages of 1947 value of shipments per *Census of Manufactures*, unless otherwise indicated.
[b] From Table III.
[c] Percentage of copper refining capacity in United States, 1947.
[d] Percentage (approximate) of total passenger car registration, 1951.
[e] Percentage of value added per *Census of Manufactures*, 1947.
[f] Percentage of value added per *Census of Manufactures*, 1947; firm percentage refers to wholesale fresh meat packing and to diversified firms.

to a similar index of the size of large plants as an indicator of optimal plant scale, it cannot be argued in parallel vein that the sizes of the largest actual firms will tend to approximate the minimum optimal scale of firms. The firm will not tend to divide, amoeba-like, to make two firms of minimum optimal scale instead of one when it has doubled the minimum optimal scale. If the scale curve is flat or relatively flat at scales larger than the minimum optimal, the firm may grow to such scales without cost disadvantage. At the same time, it may have numerous other incentives — such as increasing its monopoly power and obtaining more effective sales promotion — for wishing to reach super-optimal scales either without or with some production cost disadvantages. Firm size, in brief, has a complex rationale, in which economies of the large firm in production and distribution may play only a limited part. Statistics on actual firm sizes serve simply as a backdrop for a study of economies of the large firm and not as indicators of the extent of these economies.

The second column of numbers in Table VIII presents the mean questionnaire estimates of minimum optimal plant sizes by industries from Table III above (averages of high and low estimates), and the last column the ratio of the average size of the largest 4 firms to this mean estimate of the minimum optimal plant size. (Thus, for the cigarette industry, a firm which was the size of the average of the first four firms, and supplied 22.6 per cent of the national market, would be large enough to support 4.1 plants of estimated minimum optimal scale.) This ratio in the last column is obviously a very synthetic number, since it does not refer to the average actual number of plants per firm for the first four firms, but the average number of plants they would have if each of their plants were of the estimated minimum optimal scale. It is accordingly some index of the degree to which firm sizes among the largest firms have on the average exceeded the requirements of efficiency imposed by economies of large plants alone.

In reading these numbers, some distinction should be drawn among industries with relatively unsegmented national markets — in which certain potential economies of the multiplant firm may not be present — and those with markets segmented geographically or by product. In the former category, including copper, cigarettes, typewriters, soap, rayon, tires and tubes, distilled liquor, and tractors, for 6 of the 8 cases the ratio of average actual firm size to estimated minimum optimal plant size is 4.1 or less, and for 4 such cases it is in the general neighborhood of from 1 to 2. Only in tires and liquor is the average actual firm size a more substantial multiple of estimated optimal plant size — 9.3 and 12.5 respectively. In the 12 industries with regional or product-line segmentation of their markets, however, the median ratio of firm size to optimal plant size is 7.7, and in 4 industries the average size of the first 4 firms is from 15 to 25 times that required for one minimum optimal plant. A tentative hypothesis is that the "segmented" industry has offered the more fertile field for an extreme development of large firm sizes relative to the efficiency requirements of single-plant production. This fertility may of course be found either in economies of large firms or in other advantages of large firms not linked with production and distribution costs.

Let us now turn to the estimates submitted in answer to questions concerning the economics of large firms. These questions were directed toward determining (1) the minimum optimal scale of firm, and (2) the relationship of cost to the size of firm at smaller sizes. The information received is summarized in Table IX. In column 2 is shown the estimated size of a single plant of minimum optimal scale; in column 3 the estimated size (from questionnaire data) of a firm of minimum optimal scale; and

TABLE IX

The Extent of Estimated Economies of Multiplant Firms in 20 Manufacturing Industries

(1) Industry	(2) Estimated percentage of national industry capacity in one optimal plant (from Table III)	(3) Estimated percentage of national industry capacity in one minimum optimal firm	(4) Estimated maximum extent of economies of the multiplant firm (as a percentage of total unit cost)	(5) Estimated approximate number of optimal plants in one minimum optimal firm [a]	(6) Number of optimal plants which would be contained in the average of the largest 4 actual firms (from Table VIII)
Group 1:					
Canned fruits and vegetables	¼ to ½	¼ to ½	None	1	17.6
Petroleum refining	1¾	1¾	"	1	5.3
Meat packing (diversified)	2 to 2½	2 to 2½	"	1	4.6[b]
Fountain pens	5 to 10	5 to 10	"	1	1.9
Copper	10	10	"	1	2.3
Typewriters	10 to 30	10 to 30	"	1	1.0
Group 2:					
Flour	1⁄10 to ½	No estimate	No estimate	No estimate	24.3
Distilled liquor	1¼ to 1¾	"	"	"	12.5
Metal containers	⅓ to 2	"	"	"	16.7
Farm machines, ex tractors	1 to 1½	"	"	"	7.2
Tires and tubes	1⅜ to 2¾	"	"	"	9.3
Rayon	4 to 6	"	"	"	3.9
Automobiles	5 to 10	"	"	"	3.0
Tractors	10 to 15	"	"	"	1.3
Group 3:					
Shoes	1⁄7 to ½	½ to 2½	Small, or 2 to 4	3 to 5	21.8
Cement	⅘ to 1	2 to 10	Small, or 2 to 3	3 to 10	8.2
Steel	1 to 2½	2 to 20	2 to 5	1 to 8	6.4
Gypsum products	2 to 3	22 to 33	Small	11	8.5
Soap	4 to 6	8 to 15	½ to 1	2 to 3	4.0
Cigarettes	5 to 6	15 to 20	Slight	3 to 4	4.1

[a] Number of plants as shown in this column are not always calculated from optimal-plant-size and optimal-firm-size estimates in any simple mechanical way, since the association of differences in plant-size estimates with differences in firm-size estimates has been recognized in deriving these numbers.

[b] See note f to Table VIII.

in column 4 the estimated extent of the economies of the multiplant firm, these economies being expressed as the percentage by which the multiplant firm's costs would be below those of the single-plant firm. Column 5 shows the number of optimal-scale plants which, directly according to estimates, the estimated optimal-scale firm would include, and column 6 shows (from the last column of Table VIII) the number of optimal-scale plants which the average of the four largest *actual* firms would include.

Table IX thus gives answers to three questions as far as estimates from questionnaire data supply them: first, whether or not a firm incorporating two or more optimal-scale plants has any advantage over a single-plant firm (columns 3 and 4); second, the size of the most efficient firm (columns 3 and 5); and third, the cost advantage of the multiplant over the single-plant firm (column 4). Columns 5 and 6 permit us also to compare the size of actual firms (the average size of the first four in any industry *as measured in units of one efficient plant* in column 6) to the firm size held necessary for maximum efficiency.

Concerning the first question, it appears that in 8 industries (Group 2 in Table IX), no definite estimate could be obtained of the extent, if any, of economies of the multiplant firm. This is in spite of the fact that in five of these industries the "Big 4" firms are large enough to encompass from 7 to 25 plants of estimated optimal scale apiece, and that in two others there is a significant degree of multiplant devlopment. In 6 industries (Group 1 in Table IX), it was the consensus that economies of the scale of firm beyond the size of a single optimal plant were either negligible or totally absent. In these cases estimated cost savings of the multiplant firm cannot, according to estimates, justify concentration beyond that required by plant economies alone (either in submarkets or in the national market). It is notable, however, that in the last 3 industries in this group — fountain pens, copper, and typewriters — economies of the large plant alone are thought to be sufficient to support a significant degree of concentration by firms. In the remaining 6 industries (Group 3 in Table IX), perceptible economies were attributed to the multiplant firm. The multiplant firm was thus held to have cost advantages over the single-plant firm in 6 of the 12 cases for which any definite estimates on this question were secured. It would of course be hazardous to project this proportion to our entire sample or to larger samples.

The size of the firm of estimated minimum optimal scale is unknown in Group 2 (Table IX) and is equal to the size of one optimal plant only in Group 1. In Group 3, we find a considerable range of results in regard to the number of optimal-scale plants required for an optimal firm. In shoes, soap, and cigarettes the required number of plants per optimal firm is held to be fairly small, varying from 2 to 5; in the gypsum products industry, it is held to be high, 11. In the steel and cement industries, there is a distinct divergence of opinion among authorities. The requisite number of plants per optimal firm is held to be as small as 3 and as large as 10 in cement, and as small as 1 and as large as 8 in steel. So far as we can tell from this very small sample, there is no great uniformity in the degree of multiplant development necessary for efficiency even within those industries where a multiplant organization is held to offer some cost advantages. Two comments may be pertinent, however. First, large numbers of plants per firm are held to be needed for best efficiency only in cases (steel, cement, gypsum) where the national market is segmented into a substantial number of different regions and where also (possibly for connected reasons) a single optimal plant supplies a fairly small proportion of the national market. Second, the size of an optimal plant in 2 of the remaining 3 cases (soap and cigarettes) is enough so that from 2 to 4 optimal plants would give a firm a very sizable market share; thus the effects of much higher degrees of multiplant development may tend to remain largely unexplored.[17]

The implications of estimated economies of the firm for the size of an optimal firm as expressed in terms of its market share are shown directly in column 3 of Table IX. In Group 1, the optimal firm's national market share would be the same as that of one optimal plant, and in Group 2 the share is unknown. In 5 of the 6 cases in Group 3 (all except shoes), the optimal-scale firm could, if the top estimate were used, supply a substantial proportion of total industry capacity, ranging from 10 to 33 per cent. In 2 of these 5 cases, however — steel and cement — a much lower estimate is also available, and in shoes the proportion of the national market attributed to one optimal firm would in any event be negligible.

The shape of the scale curve for the multiplant firm is the third main question. From Table IX it appears that the curve is horizontal (showing constant unit costs) back to the scale of 1 optimal plant for industries in Group 1, and that for industries in Group 2 the shape is unknown. In Group 3, the shape of the firm's scale curve in the range between the designated optimal scale of firm and a one-optimal-plant scale, as shown in column 4, is generally quite flat. The cost advantage of the designated multiplant firm over a single-plant firm is estimated as slight, small, or at 1 per cent or less in the cigarette, soap, and gypsum product industries. In the steel, cement, and shoe industries it is placed in the range of from

[17] It is interesting to note that in three cases — steel, cement, and gypsum products — the multiplant economies were held to be realized primarily in *production*, via large-scale conduct of management and staff functions, whereas in the other three — soap, cigarettes, and shoes — the multiplant economies were represented as those of physical distribution, including outshipment freight. We will have occasion to comment further on the meaning and significance of such distributive economies in Chapter 4, in considering advantages of large-scale sales promotion.

2 to 5 per cent of costs: small but not necessarily negligible. In addition to this indication of limited variety in the shapes of firm scale curves, it is notable that in the three cases in Group 3 where the scale of the optimal firm is definitely set at a large fraction of the total market — cigarettes, soap, and gypsum — the advantage of the multiplant firm over the single-plant firm is held to be slight, thus suggesting a reduction of the net impact of scale economies upon entry, or an effective reversion to whatever importance plant economies have. In the case of steel and cement, the advantages of the multiplant firm are held to be small though appreciable, but in both of these cases there is considerable doubt as to whether any extensive multiplant development is needed for optimal efficiency.

In sum, our findings on the importance of multiplant economies (a) leave us with a blank for 8 of our 20 industries (Group 2); (b) show very slight or no multiplant economies for 9 of the remaining 12; and (c) show small but possibly significant multiplant economies for the remaining 3, although in one of these the size of the optimal multiplant firm is still held to be rather small. Although the questionnaire estimates leave large gaps in our knowledge, they create the general impression that economies of large multiplant firms will not significantly tend in very many cases to augment the entry-inhibiting and concentration-encouraging effects of the economies of large plants already discussed.

A subsidiary question is whether or not the exploitation of estimated multiplant economies in the industries in Group 3 will require the firm to control, in any individual submarket, a larger fraction of industry capacity than is required for exploitation of the economies of a single plant. The number of plants per optimal firm ranges from 2 or 3 in the case of soap to 11 in gypsum or from 1 to 8 in steel. Applying these estimates, the proportion of national industry capacity needed for best efficiency in a multiplant firm is clearly increased. But the proportion of the capacity supplying any particular regional or product submarket will not be increased if the industry market is segmented and if efficient multiplant firm includes only one optimal plant per submarket. No more than one optimal plant per region is attributed to the optimal firm in cement or in steel, and the proportion of any regional market that need be supplied for efficiency is thus not increased by the incidence of economies of the multiplant firms. In the remaining 4 cases the conclusion is different. Soap and cigarettes have relatively unsegmented national markets, and the proportion of the market required for best efficiency is doubled, trebled, or quadrupled by the emergence of economies of the multiplant firm. In shoes the assumed specialization in a single product line of the 4 or 5 plants needed for efficiency raises the requisite firm concentration on product lines by corresponding multiples. In the gypsum industry it was evidently assumed that an optimal firm would operate several plants in each of several major regions. In all of the last 4 cases, therefore, economies of the multi-plant firm tend to encourage greater *effective* concentration by firms than plant economies alone. But in these cases (possibly excepting shoes) the economies of the large firm were characterized as slight, so that the tendency in question may be a weak one.

Let us now consider the preceding information on the extent of economies of the multiplant firm in conjunction with our earlier findings on economies of large plants, in order to appraise the combined impact of the two sorts of economies on the relation of size to efficiency for the firm. On pages 81 and 82 above, we concluded that our 20 industries fell into four classes on the basis of the importance of plant economies: (1) *with very important plant economies* (automobiles and typewriters only); (2) *with moderately important plant economies* (cement, farm machinery, rayon, steel, and tractors); (3) *with relatively unimportant plant economies* (canned fruits and vegetables, cigarettes, flour, liquor, meat packing, petroleum refining, soap, shoes, and tires and tubes; (4) *unclassified* (copper, gypsum products, fountain pens, and metal containers). We need here only to consider the extent to which the preceding classification would be changed by the recognition of multiplant firm economies simultaneously with plant economies. Obviously the changes, as far as they are based on the questionnaire estimates just reported, will not be great, and will be limited to the 6 industries in Group 3.

The industries with "very important" plant economies — automobiles and typewriters — remain in the category of very important economies of the large firm, since the efficient firm is at least as large as the single efficient plant. But in neither case do we have any definite estimate of the added importance of economies of multiplant firms. Recognition of estimated economies of multiplant firms for Group 3 industries does not promote any further industries into the "very-important-scale-economies" category, since either the firm scale curves are too flat (soap, cigarettes, and gypsum products), or the percentage required in any submarket is not larger than required by plant economies alone (steel and cement), or the size of the optimal firm is too small (shoes).

The industries with "moderately important" plant economies included steel, cement, farm machinery, tractors, and rayon. For steel and cement, as we have seen, exploitation of estimated economies of multiplant firms would probably not require more than one plant per regional submarket, and therefore the net importance of scale economies as judged by the "percentage effect" on entry is not increased: a firm need build no more than one optimal plant per submarket in attaining optimal multiplant scale. It should be noted, however, that plant economies for steel and cement are judged moderately important only with reference to the largest regional submarkets; in smaller regional submarkets, supplied by smaller total capacities, plant economies may be very important.

Farm machinery, tractors, and rayon remain in *status quo*; over-all scale economies therein are judged moderately important on the basis of plant economies alone, and we lack estimates of the importance of economies of the multiplant firm. In all cases of "very" and "moderately" important plant economies, economies of multiplant firms were never denied in questionnaire replies, though they were positively claimed in only two out of seven cases.

Can any industries be promoted from the third class to the second class on the basis of estimated economies of the multiplant firm? The candidates are soap, cigarettes, and shoes (gypsum products are set aside because of lack of data on the plant scale curve). The shoe industry is more or less on the borderline in this respect. Estimates of multiplant firm economies would give the optimal firm 3 to 5 plants and from .5 to 2.5 per cent of the total shoe market, depending on the number of plants and the estimate of optimal plant size; this firm has a 2 to 4 per cent cost advantage over single-plant firms. The estimates in question, however, suppose specialization by the firm to a single major product line, and this would imply the provision of from about 2 per cent to about 6 per cent of the largest submarket output by a single optimal firm. Considering the relative flatness of both plant and firm scale curves, the critical percentages would probably be around 1 to 3 per cent for the largest submarket, although distinctly larger than this for smaller submarkets. We might thus consider the shoe industry, on the basis of plant plus firm economies, as a marginal addition to the "moderately-important-scale economies" class.

The soap industry also might be promoted marginally. It was placed in the category of "unimportant" plant scale economies because costs were estimated as only 3 per cent above the optimal level for a plant supplying 2 per cent of the market. We now have added to this the observation that a two- to three-plant firm should have cost advantages of .5 to 1 per cent over a single-plant firm. Combining these advantages, a firm with 8 to 15 per cent of the national market might have a total cost advantage of 4 per cent over one supplying 2 per cent of the market. Thus over-all scale economies may be a significant force in determining the condition of entry.

The cigarette industry, however, cannot be promoted in class. A plant supplying 1 per cent of the national market would, according to estimate, have only a 2 per cent cost disadvantage as compared to larger plants, and a multiplant firm would have "slight" cost advantages over a single-plant firm. It is difficult to make a case for "moderately important" over-all scale economies from this assortment of information. Summarizing the preceding observations, we add to the cement, steel, farm machinery, tractor, and rayon industries the soap and shoe industries as marginal members of the "moderately-important-scale-economies" class.

This leaves in the "unimportant scale economies" class the canned fruit and vegetable, cigarette, meat packing, petroleum refining, flour, liquor, and tire and tube industries. For the first 4 of these, we have positive estimates that economies of multiplant firms are absent or small. For the latter 3 no definite estimates on the multiplant matter were developed, and we leave them in *status quo* pending development of further information.

Remaining in an "unclassified" category are copper, gypsum products, fountain pens, and metal containers, for all of which insufficient data on the shape or plant scale curves were received. Of these, the fountain pen and copper industries are held to possess no noticeable multiplant economies. The estimated size of an optimal plant is large, but we lack data on relative unit costs with smaller-scale plants. For gypsum products, small economies to a large multiplant firm are predicted, but we lack data on the shape of the plant scale curve. Again, optimal plant size is a significant share of any submarket capacity. The metal container industry is in the same general category, although there is less certainty about optimal plant size and no estimate on economies of the multiplant firm. In at least 3 of these 4 industries — fountain pens, copper and gypsum — the high relative size of an optimal plant clearly leaves open the possibility that over-all economies of scale may be moderately important to very important.

In sum, our classification of industries according to the importance of over-all scale economies — those of plant plus those of multiplant firm — produces the following results:

"Very important"	2
"Moderately important"	7
"Unimportant"	7
"Unclassified"	4

In Appendix C we review supplementary sources of data to see if the picture can be further clarified. Summarizing about these supplementary data, there are no findings which clearly suggest a revision of the preceding classification of industries according to the importance of the combined economies of plant and firm. Such added information as is relevant does not alter the content of the categories there. For typewriters, the possibility of largely unexploited economies of multiplant firms is suggested, but the industry is already in the "very important over-all economies" category. The same is suggested for copper and fountain pens, but we are unable to remove these from the "unclassified" category because of the paucity of data on the shapes of plant scale curves. The existence of economies of multiplant firms in steel and cement is questioned, but this does not demote them from the "moderately important scale economies" class, because they are there primarily on the basis of the relation of the size of a single optimal plant to a single submarket. Added data on autos, farm machinery, and tractors do not suggest reclassification, since the suggested multiplant developments would leave the previously indicated percentages of product submarkets in the same categories as before. For other industries, supplementary data either corroborate previous findings, or are absent or inconclusive.

The probable effects of observed scale economies on the condition of entry

The preceding findings concerning economies of large plants and firms have intrinsic interest, but we are concerned mainly with the implications of the discovered pattern of scale economies for market organization and behavior. In the remainder of this chapter, we will consider the impact of the observed scale economies on the condition of entry to the industries in question, and also comment on the extent to which such scale economies provide a rationale for seller concentration in these industries. In discussing the condition of entry, we will refer here only to the "percentage effect" of scale economies on entry, deferring to Chapter 5 the treatment of absolute-capital-requirement effects.

In preceding pages, we have advanced a set of hypotheses as to why entry to an industry will be deterred by the fact that in order to reach optimal efficiency a plant or firm must supply a significant percentage of market output. If it must, it is likely to be able on the one hand to enter at or near optimal scale only by inducing repercussions that will either lower selling prices or result in the elevation of costs above the minimum optimal level,[18] or on the other hand to enter at insignificantly small scales only with costs well above that level. Established firms can thus elevate their long-run prices somewhat above the lowest-cost level associated with minimum optimal scale without attracting further entry, because either a price reduction or a higher-than-minimal cost will generally be expected by the entrant after his entry. Extending the argument, the larger the percentage of total market capacity or output provided by the minimum optimal scale of plant or firm, and the more steeply unit costs increase with movement to suboptimal scales, the more long-run prices can be elevated above the least-cost level without inducing entry. With oligopoly among established sellers, they may be expected to choose consciously whether to stay below or exceed the entry-inducing price thus established.

[18] Or, given product differentiation, which increase the sales-promotion outlays of established firms, thus making sales promotion (at any scale) more costly for all than it was prior to entry. This is essentially an equivalent repercussion; to simplify the following analysis, we will formally neglect it, but the general course of the argument would not be altered by its explicit recognition.

The crucial notion which emerges from this outline analysis is that of some specific maximum entry-forestalling price, which lies above the lowest-cost level associated with minimum optimal scale, and which does so because the potential entrant anticipates, on account of significant scale economies, a lower-than-current price or a higher-than-minimal cost after entry. Let us explore the theoretical presuppositions underlying this notion, confining ourselves principally to the immediately relevant case where there is an oligopolistic market structure as among established sellers.

A first corollary, then, is that there is a sort of interdependence between the actions of established sellers and the actions of any potential entrant. That is, established sellers are aware of the possibility of entry, and of the fact that their individual and collective price policies may influence potential entrants in their decisions whether or not to enter. Even a single potential entrant, moreover, may be "big enough to worry about" if there are significant scale economies. Established sellers will presumably have conjectures as to which of the alternative prices that they can set will or will not induce one or more potential entrants to enter, and may choose whether or not to exceed what they believe to be an entry-forestalling price.

Conversely, any potential entrant is aware — if economies of scale are significant — that his entry at efficient scale will not go unnoticed by established sellers, that his addition to market output may be large enough to induce an adjustment either of market price or of going market shares, and that established sellers will react in some way or other to entry made at a significant scale. He presumably also knows that established sellers are aware of the threat of entry, and are guiding their policies accordingly, and that the prices they now charge have been influenced by awareness of their effects on his disposition to enter the market.

He is thus invited to "read" their current policies in this light and, given all information, (1) to develop conjectures as to the market situation after his entry, and (2) to decide whether or not to enter the market. All of this may be clearly seen or only dimly grasped, of course, but it could hardly be completely overlooked. To summarize, in the circumstances described the potential entrant does not view the going long-run price in the industry as given and unresponsive to his entry, and knows moreover that it may have been set with his thinking in mind. Conversely, the established sellers view any disposition of the potential entrant about whether or not to enter not as fixed and beyond their influence, but as dependent, to some extent at least, on their own long-run price policies.[19]

---

[19] The following revisions in the argument are required if the assumption of significant scale economies or of oligopolistic concentration among established sellers is dropped. If there is oligopolistic concentration among established sellers but no

The next crucial question, given this interdependence of the established and potential entrant firms, is whether in fact the potential entrant will be influenced in his disposition to enter by the long-run level of going prices that are charged by established firms in the industry. The notion of specific entry-forestalling and entry-inducing ranges of price, and of a condition of entry measured by reference to them, rests clearly on the notion that the potential entrant is influenced in some way by the going level of prices. There are of course two general logical possibilities here. The first — that he will not be influenced at all — is a little hard to imagine. The potential entrant would need to have conjectures about the reactions of established firms to his entry, and in turn about the market situation after his entry, which were totally unaffected by the going prices (and corresponding sales volumes) of established firms. He might make any number of alternate conjectures concerning reactions to his entry, ranging from his acceptance as an equal member of a joint monopoly to aggressive retaliation against him, but any conjecture he had would be insensitive to adjustments in the going price policies of established firms. We regard this possibility as not very probable, and will generally neglect it in subsequent discussion.

The alternative and much stronger possibility is that the potential entrant's conjectures concerning a post-entry market and his disposition to enter are influenced by the going price policies of established firms. The major reason for such an influence is that the entrant is likely to read the current price policies of established firms as some sort of a "statement of future intentions" regarding their policies after his entry has occurred. Exactly how he will read a given policy is uncertain, and remains to be discussed, but much argues in favor of his making some reading of the implications for future actions of current price policies.

Pursuing this matter, we must recognize that there are at least two relevant dimensions to a going set of policies of established firms — the price or prices they are charging and their sales quantities or market shares. (Added dimensions such as the size of selling outlays and design of products may be neglected in a discussion of the "pure" scale-economies

---

significant scale economies affecting the entrant, the established sellers will adjust their policies in about the same way in terms of their effects on the disposition of a collectivity of potential entrants to enter, and the individual potential entrant will view the long-run going price as fixed or beyond his power to influence by entry. (This model would appear important in appraising "pure" cases of product differentiation and absolute cost advantage as barriers to entry.) If there are significant scale economies but a relatively unconcentrated group of established sellers (an improbable case), the established sellers might neglect the effects of their prices on entry, but the entrant would tend to calculate the probable effects of his entry on the going market price situation. If there are insignificant scale economies and low concentration among established sellers, the latter would disregard the influence of their prices on entry, and any entrant would view going prices as not subject to influence by his entry.

case.) As regards the going long-run level of prices, it may be argued that the entrant will in general view them as (a) viable prices for the industry; (b) prices which, if directed to discourage him as an entrant, will also be likely to be directed to discourage further potential entrants in the future; and (c) prices which the going state of rivalry or imperfection of collusion in the industry may not permit to be consistently exceeded. The circumstances in which the entrant would expect his entry probably to result in an *increase* in industry prices seem likely to be rare in occurrence. *Initially, therefore, we may suggest that going price policies of established firms are likely to be read to the effect that post-entry price is unlikely to exceed pre-entry price.*[20]

The reading of current price policies simply to the effect that post-entry price will not exceed current price, however, is in fact relatively optimistic, since maintenance of going price would imply willingness of established firms to permit an entrant to borrow a market share from them in order to maintain price. The potential entrant seems more likely to expect that established firms either will maintain their going outputs, thus causing his entry to lower industry prices, or in any event will not restrict their outputs sufficiently to maintain prices unless he, the entrant, comes in at a negligible and thus uneconomical scale. In addition to assuming that the potential entrant will not expect post-entry price to exceed pre-entry price, *we will also assume that he will see a non-negligible and perhaps dominant probability that post-entry prices will be lower than pre-entry prices if he enters at a significant scale.* His mean expectation of post-entry prices will be that they will fall somewhere below current prices.

With given conjectures concerning the disposition of established firms to hold or yield market shares, it will be true that the higher the prices which established firms set, relative to the level of minimum average cost, the higher post-entry prices the entrant will tend to anticipate and the more likely he will be to enter the market. Correspondingly, there will be some critical level of going prices above which the entrant will be inclined to enter, and below which he will not. This will be true in any case unless the character of conjectures concerning price reactions to entry is fundamentally altered by changes in the altitude of going prices, an event which would be deemed improbable in the light of the foregoing discussion.

Thus, through these assumptions and deductions, we conclude that in industries with significant scale economies, potential entrants will generally relate their anticipations of a post-entry market situation systematically

---

[20] The unwillingness of potential entrants to stake much on the possibility of higher prices after entry may also be enhanced by the fact that levels of industry price *above* the going long-run price are likely to be relatively unexplored, so that the entrant may have substantial uncertainty about the elasticity of demand (and thus of his possible market share) at such higher prices.

to the going prices of established firms, that they will generally expect post-entry prices at or below going prices, with the mean expected price below, and that in consequence there will be a systematic relation between disposition to enter and the going level of prices, such that there is a line between prices which will encourage and discourage entry.

The next question is how high will the maximum entry-excluding level of price be, relative to minimal costs, in a given situation of scale economies? Or, to put it another way, to what extent will various scale-economy situations permit an elevation of going price above the minimal-cost level without attracting entry? These are not simple questions because (a) there is an inescapable range of uncertainty concerning potential entrants' anticipations of established firms' reactions to entry; (b) there is a wide variety of possible and actual scale-economy situations, as defined in terms both of the market percentage of the minimum-optimal scale of plant or firm and of the shape of the scale curve at smaller scales; and (c) any entrant is faced with numerous alternative opportunities as to the best scale for entry. Let us examine several simplified cases suggesting the consequences of broad alternative conjectures by potential entrants and of alternative scale-economy conditions.

We may distinguish in general six possible categories of conjecture by potential entrants. The first of these (1) is based on the entrant's decision to enter at an insignificantly small scale, even though he will, in the sort of situation imagined, incur super-optimal unit costs by doing so. In this event, his entry will not perceptibly influence the market and will be "unnoticed" by established firms. Thus, the potential entrant's conjecture will be for an unchanged industry price and for no restriction (other than product differentiation, here neglected) on his ability to secure a market for his output at the intended scale. His only disadvantage will be that his unit costs will be higher than the optimal level by an amount depending on the shape of the scale curve in question.

The remaining possible conjectures assume a decision by the potential entrant to enter at a significant scale, sufficient to affect the market and to induce reactions by established firms, although the specific scale contemplated by the entrant may be either equal to or smaller than the minimum optimal or lowest-cost scale. Two general polar conjectures stand out here: (2) the potential entrant may predict that established firms will react to entry by adhering to the pre-entry level of prices (unless undercut by the entrant) and by permitting the entrant to secure such a market share as he can at this level of prices; and (3) the potential entrant may predict that established firms will react to entry by holding their pre-entry outputs constant and by permitting industry prices to be lowered by such additions to industry output as the entrant chooses to and is able to make.

The fourth possible conjecture (4) is that the reaction of established firms will be somewhere between the limits of (2) and (3) — that they will reduce output by less than enough to permit maintenance of the pre-entry prices, and will thus permit the entrant to gain a market share at a price below the pre-entry level of prices but above the post-entry price imagined in (3). This seems to be the most likely and realistic conjecture of all, although its content is best understood by examining the two limiting cases (2 and 3) which surround it.

In addition, there are two extra-polar possible conjectures, lying outside the limits of cases (2) and (3). One of these (5) would suppose "retaliation" by established firms, which we will define to mean an increase in the outputs of established firms above the pre-entry level, resulting in a greater lowering of industry prices than in (3). The other (6) would imagine an increase in the pre-entry prices of established firms, permitting the entrant to gain some market share at a level of prices more favorable than that which held before his entry. Although a certain minor probability might be assigned to either of these contingencies in a complex set of alternative conjectures, it would appear that they may be largely neglected for practical purposes. We may thus limit ourselves to the exploration of the first four possible conjectures listed above.

The second major basis for distinguishing potential-entry cases where scale economies are involved is the shape of the scale curve of the plant or firm. This shape involves in general (a) the percentage of the relevant market output that will be supplied by a firm attaining minimum optimal scale (whether with one plant or more within the relevant market); and (b) the percentages by which unit costs at various smaller scales (e.g. 75, 50, 25, or 5 per cent of optimal scale) will exceed the unit costs associated with minimum optimal scale.

A myraid of posibilities occur here, but we may proceed to identify various broad sorts of scale curves. Obviously relevant will be the distinction between relatively large and relatively small optimal-scale outputs, when these outputs are expressed as percentages of the relevant market output. Also relevant will be the difference between scale curves which rise (in terms of unit costs) relatively steeply and relatively gradually as scale is reduced below the optimal.

Given this general outline of alternative situations, let us turn to the question of how much the existence of given scale-economy situations will probably permit established firms to elevate prices above minimal average costs without attracting further entry.

The simplest model for prediction would correspond to the supposition that the potential entrant generally expects that the reaction of established firms to entry will be to hold their own outputs constant and to permit the added output of the entrant to affect industry prices ac-

cordingly (3 above). For purposes of simplicity in analysis, let us assume
certain things about relevant surrounding circumstances: first, that there
is homogeneity among the products of all established firms and the product
of any entrant firm, so that all will sell at a single common market price
at any one time; and second, that the price elasticity of demand for the
total market output (as referred to any market the entrant penetrates)
is unity, so that any increase in quantity offered for sale in the market will
result in a decline in market price for all sellers such that total market
receipts from sales will be unchanged. Given these conditions, the implications *per se* of the size of optimal-scale output as a percentage of any
going market output is obvious. Suppose that an added firm could enter
a market *only* at optimal scale, and suppose that the output of an optimal-
scale operation were alternatively 50 per cent of going market output, 10
per cent, 5 per cent, and 2 per cent. Then the addition of one firm
supplying an amount equal to 50 per cent of going market output would
lower price by one-third; the addition of one firm supplying 10 per cent
of going market output would lower price by about 9 per cent; a 2 per
cent addition to market output would lower price by a very little less
than 2 per cent, and so forth. In general, the percentage reduction in
market price attributable to an increment of entry at minimum optimal
scale would be positively related in a systematic way to the percentage
of the going market which an optimal-scale entrant would supply.[21]

This does not in strict logic lead us directly to a prediction of how
much, with various optimal scales, established firms could raise price
above the minimal-cost level without attracting entry, since optimal
scale will presumably be measured by a given absolute number of units
of output (per period of time) and since, therefore, an optimal-scale
output will represent an increasing percentage of going market output
as established firms raise price and restrict the going market output.
The logical solution is quite simple, however: established firms can restrict market output below that at which price will equal minimal average
costs by an amount equal to the output of an entrant firm of minimum-
optimal scale, provided that the entrant firm can enter only at that scale.
With a unit-elastic market demand (price varying with market output so
that total receipts from sales are always invariant), this would mean, for
example, that:

(1) Where a firm of minimum optimal scale supplies 50 per cent
of the output required when price equals minimal average costs, estab-

---

[21] The percentage price reduction here equals $1 - \dfrac{1}{1+E}$, where E is the percentage of going market output (the latter being taken as unity in the denominator of the
second term) which an optimal-scale operation will supply. Product homogeneity and
unit-elastic market demand are presupposed in this formulation.

lished firms can raise price 100 per cent above minimal average costs before attracting entry.

(2) Where a firm of minimum optimal scale supplies 10 per cent of the output required when price equals minimum average cost, established firms can restrict output 10 per cent below the latter level and raise price 11.1 per cent above minimal average costs before attracting entry.

(3) With smaller percentages, the per cent by which price can be raised above minimal average cost without attracting entry will be roughly equal to the percentage supplied by an optimal firm of the market output demanded at a price equal to minimal average cost.[22]

In terms of the usual facts about shapes of scale curves, the preceding represents an extreme estimate of the effects of scale economies on the condition of entry. Otherwise, allowance could easily be made for variations in the elasticity of market demands — e.g., more elastic demands would generally reduce the barrier to entry, and less elastic demands increase it. The lack of product homogeneity, which might result in the inability of an entrant firm to attain a scale which would be optimal or otherwise desirable, is best treated apart from the consideration of the scale-economy issue *per se*.

The estimate here is deficient, however, in that it supposes that entry can be made only at the minimum-optimal scale. In fact, the entrant may find it advantageous to enter at a smaller scale, even though unit costs are thereby higher. It will be induced to do so (as its best opportunity) if the cost disadvantage thus incurred is smaller than the accompanying price advantage it gets by affecting market price less than if it had entered at optimal scale. Let us investigate this matter, still supposing that established firms are expected to react to entry by holding their outputs constant (3 above).

Consideration of this matter naturally raises the question of how steep the scale curve is at outputs short of the optimum. It is enough here to suppose three typical shapes:

(1) "Shallow," which we will exemplify as having costs up 1 per cent at 50 per cent of minimum optimal scale, up 2 per cent at 25 per cent of minimum optimal scale, and up 3 per cent at 10 per cent of minimum optimal scale.

(2) "Medium-sloped," which we will exemplify as having costs up 3,

---

[22] The general formula here is that if the market output demanded at a price equal to minimal average costs is 1, and if e is the percentage of *that* market output supplied by an optimal-scale entrant firm, then the maximum entry-excluding price, expressed as a percentage of a price equal to minimal average cost is $\dfrac{1}{1-e}$ and the percentage by which that price exceeds minimal cost is $\left(\dfrac{1}{1-e}-1\right)$.

6, and 9 per cent respectively at 50, 25, and 10 per cent of minimum optimal scale.

(3) "Steep," characterized as having costs up 7, 14, and 21 per cent respectively at 50, 25, and 10 per cent of minimum optimal scale. (We have not found actual plant scale curves much steeper than this, or multiplant firm scale curves even approximately this steep.)

Any of these slopes may be found in conjunction with various optimal-scale conditions; for example, we might find the "shallow" scale curve for a plant with a minimum optimal scale which would supply a quarter of the total market output at minimal price, or alternatively (in another industry) for a plant with a minimum optimal scale supplying only a tenth of such an output. There may thus be various combinations of the magnitude of minimum optimal scale expressed as a percentage of total market output at minimal price and the shape of the scale curve at sub-optimal scales.

The question now is this: Given the ability of a firm to enter at sub-optimal as well as optimal scales if it so chooses, how much smaller will be the excess of the maximum entry-excluding price over minimal average costs with various shapes of scale curves and various optimal scales? Still supposing that established firms will hold their outputs constant in the face of entry, these firms can, while excluding entry, set price above minimal average costs by an amount equal to the smallest attainable sum of (a) the excess of price over minimal cost which a unit of entry will just erase; and (b) the excess of the unit costs of the entrant over minimal average costs, the scale of the entrant being variable so as to minimize this sum.

It follows that if, by reducing scale at entry below the optimal, the entrant can lessen the "price effect" of entry by more than it increases unit costs above the minimal level, its gross disadvantage from entry (the sum of a and b) will be reduced, and established firms will be able to elevate price by less while excluding entry.

Suppose, for example, that the optimal scale of an entrant's plant is such as to supply 5 per cent of market output at the minimal price. If it could enter only at optimal scale, its entry would erase an excess of industry price over minimal cost of *about* 5 per cent; therefore, established firms could set price about 5 per cent above minimal- or optimal-scale costs and not attract entry. But now suppose that the entrant can also enter at half-optimal scale (2.5 per cent of market output at minimal price) and incur unit costs only 1 per cent higher than minimum optimal costs. Then the effect of his entry at the reduced scale would be to offset an excess of industry price above minimal cost of about 2.5 per cent and at the same time to incur costs 1 per cent above the minimal level. Established firms could then presumably elevate price only about 3.5 per cent above the minimal level while excluding entry. If, further, the entrant could enter at a quarter optimal scale (thus 1.25 per cent of the relevant market output) while incurring costs of only 1.75 per cent above the minimal level, the maximum entra-excluding price would be only about 3 per cent above that minimal level.

The scale at which the entrant would incur the smallest gross disadvantage (price effect plus cost elevation) is the *critical scale* in determining the excess of the best entry-excluding price over minimal costs. The (minimized) gross disadvantage at this critical scale' is the amount of that excess, and determines the height of the barrier to entry resulting from scale economies. This is all based on the express supposition that established firms are expected by the entrant to hold their outputs constant in the face of entry.[23]

The possibility of entry at suboptimal scales will of course lower the barrier to entry if the entrant can find a scale with a smaller gross disadvantage (as defined) than it incurs at optimal scale. How shallow a scale curve will be required to offer this opportunity? Obviously this is related to the size of the optimal scale of plant as expressed in terms of percentage of total market supply at the minimal price.

In general, the larger the optimal scale in these terms, the greater is the price effect of entry at optimal scale (established firms' outputs being constant); correspondingly, the greater is the diminution of the price effect — in percentage-point terms — attributable to cutting scale below the optimum by a given fraction. Thus if optimal scale supplies 10 per cent of market output, entry at that scale will offset an excess of price over minimal cost of about 10 per cent, *and halving that scale at entry will diminish the price effect of entry by 5 percentage points.* But if optimal scale supplies 5 per cent of the relevant market output, entry at that scale will offset a price excess of about 5 per cent, and *halving that scale at entry will diminish the price effect of entry by only about 2.5 percentage points.* In effect, the price advantages of entering at suboptimal scale (advantages in the form of diminished price effects) are greater in percentage-point terms as optimal scale supplies a greater percentage of the total relevant market output.

If the last conclusion is so, it follows that to permit a reduction of the gross disadvantage of the entrant through entry at suboptimal scales, shallower scale curves will be required the smaller the percentage of

---

[23] Strictly, the price effect of a unit of entry and the cost elevation (both expressed as percentages of the same minimal-cost base) cannot be separately calculated and then simply added, since the proper base for calculating the price effect is shifted by the cost elevation. But so long as we are dealing with percentages of minimal cost not in excess of ten or fifteen per cent, the error encountered by following this procedure is slight, so that for our purposes we may speak as if this rough and ready procedure is applicable, and may rely generally on its indications.

total market output supplied by an optimal-scale unit. To look at it the other way, the entrant can absorb a greater cost increase (from a steeper scale curve) via suboptimal entry, and still reduce his gross disadvantage, the greater his optimal scale.[24]

Our interest in the preceding reasoning is in its application to the typical shapes of scale curves that we have seen above. The general nature of this application is revealed by considering "shallow" scale curves, with costs up 1 per cent at 50 per cent of minimum optimal scale (m.o.s.), 2 per cent at 25 per cent of m.o.s., and 3 per cent at 10 per cent of m.o.s. Here, if optimal scale supplies between about 2 and 4 per cent of the relevant market output, entry would have the smallest gross disadvantage at 50 per cent of optimal scale. At smaller optimal scales, entry at optimal scale would have the smallest gross disadvantage. If optimal scale supplied between about 4 and 6 (plus) per cent of the relevant market output, entry at 25 per cent of optimal scale would have the smallest gross disadvantage; if optimal scale supplied a bit over 6 per cent, entry at ten per cent of optimal scale would minimize the gross disadvantage. Steeper cost rises (and smaller scales) can of course be absorbed while reducing gross disadvantage as the optimal scale increases as a percentage of the total market.

Without considering further the permutations of this argument, let us apply it in a general way to the various types of actual scale-economy patterns we have described:

(1) *Very important scale economies*: 10 per cent or more of the un-segmented national or largest submarket output supplied by an optimal firm or plant, and costs up "significantly" at half-optimal scales.

Let us take 10 per cent as the percentage of market output at minimal price supplied by an optimal unit. If costs are up by 5 per cent at half-

---

[24] Suppose, for example, that the scale curve for each of two entrants (in different industries) is so shaped that unit costs are up 3 per cent above the minimal, optimal-scale, level at a scale equal to half the optimum — the *shape* of the two scale curves is the same over the observed range. Suppose also that for one entrant, optimal scale would supply 10 per cent of the relevant market output, whereas for the other optimal scale would supply 4 per cent. Now the first entrant (optimal scale equals 10 per cent of market output) could reduce his gross disadvantage by entering at half-optimal scale instead of optimal, since he thus would incur about a 5 per cent price disadvantage plus a 3 per cent cost disadvantage, for a total of 8 per cent, whereas by entering at optimal scale he would incur a price disadvantage of about 10 per cent. On the other hand, the second entrant could not reduce his gross disadvantage by entering below optimal scale. At that scale, he would incur a price disadvantage of about 4 per cent, but at half-optimal scale he would incur a price disadvantage of about 2 per cent plus a cost disadvantage of 3 per cent for a total of 5 per cent. Thus a given shape of scale curve is not shallow enough to give a net advantage to suboptimal entry with the second entrant, whereas it is with the first. In the first case, the effective barrier to entry (percentage excess of entry-excluding price over minimal costs) is reduced by the possibility of entry at suboptimal scale, and in the second case it is not, although with a shallower scale curve it would be.

optimal scale in these industries, the gross disadvantage of the entrant (assuming established firms hold their outputs constant) would be about the same at optimal as at half-optimal scale — i.e. about 10 per cent. If costs were up more than 5 per cent at half-optimal scale, optimal-scale entry would incur the smallest gross disadvantage (about 10 per cent); if less, half-optimal scale would offer a lower gross disadvantage. At one-fifth of optimal capacity, costs up less than about 8 per cent above the minimal level would give a smaller gross disadvantage to entry at that reduced scale than to entry at optimal scale.

It is thus evident here that the barrier to entry provided by large optimal scale will be reduced much or moderately below the maximum 10 per cent excess of entry-excluding price over minimal costs if the scale curve is "shallow" or "medium" in shape (pp. 100–101 above); only if it is steep will the maximum or 10 per cent barrier to entry result from scale economies. Even with a "shallow" scale curve as described (costs up 3 per cent at 10 per cent of optimal scale), however, about a 4 per cent excess of price over minimal costs could be consistent with exclusion of entry, and with steep scale curves, this excess ranges up to 10 per cent.

(2) *Moderately important scale economies*: 4 or 5 per cent of the unsegmented national or largest sub-market output supplied by an optimal firm or plant, with costs up "significantly" at half-optimal scales.

A 4 or 5 per cent disadvantage is the maximum gross disadvantage in these industries; thus an entry-excluding price no more than 4 or 5 per cent above minimal costs is expected. With "steep" or "medium" scale curves, this will be the effective barrier to entry. With "shallow" scale curves, a slightly smaller gross disadvantage, ranging from 3 to 3.5 per cent, will be incurred at a half, a quarter, and a tenth of optimal scale. (With even "shallower" scale curves the barrier would be lower.) Thus the effective entry barrier resulting from scale economies is at least slightly reduced by flattish scale curves.

(3) *Relatively unimportant scale economies*: small optimal scales or relatively flat scale curves (or both).

Since the percentage of the market supplied by an optimal unit in this category seldom exceeds 1 or 2 per cent — or, alternatively, costs are up only 1 or 2 per cent for units supplying negligible fractions of the market — similar percentage excesses of entry-excluding price over minimal costs are ordinarily maximal, and the actual excesses are presumably somewhat less in many cases.

The pertinent reference is, of course, to percentages of the unsegmented national market supplied by the optimal firm or of the largest submarket supplied by the optimal plant complex (usually one plant) of a firm operating in the submarket. The price disadvantage in a given submarket will not be increased if, in order to realize economies of the multiplant firm, an entrant enters several submarkets simultaneously. Economies of the large firm, except in unsegmented national markets, will not necessarily increase the entry barrier imposed by plant economies.[25]

All this discussion proceeds on the supposition that entrants expect established firms to hold their outputs constant (case 3, p. 97). This is a relatively pessimistic expectation from the standpoint of the entrant, permitting established firms to establish something like the maximum conceivable entry-excluding prices.[26] A much more optimistic expectation is that established firms will hold their prices constant (unless the entrant undercuts them), permitting the entrant to win such market share away from them as he can (case 2, p. 97). Let us examine the character of barriers to entry under this optimistic extreme, and then consider cases in between.

A *priori* prediction on this matter is beset by three main difficulties. First, there is the question of what share of the market an entrant will gain at any going level of prices set (and suppositiously maintained) by the established sellers. Will he gain a share equal to that of the average other sellers, or a smaller or larger one? The problem is complicated because actual market shares are nearly always influenced by product differentiation or market frictions, and because recognition of these would introduce product differentiation considerations into the scale-economies picture, on the whole prematurely. To consider the "pure" scale-economies case above (assuming true homogeneity among all sellers' products), the convenient though unrealistic assumption is that the entrant seller would obtain a market share proportionate to the number of sellers — if he were the eleventh seller, for example, he would secure one-eleventh of any market. This is congruent with the homogeneity assumption adopted in the examination of category 3 above. A tentative solution to our proposed problem may be developed on this assumption, although it will be subject to modification as product differentiation is recognized.

Second, there is the question of how much the total absolute industry demand for all sellers will be restricted as established sellers try successively higher alternative prices — of the rate at which the size of the pie, of which the entrant will take a given share, will be reduced as price is raised. This is a matter of the elasticity of demand for total industry

[25] In the smaller submarkets, where the percentage of submarket output supplied by an optimal plant is frequently 2 to 4 times as great than that for the largest submarket, the barrier to entry imposed by scale economies may be significantly greater if the scale curve is not very flat. Thus the barrier to entry would be great instead of moderate in small cement or steel submarkets, and medium instead of low in small petroleum-product sub-markets. But the possibility of reduction of submarket size seriously impeding entry is frequently not realized, because of flat scale curves.

[26] The possibility of an expectation of retaliation to entry is neglected.

output. Taken in conjuction with the percentage share of the entrant, it will determine the absolute output he can attain at each alternative level of price set by established sellers. His absolute share will be smaller for a given excess of price above the minimal cost level, the more elastic the industry demand is — and thus, the higher his costs will be along a given back-rising scale curve. Consequently, established sellers will be able to establish higher entry-excluding prices (other things being equal) with more elastic industry demand curves, since the greater reduction of aggregate industry demand works against the potential entrant by restricting his absolute output at higher prices. (The opposite was true where it was assumed that established sellers would hold constant outputs, as above. There, more elastic demands decreased the price effect of an entrant's addition to output and lowered the barrier to entry.)

Third, there is the derivative question of the best price established sellers can charge that will exclude entry, the property of such a price being that at all lower prices the entrant's unit costs, given his market share, will exceed price.

Any extended theorizing on this last issue would be unduly prolonged for our purposes, but some general indications may be set forth.

First, if the entrant's absolute market share, at a price equal to minimal costs, *is as large as his optimal scale*, established sellers will find that the only entry-excluding price is equal to the entrant's minimal costs. There is then no barrier to entry so long as the entrant's minimal costs equal those of established firms, as they will in the absence of absolute cost advantages. Essentially, this would result from the fact that before entry, established firms were on the average above minimum optimal scale and that entry therefore did not elevate costs and price through inadequate market shares.

This situation is illustrated diagrammatically in Figure 1. In this figure let AC be the scale curve of entrant, relating unit costs to (designed) rate of output; the output OX is the output at minimum optimal scale (costs being assumed constant at the minimal level for larger scales). Let some demand curve dd' represent the entrant's share of the total market, after entry, at each relevant alternative price (a constant fraction of some industry demand curve). Now if the entrant's share is either at d_1d_1' (just sufficient to give a price covering cost at optimal scale), or at d_2d_2' (larger than this) established sellers cannot find a price above minimal cost (above OP_m) which will exclude his entry if the entrant expects them to hold price unchanged in the face of entry.

Second, if the entrant's share of the market, at a price equal to minimal costs, *is smaller than his optimal scale output*, established sellers will be able to elevate price somewhat above the minimal-cost level without attracting entry. The amount by which they will be able to do so will depend on three things: (1) How "crowded" the industry already is, which will help determine how much short of optimal-scale output an entrant's market share will be at minimal prices, assuming he gets an equal share, (2) how "steep" the entrant's scale curve is at outputs short of the optimum, which will determine how rapidly his costs go up with a suboptimal share; (3) how elastic the industry demand curve is, which will determine how much absolute market shares are restricted with an elevation of price. In general, established firms can secure higher entry-excluding prices as the industry is more "crowded," as the scale curve is steeper, and as industry demand is more elastic.

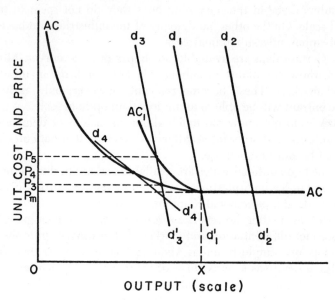

FIGURE 1

Referring again to Figure 1, suppose that d_1d_1' represents the market shares of each of 9 established sellers, prior to entry. If one entrant came in, the shares of all sellers would now be at d_3d_3'. Then established sellers could exclude the entry at prices up to P_3. Applying our principles, it is also clear: (1) that if demand were more elastic, as at d_4d_4', entry-excluding price would be higher at P_4; (2) that if instead the scale curve were steeper at AC_1, entry-excluding price would again be higher, at P_5; (3) that if the industry were initially so crowded that established firms had shares at d_3d_3' instead of at d_1d_1', entry would shift the shares to the left of d_3d_3' and result in a higher entry-excluding price; (4) that if only *two* firms established initially had shares at d_1d_1', prior to entry — so that optimal scale was larger relative to the market — a unit of entry would place post-entry shares to the left of d_3d_3', again permitting a higher entry-excluding price.

Given these general principles, what is likely to be the entry-forestalling effect of the actually discovered scale economies, if maintenance of going price by established firms is expected? Several relevant considerations stand out:

(1) If we judge by the average scale of the first 4 firms, none of the 20 industries (so far as available data reveal) is "crowded." In most of them, these 4 firms on the average have apparently superoptimal scale nationally or by submarkets; in the remaining ones they do not seem to be below optimal scale. On the other hand, many of the industries also have smaller firms of apparently suboptimal scales.

(2) Certain data are available on shapes of scale curves. Most pertinent are those for plants in submarkets and for firms in unsegmented national markets. These become relevant, however, only as it appears that the entrant will be able to attain less than optimal scale.

(3) We do not know too much about elasticities of demands for industry outputs, and other information is so sketchy that data on elasticities could not be put to much use.

(4) Data on optimal scales are available and are perhaps crucial. This is because the leading question is whether or not the entrant could attain optimal scale at a price equal to minimal cost.

On this last matter, however, *a priori* speculations seem generally idle, since product differentiation and market frictions make futile the attempt to develop any simple formula. About all we can say is that the larger the optimal scale (as a percentage of the market) the harder a time the entrant would have to attain that scale. With this in mind, the following may be offered on our twenty industries (categorized according to the importance of scale economies on pages 81–82 and 90–93):

(1) In almost every case, ability of the entrant to attain a market share comparable with those of the first 4 to 8 established firms would give him approximately optimal scale at a price approximately equal to minimal costs and result in substantially no barrier to entry, if established firms maintained prices (if not undercut) in the face of entry. Thus the expectation that they would maintain prices would tend generally to remove the entry-deterring effects of scale economies, given this good ability by entrants to attain market shares. This suggests that in the absence of all product differentiation (which accounts for the existence of many small firms in various of these industries), scale economies would be generally unimportant deterrents to entry under the optimistic expectations specified. Optimal scales are simply not large enough to make it otherwise, given the relatively ample scales of the leading firms.

(2) If the ability of the entrant to gain an adequate market share is restricted — as by product differentiation — he generally may expect higher than optimal costs in significant degree in the "important-scale-economy" industries, in a lesser degree in the "moderate-scale economy" industries, and negligibly elsewhere. Corresponding barriers to entry are raised, even though established firms maintain prices in the face of entry. It should be noted that the same product-differentiation considerations which combine with scale economies to impede entry would presumably offer a corresponding or greater impediment if entrants expected established firms to maintain outputs — this impediment being reflected in lower prices to the entrant than to established firms if he entered at optimal or substantial scale. Thus, price maintaining expectations retain their rank as generally more optimistic than output-maintaining expectations.

Let us now return to our main theme. We have appraised the prospective entry-deterring effect of observed scale economies on the alternative suppositions that, in the face of entry, established firms are expected to maintain constant outputs (case 3), and constant prices (case 2). Between these extremes lies case 4 — the more probable expectation of some output reduction by established firms, but not enough to maintain prices in the face of entry.

Under the actual scale-economy conditions observed,[27] entry barriers resulting from scale economies alone will in case 4 then lie somewhere between those found in cases 2 and 3. This would mean that (referring to the largest submarkets) established firms might be able, by virtue of scale economies alone, to forestall entry while elevating prices above minimal costs by some indeterminate amount less than 5 to 10 per cent in the 2 industries with very important scale economies, by something less than 3 to 5 per cent in the 7 industries with moderately important scale economies, and something less than 1 or 2 per cent in 7 industries with relatively unimportant scale economies. Of course, the ability to exploit these scale economies is increased if product preferences significantly favor established sellers.[28]

A final possibility regarding entrants' expectations has been described as the supposition that they would enter at very small scales (incurring such cost disadvantages as this involved) and thus expect no

[27] I.e., in all conditions except where scale curves are *much* steeper than actually found, and where in addition entrants can secure only suboptimal market shares.
[28] An operationally meaningful distinction among the three entry-barrier categories supposes that the variance in cost observations and estimates of firms is insufficient probably to forestall actual detection of the relevant differences — for example, between a 2 per cent and a 5 per cent price-cost gap. The differences among the predicted magnitudes are indeed small enough that an even grosser classification of cases might be in order.

reaction from established sellers (case 1). No perceptible price change would then result from entry, and also no perceptible output adjustments by established sellers. We now see that this may be viewed as a subsection of case 3 (outputs of established firms constant) in which the limit is reached where the increment to entry is small enough not to affect price, and in which the entrant's entire disability is in costs above the minimal level. Our analysis of case 3 suggests that this extreme adjustment in the cases in question will be relevant as the adaptation affording the entrant the smallest gross disadvantage only if there is a very flat scale curve back to very small scales. When this is true, the conclusions already developed for unimportant scale economies under case 3 are applicable — entry barriers due to scale economies will be very low.[29]

Thus we have been able to make some prediction of the height of the barriers to entry likely to result from the actual scale economies observed in the 20 industries in our sample — or at any rate of the maximum limit on these barriers. In appraising them, we have endeavored to deal with scale economies more or less in isolation, without considering the possible interacting effects of product differentiation. In the next chapter, we shall turn directly to entry barriers resulting from product differentiation. First, however, we will consider the extent to which observed scale economies in the 20 industries provide a rationale for the existing degree of seller concentration in them.

Economies of scale as a rationale for existing concentration

To what extent are existing degrees of concentration in our 20 industries "justified" by apparent economies of the large plant of firm, and, conversely, to what extent are they "underjustified" or "overjustified," in the sense that concentration is greater or less than required for optimal efficiency in scale?

Although concentration by firms ordinarily attracts the most attention in policy discussion, passing notice may first be given to plant concentration, as measured by the proportions of output or capacity provided by a given number of plants from an array of all plants in an industry. A survey of these data (presented earlier) suggests:

(1) The largest several plants in an industry — from five or ten to twenty or more — are typically somewhat larger than the estimated optimal size of plant; on the average such plants may be from less than double to five times the estimated optimal size. The observed tendency

---

[29] Throughout the preceding discussion, as noted on page 93 above, we have refrained from explicitly discussing one possible reaction of established firms to large-scale entry — namely (if products are differentiated) elevating their sales-promotion outlays. In general, the anticipation of this reaction would also impede entry, in the same general way as would an anticipated price reduction. The magnitude of such a reaction could of course vary within wide limits.

is evidently due to the duplication of optimal-scale plant facilities on single sites in large submarkets or in unsegmented national markets where freight costs are unimportant. In most of these cases, the excess of attained over optimal scale is not clearly linked with economies of the large firm, although it is or may be in some.

(2) Additional plants, next in size to the largest and of sizes varying in the general neighborhood of the optimum, are normally present in sufficient numbers so that from 50 to 90 per cent of industry output is supplied by plants not significantly below the optimum.

(3) Plants significantly below the optimal scale (in terms of percentage of the market supplied) supply the remainder of industry output — 10 per cent up to perhaps 50. But of these, plants supplying the bulk of remaining output are ordinarily close enough to the optimum so that, in view of the shapes of plant scale curves, their disadvantages in cost are probably not very big. Also of course, the existence of small plants producing specialties or operating in small isolated markets accounts for part of the small-plant phenomenon in many industries, and may be quite consistent with efficiency. Detailed data on this last matter are not available.

Typically, then, enough plants are so near optimal or larger scales that the bulk of industry output is provided by plants suffering no serious cost disadvantage because of scale. Correspondingly, plant concentration is usually somewhat "higher than needed" (for efficiency) at the top end of the size distribution of plants, and somewhat "lower than needed" at the bottom end. But generally, plant concentration plays a minor role, and multiplant developments of firms a major role, in the over-all picture of concentration by firms.

In the case of firms, attention usually centers mainly on the "top-level" concentration, as registered by the market control of the largest 4 or 8 firms in the industry, since it is for them that excessive or "unnecessary" firm size is ordinarily suspected. Referring to the first 4 firms in each of our industries, it appears that concentration by the large firms is in every case but one greater than required by single-plant economies, and in more than half of the cases very substantially greater. Generally it is only within some of the industries with very important economies of large plant — e.g., fountain pens, copper, typewriters, autos, tractors — that concentration by firms has not been much greater than required by single-plant economies. Even in these cases it may be two or three times as great as thus required. In the other cases concentration by firms tends to be a substantial or large multiple of that required by single-plant economies. Remembering that we are dealing in general in this sample with the more concentrated manufacturing industries, we may say in summary that nearly all of the industries tended to become moderately or highly concentrated (by firms) whether economies of the single plant were important or not. Some of this excess of the size of the firm over that of a single plant of minimum optimal scale is reflected in the development of plants of superoptimal scale, as we have seen just above. Much of it, however, results from multiplant development — of a moderate extent in most cases, but of a very great extent in such cases as canned goods, flour, liquor, metal containers, and shoes.

Another question is whether the existing degree of concentration by large firms is consistent or inconsistent with the existence of a single optimal plant per firm in each recognized submarket. In 6 of the 8 cases where the national market has been considered substantially unsegmented — copper, liquor, tires and tubes, rayon, soap, and cigarettes — the degree of concentration by firms within the single market is noticeably greater than required by such plant economies, although in 4 of the 6 cases it is greater by at most a multiple of 2 to 4. In 7 cases — petroleum refining, meat packing, fountain pens, cement, steel, farm machines, and gypsum products — the degree of national concentration by firms is not grossly inconsistent with the larger firms having on the average but a single optimal plant per submarket in each of several or many submarkets. (This is certainly not to deny that the largest single firms may have more than this and probably do; we refer only to the average of the largest 4 firms). In the last 5 cases — canned goods, flour, automobiles, metal containers, and shoes — the degree of concentration by firms exceeds by a significant multiple that required for each of the 4 largest firms to have on the average one optimal plant in each submarket. Thus in 11 of 20 industries the existing degree of concentration by firms as measured by the average size of the largest 4 firms is significantly greater than required for these firms to have only one optimal plant per submarket; in the other 9 cases concentration is at least roughly consistent with such a condition.

The third question concerns the extent to which the existing degree of concentration by large firms is justified by the exploitation of economies of multiplant firms. We will go no further with this question here than a comparison of the fifth and sixth columns of Table IX will take us. In Group 1 in that table, the alleged absence of any economies of multiplant firm implies that there is no justification in terms of costs for any excess of concentration by large firms over that required for single efficient plants, although in 1 case (typewriters) the existence of an excess is uncertain, and in 3 others it is not necessarily accompanied by accentuated concentration in individual submarkets. In Group 2 no estimates of multiplant economies are available; we need say no more than that in 6 of 8 cases (excluding farm machines and tractors) there is a concentration by large firms substantially greater than that required for efficient plants in each submarket. In Group 3, in only 1 of the industries (shoes) does the degree of concentration by firms seem clearly to have exceeded that required for economies of production and distribution by the large firm.

In the sample as a whole, the existing degree of concentration by the largest 4 firms lacks a clear cost justification in perhaps 12 of 20 cases, although in 7 of these we have a simple lack of any definite estimates. In 3 more cases (typewriters, fountain pens, and tractors), the multiplant phenomenon is not very important, and in the remaining 5 (the last in Group 3), a potential cost justification has been offered. Further information is needed on this matter, particularly with reference to cases in which multiplant firm organization has increased effective concentration in individual submarkets or in unsegmented national markets.

All this discussion, however, refers to concentration as measured in terms of the average size of the first four firms in an industry. A different picture of size and of the extent of unexplained or unjustified size will emerge as we look at the individual firms within the first four in any industry. As a general rule, so far as available statistics reveal, the largest single firm in an industry may control from a third to over a half of the total market share controlled by the first four firms, whereas the fourth largest firm may control from a sixth to less than an eighth of that total. Thus we find that unexplained or "unjustified" size is generally more acute and more common for "largest" firms than for the average of the four largest, and very frequently small or negligible for firms around the fourth in size rank.

Similarly, the sizes of firms below the fourth in rank are not commonly in excess of that required for optimal efficiency, and very infrequently sufficient to require more than one optimal plant per submarket. The "excess" concentration problem in an industry — in the sense that it reflects firm sizes above what is evidently needed for lowest production and distribution costs — is thus ordinarily one which involves mainly the largest two to four firms; firms below that rank do not have, except in a very minor fraction of cases, sizes in excess of those claimed as necessary for efficiency. As we proceed to still smaller firms — below the first eight, twelve, twenty, or forty — firm sizes (like plant sizes) are frequently below the estimated optimum, though the bulk of output will normally be supplied by firms with no very serious cost disadvantage due to scale.

4

PRODUCT DIFFERENTIATION ADVANTAGES
of Established Firms as Barriers to Entry

A second major class of deterrents to entry is found in the "product differentiation advantages" of established firms. Buyers may have a preference, transitory or permanent, for some or all established products as compared to new-entrant products, and this may in essence erect some barrier to entry.

Product differentiation was first emphasized as such in academic literature by Chamberlin in his *Theory of Monopolistic Competition* in 1933, although it has of course been an important phenomenon at least as long as the "ad man," and has existed as long as commerce and business. It refers in essence to buyers' preferences for one or some of a variety of very similar substitute products, such as several brands of cigarettes or several makes of automobiles, and also to the fact that different buyers have different product allegiances or preference patterns, so that the preferences in question do not result in some universally agreed-upon system of grading or rating for the competing products.

Product differentiation is propagated by differences in the design or physical quality of competing products, by efforts of sellers to distinguish their products through packaging, branding, and the offering of auxiliary services to buyers, and by advertising and sales-promotional efforts designed to win the allegiance and custom of the potential buyer. These latter efforts may turn in part on informing the consumer of the distinctive physical properties of individual products, and also in part on "convincing" him of their desirability, prestige, or superior quality.

What are the principal consequences of product differentiation? The one most often emphasized in the literature of economic theory is that the individual seller gains some independent jurisdiction over his price, relative to the prices of his rivals, which he would not have if the competing products were parts of a single homogeneous, standardized commodity. He can presumably raise his price somewhat above those of his rivals while retaining some but not all of the customers who prefer his product, and will suffer increasing loss of customers with increasing elevations of price. Correspondingly, he can lower his price to and below those of his rivals without attracting away all of the buyers who prefer their products, although his own sales should expand as his relative price becomes lower. The seller's ability to control his individual price in the way made possible by product differentiation of course complicates and somewhat alters the manner in which he may calculate or arrive at a "profit-maximizing" price.

A derived tangible consequence of this is that, once a competitive balance is struck in the market, there may be a variety of individual prices on rival products. This is not always so, however, and perhaps not so in the majority of cases. Though buyer preferences for individual products do exist, the preferences may be sufficiently vulnerable to price differences that many buyers will be "detachable" from a preferred seller by a small difference, even though rather durable buyer allegiances will persist as long as rival prices are substantially identical. In consequence, we frequently find industries with differentiated products in which all principal sellers charge substantially identical prices, and apparently would be unwilling or afraid to try any other course. Industries where there is price variety are often also found, however. One pattern appears where there are two or more classes of sellers, one enjoying general preferences for its products and charging roughly uniform prices at a higher level, and another or others charging roughly uniform prices at a lower level or levels. Not only may some prices be absolutely higher than others, but some may be more favorably related to unit costs than others, thus revealing a net advantage of some established sellers over others.

But price differences are not the only nor necessarily the most important consequence of product differentiation. Among established sellers, three added consequences stand out:

(1) Selling costs — for advertising, sales promotion, etc. — tend to be incurred, often in substantial quantity, in order to gain and maintain a share of the market against established rivals and also against potential entrants. To such selling costs are added costs incurred to improve or vary the product aimed at the same ends.

(2) Alterations in organization favoring sales promotion, such as the integration of distributive functions and facilities, may be encouraged.

(3) Given those adaptations of pricing, selling outlays, etc., that are made, different firms will in a competitive balance obtain significantly different shares of the market. Frequently, the force of existing product preferences will be evidenced more in the disparity of their market shares than in the disparity of their prices.

This has all been fairly well recognized in the existing literature of economic theory. What is generally less well recognized is the impact of product differentiation on the condition of entry.

In general, product differentiation may lead to significant buyer preferences between established products and the products of new entrant firms. There is a good *a priori* possibility, moreover, that most buyers will on balance prefer established and known products to new and unknown ones. Of four major established brands of soap flakes there may be none enjoying a clearly preferred position over the others; each may have a large following of loyal customers who will remain loyal as long as the prices of the four are closely similar. But if a new brand of soap flakes were introduced by an entrant, the great bulk of the buyers of all four established brands might very well prefer any of those four brands to the new unknown, with the result that the entrant could secure an appreciable market, if at all, only by making some financial sacrifice not incurred by the established firms. Thus a general tendency of buyers to prefer established to new products may place potential entrants to a differentiated-product industry at a disadvantage as compared to firms already established in the industry.

In general, this disadvantage may take the form of either lower price or higher selling cost. In order to secure a market, the entrant may have to accept a lower net price than established firms, relative to the cost of production, either perpetually or for an appreciable interval of time during which he establishes "buyer acceptance" for his product. Or he may have to incur appreciably higher selling costs per unit of sales volume, indefinitely or for a similar interval. Finally, he may have some combination of these two disadvantages. His total disadvantage due to product differentiation at any time will be effectively the sum (conveniently stated in per-unit-of-output terms) of his price and his selling-cost disadvantage. Not only the initial size of the disadvantage, but also its duration will of course be important. Additionally important may be an increment to absolute capital requirements, representing money which the entrant must "invest in losses" over a period of years during which he is striving to establish his product.

If the potential entrant suffers some "product-differentiation disadvantage," the established firms should, by virtue of their advantage, be able to elevate their long-run price above minimal costs by some corresponding amount without attracting entry. The gap between price and minimal cost (including selling cost) which they can establish while forestalling entry will be a measure of the barrier to entry attributable to their product-differentiation advantages. Needless to say, this gap may vary as among established sellers so far as there are differential advantages as among them, so that the entry barrier in question may be reflected in several measures which refer separately to several established sellers or groups thereof.

In its simplest form, a product-differentiation barrier to entry would occur if its height were the same, in per-unit-of-output terms, regardless of the scale at which entry was made [1] — if there were neither economies nor diseconomies of large-scale sales promotion. Then the product-differentiation barrier would be simply additive to any resulting from scale economies, and would not affect the entrant's decision as to the best scale for entry. (In the "pure" case, there would be also no production economies or diseconomies of scale.)

Suppose that all established sellers of electric shavers have equal advantage, and that an entrant to the market would either have to incur, on the average for a period of ten years, one dollar per shaver more in advertising costs or receive a price of one dollar less per shaver than established sellers, regardless of the scale which the entrant aims to attain. Suppose also that after ten years in the market, no disadvantage is anticipated. The entrant, averaging his first ten-year disadvantage over the anticipated outputs of as many years as he takes into account, and with appropriately increasing discount for interest and risk of successively more remote years, will presumably consider himself at a net disadvantage for his total future operation of something less than one dollar per shaver. Then established firms should presumably be able to set price up to a similar amount above minimal costs without attracting entry, since at lower prices the entrant would anticipate a net loss on his total future operation.

Product-differentiation barriers and scale economies

If there are neither economies nor diseconomies of large-scale sales promotion, the entrant may and presumably will enter at any scale which would otherwise be most advantageous (in view of economies in production and distribution), and his decision as to scale should not be influenced by product-differentiation disadvantages *per se*.[2] This is true at any rate except as far as the capital requirement for "investing in losses" during his break-in period might alter his decision as to scale. In fact, however, there is a clear possibility that there will be either diseconomies or economies of large-scale sales promotion in an industry, and that in consequence the net advantages of a given scale may be altered and the

[1] The same, that is, provided that established sellers do not react to large-scale entry by increasing their own promotional outlays. (If they do, this in effect raises an entry barrier attributable to the scale of entry, rather than to diseconomies of large-scale sales promotion to the entrant.)

[2] Not strictly, although the existence of product differentiation introduces the possibility that one of the reactions of established firms to large-scale entry will be an elevation of their promotional outlays. This has been taken separately into account (pp. 110 above).

entrant's decision as to the most advantageous scale for entry significantly altered.

In the first place, there may be diseconomies of large-scale sales promotion, in the sense that the gross disadvantage of the entrant in lower price plus higher selling cost per unit increases from some point as his scale increases, when promotional outlays of rivals are unchanged. A potential automobile manufacturer might be able to find a market for 10,000 automobiles per year with a price-plus-selling-cost disadvantage of only $50 per car as compared to the strongest established firms, but he might find that his disadvantage increased progressively to $150 per car as he sought successively large volumes up to 200,000 cars per year. This might result from the fact that some but not many buyers are easily detachable from the established brands by novelty or specialty in design, or have the desire to be "experimenters" with a new product.[3]

Why should such diseconomies of large-scale sales promotion be significant? Cannot any entrant simply choose to enter at the reduced scale at which the product-differentiation disadvantage is minimized, so that this scale becomes the effective scale of entry for numerous potential entrants? Aside from the fact that there may be room for a few but not many little entrants of this sort in an industry (so that the diseconomies noted would vanish and the condition of entry alter before much entry took place), a general reason for the significance of such diseconomies may be that the scale at which the product-differentiation disadvantage is minimized is so small as to be suboptimal from a production-distribution standpoint, so that the entrant would incur diseconomies of suboptimal production in order to minimize his product-differentiation disadvantage. This could be true even though the optimal scale for production and distribution would itself not supply a significant fraction of the market.

If such a situation is encountered, the scale at which entry takes place is likely to be altered because of product differentiation disadvantages. The entrant should compromise by selecting a scale which minimizes the aggregate of production-scale economy and product-differentiation disadvantages, and in the instances noted this will tend to lie between the smaller scale at which product-differentiation disadvantages are minimized and the larger scale (optimal or smaller) at which disadvantages due to the effects of production scale economies are minimized.

The preceding is significant because it suggests, where there are diseconomies of large-scale sales promotion: (1) that the product-differentiation disadvantage is not simply an invariant value to be added to other

---

[3] It should be noted that the existence of such diseconomies to the entrant is quite consistent with there being no scale at which the entrant is not at some net disadvantage as compared to established firms.

disadvantages, but a magnitude varying with scale; (2) that the relevant magnitude for analysis of entry barriers is that found where the aggregate disadvantage to entry from all causes, including production scale economies, is minimized; and (3) that the production-scale-economy disadvantage, to be added to the present one, is potentially codetermined with the product-differentiation disadvantage, and thus alterable in the light of product-differentiation considerations previously neglected.

The same practical conclusions apply in the case of the existence of the opposite potential phenomenon — economies of large-scale sales promotion — although here the direction of the effects of the variation in product-differentiation advantages with scale is different. Economies of large-scale sales promotion occur for the entrant if his gross disadvantage in lower prices plus higher selling costs per unit decreases as his scale increases through some range, when promotional outlays of rivals are unchanged. Such a condition might result from the fact that, at a given price, sales would increase more than proportionally to the sales promotion budget as the budget became large enough to support either heavy advertising in national media or a nationwide distributive system. We have already expressed some skepticism about the existence of significant economies of this sort for entrants, and have also emphasized that the product preferences between established and new entrant products may easily be such that although both established and new entrant firms enjoy economies of large-scale sales promotion, new entrant firms will have a net promotional disadvantage at every commonly attained scale.

If entrants do encounter such economies, they may be significant in two ways. The optimum scale for sales promotion toward which product-differentiation disadvantages decline may be no larger than the scale of entry at which the entrant would have minimized his disadvantage due to production and distribution economies alone. In this event, the firm will not be induced to alter its scale of entry by reason of selling economies, but the advantages of entering at the given scale may be intensified. Or the optimum scale for sales promotion may exceed (by little or much) the best scale of entry as determined by production-distribution economies alone. In this event, the entrant will probably compromise between the alternative optima; as a result, he will tend to enter at a larger scale than otherwise by reason of selling economies; and as a further result, the over-all barrier to entry resulting from all scale economies will in general be somewhat increased (as the net product-differentiation barrier is virtually decreased) by selling economies. The resultant necessity in analysis for a joint rather than separate consideration of production-distribution economies and selling economies in determining their effects on the condition of entry is again evident.

Mixed patterns of variation of economies or advantages of large-scale sales promotion are of course possible and even probable of occurrence. Economies of large-scale selling might be succeeded by diseconomies as scale was increased, and just as plausibly diseconomies might be succeeded by economies. In either case, the effect of such variations of sales-promotional efficiency with scale on the scale of entry and the impact of all scale economies on the condition of entry must be determined by considering selling economies in conjunction with the economies of production and distribution.

At least this is hypothetically so. When we come to evaluate the condition of entry for specific industries in our study on the basis of available data, we usually find a definite insufficiency of data for establishing patterns of variation of the product-differentiation disadvantages of entrants with scale. This is because respondents to questionnaires were generally not disposed to particularize on this matter, and perhaps more basically because the suspicion that established firms enjoy selling-cost-economy patterns different from those of entrant firms leaves anyone with very little basis for guessing on this matter. Our treatment of actual economies and diseconomies of large-scale sales promotion can thus lead only to rather tentative amendments to certain basic flat-figure estimates on the product-differentiation disadvantages of entrants to the various industries.

Content and organization of this chapter

The general purpose of this chapter is to determine from available data the nature and extent of the product-differentiation advantages of established over potential entrant firms, and the heights of the resultant barriers to entry, in our 20 industries. The plan of the chapter is, for each of the 20 industries separately: (1) to evaluate the nature and general importance of product differentiation, in part as an influence on intra-industry competition, but particularly as a consideration creating barriers to new entry; (2) to appraise the general extent of the disadvantages of new entrants resulting from product differentiation, relative to the most favored established firms; and (3) to inquire about the extent to which such disadvantages are variable with variation in the scale of entry, and about the manner in which the over-all impact of advantages of scale on entry may thereby be altered.

Data relevant to these pursuits have been drawn from several sources. Replies to questionnaires are the primary source, as in the case of the study of scale economies. In addition, however, we have drawn to a considerable extent from various sources on advertising and other selling costs and on prices, from data on market shares of firm, from information concerning product patents, and from miscellaneous information concerning the market behavior of buyers and sellers. Particular sources are cited as appropriate in Appendix D. Because of the relative paucity of information from any one source, it will not be fruitful in this instance to present findings based on questionnaire data separately.

The data in question are relatively unsatisfactory, or substantially less satisfactory than those dealing with scale economies. Questionnaire replies were generally more sketchy and less well documented, and seemed to reflect a greater uncertainty on the part of respondents about the quantitative magnitudes involved. Much of the advertising-cost data available refer only to "traceable" advertising, as reported by certain services covering periodicals, network radio and television time, and "nationally placed" newspaper advertisements, and these traceable quantities evidently bear a varying relationship from industry to industry to the actual total advertising expenses on all media.[4] Data on the experience of actual entrants in the last couple of decades are scarce, either because entry has been rare or because adequate records of entrants' experiences are not available. Finally, as already noted, data relating the product-differentiation disadvantages of entrants to the scale of entry are quite deficient. In consequence, any quantification of the net product-differentiation disadvantages of potential entrants to our industries is highly speculative, although we have attempted some wherever there was some basis for guessing. Similarly, modification of previous quantitative judgments concerning the effect of scale economies on entry, in the light of advantages or disadvantages of large-scale selling, is ordinarily next to impossible, although some qualitative judgments may be offered.

The remainder of the chapter presents a tabular summarization and general discussion of findings on all 20 industries with respect to extent and nature of product differentiation, resultant barriers to entry, and importance and impact of advantages or disadvantages of large-scale sales promotion, and offers some general conclusions on the absolute and relative importance of product differentiation as a barrier to entry. In Appendix D, we have given detailed comments on each of the twenty individual industries.

General evaluation of product differentiation among established firms in 20 industries

Product differentiation, as we have indicated, may have a dual effect: first, on the character of intra-industry competition among established firms, and second, on the condition of entry. The effect on intra-industry competition will take the form of supporting preferred market shares

---

[4] Traceable advertising costs referred to throughout this chapter constitute for any firm or industry the sum of periodical, radio and television, and "national" newspaper advertising costs (for space or time only) as calculated by *Publisher's Information Bureau* and by the *Bureau of Advertising, American Newspaper Publishers Association*, generally for the year 1950.

based on regular customer allegiances to certain sellers, of encouraging advertising and other sales promotion as competitive weapons, of permitting some sellers to obtain higher prices or lower unit selling costs than others, and so forth. The effect on the condition of entry will take the form of placing the potential entrant at a disadvantage, as compared to established firms, in price receivable on sales or in unit selling costs of securing a given price or volume.

The latter effect is potentially susceptible to evaluation in terms of a single quantitative measure, which we may either learn or guess at. This measure is the minimal net price-plus-selling-cost disadvantage per unit of output suffered by an entrant as compared to an established firm or firms. The effect on intra-industry competition, however, cannot be appraised in terms of a single measure, since the effects of product differentiation in this sphere are disparate. Nevertheless, it is possible in any industry to make some ranking of the effects of product differentiation on intra-industry competition, and from such rankings to make an over-all comparative rating of the industry as to how important product differentiation seems to be. Tangible evidence of the relative importance of product differentiation will be the size of advertising and other sales-promotion costs (in ratio to sales), the extent to which sellers regularly improve and vary products as a means of securing custom, otherwise unexplained disparities of market share of different sellers, dynamic shifts in such shares apparently attributable to product variations and changes in the size or quality of promotional campaigns, and distinct differential advantages among established sellers in selling prices or in unit promotional costs.

Drawing upon all evidence available, we will introduce our treatment of product differentiation with an attempt to "grade" each of our 20 industries according to the apparent importance of such differentiation as a force in intra-industry competition. Ratings, based on all sources of information and statistical data, are primarily relative; the rating terms chosen are "negligible," "slight," "moderate," and "great." Where product differentiation is held to have "great" importance, it is apparently the dominant force or pivot of market strategies in intra-industry competition. Where it is held to have "negligible" importance, it seems to affect intra-industry competition so little that it could be neglected in an analysis of such competition. The "slight" and "moderate" ratings simply represent two steps between these extremes, and have only ordinal significance.

The results of these ratings are set forth in Table X, together with an indication in each case of the primary evident basis of the existing product differentiation — that is, the primary means by which customer allegiances to particular products have been secured and held. Several things stand out in this tabulation.

TABLE X

Classification of 20 Industries According to the Influence of Product Differentiation on Intra-Industry Competition

Industry	Rating of the importance of product differentiation [a]	Evident primary bases of product differentiation
I. Producer-good industries [b]		
Copper	Negligible	——
Rayon	Negligible	——
Cement	Negligible	——
Steel	Slight	Customer service; personal sales representation.
Gypsum products	Slight	Small design differences in some products.
Flour [c]	Negligible to moderate, depending on market	(Negligible differentiation in producer-good sales; moderate differentiation in home-consumer sales.) Heavy advertising, customer service.
Metal containers	Slight or moderate	Customer service; leasing of equipment to customers; design differences in some products, based on patents.
Farm machinery and tractors	Slight to great, depending on product line	Differences in design; control of or affiliation with retail-dealer systems.
Typewriters	Great	Customer service; slight differences in design; advertising.
II. Consumer-good industries [b]		
Meat packing	Negligible to slight	Advertising; quality maintenances. (Differentiation found mainly in processed meats, not in fresh meats.)
Canned fruits and vegetables	Negligible to moderate, depending on product lines and markets	Advertising.
Shoes	Slight to moderate, depending on product and price lines	Advertising; control of or affiliation with retail-dealer systems; differences in design in women's shoes
Rubber tires [d]	Moderate	Advertising; slight differences in design; customer service; control or or affiliation with retail-dealer systems.

[a] Reference of rating is to principal product(s) of an industry.
[b] Industries identified as producer-good or consumer-good according to buyers of majority of output.
[c] Majority of output sold to producers, minority to consumers.
[d] Majority of output sold consumers, minority to producers.

TABLE X (continued)

Industry	Rating of the importance of product differentiation	Evident primary bases of product differentiation
Petroleum refining [e]	Moderate	Advertising; maintenance and subsidy of retail-dealer systems.
Fountain pens	Slight to great, depending on product and price line	(Differentiation great mainly in high-priced, "quality" pens, declining with price class.) Heavy advertising; differences in design.
Soap	Moderate or great	Heavy advertising.
Liquor	Great	Heavy advertising; quality maintenance.
Cigarettes	Great	Heavy advertising.
Automobiles	Great	Numerous differences in design; control of retail-dealer and customer-service systems; advertising.

[e] Classified primarily on basis of the principal product (gasoline).

As would be expected, the bulk of 10 [5] producer-good industries have either insignificant or slight product differentiation. This applies to such products as copper, rayon, cement, steel, gypsum products, the producer-good fraction of flour, some farm machinery, and possibly to metal containers. The clear exception to the rule for producer goods is found in typewriters, and in tractors and large or complex farm machinery; in addition there is a possibility that metal containers may also constitute an exception. The products in most of these industries are of course physically homogeneous, or nearly so; only in the exceptional cases just mentioned is this rule seriously violated. Consequently, and because producer-buyers are generally well informed and price-conscious, such product differentiation as is found is ordinarily based on the supplying of auxiliary services to customers, plus personal sales representation. Largely when important design differences emerge among sellers do we seem to find important product differentiation in this sphere.

The picture is quite different with consumer goods, where either moderately or very important product differentiation is the rule. The apparent exceptions are in meat packing (especially in fresh meats), a part of canned fruits and vegetables, inexpensive men's shoes, and cheap fountain pens. But we find moderately important differentiation in the consumer-good fraction of flour sales, some canned-goods lines, tires, and petroleum products, and very important differentiation in soap, quality

[5] Counting farm machines and tractors separately.

fountain pens, liquor, cigarettes, and automobiles. The single most important basis of product differentiation in the consumer-good category is apparently advertising; in all cases it appears in significant volume. Second in general importance is the control of or contractual affiliation with wholesale and retail distributors — especially the latter. (See the cases of shoes, rubber tires, petroleum refining, and automobiles.) Substantial differences in design or functional capacity of the product appear important only in a distinct minority of cases in this sample — automobiles, quality fountain pens, and in a lesser degree, rubber tires. In addition, however, there are some consistent quality differences among sellers, often linked with corresponding price differences, as in liquor and shoes, and there are related differences in the extent to which there is quality control or *quality maintenance* for a brand or product through time. As a general rule also, "heavy" advertising, ranging from 5 per cent of sales revenue up, is ordinarily found as a basis for great product differentiation where other bases are weak or largely lacking, as in the cases of soap, cigarettes, and liquor. Where either design differences or control of distributive systems or both are present, important product differentiation is generally secured with small or moderate advertising costs per unit of product.

Viewing our sample as a whole, we find a broad range of industries as classified with respect to the importance of product differentiation for intra-industry competition. Let us now turn to the matter of more immediate interest — the impact of such product differentiation on the condition of entry to these industries.

The effects of product differentiation on the condition of entry in 20 industries

Our findings on product-differentiation barriers to entry to the industries studied come preponderantly from questionnaire estimates, although in a few cases such estimates are supplemented or replaced by estimates from other sources. As previously indicated, economies or diseconomies of large-scale sales promotion may be encountered, and may influence the entrant in choosing the scale for entry at which he would have the minimal aggregate disadvantage relative to established firms. In consequence, the magnitude sought as a measure of the effective height of the product-differentiation barrier to entry is the height of this barrier if entry is to be made at the "least-disadvantaged" scale. Furthermore, we have followed the policy here of attempting to obtain a comparison of the most-favored potential entrant or class of potential entrants with the most-favored established firm or firms, and a corresponding measure of the extent to which the latter can elevate prices above their minimal costs (corresponding industry-wide price adjustments being assumed) without attracting the former into the industry.

From the data available, however, we cannot attain much precision in either of the preceding regards. Because the "least-disadvantaged" scale of entry is an unfamiliar and a rather refined concept, it would be difficult to induce respondents to questionnaires to relate their estimates to it. They may generally have some scale of entry in mind, but not necessarily the one we would wish to specify. It is also difficult to develop distinctions among different established firms or different potential entrants or classes thereof — both categories tend to be thought of by businessmen in "rough average" terms. About the best we can do is attempt to divine the assumptions made by estimators (or applicable to their estimates) with respect to scales of entry and identities of potential entrant and established firms compared, and then consider any modifications of their estimates that are appropriate in the light of indications concerning economies of large-scale sales promotion or differential advantages within groups of firms.

Our procedure is as follows. First, we present for the 20 industries a series of estimates of the product-differentiation barrier which are roughly related to a common or uniform assumption concerning the scale of entry — namely, that entry will take place at a scale in the general neighborhood of that required for *one plant* offering optimal production-distribution economies. (The feasibility of this is increased by the fact that most estimators in business tend to refer to actual entry experience, which has been that of entrants of relatively small scales.) Given this beginning, we consider second the extent to which apparent economies or diseconomies of large-scale sales promotion, encountered as the size of the entrant firm became larger or smaller than that just specified, would be encountered and would have an influence on the scale of entry. Our first estimates are subject to revision in the light of findings on this point, as are previous judgments concerning the impact of scale economies when only production economies were considered. We will turn to this matter in the next section.

A summary of findings on the estimated height of product-differentiation barriers to entry for the one-optimal-plant firm is presented in Table XI. Because the estimates are generally of a rather rough-and-ready character and presumably subject to appreciable margins of error, we have attempted only a three-fold qualitative classification of industries, designating industries as those where these barriers are (I) "negligible or slight," (II) "moderate," and (III) "great." In general, Class I includes industries in which the disadvantage of the entrant in terms of lower price or higher selling cost than established firms would range from "slight and transitory" to a disadvantage of a small percentage of price sustained for only a very few years after entry. Industries in Class III ("great" entry barriers) are those in which the estimated price or selling cost disadvantage of the potential entrant would loom large for many years. A 5 per cent of price disadvantage for ten years or a 10 per cent of price disadvantage for five years would be more or less minimal for industries included in this class, and significantly greater disadvantages would be found in some instances. Class II includes industries in which the disadvantage of potential entrants appears to lie between the upper limit suggested for Class I and the lower limit suggested for Class III. In typical member industries of Class II, something less than a 5 per cent price disadvantage (but above 1 or 2 per cent) for a substantial period, or a greater disadvantage for a quite limited period, is found.

TABLE XI

Classification of 20 Industries According to Height of Barrier to Entry Created by Product Differentiation (Entry at Production-Economy Optimum Scale for One Plant Assumed) [a]

Industry (1)	Basis of prospective entrant's disadvantage (2)	Estimated extent of prospective entrant's disadvantage (3)
Class I: Negligible or slight entry barriers [b]		
Copper	Customer inertia, habit, loyalty	Slight and transitory
Rayon	Customer inertia, habit, loyalty	" " "
Cement	Customer inertia, habit, loyalty	" " "
Canned fruits and vegetables (bulk of standard items) [c]	Advertising and product reputation (both unimportant)	Negligible and transitory. Lower price (if any) offset by lower advertising cost
Flour (industrial and private-label sales)	Customer inertia, habit, loyalty	Any disadvantage temporary and less than 1 per cent of price
Fountain pens (low-price and ballpoint)	Customer inertia, habit, loyalty	No significant disadvantage
Gypsum products [d]	Customer attachments to established brands or firms	"Extra" promotion costs to gain a market position
Meat packing	In processed meats, slight barriers based on advertising, product reputation. In fresh meats, negligible barriers	In processed meats, 2 to 6 per cent of price either in price concessions or extra sales promotion, for one year. In fresh meats, negligible disadvantage.
Farm machinery (simple implements and local specialties)	Product reputation, established dealer systems	"Quite small"
Steel	Customer inertia, habit, loyalty, plus customer dependence on services from established firms	2 per cent of price, either in price concessions or extra sales promotion, for the first one or two years

TABLE XI (continued)

Industry (1)	Basis of prospective entrant's disadvantage (2)	Estimated extent of prospective entrant's disadvantage (3)
Class I: Negligible or slight entry barriers (cont.)		
Shoes (women's and lower-priced men's) [c]	Advertising, product reputation, established dealer systems	Extra promotional costs equal to from one to three per cent of price for five years
Class II: Moderate entry barriers [b]		
Canned fruits and vegetables (certain specialties; e.g., soups and pineapple) [c]	Brand allegiances based on advertising, product reputations	Appreciable extra promotional expenses for at least several years
Shoes (higher-priced men's and some specialties) [c]	Brand allegiances based on advertising, product reputation; established dealer systems	"Perceptible" price disadvantage plus "higher" promotional costs for five or more years
Flour (miller's-brand consumer sales)	Brand allegiances based on heavy advertising, consumer service	5 to 7 per cent price disadvantage for an undefined period, partly offset by lower promotional costs
Metal containers [e]	Improvement and special-product patents controlled by established firms; disadvantage in supplying field service and customer equipment unless entrant is quite large	2 to 5 per cent price disadvantage for a prolonged period, possibly offset in some degree by lower costs
Rubber tires [f]	Brand allegiances based on prolonged advertising; product reputations; established dealer systems	Up to 5 per cent of price, in price concessions plus promotional costs, for a prolonged period, possibly offset by a lack of original-equipment business by the entrant
Petroleum refining	Established dealer systems, brand allegiances	5 to 10 per cent of price, in price concessions and subsidies, for three to five years in the tank-wagon market; less if an area has a developed jobber's market
Soap	Brand allegiances based on prolonged advertising	"Many years" of "higher" advertising costs, but product innovations may reduce the disadvantage

TABLE XI (continued)

Industry (1)	Basis of prospective entrant's disadvantage (2)	Estimated extent of prospective entrant's disadvantage (3)
Class III: Great entry barriers [b]		
Tractors and large, complicated farm machinery	Brand allegiances based on product reputation, customer service; established dealer sytems	"Large," but not otherwise estimated
Typewriters	Brand allegiances based on product reputations, customer service, advertising	"Substantial" promotional disadvantages for five or ten years
Cigarettes [c]	Brand allegiances based on prolonged advertising	10 to 25 per cent of manufacturer's price, probably in extra promotional costs, for seven to ten years
Liquor	Brand allegiances based on prolonged advertising, product reputations; prestige in conspicuous consumption of known brands	20 per cent of manufacturers' price in "bonds" and 15 per cent in "B" blends, "indefinitely"; similar disadvantage in "straights." Disadvantage of entry to "A" blends "prohibitive."
Fountain pens ("quality" or high-priced)	Brand allegiances based on advertising, conspicuous consumption motives	"Huge and probably prohibitive" disadvantages in promotional costs
Automobiles [c]	Brand allegiances based on advertising, product reputations, conspicuous consumption motives; allegiances to established dealer-service organizations. Lower trade-in values on used products of entrant for a long period	5 to 15 per cent of manufacturers' price, in price or extra promotion, for ten years, incurred with substantial risk of failure

[a] Data are usually from replies submitted to questionnaires by company executives, unless otherwise indicated.

[b] Reference, unless otherwise specified, is to comparison of "most-advantaged" established firms and "least-disadvantaged" potential entrants. Industries are classified in terms of principal products and markets.

[c] Questionnaire data are supplemented significantly by data from other sources — i.e. L. A. Doyle on canned goods, Bruce Cheek on shoes, Tennant (*The American Cigarette Industry*) on cigarettes, David K. Smith on automobiles.

[d] Classification of the gypsum products industry refers to the period after 1950, subsequent to an antitrust decree. Prior to then, a "great" product-differentiation barrier, based on patent control, seems to have existed. See Appendix D below.

[e] Classification of the metal container industry refers to the period subsequent to 1950, after an antitrust decree. Prior to then, a "great" product-differentiation barrier probably existed (see Appendix D below). Questionnaire data on metal containers were supplemented from data in C. H. Hession, *Competition in the Metal Food Container Industry*.

[f] Data on tires are dominantly from an unpublished manuscript of R. B. Heflebower, which incorporates much data from O.P.A. records.

In addition to classifying industries in this manner (column 1 of Table XI), we have also indicated the primary apparent basis of the prospective entrant's disadvantage (column 2), and the estimated extent of his disadvantage (column 3). As to the bases of such disadvantage, four general types stand out: (a) customer inertia, habit, and loyalty (generally not too strong and found in producer-good industries); (b) preferences for products of established firms based on advertising or on established product "reputations"; (c) allegiances to established firms based on services supplied to customers; and (d) established dealer systems, owned or more or less controlled by established firms. The inability of potential entrants to match the physical product designs of established firms does not stand out as generally important in industries within this sample, but the allegiance of consumers to established products in areas in which they are ignorant or uncertain concerning the actual properties of products is quite important.

Classified as subject to negligible or slight entry barriers resulting from product differentiation are 6 entire industries and segments of 5 others: copper, rayon, cement, gypsum products, meat packing, and steel, together with a large part of canned foods, the industrial and private-label market in flour, the low-price and ballpoint sector of fountain pens, a minor fraction of farm machinery, and low-priced men's and women's shoes. Seven of the 11 industries (or sectors of industries) are clearly engaged in supplying producer goods, and in nearly all of these the slight or negligible product-differentiation barrier rests dominantly on customer habit and on loyalties depending on long-established buyer-seller relations, gratitude of the buyer for service and consideration, and the security of dealing with sellers of established responsibility. Generally these things alone do not appear to place the entrant at very much of a disadvantage for very long. The only consumer-goods industries included are meat packing and sectors of the canned goods, shoe, and fountain-pen industries. Perhaps these have in common the fact that buyers purchase the goods (which are inexpensive per unit and not very durable) repeatedly over short time intervals, buy for use rather than prestige, and generally feel well able to make personal judgments about the relative physical qualities of competing products. Whatever the reason, sales promotion does not seem to have given established sellers very much of an advantage over entrants in these cases.

At the other extreme, we find 5 industries and segments of 2 others classified as subject to great entry barriers attributable to product differentiation. These are the typewriter, cigarette, liquor, tractor, and automobile industries, together with the "large-machinery" segment of the farm implements industry and the "quality-pen" segment of the fountain-pen industry. In this group, such entry barriers apparently range from "prohibitive" at the maximum to high enough to permit established firms to elevate prices quite substantially above minimal costs while forestalling entry at the minimum. Brand allegiances based mainly on prolonged advertising and conspicuous consumption motives offer the predominant explanation of the great barriers in cigarettes, liquor, and "quality" fountain pens, whereas established dealer chains and extended customer-service systems loom as large or larger in automobiles, typewriters, and tractors and large farm machinery. Goods in the latter category are relatively expensive per unit, durable enough to require service while in use, and infrequently purchased, and also are complicated mechanical devices poorly understood by the buyer. This combination of properties appears conducive to great product-differentiation barriers to entry in both producer and consumer good industries.

In between, with moderate entry barriers due to product differentiation, we find 4 industries and segments of 3 others. These are soap (which might be promoted to Class III), petroleum refining, tires, metal containers, the miller's-brand consumer market of the flour industry, some canned goods, and high-priced men's shoes. All are consumer-good industries except metal containers. Buyer allegiances based on product reputations and prolonged advertising seem the important bases of entry barriers in most of these cases, but these forces are apparently not as strong as in the cigarette, liquor, and fountain-pen industries. Established dealer systems and customer service also seem important in the sale of petroleum products, tires, and metal containers.

It must be remembered, of course, that the classifications rest on evaluations of the disadvantages of entrants with roughly the scale of a single optimal plant and are subject to modification in the light of evidence concerning economies or diseconomies of large-scale sales promotion. Temporarily neglecting such modifications, however, it may be useful to speculate as to about how high a barrier to entry is imposed by product differentiation in each of the three classes of industries listed in Table XI — as to how much above minimal costs established firms can, by reason of product differentiation advantages, elevate price while still forestalling entry.

Judgments on this matter are necessarily deduced from the sort of data presented in the table. If an entrant firm would receive a lower profit per unit of sales than established firms for a certain period of years, this disadvantage is presumably convertible into some average net disadvantage per unit of output applicable to all future operations. Established firms should be able to set price above minimal costs by an amount equal to the latter disadvantage and leave the entrant with the anticipated equivalent of a no-profit operation for life. Entry could be forestalled at or just below such a price, and the height of this price above minimal costs would measure the height of the product-differentiation barrier to entry.

Typically the entrant would not expect to sustain his average net disadvantage in each year of his future operations, but would rather anticipate large initial disadvantages which decreased, possibly to a vanishing point, with the passage of a certain number of years. Thence, the maximum entry-excluding price which established firms might set is effectively one which would saddle the entrant with net losses for a break-in period of a certain number of years, and thereafter permit him some supernormal profits. In deciding how large an early loss he is willing to take in order to have a chance at anticipated (but uncertain) future profits, the entrant implicitly decides how much above minimal costs the going industry price would have to be to induce him to enter. The only unique importance of the fact that an entrant would anticipate a declining disadvantage through time after his entry, and thus early losses at prices just above or below the best entry-excluding price, is that the early losses constitute an essential addition to the capital requirements for entry. The entrant must be prepared at the margin to invest a certain amount of money in losses in addition to his initial investment in plant and working capital. In cases of great entry barriers due to product differentiation this investment in losses may be absolutely large and constitute half or more of the total capital requirement. We will return to this matter when we discuss capital requirements in the next chapter.

Because of uncertainty concerning the discount factors likely to be employed in comparing early losses with later gains, only very rough estimates can be made as to the net barrier to entry imposed by product differentiation in the three classes of industries listed in Table XI. The following guesses are the best we can do for the moment.

For industries in Class I (negligible or slight barriers) it would be surprising if in most cases established firms could, by virtue of product-differentiation advantages, elevate long-run price above full minimal cost by more than about 1 per cent without attracting entry. Two per cent is a maximum which might be reached in the case of one or two industries. For industries in class II (moderate barriers), the height of the maximum entry-excluding price above full minimal cost — as far as this is determined by product differentiation — might be expected to run from 2 to 4 per cent. This is a very rough and ready guess in view of ambiguities concerning the length of break-in periods and the size of virtual advantages with which entrants may offset disadvantages. There is evidently an appreciable variation among industries in this category. For industries in Class III, the excess of the best entry-forestalling price over full minimal cost, as far as the excess is determined by product differentiation, might range from close to 5 per cent at a minimum up to maximum two to four times this great. If our estimates are correct, the threat of entry to these industries in general probably does not impose the strategic limitation on the pricing policies of established firms. This is true, at any rate, unless entrants could exploit economies of large-scale sales promotion (or similar economies of very small scale) to reduce the disadvantage here associated with entry at about the scale of a single optimal plant. A distinct and wide variety of entry-barrier situations seems to arise from product differentiation. Let us now consider how our first judgments might be modified by economies and diseconomies of large-scale sales promotion.

The effects of economies and diseconomies of large-scale sales promotion

It is unfortunate from the standpoint of our ambitions in this chapter that we have been unable to learn very much about the incidence of economies or diseconomies of large-scale sales promotion, particularly as these might affect new entrants to industries. This is in part because of a simple lack of data, but also in part, as we have indicated, because we cannot be sure for established firms whether or not the preferred sales-promotional positions of some large firms reflect any systematic association of size to promotional advantage, and because also we have no adequate basis for knowing to what extent such promotional advantages of scale as are realized by established firms are also available to entrants. About all that our findings on this matter will support are some very brief and highly speculative suggestions.

Starting from a basis of estimates of the product-differentiation disadvantages which entrants would incur if entering at the scale of one optimal plant, two questions stand out:

(1) If the firm enters at various *smaller* scales, will its net product differentiation disadvantage become any larger or any smaller than we have previously estimated? If so, how will this affect its scale of entry and its effective net disadvantage?

(2) If the firm enters at various *larger* scales, will its net product differentiation disadvantage become any smaller or any larger than we have previously estimated? If so, how will this affect its scale of entry and its effective net disadvantage?

On the first question, our information is perhaps more deficient than on the second, and particularly so on the matter of possible diseconomies of large-scale sales promotion with the variation of the entrant's scale between zero and that of a single optimal plant. There is always an open possibility that although a firm large enough to operate one optimal-scale plant might suffer a significant product-differentiation disadvantage, it could greatly reduce this disadvantage by operating at a much smaller scale. Opportunities to cater to limited local markets or to narrow markets for differently designed products — for example, to make a whiskey catering to tastes in a single locality or a sports car designed for a few thousand buyers a year — could explain this phenomenon, although these opportunities would not necessarily much modify the condition of entry to the major mass-production markets of the industries in question. The most we can say on the matter is that in industries outside Class I in Table XI the possibility that the product differentiation disadvantage might be significantly less at smaller scales is not adequately tested, but, excepting limited entry to some "specialty" segments of markets, the available indications are either neutral or negative.

What of possible economies of large-scale promotion as the entrant firm increases size toward the single-plant optimum? Such economies would seem to be unimportant in the industries listed in Table XI which have negligible or slight product differentiation — that is, in copper, rayon, cement, steel, gypsum products, and meat packing, and in designated sectors of the flour, farm machinery, canned goods, shoe, and fountain-pen industries. In these cases generally sales promotion is of small enough importance so that variation in its effectiveness as the size of the firm varies from quite small to the scale of one optimal plant is not likely to be significant. Thus, no modifications in the previously discovered production-economy patterns for plants in these industries will be suggested. For the remaining industries, there is at least a good open possibility that significant economies of large-scale promotion would be encountered over the range in question, and questionnaire replies bearing on the matter frequently state or imply that they are. But in most industries we lack any quantitative estimates of how important such economies are, and of the extent to which they may reinforce production economies.

In general, important economies in sales promotion with increases of scale up to that of a single optimal plant seem likely to be present in the automobile, typewriter, tractor, and petroleum refining industries. The reasons that such economies are strongly suspected in these industries are (1) in all of them, either extensive dealer, dealer-service, or field-service organizations are essential to effective sales promotion; (2) optimally extensive organizations of this type cannot be developed by firms greatly below the single-plant scale; but (3) the advantages of these large promotional organizations can be pretty well exploited by the time the firm has grown to the scale of a single optimal plant. Their major incidence occurs during the expansion of the single plant toward its production optimum rather than requiring extensive multiplant development.[6] In these industries it seems a good guess that the importance of plant-scale economies deriving from production considerations is sig-

[6] Of course, the entrant, although exploiting these economies, might (and generally would) be at a net product-differentiation disadvantage to established firms at every common scale.

nificantly reinforced by advantages of large-scale sales promotion. The same is also probably true of the more product-differentiated sector of the fountain-pen industry, although there it is primarily economies of large-scale advertising which are involved.

This is not to say that significant economies of large-scale sales promotion may *not* be encountered over the specified range in the other industries not already mentioned in this connection. The difficulties in deciding whether or not they are found in this range result in part from general uncertainty as to whether they exist for entrants at all, but also either (1) from the facts that such advantages as are involved are primarily those of large-scale advertising, and that it is ordinarily possible or probable that these advantages would be reaped primarily with multi-plant development carrying the firm well beyond the scale of a single optimal plant; or (2) from the fact that such advantages of large dealer or service organizations as there are may be gained primarily by reaching multiplant scale. It is for the first reason that the soap, liquor, and cigarette industries, as well as the more highly product-differentiated sectors of the flour and canned-goods industries, are groups which we hesitate to classify with respect to the incidence of sales-promotional advantages as firm scale expands up to that of one optimal plant. It is for the second reason that we hesitate to classify similarly the rubber tire and metal container industries, as well as the more product-differen-tiated sectors of the shoe and farm machinery industries. For these groups of industries, we enter no judgment as to how much sales-promotional advantage may vary as the firm expands toward an optimal one-plant size.

Let us now turn to possible economies and diseconomies of sales promotion at multiplant scales. So far as available data permit any determination, there are probably no such diseconomies *of significance* in the industries studied. Apparent production economies of the large firm can probably be fully exploited without running into significant diseconomies of promotion. So long as the latter is true, the fact that the entrant might nevertheless encounter promotional diseconomies by growing still larger — e.g. to the size of the leading one or two established firms in many instances — would have no effect on the condition of entry.

Economies of multiplant sales promotion are another matter. In a number of industries, economies either of very large scale advertising or of large dealer or service organizations are possible as the firm expands into the multiplant range. Our findings on this matter are set forth in Table XII. As this table indicates, the possibility is not very strong in 11 of our 20 industries and in sectors of 3 others (Group I), although reasons vary. For industries in Group I-A the reason is the apparent unimportance of product differentiation and sales promotion in general. In Group I-B, on the other hand, product differentiation is generally quite important, and the fact that economies of multiplant sales promotion seem unimportant evidently stems from the consideration that a single optimal plant supplies a large enough fraction of the total market (or submarket) so that the promotional economies in question can be pretty fully exploited by the time the firm expands to that scale. For industries in Group I-C, neither of the previous explanations quite fits. Product differentiation is important, and the scale of an optimal plant is not large. But the significant product differentiation is found largely in actual physical differentiation of design or style of product; design and style are rather dynamic and frequently changing, to the end that the relative importance of the established brand name *per se* is reduced; and introduction of attractive design variations is easy enough or little enough dependent on the facilities of large organizations so that small firms, entrant or established, can fairly well match the corresponding endeavors of large firms.

For industries in Group I of Table XII, therefore, we may take the estimates of product-differentiation disadvantage for a single-plant scale (from Table XI) as minimal and not subject to reduction by enlarging scale further, although a significant incidence of promotional economies as single-plant scale is approached has been tentatively predicted for the automobile, typewriter, tractor, petroleum refining, and fountain-pen industries in this group.

There is an appreciable possibility, however, that significant economies of multiplant promotion may be available to the entrant in the industries included in Group II of Table XII. In the industries in Group II-A this stems from the fact that advertising in national media is the primary pivot for product differentiation, and that these media may be more effectively exploited with very large scales and the correspondingly large advertising budgets these scales permit. The only question concerns the extent to which the entrant could reap advantages comparable to those of the largest established firms, and this is a question which we are simply not in a position to answer. In the industries in Group II-B, the pivot of product differentiation is the effective dealer system, with maximum effectiveness apparently requiring a firm scale well beyond that of a single plant. Metal containers (II-C) fall in the same general category, although here the field service and equipment-rental organization is the crucial factor. In all these cases large established firms seem to enjoy promotional advantages, but again we do not know to what extent entrants might develop comparable advantages by growing similarly large. In consequence, about all we can say is that the product-differentiation disadvantage attributed to the single-plant entrant to these industries in Table XI may very possibly be reduced somewhat by entry at larger scale, although we do not know by how much or at how much larger a scale.

TABLE XII

Classification of Industries According to the Estimated Incidence of Economies of Sales Promotion to the Multiplant Firm

---

Group I: Industries in which economies of large-scale sales promotion are very probably not significant at scales beyond that of a single optimal plant

A. *Industries with relatively unimportant product differentiation*:

Copper	Meat packing
Rayon	Flour (industrial and private label)
Cement	Canned fruits and vegetables (bulk
Steel	of standard items)
Gypsum products	Shoes (low-priced men's)
Fountain pens (low-priced and ball-point)	

B. *Industries with large optimal plant scales*:

Automobiles	Fountain pens ("quality" or high-priced)
Typewriters	
Tractors	Petroleum refining

C. *Other industries*:

Farm machinery (simple implements and local specialties)
Shoes (women's)

Group II: Industries in which significant sales promotional economies of multi-plant firms are possibly available to entrants

A. *Industries in which advantages of very-large-scale advertising are possibly present*:

Soap	Flour (miller's brand, consumer sales)
Liquor	Canned fruits and vegetables (specialties)
Cigarettes	

B. *Industries in which development of effective dealer systems may require large firm scales*:

Tires and tubes	Farm machinery (large and complicated machines)
Shoes (high-priced men's, and specialties)	

C. *Other industries*:

Metal containers

In any event, any reduction of the product-differentiation disadvantage via this route would usually be offset in some degree at least by an increased barrier to entry resting on the enlarged scale of the entrant relative to the market he entered.

Reviewing our general findings on economies and diseconomies of large scale sales promotion, two things stand out. First, there is little or no evidence to support or refute the hypothesis that an entrant (except to "specialty" segments of certain markets) would encounter diseconomies or disadvantages of large-scale sales promotion through increasing its scale from zero toward the production optimum in scale of firm. Second, as to the incidence of economies or advantages of large-scale sales promotion, our industries fall into three general classes:

I. Industries in which economies of large-scale sales promotion are generally not significant:

Copper	Flour (industrial and private-label sales)
Rayon	Farm machinery (simple implements and
Cement	local specialties)
Steel	Canned goods (bulk of standard items)
Gypsum products	Fountain pens (low-price and ballpoint)
Meat packing	Shoes (women's and low-priced men's)

II. Industries in which significant economies of large-scale sales promotion are probably encountered, but mainly in the range of scale between zero and that of a single optimal plant:

Automobiles	Petroleum refining
Typewriters	Fountain pens ("quality" or high-priced)
Tractors	

III. Industries in which significant economies of large-scale promotion, involving increases of scale to the sizes of multiplant firms, are possibly or probably encountered:

Soap	Canned goods (specialties)
Liquor	Shoes (high-priced men's and specialties)
Cigarettes	Farm machinery (large and complicated
Metal containers	machines)
Flour (miller's-brand	Tires and tubes
consumer sales)	

In the light of our findings on the incidence of advantages of large-scale sales promotion, what revisions are required in our previous conclusions concerning the effect of scale economies on the condition of entry and the net effect of the product-differentiation advantages of established firms on the condition of entry? For industries included in the first group above, no modifications are required. In all of these industries the product-differentiation barrier to entry is adjudged unimportant with entry at single-plant scale, and in addition economies of large-scale promotion seem unimportant either short of or beyond the single-plant scale of entry. For industries in the second group above, a closer look is required. In addition to the fact that the product-differentiation barrier is adjudged significant, its height has been assessed with reference to entrants entering at or about the optimum scale for a single plant. This barrier will presumably not become lower if entry is made at still larger scales, but if entry is at smaller scales, it will become higher. In consequence, the entrant finds an added sales-promotional disadvantage in entry at scales below that of a single optimal plant, in addition to the disadvantages of elevated production costs already noted. The plant scale curve effectively becomes steeper, and the entry-deterring effects of economies of large plant are increased above those noted in Chapter 3. This deterrent to entry through promotional scale economies is clearly in addition to the product-differentiation barrier associated with entry at optimal plant scale.

When the increased steepness of the plant scale curve due to economies of large-scale sales promotion is taken into account for the five industries in question, some reclassification of them in terms of the importance of the scale-economies barrier to entry is in order. Since the automobile and typewriter industries were already in the "very important scale economies" category (pp. 90 to 93), discovery of significant promotional economies of large plants reaffirms their membership in this top category, and in addition suggests that the deterrent to entry resting on scale economies may be somewhat larger than previously suggested. The tractor industry, previously classified as having "moderately important" plant scale economies in production, appears a good candidate for promotion, and tentatively joins the automobile and typewriter industries in the "very important scale economy" class. The petroleum refining industry, previously classified as having "relatively unimportant" scale economies but lying toward the upper limit of that class, may be reclassified as having moderately important scale economies. For quality fountain pens, previously unclassified as to the importance of scale economies, no definite reclassification can be proposed, but the existence of at least "moderately important" economies of large-scale sales promotion appears as a distinct possibility.

For industries in the third group above, in which promotional economies to firms of multiplant scale may be present, reclassification seems more hazardous because of the generally less definite and tangible character of the promotional economies available to entrants. If such economies are present, their realization will tend (1) to reduce the product differentiation barrier to entry somewhat below that associated with single-plant entry; and (2) to increase the scale-economy barrier to entry by reinforcing the importance of scale economies which rest on production considerations. If, therefore, we choose as our benchmarks an estimate of scale-economy barriers to entry resting on production-distribution economies alone (pp. 90 to 93), and an estimate of product-differentiation barriers to entry referring to entry at single plant scale, the introduction of promotional economies of the multiplant firm has two opposite and thus (in some degree) self-cancelling effects on the previously estimated aggregate barrier to entry, since it increases the previously estimated scale barrier only by reducing the previously estimated product-differentiation barrier.

Because of this, there is in the present state of information a very good case for not reclassifying the industries in the third category in either respect. That is, we may leave them as previously classified according to the importance of scale economies (in a classification which may understate this importance), and at the same time accept the estimate of the product-differentiation barrier to entry associated with single-plant entry (thus entering a compensating overstatement).

The classification of industries according to the importance of product differentiation barriers to entry is thus left generally as in Table XI, though with the understanding that in the soap, liquor, cigarette, tire and tube, and metal container industries, and in sectors of the flour, canned goods, shoe, and farm machinery industries (all classed as having "moderate" or "great" product-differentiation barriers), there may be an overstatement of the product differentiation compensated in a degree by an understatement of the importance of scale economies.

The corresponding and consistent classification of industries according to the importance of scale economies, revising the findings of pp. 90 to 93 in accordance with the preceding analysis, would show:

(1) *Industries with very important aggregate scale economies:*

Industry	Estimated height of product-differentiation barriers
Automobiles	Great
Typewriters	Great
Tractors	Great

(2) *Industries with moderately important aggregate scale economies:*

Cement	Slight
Rayon	Slight
Steel	Slight
Shoes	Slight to moderate
Farm machinery	Slight to great
Petroleum refinery	Moderate
Soap	Moderate

(3) *Industries with relatively unimportant aggregate scale economies:*

Meat packing	Slight
Flour	Slight to moderate

Canned fruits and vegetables	Slight to moderate
Tires and tubes	Moderate
Liquor	Great
Cigarettes	Great

(4) *Unclassified industries:*

Copper	Slight
Gypsum products	Slight
Metal containers	Moderate
Fountain pens	Slight to great

It is to be understood that this classification is correlative to and to be interpreted in conjunction with the classification according to the height of product-differentiation barriers in Table XI.[7]

The foregoing treatment is primarily a brief summary of findings on

---

[7] Before leaving the matter of economies of large-scale sales promotion, a comment on their probable content may be in order. In a strict and narrow sense they should reflect something equivalent to a reduction in promotional costs per unit of sales (generally an increase in price net of promotional cost) as the sales volume is expanded by virtue of larger aggregate promotional outlays. Most frequently such advantages tend to be and can be realized only by promoting sales on a nationwide basis, through the use of national advertising media and nationwide distributive networks; otherwise at least broad and intensive regional promotion is involved.

What may be overlooked is that the exploitation in this way of such strictly promotional advantages of scale may also be accompanied, in a sense, by a virtual reduction of physical distribution costs per unit as the total sales volume is expanded. In effect, once a nationwide or comparable sales promotion technique is adopted, the firm is committed to distributing through numerous spatially disparate nodes — e.g. wholesaling and retailing centers. At each node, physical distribution costs may decline, down to a point, with increased volume passing through the node, and also outshipment freight costs may be reduced by scattering plants geographically near the major nodes. Then it is true that, *taking nationwide or comparable sales promotion and distribution as given,* physical distribution economies may be realized until the firm is large enough to exploit all nodal economies (as large in capacity as the sum of all relevant nodal optima), and to minimize freight costs through a multiplication of decentralized plants. Thus, assuming nationwide or comparable promotion and distribution, physical distribution costs as well as promotion costs may decline as scale is increased in the pursuit of promotional advantages.

This new sort of quasi-economy of scale is clearly a very close relative of strictly promotional economies, and the two can easily be lumped (purposely or inadvertently) in assessing advantages of large-scale sales promotion. Although physical distribution economies of this general order were recognized in three cases (soap, cigarettes, shoes) in our estimates of scale economies in production and distribution in Chapter 3, the writer has the feeling that they may be present as well in many other industries just classified as probably or possibly having economies of large-scale promotion, and that they may be often a significant part of any overall advantage of large-scale, nationwide promotion and distribution. If so, strictly promotional economies have in some sense been overrated, and production-distribution economies of multi-plant firms correspondingly underrated, though the final evaluation of the total impact of all advantages of scale should not be biased by this.

product-differentiation barriers to entry. In Appendix D, we have given in greater detail the underlying findings about various individual industries.

The relative importance of product differentiation as a barrier to entry: summary

In a broad summary of these findings concerning the absolute and relative importance of product preferences as barriers to entry, three major observations emerge.

First, product differentiation is of at least the same general order of importance as an impediment to entry as are economies of large-scale production and distribution. Conclusions based on the twenty industries of our sample are (a) the product-differentiation barrier to entry differs widely among industries, ranging from "slight," through "moderate," to "great"; (b) there is a significant number of industries in each entry-barrier category so defined; and (c) this is true when the quantitative connotations of the adjectives "slight," "moderate," and "great" are roughly the same as applied to scale-economy and product-differentiation barriers to entry. We must look at least as much to product preferences as to economies of large-scale production if we are interested in the why and wherefore of impediments to entry to manufacturing industries.

Second, great entry barriers are more frequently attributable to product differentiation than to scale economies in production and distribution. Only 2 of our 20 industries qualified as having such barriers on the basis of these scale economies alone — automobiles and typewriters. But these 2 and roughly 4 more qualified as having great product-differentiation barriers. Extreme barriers to entry, ordinarily coupled with very high concentration and perhaps with the less desirable of the possible consequences of oligopoly, seem to be linked to a substantial degree with product differentiation in favor of large established firms. If this observation is correct, it may cast some new light on the true character (if not the dilemma) of the problem of public policy oriented toward an improvement of the effectiveness of competition.

Third, the sources of high barriers to entry attributable to product differentiation are varied and complex, but several things stand out as important. Although the simple force of heavy advertising plays a significant role in most cases, the strategic underlying considerations in strong product differentiation seem frequently to include (1) durability and complexity of the product (and corresponding infrequency of purchase by the individual consumer), generally associated with poor consumer knowledge or ability to appraise products, and thus with dependence on "product reputation," and also with dependence on customer-service organizations; (2) integration of retail dealer-service organizations by manufacturers, either through ownership or exclusive-dealing arrangements (related to the first phenomenon mentioned); (3) importance of "conspicuous consumption" motives on the part of purchasers, attributable mainly to the manner or surroundings in which the goods are used by the buyer. All of these things might seem to suggest the existence of fundamental technical considerations, institutional developments, and more or less fundamental consumer traits which make possible or even very probable the development of strong and stable product-preference patterns. They may also suggest that advertising *per se* is not necessarily the main or most important key to the product-differentiation problem as it affects intra-industry competition and the condition of entry. Although instances are found in which it is, we may need in general to look past advertising to other things to get to the heart of the problem. Conceptions of feasible and effective public policy may need to be adjusted accordingly.

Finally, patent controls do not seem to loom large in our sample of industries as legal protections to product differentiation, at least as of the present date. It is interesting to note, however, that in two industries (gypsum products and metal containers) such controls were evidently significant until about 1950, and were reduced in importance by decrees resulting from antitrust suits.

5

ABSOLUTE COST ADVANTAGES
of Established Firms as Barriers to Entry

A third source of barriers to entry, in addition to scale economies and product differentiation, is found in what we will call here *absolute cost advantages* of established over potential entrant firms. An absolute cost advantage exists if the prospective unit costs of production of potential entrant firms are generally, and more or less at any common scale of operations, higher than those of established firms. In the terminology of price theory, the long-run average cost or scale curve (showing the relation of scale of operations to unit costs for a firm) would then lie at a higher level for the entrant than for the established firm. The entrant firm would have higher unit costs if each were at its own optimal or minimum-cost scale, and also if each were at any other common scale.[1]

By and large an absolute cost advantage to established firms will exist because the entrant either must use inferior production techniques or must pay higher prices for productive factors such as labor, materials, plant, and money capital. The principal potential sources of absolute cost advantages are correspondingly obvious, and thus may be briefly categorized:

(1) Established firms may control superior production techniques and be able either to deny their use to entrants or to levy royalty charges for their use which elevate the entrants' costs. Control of techniques may be exercised through patents, secrecy, or both.

(2) There may be imperfections in the markets for productive factors purchased by all firms which permit established firms to secure such factors at lower prices than potential entrants can.[2]

---

[1] If there are differences in the level of cost among different established firms, the absolute cost barrier to entry must be measured by comparing the entrant to a specific established firm or group thereof. In general, it will be convenient to make the comparison between the entrant and the "most advantaged" established firm or firms — those with the lowest cost levels.

[2] The raising of the general level of factor prices in relevant markets by reason of

(3) Strategic factor supplies — especially perhaps natural-resource raw materials — may be owned or otherwise controlled by established firms, so that entrant firms might be denied access to essential materials entirely, or be forced to use inferior materials involving higher costs or to purchase materials from established firms at premium prices.

(4) The market for investible funds may be such as to impose higher effective interest costs on entrants than on established firms, or alternatively to impose a more severe rationing of funds on potential entrants.

With respect to advantages of established firms in the matter of factor supplies, some care must be used in interpretation. What is referred to is the basic unavoidable disadvantage of the entrant, after he has made the best possible adjustment to the situation in question. Disadvantages which are avoidable through adaptations in other dimensions should not be counted if the aggregate disadvantage can be lessened by such adaptations. A principal type of relevant adaptation is integration by the entrant to escape the disadvantage of a non-integrated status. Frequently, a potential entrant to an industry in which the major established firms are integrated through several productive stages will find that if it enters in non-integrated status for production in some later stage, it will have to purchase materials from established integrated firms and thus perhaps pay premium material prices. This would saddle it with an absolute cost disadvantage. This might be true, for example, of a firm trying to establish a steel rolling mill without providing its own pig-iron supply, or of an independent refiner who depended on the rental of the crude-oil pipeline facilities of established firms for his raw material transportation.

In such cases, the entrant firm can perhaps overcome or eliminate the absolute cost disadvantage associated with non-integrated status by entering as an integrated firm instead, although in so doing it will generally increase its capital requirements and may need also to increase the scale of entry. If now the increased disadvantages (attributable to scale or to capital requirements) consequent upon integration are less than the absolute cost disadvantages which are avoided by integration, the effective or least disadvantaged sort of entry will be that of the integrated firm, and it is to the entry of such a firm that we should refer in appraising the aggregate barrier to entry. In such a case, the absolute cost barriers to entry other than those due to capital requirements might be evaluated at zero, whereas the deterrents to entry attributable to scale economies and capital requirements should be scored as those encountered by the integrated entrant. In general, of course, our estimates in any industry of the effective scale-economy, capital-requirement, and factor-price barriers

---

the added demand of the entrant should also be counted, although this seems unlikely to occur in practice.

to entry should all be consistent with a single supposition concerning the horizontal scale and degree of vertical integration of the entrant.

The preceding is a good rule to follow in appraising available empirical data. Necessarily, however, the data for most industries are sketchy on crucial points, so that a good deal of guesswork is involved in attempting to decide upon the most effective scale and degree of integration of the entrant, and thus on the extent of capital requirements for most effective entry and on the net importance of other absolute cost barriers. About all we can do is to indicate the assumptions we have made along these lines in the various cases, and the general line of reasoning leading to their adoption.

In attempting to arrive at some estimate of the most effective or least disadvantaged scale and degree of integration for the entrant, the datum most difficult to deal with is the absolute capital requirement — the amount of money the entrant needs to invest to create this or that size and shape of firm. What we should like to know but generally do not is (1) the character of the supply schedule for funds to the potential entrant, showing contractual and imputed interest costs for each alternative amount of funds sought over a relevant range; (2) the corresponding amount of the disadvantage (if any) which the potential entrant incurs, as compared to the most favored established firms, in interest cost per unit of funds at various alternative scales of entry; and (3) whether and to what extent this disadvantage increases or decreases with the scale of entry.

What we generally do know is simply (1) that the most-favored established firms generally did have and now have access to internal financing or to the capital markets at relatively favorable terms; (2) that entrants would need to raise various large amounts of money to finance entry; and (3) that as the capital requirement for entry becomes larger, raising money is thought to become "more difficult," presumably in the sense that either the effective interest cost is greater, or "rationing" of funds limits more and more severely the roster of potential entrants, or both. In addition, on the postulate that established firms enjoy a generally preferred position and have not encountered diseconomies of accumulating large amounts of funds, it is frequently thought that entrants are generally at some basic disadvantage in capital costs, and that this disadvantage increases with the increase in the capital requirement. This would imply that, among industries, the barrier to entry imposed by capital requirements is higher as the capital requirement is higher, and also that there is probably some tendency within any industry toward capital-cost diseconomies of increasing scale to the entrant. But we are not actually in a position to make even roughly reliable quantitative estimates of the barrier to entry resulting from an entrant's disadvantage in securing capital, or of the variation of this disadvantage with increases in the amount of capital required.

In consequence, we will make no attempt to adjust our estimates of the most effective scale and degree of integration of entry, or of the effect of scale economies on entry, in the light of absolute capital requirements and their consequences in various industries. Any attempt to do so would rest on purely speculative judgments. What we will do is to proceed as far as possible in assessing entry barriers while provisionally neglecting the effects of capital requirements, and then comment separately on the possible impact of capital requirements on our previous conclusions.

Our primary aim in this chapter is to appraise the height and character of absolute cost barriers to entry to our sample of twenty industries. Consistent with the foregoing analysis of the character of these barriers and of the problems of measuring them, we will deal first with absolute cost barriers other than those involving capital requirements, and second with those arising from capital requirements.

The first section below is thus concerned with the extent to which (a) control of production techniques by established firms, (b) imperfection of factor markets, and (c) control of strategic factor supplies by established firms, appear to impede entry to the manufacturing industries in question. The findings are based largely on replies to questionnaires, but also on various supplementary evidence as available. In the appraisal of the net impact of these considerations on entry, it is necessary to specify assumptions concerning the degree of integration and the scale of the entrant, and to consider the implications of these assumptions for the importance of scale economies and of capital requirements. We will proceed by first summarizing our findings relative to the twenty industries, and then appending explanatory comments on certain individual industries as necessary.

The second section below will deal with the extent of capital requirements for entry to the twenty industries. We will attempt to estimate, largely on the basis of questionnaire replies, (a) the capital requirement for entry with one plant of minimum optimal scale for production, and (b) the capital requirement for entry at the most effective scale for entry in the light of all other considerations. Given these estimates, we can then speculate about the importance of the specified absolute capital requirements as deterrents to entry.

Finally, we will consider the over-all importance of absolute cost barriers to entry for the twenty industries.

Control of techniques and factor supplies, and factor-market imperfections

The absolute cost barriers to entry here considered inhere in factor-market imperfections and in the control of production techniques or of factor supplies by established firms. The importance of the control of factor supplies by established firms may in general depend upon the degree of integration attained by the entrant, and therefore it is necessary to itemize assumptions concerning such integration. In general, the specific sources of absolute cost barriers which have been found to be of perceptible importance in the industries in question may be classified under four headings:

(1) The disadvantage of entrant firms in acquiring expert management personnel.

(2) The disadvantage of entrant firms in acquiring "production know-how" of the unpatented variety, which is nevertheless not freely available because of secrecy or a lack of general dissemination of specialized knowledge.

(3) The control through patents of various production techniques by established firms — a control which permits them to exclude the entrant from access to such techniques or to assess a royalty for use that may be a disadvantage to the entrant.

(4) The control by established firms of essential natural-resource supplies (generally minerals), with the result that entrants either could not secure adequate supplies of this sort or would have to employ inferior or high-cost supplies.

The first two sources of disadvantage — difficulty in acquiring management and difficulty in acquiring know-how — are obviously closely related; similarly, lack of access to know-how and to patented processes are different only on a formal level. Other sorts of factor-market imperfection, such as would enable established firms to purchase on more favorable terms than entrants, are omitted from the preceding list because they have not been found to be important; since the passage of the Robinson-Patman Act (1936), it is generally held that such buying-price advantages to established firms as previously existed have been largely eliminated. (We report this, although conclusive evidence is substantially lacking.) Finally, control of factor supplies by established firms is listed as applying to natural-resource control only. This is because control of other factor supplies, like processed materials made from freely available natural resources, or transport facilities, is generally made ineffective by integration of the entrant, and because such integration generally seems the better alternative for him, all things considered. Wherever such integration is essential to avoid an absolute cost disadvantage, however, this fact will be particularly noted, and alternative possibilities will be considered.

As to the apparent importance of absolute cost barriers to entry in the 20 industries, we may first observe that in practically all the industries studied there would appear to be at least a nominal disadvantage to the entrant in acquiring trained management personnel and similarly in acquiring the requisite production know-how. The presence of such a disadvantage was suggested independently in questionnaire replies in the case of nearly every industry studied. Except in a couple of cases, however, this disadvantage does not appear to be great, and the resultant net barrier to entry, as measured by the cost disadvantage of the entrant, must be rated as negligible or slight. Ordinarily it would be reflected in "shakedown losses" for a very limited time, or in slightly higher over-all costs for a few years. In surveying individual industries, therefore, we will accept this base-level disadvantage as standard, and not comment on the "management and know-how" disadvantage in individual cases unless it is apparently greater than ordinary.

For a substantial list of industries there would appear to be no further absolute cost barrier to entry (capital requirements aside) than this more or less basic initial difficulty of the entrant in acquiring management personnel and know-how. These include (alphabetically):

Automobiles	Liquor
Canned fruits and vegetables	Meat packing
Cigarettes	Soap
Farm machinery	Shoes
Flour	Tractors
Fountain pens	Typewriters

Of these industries in general, questionnaire respondents made the following statements: (a) patent control of processes has in recent times been unimportant (though it may have been in the past in some cases); (b) monopolization of resource supplies by established firms is not present; (c) established firms would not have buying-price advantages in the acquisition of material and supplies; (d) the disadvantage to entrants in acquiring management and know-how is nominal or slight. This is not to say, incidentally, that the last-mentioned disadvantage is at a uniform level among all the industries just listed: it might be at a minimum for shoes and canned goods, and larger than in the other cases for automobiles. The respondents merely indicated that for all 12 industries listed, the disadvantage does not exceed the "slight" level.

The principal restrictive qualifications to the preceding generalizations concern suppositions relative to integration in 4 of the industries listed — liquor, farm machinery and tractors, and automobiles. (Outside these cases, integration choices for entrant do not seem important.) The nature of these qualifications, and their implications for judgments relative to scale economies and to capital requirements, may be summarized briefly:

(1) *Liquor.* Integration of cooperage manufacture by the distiller

may be necessary to avoid some cost disadvantage in acquiring barrels for aging whiskey. It does not appear that such integration would imply modification of our earlier judgments concerning scale economies in this industry, and such integration is evidently taken into account in estimates of capital requirements.

(2) *Farm machinery and tractors.* Some questionnaire replies indicate that it may be necessary to integrate the production of castings, forgings, and engines (instead of purchasing them) in order to avoid some disadvantage in cost. The last comment under (1) above also applies here, at least in the case of tractors, since scale-economy estimates there generally presupposed such integration. For farm machines (excepting tractors), the integration requirement might reinforce the scale economies already described, though to what extent and how much is uncertain. It does not on balance appear probable that the integration requirement and its relative importance would be such as to elevate the farm machinery industry to the status of possessing "very important" scale economies.

(3) *Automobiles.* Several sources of information suggest that a rather extensive integration of parts manufacture, going well beyond the integration of bodies and engines assumed in scale-economy estimates, may be necessary for the entrant to avoid some cost disadvantage in acquiring parts. The situation here is that the largest two firms are heavily integrated and that they, and especially General Motors, supply other firms in the industry with parts of various sorts. On such sales it is generally held that the parts-making subsidiaries or divisions of such integrated firms charge their outside customers the same prices as those at which they "bill" their own assembly divisions. However, these internal-external parts prices apparently are set to include some margin of excess profits to the parts-making branches, and if they do, the less fully integrated purchaser of such parts is at a virtual disadvantage to his more integrated large competitors. This disadvantage, the size of which (as a proportion of total cost) cannot be determined, could be avoided through extensive integration by the entrant.

If such integration were undertaken, the optimal scale for entry and the importance of scale economies would apparently be increased. Then minimum optimal scale would presumably lie at or above the upper limits previously estimated, which are 10 per cent of all auto volume or 20 per cent of the low-priced class. This would tend to push the automobile industry to an even more extreme position with respect to the importance of scale economies. If such integration were not undertaken, and the entrant instead integrated only bodies, engines, and a few other components, he would sustain some absolute cost disadvantage, although encountering a less formidable scale requirement. We have classified the automobile industry here on the supposition of extensive integration by the entrant. As far as we can tell, the gross barrier to entry (scale considerations and absolute cost disadvantages taken into account) would probably not be less if a smaller degree of integration were attempted. In any event, solution of the problem of acquiring parts probably imposes some added disadvantage on the entrant, whether because of increased scale or because of increased parts cost.

Four other industries would also seem to qualify as having slight absolute cost barriers to entry:

Metal containers   Tires and tubes
Cement   Petroleum refining

These are set apart from the previous list because factors in addition to the "management and know-how" difficulty seem to play some appreciable role. The special circumstances in these industries may be summarized briefly:

(1) *Metal containers.* For this industry, there is at least some slight problem with patents. The basic patents expired long ago, but there are numerous improvement and special-process patents which would apparently not be freely available to entrants. Industry sources hold that there are good alternative processes to those patented, and that non-infringing imitations are fairly easy to develop, so that the total barrier imposed by patents is slight. Direct and detailed information on this matter has not been developed. In this industry, incidentally, it is held by industry sources that the buying-price advantage of the Big 2 in acquiring steel — fairly well documented for earlier periods — has vanished since the passage and enforcement of the Robinson-Patman Act.

(2) *Cement.* A possible disadvantage to entrants here stems from the shortage of good limestone deposits for use in raw material. Some industry sources hold that with the best deposits already in use (quality and proximity to markets considered), the entrant would have to use inferior deposits and incur appreciably higher costs. Other industry sources tend to discount the importance of the resulting disadvantage, and we remain in a state of uncertainty about the matter. With lots of limestone in various grades and locations, of course, it might be argued that differential resource rents, not matched by differentials in contractual costs, are all that is involved.

(3) *Tires and tubes.* The larger firms in the industry show lower unit costs for tire fabric than the small firms, and this may be due to integration. If integration of fabric production is necessary for minimal costs, the scale requirements for best efficiency may be increased, but apparently not very much. (We have developed no objective basis for revising our previous scale estimates, though the matter is uncertain.) The state of availability of synthetic rubber to firms not controlling an integrated

supply is not at all clear. In addition, the whole matter is currently in flux. It does not appear that in the past non-integrated producers of tires were at a disadvantage; for the future, we eschew speculation.

Various special product and process patents are in force in the industry, but industry sources hold that they are difficult to enforce or protect, and that what they cover would generally "move with management" as the entrant acquired managers from the ranks of established firms. From the preceding, it is apparent that the tire and tube industry is a rather uncertain entry in the category of slight absolute cost barriers.

(4) *Petroleum refining.* There is uncertainty as to whether integration of crude-oil transport facilities is prerequisite to the avoidance of disadvantage in delivered raw material costs, although we have assumed transport integration in our earlier estimates bearing on economies of scale. There have been allegations aplenty for many years that the independent refiner without his own tankships or pipelines is at a great disadvantage in acquiring transport, unless he finds oil fields and market at the same place (as in Los Angeles).[3] Industry sources from the integrated-firm group generally hold that by using common-carrier pipelines and chartering tankships, the non-integrated refiner could get transport costs as low as the integrated firms which own these facilities. In general, non-integrated refiners do not appear to believe this. On balance, we are inclined to specify transport integration as a requisite for avoidance of a transport-cost disadvantage, and have shaped scale-economy estimates accordingly. This does not generally lead to larger minimum-optimal-scale requirements than non-integrated refining, but it does elevate capital requirements.

A further matter is that of refining patents. The technology of refining is dynamic, and numerous strategic patents are in effect at all times. These are generally held or controlled by the major integrated firms. Industry sources hold that there is free access to patented processes at royalties equal to perhaps .75 per cent of product price on older processes, and 2 to 3 per cent on the latest processes. They also hold that these royalties hardly cover the allocated development costs, so that an entrant would actually be at no net disadvantage. Lacking detailed statistics on either development costs or royalty rates, we report this, and are tentatively guided by it in our classification.

Sixteen of 20 industries have been tentatively classified as having no more than slight absolute cost barriers to entry, subject to various qualifications as stated. In 3 of the remaining 4, the situation appears otherwise. Briefly, the indications in these industries are:

(1) *Gypsum products.* Industry sources indicate that know-how is

[3] See George S. Wolbert, Jr., *American Pipe Lines* (1952), for an analysis of the issues.

extremely important in wallboard production, and that established firms generally have various gadgets and technical improvements protected primarily by secrecy. A new firm might be at an appreciable disadvantage for several years before acquiring or developing sufficient know-how, and in the meantime would have difficulty in establishing and controlling the quality of its wallboard. In addition, any new firm would effectively have to pay U. S. Gypsum the nominal royalty [4] of 1 per cent of sales for use of wallboard patents so long as these patents run. Finally, it is suggested by industry sources that the purchase price or royalty rate which an entrant would have to pay for gypsum rock would be higher than that paid by established firms. The extent to which this may reflect advantage of old purchases or contracts carried into a period of inflation and of rising competitive rents on gypsum deposits is not clear. All things considered, however, it appears that the absolute cost barrier to entry to this industry may exceed the "slight" level and might be rated as moderate. It is further generally indicated that the integrated production of liner paper for wallboard may be necessary for the establishment and maintenance of quality. Such integration would apparently not require the revision of previously estimated scale requirements.

(2) *Steel.* Entry to the steel industry — in the sense of entering integrated mass production of iron, steel, and semi-finished products — would be effectively possible only if the entrant could secure or have assured to him an adequate supply of iron ore. Although specialty steel production is possible with only a supply of scrap or of purchased pig iron or ingot steel, iron ore is indispensable to entering the field of mass-produced, standard steel products.

And iron ore is scarce and closely held.[5] In 1949, about 92 per cent of ore shipments from the Lake Superior region were made by 4 established integrated firms and 4 affiliated or controlled ore companies, and the remaining 8 per cent by 12 more ore firms and 4 more steel companies. The same situation of close control is in general developing in taconites, and in the exploitation of Canadian and other foreign ores. Industry testimony in general is that, in times of active demand for steel, there is little or no "open" or spot market in ore, nearly the whole supply being committed on long-term contracts to or owned outright by established steel firms. In consequence, an entrant in order to assure himself of an adequate ore supply would in general have either to "buy into" some going ore arrangement, or to invest in the development of new sources of ore.

The extent of the entrant's disadvantage in "buying in," if indeed he

---

[4] See Appendix D below.
[5] See *Hearings*, Subcommittee on Study of Monopoly Power, Committee on Judiciary, House of Representatives, 81st Cong., 2nd Sess., Serial No. 14, Parts 4–A and 4–B.

could do so, is not estimated; the prospect of developing new sources is highly uncertain, and the cost certainly high. In the circumstance in which high grade iron ore is in strictly limited and dwindling supply, it appears that the entrant would probably either have to pay in excess of the competitive rents on ore in order to "buy in," operate with inferior ore at a substantial cost disadvantage, or be very lucky in finding and developing a new source. In sum, it appears that there is a substantial absolute cost barrier to entry to the steel industry, resulting from the scarcity of iron ore and the close holding of known commercial deposits of ore. The capital requirements for securing an ore supply for a one to five million ton operation in steel are hard to estimate.

(3) *Copper.* The situation in copper is similar but probably more severe. Entry to the smelting and refining of copper, for the production of primary copper, would have as a prerequisite the securing of an adequate ore supply. Copper ore reserves are scarce, dwindling, and tightly held, with three or four firms controlling nearly all of available commercial copper reserves both within the United States and in accessible foreign areas such as South America.[6] There is substantially no open or spot market in ore, or in foreign blister copper, such as would permit an entrant to purchase his required raw materials.

Industry opinion is quite explicit on this point, as indicated by the remarks that entry would have to "start with the discovery of ore," and that "it would be folly to enter the smelting or refining business without a source of material to be treated; from a practical standpoint, there is not much possibility of this." Further, "easy surface prospecting is a thing of the past, and new discoveries would involve larger capital for drilling and underground work." Although quantitative estimates of an entrant's disadvantage are not avaliable, it would appear that the absolute cost barrier to entry resulting from the scarcity of resources is at least formidable and perhaps insurmountable. Such a judgment is of course subject to the ultimate uncertainty concerning the possible nature, location, and quality of as yet undiscovered mineral resources.

We should point out the exception that the smelting, refining, or melting of scrap is feasible for entrants intending to supply various copper products, especially brass and bronze. About 25 per cent of the total annual copper supply is currently from scrap. Aside from the fact that the yield easily producible from such scrap is not readily substitutable for primary copper, however, is the fact that the scrap melters or processors would not in general tend to expand the supply of copper appreciably, but merely to redistribute a fixed volume of business among more firms. Such entry would tend to have little effect on the volume, prices, or profits of primary copper producers. The basic scarcity and close

[6] Federal Trade Commission, *The Copper Industry* (1947), pp. 32–47.

control of copper ore reserves thus still imposes a formidable barrier to entry which would affect the major integrated producers.

The only industry so far unclassified is that producing rayon. Hesitancy in classifying this industry results from the conflicting and uncertain indications concerning absolute cost barriers to entry, especially with respect to production know-how. Although patents were once important in this industry, the basic patents expired about 1930,[7] and it is reported that various improvement patents are more or less freely licensed. The crucial factor in more recent years seems to have been know-how, based on technical experience and protected fundamentally by secrecy. Acquisition of this know-how seems to have been more difficult than in most other industries, as reflected in the fact that entrants have had to call on European talent in assembling their management and engineering staffs. Conduct and control of chemical and subsequent processes seem especially complicated, and the entrant may be subject to fatal disadvantages if he cannot acquire the apparently scarce expertise in his management and engineering staff. We hesitate to estimate the resultant barrier to entry, however, because from no source has it been possible to obtain even a rough qualitative judgment concerning the magnitude of the resultant disadvantage, or of the way in which it may have been declining over time. The rayon industry thus remains unclassified with respect to the matter of absolute cost disadvantages of entrant firms.

Given these specific conclusions, we may now summarize about the importance of the principal absolute cost barriers to entry: patents, resource control, and monopoly of expert management and know-how.

In general, such barriers would appear distinctly less important than those resulting from product differentiation or from economies of scale. In 16 of our 20 industries, no more than a slight barrier to entry appeared to result from the absolute cost considerations enumerated. In a few of these, however, some integration by the entrant was required to avoid a substantial barrier to entry, with a consequent increase in scale requirements in one or two cases.

In 3 industries and possibly 4, moderate or high barriers to entry appeared to result from absolute cost considerations. In 2 of these — copper and steel — the barrier resulted from natural-resource scarcity and the close control of known resources by established firms. In the other 1 or 2, it hinged mainly on patents or on know-how protected by secrecy. In general, if this sample is representative, it would appear that resource control is infrequently a source of an important barrier to entry. On the other hand, slight barriers to entry commonly result from the difficulty of entrants in acquiring management and know-how, and less frequently

[7] See Markham, *Competition in the Rayon Industry*.

from patents. The preceding judgments are drawn largely from industry opinion, but supplementary evidence tends to corroborate them.

The necessity for backward integration by the entrant to avoid a serious absolute cost disadvantage would appear to be confined to from 4 to 6 industries at the most — steel, copper, autos, petroleum refining, and possibly farm machinery and tractors. In the first 2 cases, integration back through the mineral ore is accepted as a fact of life, and the necessity for integrating in this way raises an important absolute cost barrier, though it does not necessarily alter scale requirements based on processing technology. In petroleum refining, integration of crude-oil transport facilities may be necessary to avoid disadvantage. This would not generally increase scale requirements based on processing technology, but would definitely increase capital requirements. If capital shortage is not severe, integrated entry seems superior to non-integrated entry. In the automobile industry, backward integration into fairly comprehensive parts production may be necessary to avoid appreciable absolute cost disadvantage, and this will increase scale requirements or reinforce the importance of economies of scale, as well as raising capital requirements. But such integration seems likely, on balance, to offer as favorable a course to the entrant as any other. In farm machinery and tractors, integration of components production may again be necessary to avoid disadvantage; the effect of such integration on scale requirements is negligible for tractors, and uncertain for other farm machines.

Absolute capital requirements and their possible effect on entry

As we have indicated, there does not seem to be very much we can do to determine the extent of an entrant's disadvantage in acquiring funds for investment, other than to estimate the absolute capital requirements for efficient or effective entry and then speculate about the consequences of the absolute amounts involved.

A first approximation to capital requirements may be made by estimating the probable investment necessary to establish one plant of minimum optimal scale in each of the twenty industries in question. Such estimates, as based on questionnaire replies, are set forth in column 2 of Table XIII. In general, these capital-requirement estimates include inventories and working capital unless otherwise specified, presuppose the degree of integration by the entrant which has previously been designated as most effective, and refer to about 1951. But in general also, they exclude the anticipated "shakedown losses" of entrants, which in some cases may be large and prolonged.

In 5 industries, more than 100 million dollars per plant would be required, and in 3 of these, the requirement is generally 250 million dollars per plant and up. Important "shakedown" losses (as noted in the preceding chapter) would also be encountered in 2 of these industries — automobiles and cigarettes. In 6 industries (provided meat-packing entry is to be of the "diversified" type) the capital requirement per plant will run generally from 10 to 50 million dollars. Only in the case of rayon (especially viscose rayon) among these industries is the 50-million-dollar line likely to be exceeded. In 4 industries, capital requirements per plant reach moderate levels — generally from 2 to 6 million dollars per plant; and in 2 industries (plus fresh meat packing) the requirement is generally small, and possibly below a million dollars per plant. Capital-requirement estimates are unavailable for 3 industries.

From these estimates it would appear that in at least 11 of 17 industries, access to organized capital markets would ordinarily be required to finance a minimum optimal plant, and that in 5 or 6 of these, extremely large issues would be involved. In the remaining industries — and especially in flour milling, shoe manufacturing, and fresh meat packing — capital requirements are for a single efficient plant small enough so that small local capital supplied by proprietorships, small partnerships, or closely held corporations might easily suffice. As to how much more difficult it is to raise 100 million dollars than 1 million, or how much differential disadvantage is thereby imposed on the entrant as compared to established firms, we may speculate, but we do not have much reliable information on the point.

Before pursuing this subject further, however, two related matters should be considered. The first is the relation of the absolute capital requirement associated with efficient plant scale to the corresponding requirement relative to the share of the market an entrant would have to supply. As we have emphasized earlier, economies of scale may have two distinct possible impacts on the condition of entry: one the "percentage effect," exercised via the proportion of the market an entrant must supply to be efficient, and the other the "absolute-capital-requirement effect," exercised via the amount of money he must raise to accomplish the same end. Although knowledge of the shape as well as the position of the scale curves relating efficiency to size is requisite to an adequate appraisal of either effect, a first index to the magnitudes of these effects is supplied by measures of (a) the proportion of the market supplied by a plant of minimum optimal scale, and (b) the absolute capital requirement for such a plant.

As we have seen, the latter information is set forth in column 2 of Table XIII. In column 3 of the same table, we reproduce (from Tables III and V) estimates of the proportion of either the unsegmented national market or the largest recognized submarket which a plant of minimum optimal size would supply in each of the 20 industries. Two conclusions obviously emerge from the comparison of columns 2 and 3. First, there is

TABLE XIII

Classification of Industries According to Capital Requirements for a Single Optimal Plant, and Related Information

(1) Industry	(2) Capital requirement for one plant of minimum optimal scale (millions of dollars)	(3) Percentage of largest submarket supplied by one optimal plant (Tables III, V)	(4) Estimated shape of plant scale curve at suboptimal scales	(5) Existence of production economies of multiplant firms (from Table IX)	(6) Incidence of economies of large-scale sales promotion
I. Industries with very large capital requirements per plant (generally above $100 million):					
Steel	265 to 665	2½ to 6¼	Moderately sloped	Yes	Negligible
Automobiles	250 to 500 ᵃ	10 to 20	Moderately sloped	No estimate	Promotional economies up to size of optimal plant
Petroleum refining	225 to 250 ᵇ	4⅓	Relatively flat	No	Promotional economies up to size of optimal plant
Tractors	125	10 to 15	Relatively flat	No estimate	Promotional economies up to size of optimal plant
Cigarettes	125 to 150	5 to 6	Relatively flat	Yes	Promotional economies of multiplant firms possible
II. Industries with large capital requirements per plant (generally $10 to $50 million):					
Rayon	50 to 75 ᶜ / 90 to 135 ᵈ	4 to 6	Relatively steep	No estimate	Negligible
Liquor	30 to 42	1¼ to 1¾	Relatively flat	No estimate	Promotional economies of multiplant firms possible
Cement	20 to 25	4 to 5	Relatively steep	Yes	Negligible
Tires and tubes	15 to 30	1⅜ to 2¾	Moderately sloped	No estimate	Promotional economies of multiplant firms possible
Soap	13 to 20 ᵉ	4 to 6	Moderately sloped		Promotional economies of multiplant firms possible
Meat packing (diversified)	10 to 20	8 to 10	Relatively flat	No	Negligible

III. Industries with moderate capital requirements per plant (generally $2.5 to $10 million):

Fountain pens	6	10 to 15	No estimate	No	Promotional economies up to size of optimal plant, for "quality" pens
Metal containers	5 to 20	2 to 12	No estimate	No estimate	Promotional economies of multiplant firms possible
Gypsum products	4 to 6	8 to 12	No estimate	Yes	Negligible
Canned fruits and vegetables	2½ to 3	2½ to 5	Moderately sloped	No	Negligible for standard items; multiplant economies for specialties

IV. Industries with small capital requirements per plant (generally under $2 million):

Flour	7/10 to 3½	⅓ to 1½	No estimate	No estimate	Negligible for promotional economies for commercial and private-label sales; multiplant economies for miller's brand sales
Shoes	½ to 2	⅗ to 1⅕	Moderately sloped	Yes	Negligible for most lines; multiplant economies for high-priced men's or specialties
Meat packing (fresh)	under 1	1/10 to 1	Relatively flat	No	Negligible

V. Nonclassified industries (capital requirements not estimated):

Typewriters	No estimate	10 to 30	Relatively steep	No	Promotional economies up to size of optimal plant
Farm machinery	No estimate	4 to 6	Moderately sloped	No estimate	Promotional economies of multiplant firms probable
Copper	No estimate	10	No estimate	No	Negligible

a Supposes integration of bodies and engines, but not of maximum range of components.
b Includes crude-oil transport facilities (average requirement).
c Acetate rayon.
d Viscose rayon.
e Excludes working capital.

no evident simple correlation between the size of absolute capital requirements for an efficient plant and the percentage of market output
supplied by it. The size of the market is evidently an erratic variable
among industries that forestalls any close correlation. Second, the absolute
capital requirement in some cases thus reinforces but in other cases
weakens the "percentage effect" on entry of economies of scale of plant.
For example, in 4 industries where this percentage effect is evidently
negligible — flour milling, shoes, canned goods, and fresh meat packing
— the absolute capital requirements for entry appear so small as to provide little added restraint on entry. But in 2 others — liquor and tires and
tubes, in which the "percentage effect" is also small — capital requirements of from 15 to 40 million dollars per plant may be sufficient to
impede entry perceptibly. Similarly, we find a large apparent "percentage
effect" of scale on entry in the automobile and tractor industries to be
reinforced by absolute capital requirements in excess of 100 million dollars
per plant, whereas with similar "percentage effects" of scale in fountain
pens and gypsum products, absolute capital requirements per plant run
around only 4 to 6 million dollars. In many of the cases, of course, the
two effects are more or less parallel, but there is no simple close association.

The second matter to be considered concerns the modification of the
capital-requirement estimates in column 2 to arrive at some notion of the
net capital requirement for an entrant making entry with the most
effective, or least-disadvantaged, scale and organization. All that column
2 contains is a series of estimates of what investment the entrant would
require to enter with a single plant of minimum efficient scale from the
standpoint of production and distribution. As we have seen in preceding
chapters, there are several reasons why the most effective scale of entry
may be other than the minimum optimal scale for one plant. (1) The
shape of the plant scale curve at suboptimal scales (reflecting the extent
of increase in unit costs at such smaller scales) may be such — in relation
to the percentage of the market supplied by a single optimal plant — that
the entrant will find a smaller disadvantage through entry at a smaller
than minimum optimal scale. (In general, flat scale curves with large
minimum optimal scales may make this true.) (2) Production and distribution economies of multiplant firms may be sufficient to make the most
effective scale of entry larger than that required for a single plant. (3)
Advantages of large-scale sales promotion may be such as to induce the
entrant to enter at a larger scale (single-plant or multiplant) than he
otherwise would. In addition, of course, the size of the capital requirement
itself — if reflected in diseconomies from acquiring larger amounts of
money — may influence the effective scale of entry and the corresponding
capital requirement.

It would be desirable, therefore, to adjust our first estimate of the capital requirement for entry to each industry (referring to one plant of minimum optimal scale) in the light of each of the three sorts of influence just enumerated. Unfortunately, the information generally available does not permit any precise adjustment. Findings relevant to such an adjustment, however, are summarized in columns 3 to 6 of Table XIII. As we have seen, column 3 of that table shows the percentage of the unsegmented national market or largest submarket supplied by a single plant of minimum optimal scale. As this percentage becomes larger, there is an increasing virtual disposition of the entrant to come in at suboptimal scales. In column 4, we characterize (from pp. 78 to 81 above) the shapes of the plant scale curve at less than optimal scales in the various industries — i.e., the extent to which unit costs are higher at smaller plant scales. These shapes are classified as either "relatively flat," "moderately sloped," or "relatively steep." [8] As we have seen, flatness of the scale curve predisposes toward, and steepness predisposes against, entry at suboptimal plant scales. The shape of the scale curve should operate together with the size of optimal scale in determining the outcome.

In column 5, we classify industries according to the estimated incidence of production and distribution economies of multiplant firms (from Table IX). Since the information on this matter is incomplete, we attempt in this resummary only to indicate whether the existence of such multiplant economies is affirmed ("yes"), denied ("no"), or not estimated. In general, of course, the existence of such economies may predispose toward larger effective scales for the entrant firm; however, the extent of such economies ordinarily seems slight enough to make us doubt that they are a major influence on the scale of entry. In column 6, we summarize findings (from pp. 134 to 138 above) on the possible or probable extent of advantages of large-scale sales promotion. Following our earlier classification, we generally categorize industries as having either (a) "negligible" promotional economies of large scale; (b) probable promotional economies of scale up to the size of a single optimal plant, but not necessarily further; or (c) possible promotional economies of multiplant scale and organization. It is clear that the existence of promotional economies of large scale may predispose toward larger effective scales of entry than might otherwise be chosen.

If the reader will consider in Table XIII the readings for each industry in the successive columns, he will get some impression of the variety

---

[8] In general, a "relatively flat" curve will find unit costs only 1 or 2 per cent higher than optimal at half-optimal scales; a "moderately sloped" curve will find them 4 or 5 per cent higher at half-optimal scales; a "relatively steep" curve will find them 8 or 10 per cent higher.

of forces bearing on the determination of the most effective scale of entry and of the corresponding capital requirement. Obviously, the information is frequently deficient, and it is also frequently very qualitative in character, especially in regard to multiplant economies and sales-promotion advantages. What can be made of this maze of data, if our aim is to arrive at estimates of net capital requirements for the most effective entry?

Reproduction in detail of our speculations concerning individual industries does not seem in order in view of the character of the data. The following general conclusions based on such speculations, however, may be reported:

(1) In 3 of the industries — typewriters, farm machinery, copper — basic estimates of capital requirements are unavailable, and no further speculations are in order.

(2) In 7 of the industries, the net capital requirement for most effective entry is, so far as we can tell from available information, probably not much different than that for a single plant of minimum optimal scale, as estimated in Table XIII. These industries are:

(a) *Automobiles* (250 to 500 million dollars). The large percentage of the market supplied by a single integrated plant of optimal scale might dispose the entrant toward entry at a suboptimal scale. But the advantages of large-scale sales promotion up at least to the size of an optimal plant probably offset this tendency, so that the estimate of the effective capital requirement is not reduced. In addition to this capital requirement, large "shakedown" losses must be considered.

(b) *Petroleum refining* (225 to 250 million dollars). The situation is roughly the same as with automobiles. A rather flat plant scale curve coupled with a moderately large percentage of the market supplied by a single plant might predispose toward entry at suboptimal scale. But advantages of large-scale sales promotion up to the size of an optimal plant probably offset this tendency.

(c) *Tractors* (125 million dollars). The situation is much the same as with petroleum refining.

(d) *Rayon* (50 to 135 million dollars). A relatively steep plant scale curve seems to discourage entry at suboptimal scales. Information on possible multiplant economies is not available.

(e) *Fountain pens* (6 million dollars). Although the shape of the plant scale curve in production is not estimated, incidence of important promotional economies up to the size of minimum optimal plant would seem to discourage entry at smaller scales — at any rate to the "quality" pen field.

(f) *Metal containers* (5 to 20 million dollars). The capital requirement for this industry is left unrevised (at that for one optimal plant) largely because we have not learned enough to justify any revision. Multiplant promotional economies are a possibility, but their extent, if any, is not known.

(g) *Gypsum products* (4 to 6 million dollars). The only definite information which would suggest a modification of previous estimates is an indication of "small" production economies of multiplant organization. Since we lack further data, no reclassification is suggested here, although an upward revision might be in order.

(3) In 2 more industries — flour and canned goods — available information does not suggest an appreciable revision of the capital requirement for a single optimal plant in order to arrive at the effective capital requirement, except for limited product lines within these industries. For these lines (principally specialties in canned goods and miller's brand consumer flour) advantages of large-scale sales promotion may be sufficient to elevate the effective capital requirement to that of a somewhat larger, multiplant firm.

(4) In 7 industries, the probable or possible existence of production economies of multiplant firms, or of sales promotion advantages of such firms, or both, *may* increase the effective capital requirement, although this is by no means certain. These industries are:

(a) *Steel* (265 to 665 million dollars). The slope of the plant scale curve in the steel industry appears sufficient to discourage entry below the lower limit of this estimate ($265 millions for a one million ingot ton plant), and it is possible that the most effective plant scale would be larger. If alleged multiplant economies in production are indeed available, they could be pretty well exploited without giving the firm more than one efficient plant in any major producing region, so that the "percentage effect" of entry at multiplant scale is not necessarily greater than that at single plant scale. It is thus conceivable that (plain shortage of capital aside) the most effective scale of entry might involve several plants to the firm and a capital requirement between 2 and 5 billion dollars. (Some industry sources, however, hold that one good plant is enough.)

(b) *Cigarettes* (125 to 150 million dollars). Indications in this industry are conflicting. The plant scale curve is apparently flat enough so that, on the basis of plant production economies alone, the effective scale for entry might be only half the minimum optimal, requiring only 60 to 65 million dollars. On the other hand, slight added production economies for a three-to-four-plant firm are predicted, and in addition there is a fair possibility of systematic promotional advantages to firms of multiplant scale. Thus the range of possible effective capital requirements might run all the way from 60 million dollars up to 200 or 300 million.

(c) *Liquor* (30 to 42 million dollars). The only thing here to suggest a revision in arriving at effective capital requirement is the possible or probable incidence of advantages of sales promotion at multiplant scale. If these are significant, effective capital requirements might range from 100 million dollars up.

(d) *Cement* (20 to 25 million dollars). The steepness of the plant scale curve seems to discourage entry with plants of less than optimal scale. Estimated production economies of multiplant operation — which could be realized without increasing the firm's percentage of the market in any single region — might lead to an effective capital requirement between 60 and 250 million dollars.

(e) *Tires and tubes* (15 to 30 million dollars). The shape of the plant scale curve probably discourages entry at less than the scale of an optimal plant. Possible promotional advantages of multiplant scale might tend to increase the effective capital requirements by some moderate multiple.

(f) *Soap* (13 to 20 million dollars). The slope of the plant scale curve would probably discourage entry at less than the scale of an optimal plant. The combination of alleged production economies of a multiplant firm (of two or three plants) and of possible advantages of sales promotion at muliplant scale might elevate the effective capital requirement to the range between 40 and 60 million dollars.

(g) *Shoes* (½ to 2 million dollars). The slope of the plant scale curve probably discourages entry at less than the scale of a single optimal plant. Small production economies to multiplant firms up to two- to four-plant size, plus sales-promotional advantages in some lines, may elevate effective capital requirements up to 2½ to 10 million dollars.

(5) In meat packing — both diversified and fresh — the relatively flat scale curves, coupled with the relative unimportance of advantages of multiplant firms in either production or sales promotion, may well mean that the effective capital requirement for entry can be smaller than that estimated for minimum optimal plants. The requirement might be 5 million dollars or less in diversified packing, and very well under 1 million for fresh packing.

The preceding comments suggest possible alterations in the earlier estimates of single-plant capital requirements which might be made in order to arrive at estimates of effective capital requirements for entry.

The sketchiness of available information bearing on the point, however, and the lack of essential quantification in various parts of this information, are such that no formal revision of capital-requirement estimates seems supportable. We will thus adhere to our single-plant estimates of column 2 in Table XIII as first approximations, subject to the following general comments:

(a) That in general (meat packing excepted) the effective capital requirements are not likely to be much smaller than those estimated for single plants.

(b) That for the 7 industries listed under (2) above — autos, petroleum refining, tractors, rayon, fountain pens, metal containers, and gypsum products — the effective requirements are also not likely to be much larger than the maximum estimates for single plants.

(c) That for the 9 industries listed under (3) and (4) above — flour, canned goods, steel, cigarettes, liquor, cement, tires and tubes, soap, shoes — the effective capital requirements may be larger than for single plants, but that this is generally fairly uncertain.

Having done our best to arrive at such estimates, what do they mean? Do very large capital requirements put the entrant at an added disadvantage, such as might be translatable into an absolute cost disadvantage in interest on funds or might force the entrant to assume a smaller scale with a corresponding disadvantage in lieu of the interest cost disadvantage? And if this is so, to what extent; and what is the quantitative progression of the disadvantage with the increase of the capital requirement? These things we simply do not know. In consequence, about all we can do, in quite a speculative way, is to honor casual empiricism and economic folklore by suggesting that there is probably *some* progression of the entrant's disadvantage and the height of the resultant barrier to entry with the increase in capital requirements. Accordingly, we may employ the ordinal ranking of industries in Table XIII — distinguishing industries with "very large," "large," "moderate," and "small" capital requirements — as a basis for comparing industries with respect to the probable relative magnitudes of entry barriers resulting from capital requirements, even though no quantitative estimate of the extent of these barriers is attempted.

Summary

In the earlier part of the chapter, we saw that absolute cost barriers to entry resulting from patents, resource control, lack of access to know-how and management, and so on, were apparently slight or small in nearly all of our sample of 20 manufacturing industries: small both absolutely and as compared on the average to barriers resulting from scale economies and product differentiation. In only 3 industries — steel, copper, and gypsum products — were there definitely apparent important absolute cost barriers to entry, and in the first two of these the barriers were due primarily to close control of scarce natural resources. It was noted also that in several other industries a substantial degree of vertical integration by the entrant was necessary to avoid absolute cost disadvantages, and that such integration frequently increased the scale requirements for efficiency. In such cases, enforced disintegration of established firms, whenever consistent with their efficiency, might ease entry by lowering the scale-economy barriers thereto and by reducing effective absolute capital requirements for entry.

To these earlier judgments, we may add the following respecting absolute capital requirements. It would appear that in at least 5 industries such requirements may be large enough to impose appreciable added barriers to entry, of the order which would permit large established firms to forestall entry while elevating price above minimal cost. These are the steel, auto, petroleum refining, tractors, and cigarettes. And in 5 more industries — rayon, liquor, cement, tires and tubes, and soap — some lesser impediment of this order may be encountered. In 7 more industries, however — meat packing, fountain pens, metal containers, gypsum products, canned goods, flour, and shoes — it seems quite doubtful that any significant barrier to entry is raised by absolute capital requirements. These highly qualitative judgments may be kept in mind as we turn to the appraisal of combined barriers to entry in each of the 20 industries.

6

THE OVER-ALL BARRIERS
TO ENTRY
and Theory as to Their Consequences

In the last three chapters, we have made three parallel analyses "in cross-section" of 20 manufacturing industries, dealing successively with the three principal sources of impediment to entry. For each source we have considered the height of the resultant barriers to entry, the ways in which they are manifested, and the extent to which they differ among the industries of our sample. By following this procedure, however, we have so far eschewed the task of summarizing for each individual industry the combined effects of the three different sorts of barrier to entry, to arrive at some estimate of the aggregate barrier to entry for each industry. We thus turn now to a rapid summarization of previous findings on individual industries in order to develop this estimate. This procedure leads to the development of a final summary cross-section, classifying the sample according to the relative and absolute heights of the aggregate barriers to entry.

Such a summary classification provides a basis for undertaking a further task. In Chapter 1, we surveyed the content of theoretical predictions of the consequences of different sorts of barriers to entry. As soon as we have catalogued our industries according to the height and type of the aggregate barrier to entry, we will "apply" the theory of Chapter 1 by determining what sorts of market performance may be theoretically expected from each of our 20 industries (or from groups thereof) in the light of entry conditions to them.

The aggregate barrier to entry in 20 industries

In the preceding chapters, discussion of a particular type of barrier to entry has culminated in a classification of our 20 industries according to the height of the entry barrier in question. Thus in Chapter 3 industries were generally classified into three groups, as having either "very important," "moderately important," or "relatively unimportant" barriers to entry resulting from scale economies, and this classification was revised in Chapter 4 (pp. 139 to 141) in the light of findings on advantages of large-scale sales promotion. In Chapter 4 also industries were again categorized as having either "great," "moderate," or "slight" barriers to entry resulting from product differentiation. In Chapter 5, they were classified as having either "slight" or "important" absolute cost barriers to entry (pp. 148 to 156) and were again classified according to whether the capital requirements for entry were "very large," "large," "moderate," or "small."

We are on the safest attainable ground when we view each of these classifications as having primarily an ordinal significance — as simply ranking industries according to the relative importance of a particular barrier to entry, without implying anything definite about the absolute height of the barrier in any rank. We have attempted, however, in the case of scale-economy and product-differentiation barriers to estimate at least roughly the absolute quantitative barrier to entry approximated in given classes of industries. Information respecting the size of absolute cost barriers and the significance of capital requirements has not been sufficient to support similar estimates, other than the observation that the "slight" absolute cost barriers are probably no higher absolutely than other sorts of barriers characterized as slight or relatively unimportant.

Using these specific classifications and the underlying data, we may now make some appraisal of the aggregate barrier to entry in each of our 20 industries, and some ranking of them in terms of the height of this barrier. A first step is to summarize in a single table the previous rankings of the various industries with respect to the importance of different sorts of entry barriers. In doing this, we will adopt a uniform notation, designating a particular entry barrier as either "I," "II," or "III." The designation "III" will connote either "very important" for scale economies, "great" for product differentiation barriers, "important" for absolute cost advantages, or "very large" for capital requirements — the highest ranking in each case. The designation II and I will refer to the medium and low rankings in each instance; in the case of absolute cost advantages, where there is no "medium" rank, "slight" barriers will be designated by "I." In the case of absolute capital requirements, where there are four ranks, the smallest will be designated by ϕ. This summary of rankings, alphabetically by industries, is presented in Table XIV.

A rough general impression of the relative heights of the aggregate barriers to entry to the various industries may be gained from a careful perusal of this table, particularly for the extreme cases. If an industry draws a III (high barrier) rating under three of four possible headings —

as in the cases of autos and tractors — we may be pretty certain that it will have one of the highest aggregate barriers to entry. Similarly, a low or I rating in every category — as for meat packing or flour — places an industry rather unmistakably at the other extreme. But there are numerous in-between cases, and here casual observation plus casual mental calculations will leave one in some doubt about relative rankings.

TABLE XIV

Summary of Relative Heights of Specific Entry Barriers in 20 Industries
(Higher Numbers Denote Higher Entry Barriers)

Industry	Scale-Economy Barrier	Product-Differentiation Barrier [a]	Absolute-Cost Barrier	Capital-Requirement Barrier
Automobiles	III	III	I	III
Canned goods	I	I to II	I	I
Cement	II	I	I	II
Cigarettes	I	III	I	III
Copper	n.a.	I	III	n.a.
Farm machinery	II	I to III	I	n.a.
Flour	I	I to II	I	ϕ
Fountain pens	n.a.	I to III	I	I
Gypsum products [b]	n.a.	I	III	I
Liquor	I	III	I	II
Meat packing	I	I	I	ϕ or I
Metal containers [b]	n.a.	II	I	I
Petroleum refining	II	II	I	III
Rayon	II	I	I	II
Shoes	II	I to II	I	ϕ
Soap	II	II	I	II
Steel	II	I	III	III
Tires and tubes	I	II	I	II
Tractors	III	III	I	III
Typewriters	III	III	I	n.a.

[a] Alternative ratings refer generally to different product lines within an industry.
[b] Product-differentiation rating refers to the period subsequent to 1950. A rating of III is probably indicated for earlier periods. (See Table XI above.)

One way of developing systematic observations would be to calculate "average" or "aggregate" ranks, by averaging or summarizing the four individual ranks for each industry. We have not done this because the procedure is unsatisfactory. The absolute height of the barrier to entry for individual industries within a given rank is not always roughly the same. In the top or III ranks in particular, we have open-end categories in which the only condition for inclusion is that the barrier exceed some level; among industries included, the excess sometimes differs significantly. Also, a legitimate aggregation or averaging would have to presuppose that similar rank numbers in different columns denoted similar absolute heights of the barrier to entry. Although this is roughly true where absolute magnitudes have been estimated, we lack meaningful estimates of the absolute height of the barrier to entry resulting from absolute cost considerations (where these are important) and from the size of capital requirements.

In order to develop a ranking in terms of aggregate barriers to entry, it has been necessary to go back to the specific estimates on individual industries, as they are set forth in the three preceding chapters and in the appendices, and to consider these in combination for determining the probable rank of each individual industry according to the absolute height of the aggregate barrier to entry. (In this procedure, no specific value has been assigned to entry barriers resulting from capital requirements.) The results of these determinations are set forth briefly in Table XV, in which industries are ranked as having aggregate entry barriers either "very high," "substantial," or "moderate or low." It is hazardous to assign any absolute values to the entry barriers corresponding to these three rankings, but the very roughest sort of a guess would be as follows: (1) that in the "very high" category, established firms might be able to elevate price 10 per cent or more above minimal costs while forestalling entry; (2) that with "substantial" barriers, the corresponding percentage might range a bit above or below 7 per cent; (3) that in the "moderate to low" category the same percentage will probably not exceed 4, and will range down to around 1 per cent in the extreme entries in this group. All

TABLE XV

Ranking of 20 Manufacturing Industries According to the Estimated Height of the Aggregate Barrier to Entry

A. *Industries with very high entry barriers*:

Automobiles	Liquor
Cigarettes	Tractors
Fountain pens ("quality" grade)	Typewriters

B. *Industries with substantial entry barriers*:

Copper	Shoes (high-priced men's and specialties)
Farm machines (large, complex)	Soap
Petroleum refining	Steel

C. *Industries with moderate to low entry barriers*:

Canned fruits and vegetables [a]	Meat packing [a]
Cement	Metal containers [b]
Farm machinery (small, simple)	Rayon
Flour [a]	Shoes (women's and low-priced men's)
Fountain pens (low-priced)	Tires and tubes
Gypsum products [b]	

[a] The barriers to entry for meat packing generally, and for major segments of the flour and canned goods industries, lie at the "low" extreme.

[b] Refers to period subsequent to 1950. Classification under group B is indicated for earlier periods.

the absolute magnitudes are quite speculative, because both of the "guess-estimated" character of much of the basic data and of theoretical uncertainty concerning the effect on entry of certain estimated situations.

Since in any industry the height of entry barriers due to product differentiation and to absolute-cost consideration may be in some degree dependent on the scale of entry, and since estimates of them should in general be related to a single assumption concerning the most effective probable scale of entry, we have taken some pains to analyze the extent of interdependence of the various specific barriers and to use this analysis in arriving at a meaningful aggregate. Some comments on the resulting classification of particular industries may be illuminating. The inclusion of the automobiles, tractors, and typewriters in the "very high" entry barrier category is fairly automatic, since in each of them very important scale economies in production and selling combined are coupled with high apparent product differentiation barriers to entry. (In addition, extremely large capital requirements are noted for autos and tractors.) Cigarettes, liquor, and "quality" fountain pens are placed in this category, however, largely on the basis of extremely high estimates of the product-differentiation barrier to entry. In addition, of course, large or very large capital requirements are found for liquor and cigarettes.

In the "substantial" entry barrier category, comment is required mainly on steel and copper. Neither of these industries would merit the rating of so high an entry barrier on the basis of available information, were it not for absolute-cost barriers resulting from scarcity and close control of essential natural resources. Yet we lack an estimate of how much of a barrier resource control actually imposes, other than that the barrier is large. It is conceivable that either industry might fall in the highest category of entry barriers, and their classification here represents the roughest sort of guess. The quantitative precision of our basic estimates is hardly sufficient to support very many fine distinctions among the industries listed as having "moderate to low" entry barriers. It is worth noting, however, that the inclusion of the metal-container industry is subject to doubt and that it might go one class higher, and also that meat packing, industrial and private-label flour making, and most fruit and vegetable canning probably have the lowest entry barriers discovered for the entire sample. Both the metal-container and gypsum-product industries would be placed in the "substantial-barrier" class B prior to 1950.

A further comment concerns the theoretical significance of the classification adopted in Table XV. This classification, which designates the aggregate barrier to entry to industries as "very high," "substantial," or "moderate to low," refers primarily to the absolute height of the barrier to entry, as measured by the extent to which established firms can probably elevate price above minimal average costs while still forestalling entry. It is not, therefore, the same as and should not be confused with the classification introduced for theoretical purposes in Chapter 1. The latter, which designated possible conditions of entry as "ineffectively impeded," "effectively impeded," and "blockaded," referred directly not to the absolute height of entry barriers but to established firms' reactions to these barriers. Thus, a barrier which "ineffectively impeded" entry was one low enough so that established firms acting in concert would find it unprofitable to set price low enough to exclude entry. A barrier which "effectively impeded" entry was one such that under similar suppositions established firms would find it profitable not to exceed the entry-forestalling price, and thus would exclude entry at a "limit" price, even though this price was below a monopoly price for the industry. A barrier "blockading" entry was one such that the maximum entry-excluding price was above the monopoly level, permitting blockaded entry with monopoly pricing. Since we cannot say in any general terms just how high an absolute barrier to entry must be to blockade, effectively impede, or ineffectively impede entry, and since considerations other than the absolute height of the entry barrier in some cases determine the classification, it is impossible to establish *a priori* any one-to-one or other very simple correspondence between the categories of Table XV and those developed in Chapter 1. A movement upward through the first classification would tend to be accompanied, on the average, by a movement upward through the second. But it does not necessarily follow, for example, that all the industries with "very high" entry barriers per Table XV have "blockaded" as opposed to "effectively impeded" entry. It does follow that, in projecting the theoretical consequences of data presented in Table XV, we must engage in some additional theorizing about the probable impact of various absolute levels of the condition of entry on the market conduct and performance of established firms.

The predictable consequences of existing aggregate barriers to entry

Predictions of the differing consequences of differing conditions of entry run conveniently in terms of the implications of "ineffectively impeded," "effectively impeded," and "blockaded" entry. As we saw in Chapter I the market performance of an industry may tend to be determined in the main jointly by the "level" of the barrier to entry (in these terms) and by the degree of seller concentration in the industry.

The theoretical picture is somewhat complicated because we must look not only at the "immediate" condition of entry as pertaining to some given point in time and industry structure, but also at the "general" condition of entry, which represents the succession of "immediate" conditions as successive entry occurs. Also, different absolute values of the condition of entry may be associated with a given "level" as defined. These complexities are actually very serious, however, only for cases involving "ineffectively impeded" entry, especially for the case where the attraction of entry tends to be undertaken and to result in the development of serious diseconomies of scale. For remaining cases, simplifications to adapt to available data are not hard to devise. By way of simplification, the following is offered regarding immediate conditions of entry:

(1) All analysis suggests that, with typical price elasticities of demands for industry outputs, barriers which "blockade" entry are also barriers which are relatively high in absolute terms, representing relatively large percentage excesses of the maximum entry-forestalling price over minimal costs. Conversely, absolutely high entry barriers will all tend to approach or reach the "blockaded" status unless an overcrowded industry has produced serious diseconomies of small scale plant and firm (an apparently rare phenomenon, to judge from our sample).

(2) In general, "effectively impeded" entry will involve barriers which in absolute terms run from substantial down to barely sufficient to make the forestalling of entry a preferred policy to established firms. Conversely, absolute entry barriers which are in the "substantial" and "moderate" range, but are deemed unlikely to qualify as "blockading," will generally also be "effectively impeding" in the sense mentioned. But the lower limit of absolute values which will qualify as effectively impeding entry is uncertain, and will probably vary somewhat from industry to industry. Also, of course, barriers which are moderately high in absolute terms may qualify as "ineffectively impeding" entry if there is an overcrowded industry with inefficiently small scales.

(3) Analysis suggests that "ineffectively impeded" entry may involve barriers of two sorts: (a) absolutely low barriers, where the entry-forestalling price exceeds minimal costs by only a very few percentage points at most; and (b) barriers which are moderate to quite high in absolute terms, encountered where overcrowding and inefficiently small scales have elevated the costs of established firms so that they find even relatively high entry-forestalling prices unprofitable. (An overcrowded industry with inefficiently small firm scales would be a necessary condition for the existence of the second sort of "ineffectively impeded" entry.) Conversely, barriers to entry below some minimal absolute level will qualify as "ineffectively impeding," although some higher absolute barriers may qualify also.

Given this guide, deciding which industries have entry barriers of sufficient absolute height to qualify, *ceteris paribus*, as effectively impeding or blockading entry is a first and a difficult task. An ultimately accurate decision could be developed, if at all, only through an intensive investigation of individual firms and industries, centering on such things as anticipated lags in inducing entry, the effective time preference of the managements of various firms as between immediate and future profits, the character of their expectations regarding much future market data, the degree and the type of their uncertainty concerning the values of such data, and so forth. Lacking all this, we can at best engage in a little guessing.

For purposes of this guessing, we will be guided by a few uniform assumptions concerning all the industries — adopted on the basis of various casual observations — and will not endeavor to vary the assumptions in the cases of individual industries. The assumptions are as follows: (1) If entry were induced, it would be accomplished with relatively short lags — generally in not more than two or three years. This would mean that extra profits earned through high entry-inducing prices would be relatively short-lived. (2) If entry were induced, it would generally be induced in important quantities, such that the loss of market shares to established firms (or reduction of industry price) would be of significant magnitude. This would mean that the post-entry profits of established firms would be smaller than the pre-entry profits obtainable at entry-forestalling prices by a significant fraction. (3) Established firms tend to discount future profits (as compared to present profits) at a rather low rate, reflecting a rate of time preference plus "risk" plus liquidity preference not significantly in excess of (and possibly smaller than) the corporate bond rate in the industry in question. These assumptions as a group describe a general milieu in which established firms weigh long-run profits, over many future years, more or less heavily against current profits; are not too uncertain in their anticipation of the future; and view induced entry as having a major and early impact on future profits. We rest our adoption of these assumptions simply on our own belief in their general accuracy, based on extended general observations of industry conduct and performance.

If these assumptions are generally valid, and if in addition diseconomies of overcrowding and inefficiently small scales are not present in the industries in question, it seems very likely that the industries included in groups A and B of Table XV will tend to have at least "effectively impeded" entry. Given reasonably efficient scales, that is, established firms should find it more profitable in the long run to charge prices low enough generally to forestall entry and to maintain a more or less stable industry structure. If the best entry-forestalling price in group B runs on the average from 6 to 8 per cent in excess of minimal costs (as suggested), and in group A runs higher, this outcome seems highly probable under the assumptions stated. Profits available while forestalling entry are substantial; the loss in long-run profits through inducing entry is also probably substantial as compared to the short-run gains which might be made.

With effective collusion (express or tacit) we might then expect those industries in groups A and B with "effectively impeded" entry to have precisely or close to the maximum entry-forestalling price; with less effective collusion, price might be lower than this. Some of these industries, of course (especially in Group A), might have "blockaded" entry, so that the established firms would tend even with effective collusion to maximize joint profits at prices below the maximum entry-forestalling level. Whether or not particular industries in groups A and B actually have "blockaded" entry, however, we are not in a position to determine, or even guess very well. In general we will assume (since monopoly prices are probably very high) that all or nearly all the entry barriers are no higher than "effectively impeding," though of differing absolute height.

Specific predictions for these industries will turn on whether or not significant diseconomies of overcrowding and small scale are present among established firms in them. On the basis of available information, they are probably not present to any important degree in the industries in groups A and B. The principal firms in all of them seem to be as large as or larger than required for best efficiency (see Table VIII) and the bulk of the industry outputs come from firms of such scales. The predictions must also turn on our expectations with respect to the existence or absence of "effective collusion (express or tacit) such as would permit established firms in an industry to exploit entry barriers to the full while forestalling entry. In general, very high seller concentration seems conducive to such collusion, whereas with lesser concentration the emergence of imperfections of collusion, and of lower prices, seems more probable.[1] The dividing line between "very high" and "lesser" seller concentration is subject to argument, although we have tentatively estimated it, in an earlier study, very roughly in the neighborhood of 70 per cent control of the market by the largest eight firms.[2]

Following this guide and the earlier ones developed, a more or less uniform prediction is forthcoming for the industries in group A of Table XV — autos, cigarettes, "quality" fountain pens, liquor, tractors, typewriters. In addition to having very high entry barriers, all of these industries have very high seller concentration, ranking at the top of highly concentrated oligopolies.[3] In all of them, therefore, oligopolistic interdependence seems likely to be high enough probably to lead to effective tacit or express collusion. Also, in each of them the product-differentia-

[1] Cf. J. S. Bain, "Relation of Profit Rate to Industry Concentration," *Quarterly Journal of Economics* (August 1951), pp. 293–324.

[2] Bain, "Relation of Profit Rate to Industry Concentration."

[3] For autos, cigarettes, and quality fountain pens, 90 per cent or more of the market is supplied by the largest four sellers, and competitive smaller sellers are insignificant in number. For tractors, liquor, and typewriters, the percentage control by four firms is slightly less (67 to 80 per cent, roughly) but the control of the market by the first eight firms was respectively 88, 87, and 96 per cent in 1947, again with the absence of any very large competitive fringe.

tion barrier to entry is rated as "great." For all the industries in group A, therefore, the following predictions would seem to be in order:

(1) Prices very substantially in excess of minimal costs.

(2) Excess profits of very substantial size and generally at the highest levels to be observed.

(3) Substantial selling costs for advertising, maintenance of distributive facilities, etc.

(4) Relatively stable industry structures with very little entry occurring over time (unless occasionally through major innovations in product).

This list of predictions clearly does not cover all important dimensions of industry performance; nothing, for example, is said of the degree of "progressiveness" in product and technique within the industry. But it carries us about as far as available *a priori* theory (as opposed to casual empirical observation) can.

The situation with respect to industries in Group B (with "substantial" entry barriers) is a bit more diverse. Product differentiation barriers are rated as "great" only for "large and complex" farm machinery; they are classed as "moderate" for soap, petroleum refining, and high-priced men's shoes, and as "slight" for steel and copper. As to seller concentration, it is again at the highest level for copper, soap, and large, complex farm machinery, but for steel and for petroleum refining it would appear to fall close to the "70 per cent by 8 firms" line in the principal geographical submarkets, whereas in the high-priced men's shoe field a specific concentration figure has not been obtained but is probably in the same concentration category or below. In the latter three cases, moreover, more numerous and stronger competitive fringes are in evidence than in industries so far discussed, and concentration is enough less than in the other cases that we may at least begin to wonder seriously about tacit or express collusion being effective enough to permit maximum exploitation of the entry barrier when entry is forestalled.

Accordingly, we are inclined to differentiate our predictions in the following fashion:

(1) For copper, soap, and large, complex farm machinery manufacture, the evident prediction is for a tendency toward:

(a) Prices substantially in excess of minimal costs, but not by so much on the average as for industries in Group A.

(b) Significant excess profits, though on the average lower than in Group A.

(c) Relatively stable industry structures, with little entry occurring over time (unless occasionally through product innovations).

(d) Large selling costs for soap and farm machinery, but not for copper.

(2) For steel, petroleum refining, and high-priced men's shoes:
  (a) Increased uncertainty, *a priori*, about the level of prices and of excess profits. Both might be as high as for the three industries mentioned just before, but there is also some significant probability that they might range downward toward a competitive level.
  (b) Relatively stable industry structure, with little entry occurring over time.
  (c) Large selling costs might also be expected for petroleum refining and high-priced men's shoes, but not for steel.

The industries in group C of Table XV present an even more difficult problem in the prediction of performance. In general, the entry barriers are absolutely low enough so that there is at least a distinct possibility that they will qualify as "ineffectively impeding" barriers, in the sense that established firms would prefer (if acting in concert) to have the extra immediate profits resulting from the high prices which would attract entry, as against having the rather small excess profits corresponding to the prices at which entry could be forestalled. In the case of the industries in this group with the lowest apparent entry barriers — meat packing, standard canned fruits and vegetables, and commercial flour — this possibility would seem to become a dominant probability.

In general within this group, therefore, we would seem to have two alternative general predictions, provided the established firms did act in effective collusive concert: (a) for prices stable and relatively low in relation to minimal costs, and for quite low excess profits, with entry largely forestalled and a rather stable industry structure; or (b) for unstable industry structure, with entry periodically induced, for inefficiencies of excess capacity, and for periodically high prices and profits followed by readjustments to lower levels.

The second alternative, however, is very likely to emerge only if there is some approach to effective collusion; if competition is generally strong or collusion quite imperfect, entry is relatively more likely to be more or less forestalled at low prices and profits even though a collusive monopoly industry might not desire this result. It is therefore important to look at the existing situation in regard to seller concentration, in order to get some notion of the relative probabilities in this respect.

In five cases in group C, seller concentration is distinctly low compared to the other industries of the sample, generally ranging below a 50 per cent control by 4 firms. These are cement, meat packing, women's and low-priced men's shoes, canned goods (excepting some specialties), and flour (excepting miller's-brand consumer sales). Although all of these industries might qualify as "low-grade oligopolies" rather than as "atomistic" in structure, the seller concentration is sufficiently low, and the competitive fringe of small firms numerous enough, so that serious departures from effective collusion on pricing would seem to be a major probability. In 4 other cases — gypsum products, metal containers, rayon, and tires and tubes — there is generally very high concentration, exceeding 80 per cent control of the market by the first 4 firms. In these cases, effective collusion would seem *a priori* to be roughly as feasible as in our group A industries, though the effective barriers to entry are generally much lower. For the remainder, it may be indicated (a) that concentration in small and simple farm machinery is moderately low, but not as low as in the 5 lowest cases; (b) that concentration in low-priced fountain pens cannot be closely approximated, but is apparently at least moderately low; and (c) that for miller's-brand consumer flour and certain specialties in canned goods, seller concentration is quite high.

The resultant theoretical predictions might run somewhat along the following lines:

(1) For gypsum products (after 1950), metal containers (after 1950), rayon, and tires and tubes — and perhaps as well for miller's-brand consumer flour and certain specialty canned goods — there is an alternative between an outcome involving a moderately low price and moderate to low excess profits, with forestalled entry, and a market-instability outcome with fluctuating prices and profits and inefficiencies of excess capacity. Because the absolute entry barriers for this class are at the high end of group C, the former seems quite possible or on the balance more probable than the other, although there must be a good deal of *a priori* uncertainty about this. Of these industries, metal containers, tires and tubes, and the indicated segments of the flour and canned goods industries have moderate product-differentiation barriers, and important selling costs might also be anticipated in them. Small and simple farm machinery may generally fall in the same category.

It should be noted that for periods prior to 1951, the predictions for metal containers and gypsum products should be about the same as for copper, soap, etc. (Table XI above).

(2) For cement, meat packing, women's and low-priced men's shoes, standard canned goods, and commercial flour, as well as low-priced fountain pens, the prospect is pretty well split between two alternatives — a low entry-forestalling price either chosen or enforced by competition, and an unstable price with periodic excessive entry and excess capacity. The choice is not an idle one from a social standpoint, since it is one between reasonably workable and seriously unworkable competition. But the *a priori* indications are uncertain. We do not know enough about whether the entry barriers would qualify as "effectively impeding" or "ineffectively impeding," or enough about the potential effectiveness of

tacit or express collusion, to do more than indicate that there are two distinct possibilities. It is also indicated, with slight product-differentiation barriers to entry in every case, that high selling costs are not generally to be anticipated in these industries.

Let us now summarize our predictions for the twenty industries, grouping them under three major patterns:

(1) *Industries in which forestalled entry with prices substantially in excess of minimal costs, and substantial excess profits, are major probabilities.*

    (a) With the expectation of substantial selling costs:

Automobiles	Tractors
Cigarettes	Typewriters
Fountain pens (quality)	Soap
Liquor	Farm machinery (large and complicated)

    (b) Without the expectation of substantial selling costs:
        Copper

(2) *Industries in which forestalled entry is a major probability, but either with substantially high prices and profits, or with lower prices and profits.*

    (a) With large selling costs:
        Petroleum refining
        Shoes (men's high-priced and specialties)

    (b) Without large selling costs:
        Steel

(3) *Industries in which forestalled entry with prices moderately to slightly above minimal costs, and moderate to very low excess profits, are more probable or as probable as any outcome, but in which there is at least a strong minor probability of recurrent induced entry, inefficiency of small scale, structural instability, and unstable prices and profits.*

    (a) With large selling costs:

Metal containers [4]	Tires and tubes
Flour (miller's-brand consumer market)	Canned goods (specialties)

[4] Applies to period after 1950. Classification under group 1 just above is indicated for earlier periods.

(b) Without large selling costs:

Gypsum products [5]   Shoes (women's and low-priced
Rayon   men's)
Cement   Canned goods (standard)
Meat packing   Flour (commercial)
                                 Fountain pens (low-priced)

In the light of the degree of precision of our estimates and of the character of oligopolistic pricing theory, *a priori* analysis will not take us much further than the outline above. Our predictions thus are limited, since they are extremely rough and in a significant degree indefinite in many cases. Moreover, they do not touch upon certain important dimensions of market performance.

The roughness of the groupings is the inescapable consequence of the imprecision of our basic estimates relative to the condition of entry, and cannot be remedied at this time on either the empirical or the *a priori* level, although future improvement of data is to be hoped for. The indefiniteness of predictions is in larger part a product of the state of oligopoly theory; this is likely to be remedied only by further research combining empirical generalization with deductive rationalization, although empirical tests of predictions in their present indefinite form may provide some useful leads. We will take some small steps along the testing line in the next chapter.

The fact that our predictions do not immediately bear on certain important dimensions of market performance is primarily due to the ambivalent character of theoretical indications on certain strategic matters, including efficiency in scale of firm and progressiveness in technique and product through time. On the first matter, strictly *a priori* predictions have a decidedly "iffy" character, since they leave open the possibility (though not usually the probability) of the development of inefficiently small scales in overcrowded industries, whenever scale economies are at all significant. Given this uncertainty, we have chosen to simplify things by direct reference to the fact, empirically observed, that in the industries of our sample this possibility appears not to have been realized. This, however, is empiricism and not theory, and perhaps the conclusion arrived at should not be extended casually to industries outside the sample.

On the matter of progressiveness, the plain fact is that *a priori* theory gives us no reasonably definite indications about the probable relative performance of industries with great, medium, and small entry barriers, particularly within the broad and very general category of oligopoly,

[5] Applies to period after 1950. Classification under group 1 just above is indicated for earlier periods.

within which substantially all of our sample lies. The product of theorizing along this line is full of contrary indications, the relative weight of which cannot be assessed on *a priori* grounds. We thus have little to offer on this point, and unfortunately, available empirical data tend to yield similarly little in the way of evidence having any probative value. This leads to a notable deficiency in our predictions and findings on performance.

Thus we are in no good position to predict the relationship of market structure — and particularly of the condition of entry — to the over-all workability of competition as judged by performance. About all we can do is to suggest some indicated relationships of the condition of entry to certain selected dimensions of performance: namely, the relation of price to minimal costs, the height of profits, and the size of selling costs.

The following relationships thus appear, in reference solely to the industries of our sample and to the sorts of situations discovered there:

(1) Industries with very high or substantial aggregate barriers to entry and with very high seller concentration in general have a tendency toward unworkable performance in terms of the relation of price to minimal cost (and thus in monopolistic output restriction) and of excess profits. In addition, practically all of the industries in this group would appear from our sample to have a tendency to large or very large selling costs — probably in excess of the social optimum.

(2) Industries with high entry barriers but more moderate concentration may tend to give a more workable performance in terms of prices, outputs, and profits, but the prospect is uncertain. Selling costs may still be a problem if product-differentiation is important.

(3) Industries with moderate to low entry barriers offer at least a fairly good prospect of workable performance in prices, outputs, and profits, and one which is better if seller concentration is moderate to low instead of high. Even with high concentration, however, relatively workable results are quite conceivable.

There is always a significant danger in these cases, however, of unstable and inefficient market structures, induced through periodic collusive monopoly pricing. Although important product differentiation appears to occur infrequently in these cases, there is a danger or large selling costs in some instances. With respect to this category in particular, empirical investigation is in order to determine which of the major theoretical possibilities is realized.

(4) So far as we can see empirically, inefficiently small firm scales are not generally a problem in the industries of our sample.

So much for theoretical speculations concerning effects of the condition of entry. Before considering their implications for public policy, let us turn to some evidence of performance in the industries of our sample.

7

EMPIRICAL EVIDENCE OF
THE MARKET PERFORMANCE
in Industries Under Various Conditions of Entry

In preceding chapters we have appraised conditions of entry to 20 manufacturing industries and developed predictions of how their market performance should respond to or be associated with the conditions of entry to them. Ideally we might now round out the treatise by reporting on comprehensive empirical tests for the predicted associations. But this ideal is at present not even approximately attainable. We simply lack systematic data on the market performance of most of our 20 industries, and development of the requisite data cannot be undertaken at this time. To do that, it would be necessary in all but 3 or 4 of our twenty industries to undertake *de novo* full-fledged industry studies, which neither time nor funds presently allow.

As a makeshift, we can carry the testing procedure as far as presently available data permit, conducting some limited and partial tests for the relation of the condition of entry to certain general measures of performance provided by data generally available for most or all of our industries. But let us emphasize at the outset that the data are inadequate, that the tests are somewhat inconclusive, and that their results are thus not only limited in scope but also tentative in character.

The theoretical predictions which we have developed in Chapters 1 and 6 concerning the association of the condition of entry to performance have referred primarily to the following dimensions of the market performance of industries: (1) the degree to which plants and firms approximate optimal efficiency in scale; (2) the degree to which there is chronic excess capacity of plant; (3) the long-run relationship of price to the minimal cost of production; (4) the relationship of price to average costs, as reflected in rates of profit; and (5) the size of selling costs. All these predictions are in some degree indefinite, especially as they concern the degree of efficiency in scale of firm which will emerge where significant scale economies are present. Correspondingly, empirical testing should be useful not simply in verifying specific predictions, but also in finding which of several alternative predictions is usually confirmed in practice. Further, empirical study may be useful in converting the *qualitative* distinctions drawn in theoretical predictions into *quantitative* distinctions.

To what extent will the readily available data on performance permit the sort of testing in which we should like to engage? The principal sorts of data available, and the tests they will support, are as follows:

(1) Combining findings on optimal scales of plants and firms with various statistics on actual plant and firm sizes, we have tentative but fairly systematic indications of the relationships of actual plant and firm scales to optimal scales in our twenty industries. These indications can be employed to run a rough test of the relationship of the relative efficiency of industry organization (as it is affected by scales) to the condition of entry. More fragmentary data on the incidence of excess capacity within the industries can likewise be examined to see if the showings are consistent with hypotheses concerning the relation of the condition of entry to the development of excess capacity.

(2) There is a substantial scattering of data on the profit rates earned over significant time intervals by the member firms of our industries. These data can be used to develop rough tests for the association of profits to the condition of entry and to other dimensions of market structure. Given findings on the relative efficiency in scale and capacity of the firms involved, they may also cast light on the association of the condition of entry to the relationship attained between price and minimal average cost.

(3) There is a much less adequate scattering of data on advertising costs incurred in the twenty industries. These data may be examined in the light of hypotheses concerning the relationship of the condition of entry to selling costs.

Some tentative testing of some hypotheses is thus feasible. On numerous dimensions of performance, however, we have no adequate data, and those which we do have are deficient in various degrees. In consequence, no adequate over-all appraisal of the relationship of the condition of entry to the workability of market performance can be developed here. We are perforce content with a few partial tests which, even though they were conclusive with respect to specific issues, could not be conclusive with respect to the impact of the condition of entry on the over-all workability of competition.

Efficiency in scale, and in adjustment of capacity to demand

Three initial questions are posed with respect to the efficiency of industry organization:

(1) What is the relationship of the scales of existing *plants* to the most efficient scales, and how much do observed deviations from optimal plant scales increase unit costs?

(2) What is the relationship of the scales of existing *firms* to the most efficient scales, and how much do observed deviations from optimal firm scales increase unit costs?

(3) What, if any, is the degree of chronic excess capacity of plant, and what is its apparent effect on costs?

These queries simply request a measurement of the performance in the dimension of efficiency. Given the information thus sought, two added questions may be posed:

(4) To what extent is the performance of an industry in each of these regards apparently associated with the condition of entry to it, or with other aspects of its market structure?

(5) Is the observed pattern of association (or non-association) of the condition of entry to such performance consistent with our theoretical hypotheses concerning such association? Also, where theoretical predictions in this regard are indefinite or suggest alternative possibilities, which possibilities seem to be fulfilled in fact?

Let us try to answer these questions by considering performance and its association to the condition of entry with respect successively to plant scales, firm scales, and the incidence of excess capacity.

1. *Efficiency in scale of plant*

As already suggested in Chapters 3 and 6, no general or chronic deficiency in scale of plant appears to be found in the twenty industries under study. In every case, plants supplying the bulk of the industry output appear to be large enough to attain minimal production costs per unit of output. For these plants, departures from optimal plant scale are apparently either absent or insufficient to elevate costs significantly.

This finding was obtained for each industry by (1) setting up as a standard the estimates of optimal plant scale and of the shape of the plant scale curve developed from questionnaire replies and other sources; (2) calculating, from *Census of Manufacturers* data on plant outputs for 1947 and from various data on actual plant capacities the probable size distribution of actual plants; and (3) placing the second finding against the first to determine the percentage of industry plant capacity which is probably found in plants either as large as the estimated optimum, or not enough smaller that unit costs would be perceptibly elevated; that is, the percentage of total plant capacity having close to optimal efficiency. Since we have relied rather heavily in determining the size distribution of plants on a size measure referring to output rather than to capacity *per se*, no great precision in findings is to be expected and only rough general statements are justified. At least the following, however, seem reasonably clear.

First, the share of an industry's output supplied by plants of optimal or near-optimal scale generally falls between 70 and 90 per cent. In none of the 20 industries of our sample does it apparently fall much below 70 per cent; the modal share is around 80 per cent; in only 1 or 2 cases is the share possibly above 90 and approaching 100 per cent. Thus firms supplying the preponderance of an industry's output more or less uniformly supply it from plants of efficient scale.

Second, from 10 to 30 per cent of the outputs of the various industries comes from plants which suffer a significant degree of inefficiency due to small scale. These plants are apparently enough short of the optimal scale to elevate unit costs by at least several percentage points, and, in the case of the smallest plants, by more than that. Coupled with the preceding finding, this very evidently does not mean that we have a chronic overcrowding of our industries resulting in the general incidence of undersized plants — a possibility sometimes anticipated in the conventional theory of oligopoly. But it does mean that, at least within our sample, we commonly find a *fringe* of inefficiently small plants surrounding a core of plants of efficient size. And the size of the fringe is such that from a tenth to perhaps a third of industry output may come from plants of relatively inefficient scale.

Not all of this apparent inefficiency is necessarily net waste. In part, the existence of the inefficiently small plants may be explained as a rational and economical adjustment to supplying small "pockets" in the market. These pockets may consist of limited demands for specialized products, or for standard products in remote localities, the demands being so limited that production at optimal plant scale would not be justified. Examination of the character and location of undersize plants in various industries, however, suggests that no major share of the apparent departure from efficient organization can be explained away in this fashion. We are apparently faced with the more or less general phenomenon of an inefficient fringe of unduly small plants. Moreover, although evidence on this point is incomplete, these fringes appear to persist over time. And the small plants apparently cannot be identified in the main as operations in the process of growth toward more efficient scale, although this is evidently true in some minor proportion of cases. So far as the sketchy data reveal, continuation of small plant operation within a relatively inefficient range of sizes is quite common.

We thus arrive at the general picture of a dominant core of plants of efficient scale, surrounded by a fringe of relatively inefficient small plants.

It is therefore not legitimate to assume, for purposes of theorizing about the impact of the condition of entry on pricing, that *all* plants and firms in an industry are of relatively efficient scale. But the findings do tend to confirm a crucial provisional assumption which was made in Chapter 6 in connection with predictions of market performance under various conditions of entry — that in general the dominant firms of the industry are operating at efficient plant scales.

Our next question is whether the size of the "inefficient fringe" of small plants is in any evident fashion systematically related to the condition of entry or to other aspects of market structure. With the variation of the size of the fringe among industries being apparently rather small, with the imprecision found in crucial basic estimates, and with the relatively small sample of industries at hand, it is very difficult to establish any such association, and certainly impossible to prove one. We have, however, made a very rough test for any visible or apparent association of the size of the inefficient fringe of plants in an industry to the height of the over-all barrier to entry, to the degree of seller concentration, to the relative importance of product-differentiation barriers to entry, and to the relative importance of scale economies. The finding in general is that there is no clear or convincing association of the size of the inefficient fringe to any of these structural variables. As far as we can tell from the evidence, the distribution of the magnitude of the inefficient fringe of plants may well be random as among groups of industries classified according to any of the four principles just mentioned.

There is only one possibly significant straw in the wind. Industries with low product-differentiation barriers to entry (the height of the aggregate barrier aside) have on the average a substantially smaller inefficient fringe of plants than those with higher product-differentiation barriers to entry. Although several industries with important product-differentiation barriers have relatively small inefficient fringes, 5 out of 7 industries in which the inefficient fringe apparently accounts for 25 per cent or more of industry output have either moderate or great product differentiation barriers to entry. (These are the tractor, farm machinery, metal container, tire and tube, and soap industries; only cement and shoes, with low product-differentiation barriers, have equally large inefficient fringes.

This finding is quite consistent with the familiar theoretical hypothesis that strong product differentiation among established sellers will favor the survival of firms with significant production-cost disadvantages, since the vagaries of product differentiation and sales promotion are then more likely to permit them to compensate for such disadvantages.

It may be noted in passing that inefficiency in plant scales is often combined with a lack of the most efficient or effective degree of integration, and that both horizontal expansion and vertical integration would be required for the plants in question to reach maximum efficiency. This appears to be true, for example, with respect to the inefficient fringes in the shoe, steel, petroleum refining, farm machinery, tractor, and automobile industries, although in many of these cases the advantage of integration lies at the level of promotional rather than production costs.

The preceding findings about the relation of the size of the inefficient fringe of plants to the condition of entry to the industry do not bear directly on any major theoretical hypotheses previously advanced, since those hypotheses refer directly to the relative efficiency of firms rather than of plants. But so far as plants and firms may be identified, as in the case of one-plant firms, findings do *not* tend to confirm the suspicion that overcrowded industries of inefficiently small firms may tend to result more frequently with low than with high aggregate barriers to entry. Nor, with small sample and sketchy data, do the findings disconfirm it in any conclusive fashion. We can only say that a systematic relation between the height of the barrier to entry and the incidence of diseconomies of small plant has not been empirically established here.

2. *Efficiency in scale of firm*

It has been suggested earlier that what is true of efficiency in plant scales in the sample of industries is, as far as we can tell, also apparently true of efficiency in the scale of firms. So far as expansion of firms to multiplant scales has the effect of significantly reducing costs, the firms supplying the bulk of the output of any industry appear, where data are available, to have enough plants to attain or closely approximate minimal production and distribution costs per unit of output.

This tentative conclusion stemmed initially from a comparison of the estimated optimal scales of firms (Table IX) with data on the actual scales of the principal firms.[1] In addition, estimates of the incidence of advantages of large-scale sales promotion were taken into account. The conclusion does not have too firm a base, however, because of the lack of any definite estimates concerning the extent of multiplant firm economies for 8 of the 20 industries. But there are some statements that we can offer definitely.

First, for the 6 industries in Group 1 of Table IX for which the existence of multiplant economies is denied, there is apparently no inefficiency in production and distribution due to inadequate scale of firm, other than that already attributed to small plants. The recognition of the possible or probable incidence of economies of large-scale sales promotion, moreover,

---

[1] The latter data are in part direct measures of individual firm size, from a variety of sources, and in part estimates of firm size developed from concentration data from the 1947 *Census of Manufactures*.

does not significantly alter this judgment. We thus find for these 6 industries no departure from efficiency due to a failure to attain multiplant scales (though large firms have attained such scales in most cases); such inefficiency as occurs seems fully represented in the fringe of inefficiently small plants alluded to in the immediately preceding section.

Second, for the 8 industries in Group 2 of Table IX for which no estimates of multiplant economies were developed, we must be somewhat uncertain about the possible incidence of diseconomies of inefficiently small firms. It is worth noting, however, that concentration and related data suggest that firms supplying the bulk of the output in these industries are generally large enough to exploit any probable economies of multiplant development, including those of large-scale sales promotion. The incidence of significant diseconomies of small firms (other than those already associated with small plants) thus appears likely to be slight in the industries of Group 2.

Third, for the 6 industries of Group 3 of Table IX for which some economies of multiplant development were suggested in estimates, some net inefficiencies due to the small scale of firms may be present, in addition to inefficiencies already attributed to the small scale of an inefficient fringe of plants. Examination of individual-industry data suggests that this possibility is not realized to any significant degree in the gypsum-product, soap, and cigarette industries. In each of these a very few firms supplying a predominant share of industry output are all amply large by any standard, and the inefficient-firm fringe cannot be significantly greater than the inefficient-plant fringe already referred to. In the steel, cement, and shoe industries, however, it appears that some net diseconomies of small firm — attributable to an insufficient degree of multiplant development — may be present if the high estimates of the extent of multiplant economies are accepted. If they are, it might appear that as little as 50 to 60 per cent of industry output in these cases may come from firms of optimal scale, the remainder coming from firms with insufficient multiplant development, or with this plus insufficient plant scale. Such inefficiencies of insufficient multiplant development might, according to estimates, elevate costs by two or three or more percentage points.

The possibility of some augmentation of the inefficient fringe through insufficient multiplant development is thus suggested for some part of the 20 industries under examination. In general, however, the available data do no more than suggest the possibility, and indicate that if it is realized it will be so only for a minor fraction of the cases in question. The data will certainly not support even rough tests for the association of diseconomies of small firm to the condition of entry, or judgments concerning how such associations correspond to theoretical predictions. We are left with these general impressions: (1) that in most industries there is a fringe of inefficiently small operations, generally not exceeding 30 per cent of the capacity of an industry; (2) that the inefficiency involved is principally attributable to small plant sizes, generally though not always found in single-plant firms; (3) that the disadvantage of small plants may in a few cases be augmented by a lack of multiplant development, and that in a few cases firms with efficient individual plants may suffer this lack;[2] (4) that there is little evident association of the incidence of inefficiencies of small scale with the condition of entry, although the data will not support any very firm conclusions on this matter. Available data definitely do not confirm the suspicion that inefficiencies of small scale of plant and firm may tend to occur more frequently with low than with high entry barriers; conversely, there is no conclusive disconfirmation of this hypothesis.

It is possibly worth noting that, in the absence of anti-trust laws which tend to discourage monopolization or very high concentration via the merger process, more or less permanent elimination or drastic reduction of inefficient fringes might have been expected in industries surrounded by high barriers to entry, whereas their persistent suppression in other cases would have been less probable.

3. *Excess capacity*

A principal hypothesis developed in the analysis of the effects of the condition of entry is that with "ineffectively impeded" entry (with barriers not high enough to make entry-forestalling price policies desirable) there is a significant probability of price policies leading to structural instability, excessive entry, and chronic or quasi-chronic excess capacity — all this provided that for some reason or other seller concentration becomes fairly high and competition among established sellers can become significantly restricted. This prediction is related to but not precisely the same as that of inefficiency in plant or firm scale under the same conditions.

Data available for testing this hypothesis are unfortunately scanty and incomplete. For 11 of the 20 industries — canned goods, liquor, metal containers, meat packing, gypsum products, farm machinery, tractors, soap, cigarettes, fountain pens, and typewriters — there are simply no adequate data on the incidence of chronic excess capacity. In some of these — e.g., liquor, farm machinery, gypsum products — there is evidence of transient excess capacity due to cyclical or seasonal fluctuations in demand or to

[2] A possible extension of this observation is that in a few further industries, selling differentiated products through nationwide sales promotion, even some of the larger firms may not be large enough to exploit the scale economies of physical distribution as conducted on a nationwide basis. (Cf. p. 141n. above.) It has not been possible really to test this hypothesis.

occasional errors in estimates of future demand, but no revealing data on the extent, if any, to which chronic excess capacity exists.

For 6 of the remaining industries — petroleum refining, steel, automobiles, tires and tubes, cigarettes, and copper — there is some evidence on the relation of capacity to demand, and it suggests that chronic excess capacity has not plagued these industries. Cyclical excess capacity is encountered, as in steel and automobiles, and the tire and tube industry went through a period of excess capacity apparently attributable to a serious miscalculation of demand, but it does not appear that in any of these cases there has been a persistent tendency toward redundant capacity at times of maximum or peak demand. It is noteworthy that all but one of these industries (tires and tubes) were rated in Chapter 6 as having either substantial or very great barriers to entry prior to 1950.

The other 3 industries (shoes, flour, cement) show definite evidence of substantial chronic excess capacity — in fact, of a 20 per cent or more apparent redundancy of capacity in intervals of peak demand. Quantitative appraisals are difficult because we do not know how much allowance to make for obsolescent or obsolete plant included in capacity tabulations, but there seems little doubt that there is significant chronic excess capacity in these industries. It is again noteworthy that all of these industries were classified in Chapter 6 as having "moderate to low" barriers to entry.

We have at hand nothing more conclusive than the preceding. However, we may note that our findings such as they may be are generally consistent with the theoretical hypothesis concerning the probable association of the condition of entry to the incidence of chronic excess capacity. A good deal more research would be required to test this hypothesis thoroughly.

Profits or price-cost margins and the condition of entry

A principal hypothesis emergent from the analysis of Chapter 1 concerns a relationship of the condition of entry to an industry to the price-average cost margin which will be attained in it — and thus indirectly to the degree of monopolistic output restriction and to the size of excess profits. The general conclusion of the argument is that, at least to the extent that oligopolistic concentration is sufficient to support effective express or tacit collusion in pricing, the long-run average gap between price and minimal average cost of production will tend to be greatest where "blockaded" entry is encountered (possibly approaching the joint-monopoly level), and less where "effectively impeded" entry is encountered. Where entry is "ineffectively impeded," the gap in question may be least, but may also be dynamically unstable with occasional high periods. If in addition firms are generally operating with minimal or close-to-minimal costs of production, there should be a similar relationship of the height of the barrier to entry with the profit margins between actual average costs and prices. Finally, as far as there is some generally systematic relationship of the rate of excess profit on sales (describing the price-average cost gap) and the rate of profit on equity, a relationship between profit rates on equity and the height of the barrier to entry might be anticipated.[3]

This predicted influence of the condition of entry on the size of price-cost margins and profits is clearly subject to the concomitant influence of the degree of seller concentration within the industry. Specifically, it is expected to be evidenced in a verifiable simple association of the condition of entry to profits mainly as far as seller concentration throughout is high enough to support effective collusion in industries with both high and medium entry barriers. If there are significant variations in the degree of seller concentration into the range where intra-industry competition among established firms becomes a dominant force, the potential influence of the condition of entry may become inoperative or at least may be modified and obscured. Statistically, therefore, we would anticipate some complex relationship of at least three variables — profit rate, degree of seller concentration, and condition of entry — of such a character that some net positive association of the barrier to entry and the profit rate would be apparent.

In regard to the appearance of the predicted association of the condition of entry to profit rates, it would be expected to be evident most definitely for the largest or dominant established firms in an industry, which will in general have the maximum aggregate advantage over potential entrants, and are most likely to be operating with minimal or close to minimal average costs. The profit rates of smaller firms, with inefficiently small plants or firm scales or with smaller product-differentiation advantages over entrants, might be expected to show a less certain or distinct relationship to a condition of entry calculated primarily with reference to the positions of the dominant firms. Thus the profit rates of the dominant firms alone provide the most acceptable data for testing the hypothesis in question.

This hypothesis was given specific implementation in Chapter 6. After tentatively identifying various absolute aggregate barriers to entry as "blockading," "effectively impeding," and so forth, we projected a probable relative profit-rate behavior for each of three groups of industries,

---

[3] There is clearly no simple proportional relationship between the two rates, since this relationship varies generally among firms or industries with the ratio of sales to equity. We have argued at another place, however (Bain, "Relation of Profit Rate to Industry Concentration," pp. 296–297), that *on the average* and subject to the random disturbance specified, upward and downward variations in sales rates will be accompanied by upward and downward variations in equity rates.

classified according to the height of the absolute aggregate barrier to entry. Direct testing is possible only with respect to the derived hypothesis concerning association of the condition of entry to rates of profit on equity, since independent data on minimal costs and on rates of excess profits on sales are not available. To conduct this direct test, we have first identified for each industry four or fewer dominant firms (fewer if the core of dominant firms is smaller than four in number) and have tabulated profit-rate data for each of these firms for which such data were available.[4] These profit-rate data in the case of each firm include (a) a simple average of the annual profit rates on equity (after income taxes) for the five-year period 1936 through 1940; and (b) a similar simple average of annual equity rates for the five-year period 1947–51.[5] The basic profit-rate data thus developed are contained in Table XVI below.

TABLE XVI

Profit Rates on Equity (after Income Taxes) for Dominant Firms in 20 Industries, 1936–40 and 1947–51

Industry and Firm	Average Annual Profit Rate 1936–40 [a]	Average Annual Profit Rate 1947–51 [b]
Industries with very high entry barriers:		
Automobiles		
General Motors	18.1	25.7
Chrysler	32.3	22.1
Cigarettes		
American Tobacco	11.5	12.3
Ligget & Myers	15.0	12.4
Reynolds	18.5	12.8
Philip Morris	39.3	12.8
Liquor		
Schenley	12.5	14.8
Seagrams	14.3	22.5
National Distillers	18.2	16.4
Hiram Walker	15.9	20.5
Typewriters		
Remington-Rand	15.5	22.7
Royal	23.9	21.7
Underwood	14.6	14.4
L. C. Smith	8.9	13.0

[4] Dominant firms for which adequate profit data are unavailable are perforce omitted. Profit-rate data are considered inadequate and are omitted if the firm does not do a major share of its business in the industry in question.

[5] Rates for 1936–1940 are generally drawn from S.E.C., *Survey of Listed Corporations*; for 1947–51, the rates have been individually calculated from data in Moody's *Industrials*.

TABLE XVI (continued)

Industry and Firm	Average Annual Profit Rate 1936–40 [a]	Average Annual Profit Rate 1947–51 [b]
Fountain pens (quality grade)		
Parker	12.5	23.1
Sheaffer	22.4	20.5
Industries with substantial entry barriers:		
Copper		
Anaconda	4.4	7.1
Kennecott	10.4	15.7
Phelps-Dodge	7.0	19.2
American Smelting & Refining	12.3	16.4
Steel		
U. S. Steel	4.0	8.5
Bethlehem	5.2	12.6
Republic	3.9	13.4
Jones & Laughlin	2.0	10.4
Farm machines (large and complex) and tractors		
International Harvester	7.7	10.2
Deere & Co.	14.7	16.3
Allis-Chalmers	7.4	10.3
J. I. Case	5.8	16.7
Petroleum refining		
Standard Oil (N. J.)	9.0	13.4
Socony-Vacuum	6.4	11.1
Standard Oil (Ind.)	6.1	10.8
Standard Oil of California	4.9	16.3
Soap		
Procter & Gamble	18.5	17.7
Colgate	7.4	13.8
Shoes (high-priced men's)		
Florsheim	10.2	14.3
Nunn-Bush	11.0	12.5
Gypsum products		
U. S. Gypsum	9.9	16.0
National Gypsum	12.4	14.8
Metal containers		
American Can	10.5	12.3
Continental Can	8.1	9.1
Industries with moderate to low entry barriers:		
Canned fruits and vegetables		
Cal-Pak	5.3	11.7
Stokely-Van Camp	3.8	11.7
Hunt	(3.7) [c]	7.7
Libby	7.4	8.0

TABLE XVI (continued)

Industry and Firm	Average Annual Profit Rate 1936–40 [a]	Average Annual Profit Rate 1947–51 [b]
Cement		
Lehigh Portland	4.9	12.0
Lone Star	8.3	14.6
Alpha Portland	3.0	11.6
Penn Dixie	4.6	19.1
Flour		
General Mills	9.3	12.8
Pillsbury	4.9	7.4
Meat packing		
Swift	3.4	6.4
Armour	3.1	3.5
Cudahy	0.1	2.9
Wilson	5.3	7.6
Rayon		
Celanese	11.6	18.3
North American	14.7	17.6
Shoes (diversified)		
International	8.2	12.2
Endicott-Johnson	4.5	6.2
Brown	4.9	11.6
General	14.6	13.9
Tires and tubes		
Goodyear	7.6	10.5
U. S. Rubber	10.1	12.5
Firestone	7.4	14.6
Goodrich	5.9	13.2

[a] From S.E.C. *Survey of Listed Corporations.*
[b] Calculated from Moody's *Industrials.*
[c] Loss.

For this tabulation, the following explanatory comments are in order. First, the farm machinery and tractor industries have been combined because of the participation of the same dominant firms in both; the shoe industry has been subdivided into high-priced men's shoes and other shoes; the fountain-pen industry has been restricted to so-called quality or high-priced fountain pens. Second, the gypsum-product and metal-container industries have been classified as having substantial entry barriers, since they did in the periods to which the profit data refer, although the post-1951 classification of Chapter 6 recognizes that these barriers have subsequently been lowered. That the data are incomplete in a number of cases, and not of such a character as to justify extensive treatment by formal statistical techniques, must once again be emphasized.

A next step has been to develop a rough summary of individual-firm showings by computing for each industry an average profit rate for the dominant firms listed. The average profit rate in each case is a simple (unweighted) average of firm average profit rates, referring to 1936–40 and 1947–51.[6] The resultant industry average profit rates (referring only to dominant firms listed in Table XVI) are as follows:

| | Average Profit Rate | |
Industry	1936–40	1947–51
Automobiles	25.2	23.9
Cigarettes	21.1	12.6
Liquor	15.2	18.6
Typewriters	15.7	18.0
Fountain pens	18.0	21.8
Copper	8.5	14.6
Steel	3.8	11.2
Farm machinery and tractors	8.9	13.4
Petroleum refining	6.6	12.9
Soap	13.0	15.8
Shoes (high-priced men's)	10.6	13.4
Gypsum products	11.2	15.4
Metal containers	9.3	10.7
Canned fruits and vegetables	3.2	9.8
Cement	5.2	14.3
Flour	7.1	10.1
Meat packing	3.0	5.1
Rayon	13.2	18.0
Shoes (diversified)	8.1	11.0
Tires and tubes	7.8	12.7

Given these data, our problem is to seek for the relation of profit rates to the condition of entry and to seller concentration in the two time intervals in question.

Whatever the influence of the condition of entry, there is evidently a clear association between the rate of profit earned in an industry and the degree of seller concentration in it. This finding emerged clearly from an earlier study.[7] In general, it was found there that for a 40-industry sample (including nearly all of the 20 industries considered here) there was a statistically significant difference in the period 1936–40 between the average profit rates for industries in which 8 sellers controlled more than 70 per cent of industry sales and for industries in which 8 sellers controlled less than 70 per cent. This relation of profits to concentration may reflect the influence of concentration alone, but may with at least equal probability reflect the dual influence of concentration and the con-

[6] The data are hardly complete enough to justify the arduous task of weighting individual observations.

[7] Bain, "Relation of Profit Rate to Industry Concentration."

dition of entry — if the latter two "determining" variables are substantially intercorrelated.

The simple relation of profit rate to concentration is apparent when, drawing on the average profit-rate data immediately above, we compare the average profit rates of the dominant firms of industries with "high" concentration (over-70-per-cent-by-8-firms) and "moderate to low" concentration (under-70-per-cent-by-8-firms) for our 20 industries for the periods 1936–40 and 1947–51. Table XVII below presents such a comparison, drawing upon Census national seller concentration data for 1935 and 1947 in most cases, and on generally equivalent data (for copper, automobiles, and quality fountain pens, for example) where Census data will not suffice. Clearly suggested is a possible or probable association of concentration to profit rate of the sort designated; when extensive calculations based on weighted average industry profit rates for 1936–40 were made,[8] a statistically significant association was found. There is thus probably a significant simple association of profit rates to concentration, of the sort specified, in both the prewar and postwar periods.

Let us now see if there was also a similar simple association of the condition of entry to the rate of profit by industries. Employing the same industry average profit-rate data, based on dominant-firm profits, we compare, in Table XVIII, the prewar and postwar profits of industries with "very high," "substantial," and "moderate to low" aggregate barriers to entry.

This tabulation suggests (1) that there is a distinct cleavage in average profit rates between industries with "very high" entry barriers and all other industries; but (2) that a similarly distinct difference within the "all other" group is not apparent between industries with "substantial" and "moderate to low" barriers. The first difference would almost certainly prove to be statistically significant; the second probably would not. It thus appears that our prediction of the association of the condition of entry to the profit rate is confirmed as far as it distinguishes "very high" entry barriers from others, predicting higher profits with the first sort of barrier.

The tentative finding of no great difference in profit rates between industries of "substantial" and "moderate to low" entry barriers would potentially accord with our predictions *if* in most of the industries in the latter category the firms involved viewed entry as "ineffectively impeded" — that is, viewed the barriers as low enough to encourage them to strive for relatively high, entry-attracting prices rather than to set prices sufficiently low to forestall entry. This could lead at least periodically to profit rates in this latter category roughly as high as those resulting from the entry-forestalling limit prices anticipated in industries with "sub-

[8] Bain, "Relation of Profit Rate to Industry Concentration."

TABLE XVII

Number of Industries of "High" and of "Moderate to Low" Concentration Which Have Industry Average Profit Rates [a] on Equity of Specified Sizes, 1936–40 and 1947–51

Size of industry average profit rate on equity (after income taxes) in percentage points	Number of industries with average profit rates in specified ranges of percentage points			
	1936–40		1947–51	
	Industries of "high" seller concentration	Industries of "moderate to low" seller concentration	Industries of "high" seller concentration	Industries of "moderate to low" seller concentration
25–25.9	1			
24–24.9				
23–23.9				
22–22.9			1	
21–21.9	1		1	
20–20.9				
19–19.9				
18–18.9	1		3	
17–17.9				
16–16.9				
15–15.9	2		2	1
14–14.9			1	1
13–13.9	2		1	1
12–12.9			2	2
11–11.9	1			1
10–10.9		1	1	1
9– 9.9	1	1		
8– 8.9	2	1		
7– 7.9	1	1		
6– 6.9		1		
5– 5.9		1		1
4– 4.9				
3– 3.9		3		

[a] Industry average profit rates are simple averages of the profit rates of dominant firms, as identified above.

TABLE XVIII

Number of Industries with "Very High," "Substantial," and "Moderate to Low" Barriers to Entry Which Have Industry Average Profit Rates [a] on Equity of Specified Sizes — 1936-40 and 1947-51

Size of industry average profit rate on equity (after income taxes) in percentage points	Number of industries with average profit rates in specified ranges of percentage points					
	1936-40			1947-51		
	Industries with very high entry barriers	Industries with substantial entry barriers	Industries with moderate to low entry barriers	Industries with very high entry barriers	Industries with substantial entry barriers	Industries with moderate to low entry barriers
25–25.9	1					
24–24.9						
23–23.9				1		
22–22.9						
21–21.9	1			1		
20–20.9						
19–19.9						
18–18.9	1			2		1
17–17.9						
16–16.9						
15–15.9	2					
14–14.9			1		2	1
13–13.9		1		1	1	
12–12.9		1			2	1
11–11.9		1			1	1
10–10.0		1			1	1
9– 9.9		2				1
8– 8.9			1			
7– 7.9			2			
6– 6.9		1				
5– 5.9			1			1
4– 4.9		1				
3– 3.9			2			

[a] Industry average rates are simple averages of the profit rates of dominant firms, as identified above.

stantial" entry barriers, although such profits in the "moderate to low" barrier category would then be expected to be associated with structural instability and recurrent excess capacity. This last condition is apparently met in at least 3 of the 7 industries in the "moderate to low" barrier category — cement, flour, and shoes — and it is not ruled out in the case of meat packing and canned goods.

The findings are thus potentially consistent with our hypothesis about the association of profit rates to the condition of entry in this crucial range. The available data, however, are not sufficient to permit us to say that the hypothesis (as far as it distinguishes "effectively impeded" from "ineffectively impeded" entry) has been either confirmed or disconfirmed. The only clear finding relates to the distinction between industries with "very high" and lower absolute entry barriers. Industries with very high absolute barriers (and probably either "blockaded" or "effectively impeded" entry) seem to earn systematically greater rates of profit.

With respect to this finding, however, there remains a question. Is there an ascertainable *independent* influence of the condition of entry on profits, or on the contrary is there such an intercorrelation of the condition of entry and seller concentration that the separate importance of either alone cannot be ascertained? Apparently, some independent or net influence may be ascribed to the condition of entry as apart from concentration. If the seller concentration of industries in the different entry-barrier categories in Table XVIII is examined, the following appears. Although *all* 5 industries with "very high" entry barriers have high seller concentration, it is also true that 7 industries with only "substantial" or "moderate to low" entry barriers also have high seller concentration — not significantly different numerically from that of the first 5 — and that these 7 have systematically lower profit rates than the first 5. Among industries of high seller concentration, that is, the height of the barrier to entry seems to make a perceptible difference in profits.

Conversely, some independent influence may be ascribable to seller concentration *per se*. Within the "substantial" entry barrier category the industries of high seller concentration seem on the average to have significantly higher profits than those of medium seller concentration, and within the "moderate to low" category, a rough relationship of seller concentration to profits is again apparent. In effect, condition of entry and seller concentration are by no means perfectly intercorrelated, and both variables appear to have some independent influence on profit rates. All these conclusions, of course, rest on visual appraisal of tables and charts and not on statistical averaging and significance-test procedures.

The apparent independent influence of the condition of entry is illustrated in Table XIX, which classifies the profit rates of the 12 industries *of high seller concentration* according to the heights of the barriers to

TABLE XIX

Number of Industries, All of High Seller Concentration, with "Very High," "Substantial," and "Moderate to Low" Barriers to Entry, Which Have Industry Average Profit Rates[a] on Equity of Specified Sizes – 1936-40 and 1947-51

Size of industry average profit rates on equity (after income taxes) in percentage points	Number of industries with average profit rates in specified ranges of percentage points					
	1936-40			1947-51		
	Industries with very high entry barriers	Industries with substantial entry barriers	Industries with moderate to low entry barriers	Industries with very high entry barriers	Industries with substantial entry barriers	Industries with moderate to low entry barriers
25–25.9	1					
24–24.9						
23–23.9						
22–22.9						
21–21.9	1			1		
20–20.9						
19–19.9						
18–18.9	1			2		1
17–17.9						
16–16.9						
15–15.9	2				2	
14–14.9					1	
13–13.9		1	1		1	
12–12.9				1		1
11–11.9		1			1	
10–10.9						
9– 9.9		1				
8– 8.9		2				
7– 7.9			1			

[a] Industry average rates are simple averages of the profit rates of dominant firms, as identified above.

entry to these industries. (It may be noted that no systematic or significant difference in seller concentration appears among the different entry-barrier categories.) There is a general appearance (stronger in 1936–40 than in 1947–51) that among industries of high seller concentration, those with very high entry barriers tended on the average to earn significantly higher profit rates than those with lesser entry barriers. This tends to confirm a part of our hypothesis concerning the relation of profits to the condition of entry. *It also suggests that seller concentration alone is not an adequate indicator of the probable incidence of extremes of excess profits and monopolistic output restriction.* The concurrent influence of the condition of entry should clearly be taken into account. When the possible association of the condition of entry to profits among the 8 industries with moderate to low seller concentration is examined, no clear relationship is found. Since all of these industries have either "substantial" or "moderate to low" entry barriers (none have "very high" barriers), and since an impact of the condition of entry on profits within this range was not found in Table XVIII, this finding was to be anticipated.

The preceding findings are of course based on data so incomplete and on a sample so small that no conclusive confirmation or disconfirmation of our theoretical hypotheses has been possible. Two tentative judgments, however, emerge. First, dominant firms in industries with very high entry barriers tend systematically to earn higher profit rates than those in industries with lower barriers, even after the separate influence of seller concentration is allowed for. Second, dominant firms in industries with "substantial" entry barriers do not appear to earn higher profit rates than those in industries with "moderate to low" barriers. This is potentially consistent with our hypothesis, if in fact the entry barriers in the "moderate to low" category are low enough so that the dominant firms find entry-forestalling price policies unattractive. Whether or not this crucial condition is fulfilled cannot be adequately demonstrated from available data.

Selling costs and the condition of entry

One seemingly obvious hypothesis developed from our analysis of Chapters 1 and 6 was that there should generally tend to be a positive association between the height of the product-differentiation barrier to entry to an industry and the size (measured probably as a percentage of sales) of its costs of sales promotion. This association would presumably rest on the suppositions (1) that stronger product differentiation is ordinarily accompanied by or rests upon larger selling costs; and (2) that higher product-differentiation barriers to entry are generally erected and maintained by higher selling costs.

Testing of this hypothesis is made difficult by the inadequacy of available data. As regards advertising, we have data for about three-quarters of our 20 industries from the Federal Trade Commission report entitled *Distribution Methods and Costs*,[9] but these in general refer to a single prewar year and the basis of their calculation is not always apparent. In addition, we have been able to develop, again for about three-quarters of the industries, data on *traceable* advertising costs (periodicals, newspapers, radio, and television) for the period around 1950. But these "traceable" costs are, because of the basis of compilation and counting, short of actual advertising costs by varying and unpredictable margins, so that they do not lend themselves well to analyses involving inter-industry comparisons of advertising costs. In addition, there is the problem of sales-promotional costs other than advertising, which may be quite important in some industries. Here we have mainly the F.T.C. estimates (from the source just mentioned) of "selling and delivery" costs other than advertising, or alternatively of "selling and general administrative costs" for about three-quarters of our industries. The difficulty with these data is that it is impossible to determine what proportion of the designated costs are properly classifiable as "sales promotional," and what proportion ascribable to routine physical distribution. In consequence, only the roughest sorts of judgments can be made concerning the relation of actual sales promotion costs to the height of the product-differentiation barrier to entry.

The general findings of our analysis of this matter are as follows:

(1) Industries previously classified as having slight product-differentiation barriers to entry generally have the lowest advertising costs. These include the copper, rayon, commercial flour, gypsum products, meat packing, cement, steel, low-priced men's and women's shoe, and standard canned goods industries. Nearly all of these have apparent actual advertising costs under 1.5 per cent of sales; in no case do the costs apparently run above 2.5 per cent of sales.

(2) Industries classified as having moderate product-differentiation barriers to entry on the average have somewhat higher advertising costs in most cases, but generally not very large ones. These include the specialty canned good, high-priced men's shoe, metal container, tire and tube, petroleum refining, soap, and consumer-brand flour industries. Generally, actual advertising costs would appear to run from 2 to 5 per cent of sales in these industries. They are higher, however, for the soap industry (6 to 10 per cent of sales) and lower for metal containers and petroleum refining, although in the last case non-advertising promotional costs appear to be fairly important.

(3) Among 6 industries with great product-differentiation barriers to entry, there are 3 for which apparent actual advertising costs are high —

[9] Part V, 1944.

running from 5 to 8 per cent of sales. These are the cigarette, liquor, and quality fountain-pen industries. In 3 others, however — autos, tractors and farm machinery, and typewriters — apparent actual advertising costs run only from 1.5 to 3 or 4 per cent of sales, although in each of these cases qualitative evidence suggests that non-advertising sales-promotion costs are quite substantial. If this is so, all industries in this category have selling costs in the highest range.[10]

Unfortunately, data on non-advertising sales-promotion costs are so sketchy that no more precise judgments are possible. These tentative findings are not inconsistent with our hypothesis, but they could scarcely be said to verify it in detail.

The condition of entry and the workability of competition

Because of the incomplete nature of the check on our predictions of the association of performance to the condition of entry, as well as the limited scope of these predictions, it is not possible to state any definite conclusions on how the condition of entry affects the workability of competition. A few extremely tentative indications are apparent, however.

First, industries with very high barriers to entry tend more toward high excess profits and monopolistic output restriction than others. If in addition they have great product differentiation barriers to entry (they do in 5 of 6 cases), they probably tend toward high and possibly excessive costs of sales promotion. In their favor it may be said that wastes of inefficiently small scale and excess capacity are not beyond the normal limit among them.

Second, industries with somewhat lower though still substantial barriers to entry tend toward smaller excess profits, smaller selling costs, and a lesser degree of monopolistic output restriction. In addition, they generally have a reasonably efficient adjustment of plant and firm scales and of total capacity relative to demand. Some "degree of monopoly" is usually apparent in the performance of these industries, but it is clearly moderated in comparison with those in the first group. Competition seems, on the basis of the limited range of criteria here applied, "more workable" than in the first group — apparently or possibly because of the greater force of potential competition.

[10] A possible qualifying argument is that by incurring these large advertising costs, and concurrently exploiting advantages of large-scale promotion, firms in these industries attain lower physical costs of nationwide distribution than they otherwise might. This is not impossible in one sense — namely that there are conceivable alternatives, retaining product differentiation and nationwide promotion but restricting the promotional budgets of individual firms, which would possibly elevate distribution costs. But it could hardly be argued — theoretically or from the evidence — that distribution costs would be higher in the substantial absence of product differentiation and

Third, industries with "moderate to low" barriers to entry do not appear to score significantly better in the matter of excess profits and output restriction than those with "substantial" barriers, though they do no worse and perhaps better in the matter of selling costs. Some of them at least, however, are apparently plagued with the inefficiency of chronic or recurrent excess capacity, the possible origin of which has been rationalized above. It is not generally clear that the lower barriers to entry in this category are associated with a more workable competition than is found in the middle category, and the reverse is possibly true.

Fourth, seller concentration may tend to affect the workability of competition within given categories of industries as identified according to the height of the barrier to entry. In particular, performance may be generally more satisfactory among industries with "substantial" or "moderate to low" entry barriers if seller concentration is moderate or low rather than high. But seller concentration alone does not appear to be an adequate criterion of the workability of competition, since high seller concentration seems to be connected with significantly different sorts of performance, depending on the height of the barrier to entry.

Finally, as indicated in previous chapters, the main culprit in establishing excessive or very high barriers to entry would appear to be product differentiation. It is a strong contributing factor in 2 cases where such barriers are found (automobiles and typewriters) and the dominant factor in the other 3 (cigarettes, liquor, quality fountain pens). Extremes in differentiation between established and potential-entrant products spell difficulty with respect to the barrier to entry. On the other hand, moderate product-differentiation barriers to entry may be relatively innocuous. Extreme scale economies pose a serious problem in perhaps only 2 of the 20 industries studied.

---

sales promotion, or under every conceivable alternative pattern of product differentiation and promotion. This distinction is clearly relevant to regulatory problems.

8

THE CONDITION OF ENTRY
AND THE PUBLIC POLICY
Designed to Secure Workable Competition

Although the primary orientation of this volume is toward theoretical prediction and its implementation and testing with empirical data, some brief attention may be given to the implications of our findings for public policy.

Such implications as there are have bearing primarily on the antitrust, anti-monopoly, or pro-competitive policy of the federal government as it deals with the organization of markets and the market behavior of business firms. This policy, stemming from the Sherman Act and from later legislation in the same tradition, may undertake generally to secure or preserve market structures conducive to workable competition, and also lines of market conduct by sellers or buyers having the same tendency. Revision of market structures, and the prevention or discouragement of certain changes in them, particularly in the dimensions of horizontal seller concentration, vertical integration, and the condition of entry have all been important though perhaps not dominant aspects of past antitrust policy.

Since the condition of entry is a dimension of market structure that may have a distinct impact on the character and workability of competition, it seems reasonable that an antitrust policy, under either existing legislation or new law, might give more systematic attention than it has previously to revisions of the condition of entry which would favor more effective competition, and to the prevention of changes in the condition of entry which would adversely affect the workability of competition. Some actions along these lines are of course already a part of established policy. For example, attacks on "exclusionary tactics" designed to exclude new competitors, on exclusive dealing and tying contracts with distributors having the same effect, and on certain types of administration of patent rights designed to deny to potential entrants necessary access to techniques or product designs, are well known. What is suggested here is that a somewhat more general and comprehensive attention might be given under the law to the preservation of a socially desirable condition of entry to our industries — the preservation of an effective degree of *potential* competition.

Our comments here will not pretend to contain even a cursory survey of antitrust policy as a whole or any outline prescription for the future of that policy in all its aspects. They will be confined rather to suggestions as to the extent to which and the manner in which the pro-competitive policy might deal with the condition of entry in order to improve the workability of competition. Even within this restricted sphere, such suggestions as we may make are highly tentative or provisional. They are based either on tentative and only partly tested theories or on the results of an empirical study of only 20 industries. Their factual foundation is thus not overly firm, and in addition they rest on an evaluation of the condition of entry almost solely in terms of its effects on long-run tendencies in monopolistic output restriction, excess profits, efficiency in scale of firm and plant, and selling costs. The condition of entry has not been evaluated in terms of its possible effects on progressiveness in technique or product, on cyclical stability, or on other dimensions of market performance. In consequence, these policy suggestions are potentially subject to revision or qualification if the association of the condition of entry to the neglected aspects of market performance should turn out to be of a certain sort. With these disclaimers on record, let us proceed to the implications of our findings for public policy.

General indications of a priori analysis

It may as well be emphasized at the outset that a great deal of what we can say on policy could have been offered on the basis of the underlying theoretical analysis, as reviewed in Chapter 1, without undertaking the empirical study presented above. The empirical study is important mainly in offering some tentative confirmation of the assumptions and theories on which the policy recommendations rest, in giving some quantitative implementation to qualitative judgments, and in establishing findings in areas where *a priori* predictions were quite indefinite. These contributions are perhaps not inconsiderable, although they are of a provisional sort; we merely wish to emphasize that the general character of the policy suggestions now offered was apparent in suggestions developed from the theoretical analysis alone.

In 1951, the present writer sketched out the basic theory involved and included some tentative policy suggestions.[1] The recommendations for policy were roughly as follows.

[1] See J. S. Bain, "Conditions of Entry and the Emergence of Monopoly," *Monopoly*

First, since higher barriers to entry tend in general to be associated with higher degrees of monopolistic output restriction and larger excess profits, given the extent of seller concentration probably accompanying them, a good beginning rule for policy should be to reduce high barriers to entry wherever this is feasible — striving for "effectively impeded" rather than "blockaded" entry, and for lower absolute barriers within the "effectively impeded" range. This should in general tend to bring entry-forestalling limit prices closer to the competitive level. Second, the principal exception to this general rule would be that if "effectively impeded" entry already existed, reductions in the barrier to entry to an "ineffectively impeded" status (where entry-forestalling limit pricing policies would cease to be attractive to established sellers) might be avoided, since if concentration were to remain fairly high, structural instability and related inefficiency might result. This suggestion is consistent with the observation that "effectively impeded" entry with barriers of moderate absolute heights may on balance be preferable to "ineffectively impeded" entry, at least in industries of fairly high seller concentration.

Third, as to the sorts of entry barriers which may be legitimately attacked, it was observed that those resting on real economies of large-scale plant and firm (whatever their importance) should not and probably could not be removed, because of the adverse effects on efficiency of such removal. On the other hand, the bases of strictly pecuniary economies of scale might be likely candidates for attack. As a result, the possibilities of reducing entry barriers based on scale economies would depend in large part on the relative importance of real and strictly pecuniary economies in the cases in question. It was added that there might be a great deal of administrative difficulty in devising a policy which would selectively eliminate strictly pecuniary economies without impairing the realization of real economies.

Fourth, it was suggested in consequence that the major part of a policy designed to reduce entry barriers would perforce be directed toward product-differentiation barriers and absolute cost barriers to entry. The techniques of policy having this aim were not discussed, but casual reference was made to patent-law reform, a policy designed to ease the supply of funds in the capital markets, attacks on resource monopolization by integrated processing firms and on unnecessary integration generally, consumer education, and grade labelling. Quantitative guesses as to the relative importance of the two sorts of entry barriers involved were not developed, but the writer must admit to an initially excessive estimate of the probable relative importance of absolute cost barriers other than those involving capital requirements.

and Competition and Their Regulation, edited by E. H. Chamberlin (London, 1954), pp. 215–241, and especially pp. 237–240.

Fifth, it was suggested that any policies tending to shorten entry lags (the interval between the emergence of an entry-attracting price and the establishment of a new producer in satisfactory operating condition) would be desirable, since the shorter the entry lag the less a barrier to entry of given height is likely to induce established sellers to follow high entry-attracting price policies as opposed to relatively low entry-forestalling limit price policies.

Sixth, it was suggested that reduction of seller concentration was by no means the sole key to a pro-competitive policy involving alterations of market structures. On the contrary, the results of fairly high seller concentration might vary widely according to the condition of entry to the industry, and alteration of the condition of entry might constitute a generally more feasible regulatory technique than dissolution and dismemberment policies aimed just at reducing seller concentration. In any event, an anti-concentration policy alone would probably prove to be insufficient.

The preceding constitutes a basic tentative outline of the suggestions for policy contained below. Let us see how much it has been elaborated, implemented, and revised in the light of our empirical study.

General reduction of entry barriers, to some limit

The leading suggestion for policy drawn from *a priori* analysis was that barriers to entry should be reduced, consistent with maintaining efficiency in production and distribution, at least to the lower end (in absolute values) of the "effectively impeded" range, as a means of lessening the incidence of monopolistic output restriction and excess profits. To this it was added that reducing barriers to the "ineffectively impeded" category might not be so desirable; very moderate barriers qualifying as effectively impeding entry might be conducive to better over-all performance in an industry.

This suggestion can be to a considerable degree reaffirmed in the light of our investigation. In effect, it appears that industries with aggregate absolute entry barriers classified as "very high" do indeed have on the average significantly higher excess profit rates than industries with only "substantial" or lower barriers to entry, and higher degrees of monopolistic output restriction. It was our guess that the "very high" barriers probably qualified either as blockading entry or as in the higher absolute range of effectively impeding it: entry could be forestalled either at industry profit-maximizing prices or at prices somewhat lower than that but still quite high relative to costs. On these assumptions, the finding in question appears to confirm in part our basic prediction. Correspondingly, we can reaffirm the suggestion that reduction of barriers to entry as high as those we have called "very high" should improve performance in the respects emphasized. Even without accompanying de-concentration actions, such a reduction might increase the workability of competition.

The light cast on our predictions and initial suggestions by a compari-son of the profit rates of industries of "substantial" and "moderate to low" aggregate barriers to entry is less distinct. Given our findings in Chapter 6 as to the aggregate entry barriers in various industries, it was our guess that the "substantial" barriers would probably qualify as effectively im-peding entry — that is, entry could and probably would be forestalled at prices below the monopoly level and with moderate excess profits. Fur-ther, our "moderate to low" entry barriers would probably qualify as either in the lower range of effectively impeding (adoption of relatively low entry-forestalling price, with lower excess profits than with substan-tial barriers, would be probable), or ineffectively impeding (with entry barriers slight enough that entry-attracting prices and at least periodic excess profits of significant size should emerge). What we found was (1) no apparently significant difference in profit rates between "substan-tial-barrier" and "moderate-to-low-barrier" industries; and (2) inclusion of chronic excess capacity in a part of the latter category of industries. Our difficulty is that this finding is subject to a variety of interpretations, and that we are unable to say which interpretation is valid. In conse-quence, the validity of our basic predictions as they affect this range of barriers to entry to industries cannot be confirmed or disconfirmed.

It is equally possible, for example, that:

(1) The "moderate to low" barriers to entry as identified ineffectively impede entry in most cases, so that entry-attracting price policies yield-ing moderate excess profits in the periods observed have resulted. This notion is given some support by the finding of chronic excess capacity in the cement, flour, and shoe industries, though it is uncertain in view of the general inadequacy of data on excess capacity. If this is true, the findings are potentially consistent with our theoretical hypothesis. The implication would be that though it would be desirable to reduce entry barriers to the low end of the "substantial" range as identified, it would not necessarily be desirable to drive them much lower — at any rate unless rather low seller concentration were simultaneously assured, and perhaps not even then. As this prognosis develops, perhaps the word "substantial" turns out to be a little strong as a description of entry barriers in the middle category of industries classified according to the absolute height of these barriers.

(2) Our empirical data are imprecise enough so that an invalid distinction has been drawn between the heights of entry barriers to industries classified as having, respectively, "substantial" and "moderate to low" barriers. This would make our findings potentially consistent with

our theoretical hypothesis, but would confine the reaffirmation of our policy suggestions to that based on a distinction between "very high" entry barriers and others.

(3) The rates of profit on equity are sufficiently imprecise measures of price-average cost discrepancies to cast doubt on the quantitative findings in question.

(4) Sellers in general are less sensitive to the threat of entry and to the opportunities for forestalling entry than our theory assumes, and thus do not react systematically to the relatively small differences between "substantial" and "moderate to low" barriers. This would tend to undermine the basis of our predictions, as well as at least part of the policy suggestions based on them.

With the data at our disposal, we are unable to determine which of these (or other) explanations of the empirical findings is valid. In consequence, we can only affirm our earlier suggestion that a reduction (consistent with efficiency) of "very high" entry barriers down only to a "substantial" status should be good policy as far as monopolistic output restriction and related phenomena are the objects of action, and leave quite uncertain the extent to which, if at all, it would be generally desirable and worthwhile to drive entry barriers below the "substantial" and into the "moderate to low" level. One possibility is that the drawing of unattainably fine distinctions would be required to implement a policy involving these further reductions of barriers to entry.

To our general positive conclusion, moreover — i.e. reduction of the very high barriers to entry — one qualification is suggested by our detailed empirical findings. That is, lowering a high entry barrier about enough but not too much is not necessarily a simple thing in practice; it is not quite so easy as drawing a window blind halfway down but not to the bottom. Considering the techniques of revision available, it would be fairly easy inadvertently to go so far with remedies that entry barriers would be lowered enough to encourage excessive entry and structural instability. And it is not impossible that in some cases no safe technique will be available.

Our general prescription for reducing very high barriers should thus not be construed as a recommendation for every action that influences matters "in the right direction." The varying potential results of any measure should be weighed (and potentially "over-efficacious" measures placed in a doubtful category). Also, the "side effects" of any measure on efficiency should be carefully scrutinized, in the light of the full complexity of actual situations, before accepting it.

Given this amendment to our earlier judgments on policy, let us turn to the relative importance of different sorts of entry barriers, and the means of treating them.

Scale economies, and other advantages of scale

A priori speculations about the policy problem of maintaining competition frequently emphasize the possibility or probability that in a fair share of manufacturing industries economies of scale of firm are so important that highly concentrated oligopoly is a prerequisite to efficiency. Hence, it is argued, the relatively unsatisfactory competitive conduct which is associated with high concentration must be accepted unless we are to reduce efficiency or to regulate directly. In industries where this was true, it would also hold that the scale economies in question would raise considerable barriers to entry, making the dilemma of the competitive policy more acute. Therefore, a very important question in appraising the over-all policy problem is what proportion of industries are affected by scale economies of such great importance.

The general finding based on our sample of 20 manufacturing industries (mostly either highly or moderately concentrated) is that very important economies of scale are found in a rather small proportion of the industries. Economies of scale were found clearly sufficient to impede entry substantially and lead to very high concentration in only 3 or 20 industries. Of 4 more industries for which systematic scale-economy data are not available, only one seems likely to qualify for the same category. Around 20 per cent of the industries in our sample thus present serious scale-economy problems. For the remainder, the economies in general probably do not require more than moderate concentration nor will they raise high barriers to entry. This is not to deny that perceptible (though moderate to small) barriers to entry are raised by scale economies in at least half of these remaining industries.

The scale economies in question that can be most definitely established are those of production and physical distribution. Such economies appear in a number of industries to be significantly reinforced, however, by advantages of large-scale sales promotion. These advantages are most evident in cases where integrated or quasi-integrated distribution has been used to advantage by manufacturers — as with autos, typewriters, farm machines and tractors, and petroleum products. In addition, there is the unproven possibility of advantages of large-scale advertising in the case of a number of consumer goods. In both cases, such promotional advantages of scale may be reinforced by some economies of physical distribution at multiplant scale, which are effective so long as nationwide or comparable distribution — required by optimal promotional techniques — must be presupposed.

The extent to which the economies in question are alternatively real and strictly pecuniary has been rather difficult to establish. The existence of strictly pecuniary economies of scale in production and distribution was frequently denied by our sources of information, and the enforcement of the Robinson-Patman law was given as a reason for the obliteration of certain strictly pecuniary economies formerly enjoyed. By and large, however, we have been unable to establish at all firmly the relative importance of the two sorts of economies in production and distribution. On the other hand, it appears that the bulk of the advantages of large-scale sales promotion are probably of a strictly pecuniary character, enhancing the revenues of the firms involved rather than actually reducing costs.

That economies of scale in production and distribution do not loom large as the basis of barriers to entry is fortunate for the policy-maker, because there is relatively little that can or should be done about them. In general, they establish entry barriers which we have to accept in order to get efficiency. To this generalization, however, there are at least two exceptions. First, it is legitimate and, from the standpoint of our problem, desirable to attack the bases of strictly pecuniary advantages of size such as are derived from monopsonistic buying power through the enforcement of legislation like the Robinson-Patman law. Second, the importance of scale economies is sometimes increased if the entrant is effectively forced to integrate backward or forward into an added stage of production in order to attain efficiency, for the reason that in the prior or succeeding stage, integrated established firms dominate the supply or the outlets. (We reserve the case of forward integration into final marketing outlets for separate consideration.) Now in this case, *if it is found that the integration is not required for real economy and does not reduce costs*, enforced disintegration of established firms, resulting in the establishment of non-integrated industries at both stages of production, may reduce the importance of scale economies at one or the other stage of production without offsetting disadvantages. Undoing of integration which is found to have neutral effects on costs may thus actually reduce barriers to entry without offsetting social loss and be conducive to more workable competition. The crucial question, of course, is whether or not in any particular industry the integration is economical. It is suggested that disintegration proposals be viewed under this added light, as well as in the light of more traditional standards.[2]

Sales-promotional advantages of scale appear in general to be private rather than social. They enhance profits without enhancing the general welfare, and at the same time they result in higher barriers to entry. Policies aimed at reducing these advantages may therefore appear virtually desirable in cases where existing entry barriers are currently excessive. The major difficulty is that such policies are not easy to devise.

[2] Of course, side effects of any disintegration, such as might engender distributive or other diseconomies of scale, should be watched, and compensating or correlative measures adopted, as a part of the disintegration policy, to forestall them.

In instances where the advantages of large-scale sales promotion to the manufacturer hinge on distributive integration, and where real economies of such integration are not apparent, a policy seeking distributive disintegration might be indicated (presuming entry barriers are excessive). Thus in cases like those of the automobile, farm machine, and petroleum-refining industries, the elimination of integration, and of quasi-integration through contractual exclusive-dealing arrangements, would tend to reduce the over-all advantages of large scale at the manufacturing level and to lower the barriers to entry perceptibly. If in these or other cases it were true that real economies were not realized from integration and that aggregate entry barriers were excessive, such disintegration policy might be indicated. The disintegration remedies in the recent movie antitrust cases suggest a movement along this line. (We expressly do not undertake here to pass on the question of real economies of distributive integration in the industries mentioned as examples, or to recommend any particular policy with respect to them.)

As we have argued in Chapter 4, the existence of net advantages of large-scale advertising *per se* is in doubt. As far as such advantages do exist, they could also be attacked. We defer discussion of policy measures appropriate to this phase of possibly undesirable advantages of scale until a later section.

Two qualifying provisos must be added to the preceding. First, incursions on existing promotional advantages of scale could conceivably result in some industries in a market structure wherein physical distribution would become less economical. This would be a possibility, for example, if (a) existing firms in these industries still (after the incursion) had enough advantage from nationwide promotion and distribution to induce them to promote and distribute nationally; but (b) their advantages were reduced in such manner and degree that they could no longer maintain as efficient a distributive volume as previously through various "nodes" in the distributive system — essentially because of deconcentration consequent on the reduction of promotional advantages of scale. It follows that the ultimate impact on the organization of an industry of any regulative measure that affects promotional advantages of scale must be carefully appraised before it is approved. As indicated, certain "in-between" measures could lead to waste in some industries. The desirable measures there would be those which either (a) lowered barriers to entry somewhat without in effect undermining national (or comparable) sales promotion or the organization of the industry as it affects distributional economies; or (b) disrupted the processes of sales promotion enough so that firms in the industries in question would find it profitable thereafter to promote and distribute locally or regionally, thus no longer encountering those scale economies in distribution predicated solely on nationwide promotion and distribution. Needless to say, distinguishing appropriate from inappropriate measures may be no easy task.

Second, certain distributional economies of the multiplant firm — "real" though they may be — are recognizable only "as of" the acceptance of nationwide distribution, which is in turn generally a corollary of nationwide sales promotion. Given measures affecting promotion which would thoroughly erase the advantages of nationwide promotion, these real distributional economies would drop out, and scale economies of the multiplant firm would become a less important deterrent to entry than they are, and have been represented, in the contemporary scene. The interaction between real scale economies and the institutions facilitating sales promotion is especially interesting to the serious student of anti-monopoly policies.

Absolute cost advantages of established firms

It is a commonplace in dissertations on the competitive policy that "artificial impediments" to entry should be attacked and as far as possible removed. The impediments usually cited stem from administration of patent rights and from resource monopolization via backward integration of processing firms. Such proposals are in our terms suggestions for the removal of the principal absolute cost barriers to entry.

Generally we are not inclined to disagree with these proposals. There is a serious question, however, about how far the recommended policy would take us in reducing excessive barriers to entry — in what proportion of cases these "artificial impediments" are an important source of barriers to entry. In our sample of 20 industries, such impediments do not appear to be of dominant importance. In only 3 industries — all of them involving resource control through backward integration by processors — were absolute cost barriers adjudged large; in the remainder, they were rated as slight to negligible. In none of the 20 cases was patent control found to be currently the source of a serious impediment to entry, although in two cases (gypsum products and metal containers) such impediments had been significant prior to the conclusion of antitrust actions around 1950. In a complete coverage of manufacturing industries, of course, added instances of entry barriers resulting from patent or resource control will be discovered. But it is our general impression that these "artificial impediments" are not pervasive sources of excessive barriers to entry, and that a policy directed primarily at them as the sources of such barriers would fall far short of the desired goal.

So far as these impediments are found to be strategic sources of excessive entry barriers, the appropriate public policy is fairly clear. First, regarding impediments resulting from resource monopolization by integrated established firms, disintegration movements are indicated *if the integration is not essential to efficiency in production or to effectiveness in the exploration for and development of new resources.* If it *is* essential, the resultant barrier to entry will almost have to be accepted. A considerable burden of investigation and proof would probably rest upon that public authority undertaking to implement a selective disintegration policy of the sort suggested.

In regard to patents, the sort of policy applied in the *American Can* and *U. S. Gypsum* cases (and also in the *National Lead* case) seems appropriate. That is, discriminatory administration of patent rights to exclude entry — either absolutely or through excessive royalties — should be attacked, and a practice of open licensing of all comers at fair and reasonable royalty rates should be secured. The developing trend in antitrust-law interpretation may suffice to secure this end; otherwise, legislative amendments of patent or antitrust laws might be required. (It is possible, though not certain, that in some cases compensating adjustments of institutions that encourage nationwide sales promotion would be required in order to forestall inefficient spreading of small or middle-sized firms over too large a market area.)

A final source of absolute cost barriers to entry is found in the size of capital requirements for efficient entry. Generally we have found that in a high proportion of the industries examined the absolute capital requirement is very large. It is suggested that large capital requirements place the potential entrant at a disadvantage, because he cannot secure the requisite funds at a rate as low as that available to established firms through the capital markets or through internal financing. What can be done about this barrier to entry?

It can hardly be removed entirely, and probably cannot be greatly reduced in the average case. Some suggestions, however, are appropriate:

(1) Disintegration and the prohibition of integration in cases where real diseconomies would not result therefrom may not only lessen the scale-economy barrier to entry but also reduce the effective absolute capital requirements for entry very significantly, thus lowering the barrier to entry.

(2) Since established firms operating *in other industries* frequently have the least disadvantage of all potential entrants to a given industry in acquiring the requisite capital, we should perhaps go slow in frowning officially on expansion of large firms via diversification to enter new fields. To discourage or prohibit this sort of diversification may well tend to raise the barriers to entry to industries generally, with adverse effects on competition. This disadvantage of an anti-diversification policy *vis-à-vis* large firms must be weighed carefully against the alleged dangers of the growth of gigantic firms *per se.*

(3) Government measures to ease the supply of capital to new firms —

via loan insurance, extra-fast depreciation writeoffs for tax purposes, etc. —
might be extended or developed, on the basis of a careful preliminary
study.

In other words, something at least can probably be done to lower
capital-requirement barriers to entry.

Product-differentiation barriers to entry

Perhaps the most surprising finding of our study — if previous casual
comment on barriers to entry is taken as the standard — is that the most
important barrier to entry discovered by detailed study is probably
product differentiation. That is, the advantage to established sellers
accruing from buyer preferences for their products as opposed to potential-entrant products is on the average larger and more frequent in occurrence at large values than any other barrier to entry. This is in any
event apparently true in our sample of 20 industries, and the writer is by
now prepared to guess that it is true in general. In 5 of 20 industries and
in dominant segments of 2 others, product-differentiation barriers were
found to be great; in only 6 industries, plus segments of 4 others, were
they found to be slight.[3] The impact of product differentiation on entry
thus appears stronger than that of either scale economies or absolute
cost advantages. In some cases — e.g., cigarettes, liquor, and quality
fountain pens — product differentiation almost alone is responsible for
very high aggregate entry barriers. In others — automobiles, tractors,
typewriters — it combines with very important economies of scale in
production to produce extremely high barriers. Any general policy designed to deal with the entry problem must pay major attention to the
impediments to entry raised by product differentiation.

But a feasible type of policy to deal with the problem is not easily
apparent. There is an evident propensity of the profit-seeking enterprise
to attempt to enhance profits through product differentiation, via the advantages it gives it over both established rivals and potential rivals.
Moreover, the enterprise tends to pursue a product-differentiation policy
unilaterally, and without the necessity of any sort of consensual action
that might run counter to laws against collusion or concert of action by
competitors. Furthermore, the psychology of consumers is very evidently
such that they are frequently susceptible to the blandishments of product-
differentiating sellers, so that we come at last to a presumably fairly
stable characteristic of human nature as the root of the trouble. For all
of these reasons, it is difficult to attack this sort of barrier to entry under
laws in the anti-monopoly or anti-collusion tradition, or to legislate it
away. Then too, it is difficult to organize any substantial political support
for measures designed to attack extremes of product differentiation.

[3] See Table XI above.

Given all these difficulties, we can offer no more than a few tentative comments. These all stem from the central observation that there is a good deal of institutional implementation for private policies of product differentiation, and that the institutions in question are not necessarily immutable. The strategic institutions are perhaps those of distributive integration and support of entertainment and news media through advertising expenditures of commercial concerns. In addition, we may mention the lack of an institution — adequate information services (governmental or otherwise) designed to disseminate detailed product information to buyers and to improve their knowledge of what they buy.

Our comments, then, are as follows:

(1) Where product-differentiation advantages of established firms rest heavily on distributive integration, either through ownership or through contractual arrangement, disintegration and prohibition of further integration would tend to reduce product-differentiation barriers to entry. Such a policy would seem desirable provided that it did not entail perceptible real diseconomies, and provided that it did not result in a "in-between" situation whereby firms were encouraged to undertake nationwide or comparable promotion and distribution with over-all scales inefficient for the performance of this task. The net impact of distributive disintegration on industry organization should be carefully analyzed and predicted before measures are taken along this line.

(2) Measures to restrict advertising expenditures, either absolutely or by taxation, may be considered as potentially in the public interest. But the qualification just stated applies; "in-between" outcomes are a danger to be avoided.

(3) Measures such as comprehensive grade-labelling or its equivalent, plus perhaps wide public dissemination of product information, would also be salutary, especially if they proceeded far enough to dissipate the advantages of nationwide sales promotion. The writer does not suggest that any or all of these measures is politically feasible, but they seem to embody the only apparent means of attack on excessive product-differentiation barriers to entry.

The policy toward seller concentration

We have recognized throughout that seller concentration has a concurrent influence — and probably an equally important one — with the condition of entry in determining the workability of competition in an industry. In other words, both actual competition and potential competition are important. Existing antitrust policy implicitly more or less recognizes this, although the economist commentators on that policy are inclined to give a preponderant emphasis to the effects of seller concentration, and then to append a few remarks on the problem of entry. Similarly, a great deal of attention has been given in antitrust actions of the Justice Department since 1941 to horizontal dismemberment as a proposed remedy for ineffective competition, and relatively less to the easing of entry.

Generally, this writer would subscribe to a policy of reducing very high seller concentration and keeping it from developing, subject to a freedom from diseconomies of such action and also subject to a careful interpretation of what is unduly high seller concentration. Tentative indications of studies cited above are that if we can secure situations where the first eight sellers (for example) control less than two-thirds of the market, the probabilities for effective competition are better than where the first eight firms control 80 to 90 per cent or more of the market. On the other hand, neither available evidence nor *a priori* logic support the notion that significant improvements in market performance would be likely to stem from turning a two-firm industry into a four-firm industry, or a four-firm industry into a six-firm industry (in both cases concentration remains in the very high range and alteration of behavior is improbable), or from dismembering the "big four" firms of an industry when together they control perhaps two-fifths of the market (concentration is probably already so low that further deconcentration is unnecessary or pointless). But some carefully calculated controls on concentration are probably supportable, though further study is needed to establish the character of such controls.

In devising a policy toward seller concentration, in any case, the following should be kept in mind with respect to the condition of entry, especially since dissolution and dismemberment policies may be costly and hard to secure under existing judicial interpretations of the law: The market performance of the highly concentrated industry may be much better from a social standpoint if it is not protected by very high barriers to entry. In consequence, policies designed to reduce excessive barriers to entry may be considered as *alternatives*, as well as supplements, to a policy designed to reduce seller concentration. High concentration may be a relatively innocuous phenomenon if entry barriers can be reduced to a moderate level.

Comments on the existing competitive policy

To what extent is the existing competitive policy, as embodied in our antitrust and related laws, adequate to deal with the problem of barriers to entry? No detailed analysis of this issue will be attempted here, but some suggestions may be briefly presented. The existing law has several evident applications to reducing excessive barriers to entry or to preventing their erection in the first place. These include:

(1) The application of the Sherman Act to exclusionary tactics (di-

rected against potential entrants), as exercised unilaterally by a dominant firm or in concert by an oligopoly of leading firms. This application might conceivably extend to the prohibition of resource monopoly via backward integration and to some limits on selling expenditures (see the last *Tobacco* case), but to date we are without clear precedents for the application of positive remedies in these areas by the courts. Whether the application of the Act could be extended by interpretation is a matter for speculation.

(2) The application of the Sherman Act to a restrictive administration of patents which is designed to exclude entry. Numerous actions, some apparently effective, have been undertaken, and a considerable extension of this policy under existing law seems possible.

(3) The application of the Sherman Act to vertical integration by dominant firms, seeking disintegration under a joint monopoly charge. As in the movie cases and in the pending case involving the Pacific Coast petroleum industry, the entry-impeding effects of scale economies might be reduced by enforced disintegration. It is not as yet apparent, however, that under existing law, remedies could generally be secured for integration having noxious effects on the condition of entry.

(4) The application of the revised Section 7 of the Clayton Act, prohibiting mergers having the tendency (incipient or actual) to create monopoly or lessen competition. Although this is a new law in its revised form, its application could conceivably have a tangential effect on heading off integrations which would impede entry, and a direct effect in forestalling the establishment of large firms which would be likely to succeed in erecting more formidable product-differentiation barriers to entry.

(5) The application of Section 2 of the Clayton Act (the Robinson-Patman Amendment) to the elimination of strictly pecuniary advantages of large scale, such as inhere in the monopsonistic power of the large buyer.

(6) The application of Section 3 of the Clayton Act (involving tying and exclusive-dealing contracts) to the prohibition of quasi-integration into distribution, where that would have the effect of heightening product-differentiation barriers to entry or enhancing the advantages of large scale. Until recently, a mild policy has been followed under this section, principally as a result of conservative judicial interpretation. The *Standard Stations* and *International Salt* decisions, however, suggest that a much more aggressive policy may have now become feasible.

If we view the potentialities of existing legislation as a whole, it is apparent that it might well be stretched in its application to deal fairly effectively with barriers to entry resulting from some advantages of large-scale sales promotion, from some product-differentiation advantages of large firms, and from most absolute cost advantages of large firms. But by no means can this be done with certainty, and if at all, perhaps with such crudity that losses might outweigh gains. The probability is that legislative supplementation of existing law would be required on a number of points in order to support an effective policy regarding the limitation on barriers to entry, and the precise character of desirable supplements could be specified only after detailed further study.

The principal basic deficiency of policy based on existing legislation is its substantial inability to deal (except through disintegration under joint monopoly charges, and then perhaps crudely) with the very important product-differentiation barriers to entry. Bases for action are shaky, and remedies are not apparent. In this area it would appear that a novel approach in regulatory legislation and in the assumption of functions by the government is probably required to bring serious pressure to bear on some of the most embarrassing excessive barriers to entry. But the development of an adequate policy must presuppose a fair adjudication and balancing of all interests and views, economic and otherwise, which bear on the whole matter.

Lacking or pending various sorts of legislative innovation, however, it seems probable that vigorous but careful use of existing law, within the clear orientation of the condition-of-entry problem, could go a considerable distance toward lowering excessive barriers to entry and thereby enhancing the workability of competition in American industry.

APPENDICES

APPENDIX A

Examples of Individual-Industry Questionnaires

The following lists of questions, submitted to firms in the rubber tire and cement industries, are examples of the various individual-industry questionnaires employed. Omitted from the following are (a) explanatory preambles and covering correspondence; and (b) examples of "follow-up" questions, sometimes presented orally or in writing after initial responses had been received.

I. Rubber tire industry questions

1. Concerning the size of plant or firm necessary for efficiency in the rubber tire industry:

   A. What, in your opinion, is the most efficient size for a single plant (in terms of daily or annual output capacity) devoted to producing tires and tubes?
   (1) In a wide range of sizes?
   (2) Specializing in a few popular sizes?
   B. What is your estimate of the percentage increase in production costs per tire (as compared to those of the plant of the most efficient size) which would result from using plants with respectively one-fourth, one-half, and three-fourths the capacity of the most efficient plant?
   C. Various published data show the largest four firms in the industry as obtaining significantly lower production costs per tire of given grade than smaller firms. If these data accurately represent the true situation, to what is this lower cost attributable:
   (1) Large plants, which are more efficient because of their size?
   (2) Multiplant operation, with resultant economies of management?
   (3) Just higher quality management and production organization, unconnected with size?
   (4) Lower material costs?
   D. If a new firm can lower its production costs by becoming large enough to operate several plants, how many plants, and what total output capacity, would probably be necessary to realize fully these cost advantages?

E. Do the wholesale distribution costs per tire of large firms (like the Big 4) — exclusive of advertising — tend to be the same, larger or smaller, than those of smaller firms, on replacement tire business? What reasons account for any difference, and how large is the usual difference?

F. Does growth to a size which permits extensive use of national advertising media lead to any net advantage, as in realized selling price net of sales promotion cost for a tire of given grade?

G. A general impression gathered from published data is that the Big 4 tire producers as a group have (a) lower production costs, and (b) a better relation of net realized price of replacement tires to production plus selling (i.e. full) cost, then smaller firms as a group — but that they do not show larger earning rates on investment than smaller firms because they average in their original equipment business, on which profits are negligible, zero, or negative.

(1) Is this an accurate characterization of the relative positions of large and small firms vis-à-vis earning power?

(2) Are the low-profit or no-profit original equipment sales of the Big 4 probably a necessary device for sustaining the more profitable volume in replacement tires? That is, is the maintenance of original equipment volume — presumably possible only at low prices — a prerequisite sort of indirect sales promotion without which the large companies could not easily maintain their relative positions in the replacement market?

If not, why should they have continued to accept, and maintained capacity to supply, the unprofitably original equipment business?

H. What is your estimate of the current total investment, including working capital, necessary to establish:

(1) A single plant of the most efficient size in the tire industry?

(2) A single firm of the most efficient size?

2. Concerning advantages of established firms which result from established brand preferences of buyers:

A. In your opinion, are replacement tire buyers strongly enough attached to individual brands to permit some sellers (e.g. the Big 4 and one or two others) to secure a higher net price for a tire of comparable quality than its competitors can? If so, to what extent is this higher price offset by added sales promotion and service expenses?

B. If a new firm were to enter the industry at a relatively efficient size, what would be likely to be its net disadvantage (as compared to the more successful firms in the industry) over a ten-year period, in either net selling price or in sales promotion cost per unit, in order to secure a share of the market proportional to its capacity?

(1) If it sold its own brand in replacement channels?
(2) If it catered largely to mass-distribution houses affixing their own brands?

3. Concerning advantages of lower production costs to established firms:

A. Assuming that a new firm built to a size comparable with that of the more efficient established firms, would it nevertheless tend to incur higher production costs for any reason? For example:

(1) Higher costs of financing?
(2) Inability to obtain expert management personnel?
(3) Lack of production "know-how"?
(4) Lack of access to patented processes?
(5) Higher costs of natural or synthetic rubber or of other materials?
If so, what would be the magnitude of the disadvantage from any of these sources?

4. What category of organizations would you regard as presenting the most active "threat of entry" to rubber tire manufacturing — i.e. as the most likely to enter if there were a favorable price and profit situation:

A. Mass-distribution organizations, like mail-order houses or oil companies?
B. Automobile manufacturers?
C. Firms now engaged in other lines of manufacture?
D. "New" firms not now engaged in manufacturing?
Is there thought to be any crucial maximum profit margin on tires which could not be exceeded persistently without attracting considerable entry:
(1) To the production of original equipment tires?
(2) To the production of replacement tires?

II. Cement industry questions

1. Concerning the size of plant or of firm necessary for maximum efficiency in the cement industry:

A. What, in your opinion, is the most efficient size of a single plant (in terms of daily or annual output capacity) for producing cement?
B. How much higher would costs per unit of output be with plants of successfully smaller size — e.g. one-half or one-fourth of the most efficient size?
C. What would be the current investment, including working capital, necessary to establish a single plant of the most efficient size?
D. Are there evident reductions of *production* cost attainable by a

firm through growing to a size where it operates several plants of efficient size? Of *distribution* cost? If so, how large, in terms of overall output capacity, would the firm need to become to attain maximum efficiency? How much lower costs could it then attain than an efficient single-plant firm?

E. What would be the principal sources of production or distribution cost reduction to such a large firm?

F. What would be the current investment necessary to establish a cement firm of the most efficient size?

2. Concerning advantages of established firms which result from established brand-preferences or company goodwill.

A. Is there *any* significant attachment of buyers to the cements of individual manufacturers?

B. Is this attachment strong enough to permit one cement manufacturer to obtain a perceptibly higher price than his competitors?

C. If a new firm were to enter the industry at a single-plant size, what disadvantage would it tend to have, either in net selling price or in per unit sales promotion costs, as compared to efficient established firms, in order to gain a share of the market proportional to its capacity, and for how long would it suffer this disadvantage?

D. What would the answer to these questions (in C above) be for a new firm of efficient multiplant size?

3. Concerning advantages of lower production cost to established firms.

A. Assuming that a new firm were to build to a size comparable with that of the most efficient established firms, would it nevertheless tend to incur higher production costs for any reason, and if so, by about how much? For example, would it suffer perceptibly from:

(1) Higher costs of financing?
(2) Inability to obtain expert management personnel?
(3) Lack of production "know-how"?
(4) Higher costs of any raw material or equipment item?

4. What category of organizations would you regard as presenting the most active "threat of entry" to the cement industry:

(1) Construction companies?
(2) Firms engaged in other lines of manufacture?
(3) "New" firms not now engaged in manufacture?

APPENDIX B

Economies of Large Plants: Supplementary Data

In addition to replies to our questionnaires, we have as a source of data on plant economies some analysis of historical costs of various plant sizes, some qualitative appraisals of such economies by authors of industry studies, and some relatively detailed statistics on plant sizes. It is unfortunate that only for 8 industries have any reasonably extensive supplementary data been found. Nevertheless, it may be useful to discuss such findings as are available, if only as a partial check of the accuracy of the questionnaire findings reported above.

The findings on plant economies from these miscellaneous sources are generally consistent with those already developed. Disagreements with previous findings are in general minor ones of detail, and in no case is a major revision in general qualitative conclusions concerning the size of a minimum optimal plant or the shape of the plant scale curve suggested. In addition, we may note the following by way of introduction.

First, a main reason for the paucity of supplementary data on plant economies is that many of the size-cost analyses which have been prepared from Federal Trade Commission, O.P.A., and similar records actually apply to firms and not to plants, and are in such form that it would be unduly hazardous to infer from them much concerning the relation of cost to plant size. The multiplant organization of many of the firms studied is a principal reason for this. Thus, for example, cost data for tires and tubes and for cigarettes from O.P.A. records, and for farm machines and tractors from *T.N.E.C. Monograph No. 13*, are perhaps more appropriately applied to analyzing economies of the large firm (subsuming economies of large plants). Were it not for this limitation, more adequate data or at least some data on plant economies would be available for four or five additional industries.

Second, profit data are unsuitable for analyzing plant economies, not only because they are available almost entirely only by firms, but also because profits are presumably influenced and not infrequently dominated by factors other than plant scale economies.

Third, the historical cost data upon which some of the ensuing size-cost analyses rest generally relate unit costs to the actual outputs of plants in a given year or for the average of several years. The recorded costs are influenced to an unascertained degree by a number of forces other than the net or true relationship of plant scale to unit costs. These other forces would include (1) differing rates of plant utilization among different plants; (2) differing plant designs; (3) differences in factor prices (both those currently paid and those paid in the past for fixed equipment); and (4) unascertained or "random" forces. Unless the cost data refer to numerous plants and numerous years, therefore, and size-group average costs of demonstrated statistical significance can be developed, not too much importance should probably be attached to these historical cost data.

Unfortunately, the authors of *T.N.E.C. Monograph No. 13*, in which much of the available cost data are found, committed the grievous statistical sin of attributing importance to the mere size identity of the lowest-cost plant (or firm) within an isolated year or two — although they probably did not mislead many persons by this device — and even when they calculated size-group averages, they did not trouble to learn whether differences among size-group cost means were significant in the light of intra-size-group cost variances. (Apparently they are not in many instances.) Cost data have been used with more discretion by some, as we will see when we discuss Richard Tennant's use of them in connection with the cigarette industry. But in general, we must interpret with extreme caution historical cost data of the sort ordinarily available.

With this preamble, let us turn to the further sources of data bearing on economies of large plants, considering industries in the order in which they occur in Table III.

1. *Flour.* Estimates developed from questionnaire data placed the optimal daily capacity of a plant at from 0.1 per cent to 0.5 per cent of national capacity, which amounts to from 1,000 to 5,000 cwt. daily capacity. No definite estimate was developed on the rise of the plant scale curve at smaller capacities.

The principal source of additional data on flour is *T.N.E.C. Monograph No. 13*, which shows average milling costs for various size groups of flour mills in the periods 1926–28 and 1935–38.[1] Costs are stated to exclude wheat but to include manufacturing, selling and administrative, and paid interest expense; the total number of plants covered varies from year to year in a range from 57 to 146. These data recognize only four size categories for 1926–28, lumping all mills below about 1,300 cwt. daily capacity in the smallest size class. They show no relation of cost to plant size which one would judge, in the absence of detailed analysis, to be likely to have statistical significance.

[1] Pp. 60–61; the primary source cited is *Miller's National Federation*.

For 1935–38, however, 7 size classes are used, with the smallest covering plants with capacities below about 330 cwt. daily and the next smallest between 330 and 670 cwt. (approximately). Here, among size groups of plants down to the line of 670 cwt. daily capacity, there is no systematic cost difference which one would judge to be likely to be statistically significant, although the largest size class is above 10,000 cwt. daily capacity. For the 330–670 cwt. class, unit costs are about 8 per cent higher than the average for all larger groups, and for the below-330 cwt. class, they are about 20 per cent higher. Intraclass variance data are not available to test the significance of these differences, but costs do jump up markedly in the two smaller size classes, whereas they vary aimlessly and in a moderate range from class to class in the larger classes.

These findings are placed against the questionnaire findings that optimal plant scale in flour milling might run from 1,000 to 5,000 cwt. daily capacity. So far as they are accepted, they tend to modify and amplify the questionnaire findings to the extent of suggesting:

(1) That the minimum optimal capacity is probably not beyond 1,000 cwt. (our previous lower-limit estimate) and may be as small as two-thirds of this.

(2) That costs may be up from 5 to 10 per cent at one-half of optimal capacity and as much as 20 per cent at one-fourth of optimal capacity.

The general qualitative conclusion that plant-scale economies are quite unimportant in flour milling is unmodified by these data.

Plant-size statistics suggest that the largest actual plants in the industry — including perhaps the first 10 or 15 — are on the average two or three times larger than our top estimate of the minimum optimal scale. The first 6 plants in 1947 (*Census of Manufactures*) had a value added of output averaging 1.6 per cent apiece of the national total, as against our top estimate of 0.5 per cent. The next 16 plants averaged about 0.8 per cent apiece, and the next 77 plants just under 0.5 per cent. Nine large plants in the industry as identified [2] had capacities ranging from 0.4 per cent to 2.7 per cent of national capacity. At the other extreme, of course, there are many very small mills; 84 per cent of the number all reported mills (about 2,500 in all) had capacities of from 50 to 400 cwt. daily in 1939. These accounted for about a fourth of all industry capacity. But 47.6 of all capacity in 1939 was accounted for by about 520 mills with from 800 to 10,000 cwt. capacity.[3] Further information indicates that the mills below 400 cwt. capacity were generally underutilized to a point

[2] Federal Trade Commission, *Report on Growth and Concentration in the Flour Milling Industry*, 1947, pp. 2 ff. These are apparently the largest plants of General Mills, Pillsbury, Commander-Larabee, and Standard Milling.

[3] See H. G. Vatter, "The Problem of Small Enterprise as Seen in Four Selected Industries" (unpublished doctoral dissertation, University of California, Berkeley) pp. 278 ff.

approaching discontinuance. This array of plant-size statistics is potentially consistent with previous findings.

2. *Shoes.* The range of questionnaire estimates of optimal plant scale ran from 0.14 to 0.5 per cent of total national shoe output or from about 2,500 to about 10,000 pairs per day on the basis of a 250-day-per-year operation. At smaller scales, estimates have the plant scale curve ranging from quite flat to moderately sloped.

Additional information has been supplied by Mr. Brúce Cheek, at the time he was preparing a doctoral dissertation on the men's shoe industry at Harvard University. On the basis of field investigation and interviews, Cheek tended to place optimal plant scale for men's dress shoes in general at 2,400 pairs per day (there being little rise in costs back to 1,500 pairs per day), with the amendment that for *low-priced* men's dress shoes the optimum might go as large as 6,000 pairs per day. This more or less agrees with industry sources, which place the optimum as low as 2,400 pairs per day only for high-priced men's shoes or for women's shoes, and typically estimate the optimum to be in the neighborhood of 4,000 to 5,000 pairs daily otherwise. Clearly, the qualitative character of previous conclusions is not altered: plant scale economies are unimportant in the shoe industry with the possible exception of one or two relatively small product-price lines.

Plant-size statistics are not very revealing for the shoe industry. The first 15 plants in 1947 supplied on the average about 0.7 per cent of national value added, and the next 71 plants supplied about 0.2 per cent on the average.

3. *Canned fruits and vegetables.* Estimates from questionnaire data place optimal plant scale at from 0.25 to 0.5 per cent of national capacity, and suggest that the plant scale curve is at least moderately flat at smaller scales. According to Professor Leonard A. Doyle, who has made an extensive study of the canning industry, economies of plant scale are not pronounced in this industry, and considerations other than these economies ordinarily dominate the choice of plant sizes. More detailed quantitative information on the plant scale curve in canning has not been available. Plant concentration data show that, for canned fruits and vegetables, the largest 3 plants supplied about 4.3 per cent apiece of national value added, the next 3 about 0.9 per cent apiece, the next 21 about 0.6 per cent apiece, and the next 70 about 0.3 per cent apiece.

4. *Cement.* Estimates developed from questionnaire data placed the optimal annual capacity of plant roughly at between two and two and one-half million barrels — ranging from 0.8 to 1 per cent of national

capacity or 4 to 5 per cent of the largest regional submarket. Estimates also showed cement costs at 105 at about 70 per cent of optimal capacity, 115 at 40 to 50 per cent of that capacity, and 135 at about 20 per cent of that capacity, reflecting a relatively steeply rising plant scale curve.

The principal available further data here are again from *T.N.E.C. Monograph No. 13*,[4] the same or similar data being elaborated and summarized graphically in A. D. H. Kaplan, *Small Business: Its Place and Problems*.[5] These data refer to the actual costs and actual outputs of a large number of cement plants (102 are listed in *T.N.E.C. Monograph No. 13*), apparently for the one year 1929. Costs include all plant costs, administrative costs, and imputed interest on investment, but do not include selling costs or outshipment freight. In the cases where it is revealed at all, intra-class variance of costs seems to be quite large [6] relative to inter-class variance of means.

Calculations based on the data in *T.N.E.C. Monograph No. 13* suggest that costs for plants with production above one million barrels annually did not vary significantly with size — a finding based on a three-class breakdown (above two million barrels, below one million, and in between). Applying a 3/2 correction for underutilization, this would put optimal scale at from one and a half to two million barrels annual capacity, or a little lower than our questionnaire estimates. The huge intra-class variance casts some doubt on any findings drawn from this analysis, however.

The breakdown of these or similar data into 15 size classes, with an average cost for each class,[7] suggests that the optimal scale is at about a 3-million-barrel capacity, that costs are only 3 per cent higher at a 2-million-barrel capacity, but that they are definitely higher at a 1½-million-barrel capacity. These findings square fairly well with our questionnaire estimates so far as the minimum optimal scale is concerned, but suggest a somewhat steeper rise of the scale curve at smaller scales, as follows:

Optimal plant capacity as a percentage of the largest submarket capacity	6%	5%	3.5%	2%	1%	0.5%
Costs per consensus questionnaire estimates	100	100	105	115	135	"Prohibitive"
Costs per Kaplan and Blair	100	102	108	128	154	—

[4] Pp. 22 ff.

[5] New York, 1948, p. 83. The original data are attributed to the U. S. Tariff Commission and the graph to J. M. Blair, *Review of Economic Statistics*, Vol. 24, p. 129.

[6] See, e.g., *T.N.E.C. Monograph No. 13*, Table 1, p. 22.

[7] See Kaplan, *Small Business: Its Place and Problems*.

Again, modification of the general character of our previous findings is not suggested, but some added details are supplied. Variation in the rate of utilization of plants is apparent from some supporting data in the Blair-Kaplan series,[8] and it is uncertain how much this may have distorted the findings.

Some statistical data are available from other sources.[9] These indicate that the largest 7 plants in 1947 averaged 1.9 per cent of the national value added, and that the next 43 plants averaged 0.85 per cent (cf. our 0.8 to 1.0 per cent). Although statistics on individual plant sizes are not available, the average capacity of all cement plants in the United States is about 1.5 million barrels apiece, or a bit above 0.6 per cent of national capacity. It would appear that an appreciable minor fraction of cement was produced by plants with significant diseconomies of small scale.

5. *Distilled liquor.* Estimates from questionnaire data placed the minimum optimal plant scale (distilling through bottling, allowing for typical seasonal fluctuations) at from 1.25 to 1.75 per cent of national capacity, or from 22,500 to 32,500 gallons daily capacity (when operating). A very slight rise in costs was predicted for plant scales back to a sixth of the optimum.

The only supplementary data here concern actual plant capacities and outputs. In 1947, the largest 7 plants in the industry averaged 5.2 per cent each of national value added of shipments, and the second 9 plants averaged 2.9 per cent apiece. The first 16 plants thus accounted for 63.1 per cent of the total value added of shipments. These are of course shipments and not capacities, in an industry with a heavy average load of excess capacity. Figures on 1945 individual plant capacities are somewhat more revealing.[10] They show 139 whiskey distillers in all, with 43 operated by the "Big 4" multiplant firms. Of these plants of the big companies, eight have more than 2 per cent apiece of total national capacity, and two are above 6 per cent apiece. However, 29 of their plants are below 1 per cent apiece of the total national capacity. The wide diversity of plant sizes among large multiplant firms suggests that the scale of plant, at least down to 0.5 per cent or less of the national total, is not a very important consideration in overall costs and revenues.

6. *Farm machinery.* Estimates from questionnaire data describe the size of an optimal plant as sufficient to produce perhaps 1 or 1.5 per cent of the total value of farm machinery (excluding tractors), or, perhaps

[8] *T.N.E.C. Monograph No. 13*, pp. 24–25.

[9] See, especially, in addition to the 1947 *Census of Manufactures* and the *Minerals Yearbook, Federal Trade Commission vs. Cement Institute, Respondent's Brief, Appendix A, Volume I*; also the Circuit Court opinion in 57 F (2nd) 533.

[10] 79th Congress, 1st Session, Senate Judiciary Committee, *Hearings*, pp. 267 ff.

4 to 6 per cent of the value of any one major product category of the sort in which a single plant frequently specializes. The over-all estimate definitely excludes tractors and is also limited to "large and complicated" farm machinery such as combines, binders, threshers, mowers, tractor-drawn cultivators, haying machinery, etc.; it does not include small equipment such as horse-drawn plows, barnyard equipment, and ensilage cutters. The principal recognized categories of large equipment would probably include harvesting machinery, haying machinery, planting, seeding, and fertilizing machinery, and such things as tractor-drawn tillage tools. In a very rough way, the principal firms have specialized plants for individual broad categories of this general order, and the 4 to 6 per cent estimate refers to the proportion of value of output in such a single category which such a specialized plant, at minimum optimal scale, would supply. Economies of scale of plant are felt to be distinctly less important in the manufacture of relatively "small and simple" farm machinery.

Supplementary data referring to plants are extremely sketchy and refer only to aggregate values of all farm machinery. For all farm machinery other than tractors, the largest 20 plants in 1947 averaged 1.9 per cent apiece of national value added, the next sixteen 0.9 per cent, and so on. Obviously, these data reveal little of significance for our purposes.

7. *Petroleum refining.* Estimates from questionnaire data placed the optimal scale of a refining plant at about 120,000 barrels per day of crude oil throughput (raw material used), amounting to roughly 1.75 per cent of total United States throughput capacity. The scale curve estimate showed a very slight rise in costs back to half of optimal scale and a moderate one (5 per cent on costs) at a quarter of optimal scale.

This estimate assumed production with diversified facilities at a seaboard location, with crude oil brought in and products shipped out mainly by tankship (alternatively, shipped out by land to a *very dense* market near the refinery). Integrated transport by water was also assumed. In this setting, scale requirements in transport are not strategic in determining the optimal scale of the overall operation or the shape of the scale curve, since (according to questionnaire estimates) only a fraction of optimal refinery scale would be needed for efficiency in the use of tankships. For inland operations, costs of outshipment by land in even moderately dispersed markets ordinarily make a refinery of somewhat smaller scale more economical, but at the same time the optimal scale and the shape of the refinery scale curve at suboptimal scales are also influenced by crude oil transport costs if long trunk pipelines (e.g. 500 miles and up) are used to import crude oil. The latter effect offsets somewhat the effects of high outshipment costs in limiting optimal scale and makes the scale curve steeper at suboptimal scales.[11] In the estimates of percentages of regional capacities in optimal plants in Tables V and VI, variations in minimum optimal scales of refineries among areas have been recognized, but in Table VII the scale curve refers directly to a seaboard operation (such as those in New Jersey) only.

Detailed evidence on plant economies from sources independent of respondents to questionnaires (or other than secondary sources they cite) are not plentiful. The so-called Wilson data presented before the Temporary National Economic Committee and concerning refinery operating costs [12] are well known, but are from the same sort of source, are lacking in detail, and as far as ascertainable are in general agreement with our questionnaire findings. As suggested above, some interesting data from which scale curves for trunk pipeline transportation could be constructed are available, and these could be put to use in constructing detailed scale curves for numerous inland refinery locations variously related geographically to oilfields and customers.[13] Such an intensive enterprise for a single industry is not within the plan for this volume, and we will thus not pause further on this matter.

The major source of additional evidence applying to economies of large plant in petroleum refining is therefore found in detailed statistics of actual plant sizes — generally available in a form revealing actual net capacities only for refining proper and not for transport facilities. The *Census of Manufactures* showing that the average value added of the 55 largest refineries was about 1.2 per cent of the national total in 1947 (equivalent roughly to 85,000 barrels per day capacity apiece) is initially revealing. (The next 50 refineries average about 0.3 per cent, or a bit

[11] See, e.g., the implications in terms of costs per barrel of crude oil of the data presented in George S. Wolbert, Jr., *American Pipe Lines* (Norman, Okla., 1952), p. 10.

[12] *T.N.E.C. Hearings, Part 15*, p. 8636.

[13] See Wolbert, *American Pipe Lines*, p. 10. For example, calculations based on his figures would suggest the following *approximate* interest-plus-depreciation charges per barrel of delivered crude oil for a 1000-mile-long trunk pipeline (all fixed gathering, storage, and terminal charges and all operating costs neglected) of the designated alternative capacities:

Trunk pipeline capacity in barrels per day	Approximate interest and depreciation on trunk line, per 42-gallon barrel of delivered crude oil
10,000	$ 0.35
20,000	0.20
50,000	0.14
100,000	0.10
180,000	0.08
300,000	0.07

Direct applicability of such figures to a single refining operation would depend of course on the extent of the effective opportunity for joint use of a line by more than one refinery.

under 25,000 barrels per day capacity in equivalent terms.) More revealing are the detailed statistics of individual refinery sizes.[14] The following
table presents frequency distributions of refinery sizes by broad areas for
nearly all United States refineries in 1952: [15]

Size class of plant in barrels per day of throughput capacity	Number of plants in designated size class in:						
	East Coast area	Gulf of Mexico area	Mid-west area	South-west area	Cali-fornia area	Rocky Mountain area	Total
Above 150,000	1	6	1	—	—	—	8
100,000 – 150,000	4	2	1	—	4	—	11
50,000 – 100,000	5	6	3	4	5	—	23
25,000 – 50,000	2	7	17	4	1	3	34
10,000 – 25,000	2	6	12	24	4	4	52
5,000 – 10,000	3	3	15	22	12	11	66
Under 5,000	3	5	31	46	20	23	128
Total frequency	20	35	80	100	46	41	322
Percentage of U.S. capacity	15.0	31.5	21.0	14.0	15.0	3.5	100.0

From this summary it is clear that large refineries (above 50,000 barrel
capacity) are strongly favored in the three areas where water transport
can be extensively used — the Eastern seaboard, the Gulf, and the Pacific
Coast — though refineries of smaller sizes also persist in these areas. In the
interior market areas, on the other hand, refineries with capacities somewhere between 10,000 and 50,000 barrels per day are relatively more important, and a 100,000 barrel capacity is seldom reached or exceeded.

A breakdown of these data to show the plants of the typically multiplant "major" firms separately is also revealing. For the Eastern seaboard,
Gulf, and California areas combined, the majors had 49 refineries alto-
gether. Of these, 17 had 100,000 barrels per day or more capacity apiece;
15 more had capacities between 50,000 and 100,000 barrels; and only 12
had capacities below 25,000 barrels daily. Even in the Midwest, 19 out of
26 major refineries were above 25,000 barrels per day, so that only in the
rather dispersed inland markets of the Southwest and Rocky Mountain
area were refineries below the 25,000-barrel size common for multiplant
major firms. All of this seems to fit reasonably well with our finding that
optimal efficiency may be reached around 100,000 to 120,000 barrels of
capacity with relatively ideal transportation and market-density conditions, but that over-all costs of refined products are not too much elevated
back to a half and perhaps a quarter of this optimum.

[14] From Bureau of Mines, *Information Circular* 7646, 1952.
[15] Omits only about .75 of 1 per cent of total U. S. capacity — this in scattered
areas. The various areas are construed broadly for expository purposes here.

8. *Steel.* Estimates from questionnaire data placed the capacity of a fully integrated steel mill of optimal size at from 1 to 2.5 per cent of the national total circa 1950, or (roughly) at from 1 to 2.5 million ingot tons annually. It was also suggested that for the integrated operation, unit costs might be up as much as 5 per cent at a ½ million-ton capacity. Elaborating on this theme a bit, questionnaire replies also suggested that:

(1) In general, there would be some cost disadvantage to a semi-integrated operation featuring flat-rolled products without blast furnaces, the size of the disadvantage depending on the going rate of demand for blast-furnace capacity.

(2) A minimum size for an efficient semi-integrated operation making flat-rolled products would be about ½ million ingot tons annually and might be as large as 1 million tons.

(3) A range of products *outside the flat-rolled category* — produced from open-hearth, electric-furnace, and crucible processes — can be made fairly efficiently with semi-integrated operations depending on scrap iron or purchased pig iron or with integrated operations at capacities of from 100,000 to 500,000 annual ingot tons. The best lines for such operations are generally in the specialty steels, but they may survive well even in producing carbon steels in "regional spots" where, for example, local scrap prices are favorable in the light of shipping distances from major producing centers. The plant-economy picture in steel production is thus moderately complex.

The only supplementary source of information of much value here is found in statistics on steel-mill size. The *Census of Manufactures* for 1947 shows the largest 65 mills averaging about 1.1 per cent apiece of the total national value added of steel mills. Copious data on individual plant capacities are also available from industry sources. For the 8 largest steel firms (U. S. Steel, Bethlehem, Republic, Youngstown, Jones and Laughlin, National, Inland, and American Rolling Mill) a total of 51 steel-making plants were classified as to size in 1952: [16]

Annual capacity in millions of ingot tons	Number of steel mills
6.0 – 6.9	1
5.0 – 5.9	1
4.0 – 4.9	3
3.0 – 3.9	2
2.0 – 2.9	9
1.0 – 1.9	15
0.8 – 0.9	7
0.5 – 0.7	4
0.2 – 0.4	6
Under 0.2	3
Total	51

[16] Iron Age, *Official Steel Industry Capacities*, 1952.

The major firms, most of them multiplant to a significant degree, clearly have the bulk of their steel capacity in plants above the 1-million-ton line. On the other hand, there are about 30 semi-integrated steel producers (no blast furnaces) with capacities above 100,000 tons, plus a number of tiny producers, and of these 30, about 25 are between 100,000 and 500,000 tons annual capacity. Here we observe the role of the specialty steel and allied producers. In general, actual plant sizes correspond to expectations based on questionnaire estimates.

9. *Metal containers.* Estimates from questionnaire data placed optimal plant capacity at from 1/3 to 2 per cent of the national total (packers' and general-line cans together), or 2 to 12 per cent of the largest submarket (packers' cans only). This would have been roughly from 100 million to 600 million cans, with specialization of plant by product line assumed. Estimates were not made of the shape of the scale curve at smaller capacities. Industry sources did indicate, however, that technical plant economies continued to be realized beyond the stated minimum optimal scale, that plant size was strongly influenced by outshipment freight costs as related to the size and density of the particular market, and that the effective minimum optimal plant scale was thus variable, at least within the indicated limits, among areas.

The principal further source of information is Charles H. Hession's *Competition in the Metal Food Container Industry.*[17] Hession cites two estimates by industry sources: one to the effect that an annual demand of 24 million packers' cans will support a plant, and the other (attributed to American Can) that a firm would be willing to build a plant for a 100-million-can demand. By and large, not too much is added to our previous estimates.

Census statistics show that the largest 7 plants in the industry averaged about 3.3 per cent apiece of total industry value added in 1947, and the next 17 about 0.3 per cent apiece. American Can, in accounting for about 55 per cent of the dollar sales of packers' cans of the industry, is revealed by one source to have had 18 packers' cans plants in 1944, or about 3 per cent per plant, whereas its 14 general-line can plants accounted for about 56 per cent of the market or 4 per cent apiece. Continental can had 10 or 11 packers' cans plants and 31 per cent of the market in packers' cans, and 7 general-line can plants accounting for 25 per cent of that market. But Crown Can, for example, gets only about 1 per cent apiece of the market with its packers' can plants.[18] This about exhausts the available statistical data.

[17] Brooklyn, 1948, pp. 185 ff.
[18] Hession, pp. 67 ff.

10. *Meat packing.* Estimates from questionnaire data placed the optimal scale of meat-packing plants variously between 50 and 400 hogs per day and between 10 and 120 cattle per day in fresh meat packing, or between 3,000 and 5,000 hogs daily and between 150 and 1,200 cattle daily in diversified meat packing including curing, canning, and so forth. When these quantities are expressed roughly as percentages of the total non-farm slaughter of the animals involved, we find optimal plant scale in fresh meat packing running from 1/50 to 1/5 per cent of the national market, and in diversified meat packing at from 2 to 2.5 per cent. These estimates are coupled with the observation that the plant scale curve — especially in diversified meat packing — is quite flat back to much smaller scales.

In spite of numerous popularized and specialized writings on the meat-packing industry, there is very little supplementary information available on this point. Census statistics show that the largest 12 meat-packing plants supplied 1.8 per cent apiece of the value added of fresh, wholesale meat-packing in 1947. The next 35 plants supplied 0.7 per cent apiece; the next 39 about 0.3 per cent, the next 94 about 0.1 per cent. And 32 per cent of the total supply was provided by plants smaller than the 180 plants already mentioned. These figures cover the great bulk of wholesale slaughter of beef, veal, and lamb, but exclude about 80 per cent of wholesale slaughter of pork, together with all "retail" slaughter. Again, however, actual plant sizes seem to provide confirmation of estimates concerning the general effects of plant size on efficiency.

11. *Rubber tires and tubes.* Estimates from questionnaire data placed optimal plant scale at from 1.37 to 2.75 per cent of national capacity, or roughly 5,000 to 10,000 tire casings per day (passenger plus truck tires). The plant scale curve reflecting all costs (materials plus processing) was found to be quite flat back to a half of optimal scale, but up about 5 per cent in unit costs at a quarter of optimal scale.

Considerable miscellaneous information is available on actual plant sizes and costs in the tire industry. As to plant-size statistics, the 1947 Census shows that the first 13 plants supplied 5 per cent apiece of industry value added in tires and tubes, the next 16 plants 1.6 per cent apiece, the next 9 plants 0.7 per cent apiece, and the remaining 6 plants 0.4 per cent apiece. The dominance of plants as large or larger than our minimum estimate is evident. Another source [19] indicates that the largest Goodyear plant has roughly 14 per cent of total industry capacity, the 3 largest Firestone plants roughly 7, 4, and 3 per cent each, and the largest General

[19] 79th Congress, 1st Session, H. R., Committee on Judiciary, Subcommittee No. 3, *Hearings on H. R. 2357,* 1945, pp. 288 ff., testimony of Edward Fischer of the Federal Trade Commission.

plant 3.5 per cent. The *average* size of all plants for the "Big 4" companies is about 4.5 per cent of industry capacity for Goodyear, Firestone, and U. S. Rubber, and about 2.5 per cent for Goodrich. These "Big 4" plants (totalling about 18) apparently account for all or nearly all of the plants in the largest size group in Census data plus a few others, whereas the "independents" of the industry will except for the two or three largest have capacities at or below 1.5 per cent of industry capacity.[20]

Given the preceding understanding of the sizes of plants being compared, it is possible to draw some inferences from certain historical cost data in OPA records.[21] These data compare — primarily for 1941 — the factory costs per tire of given design and quality of a group made up of the "Big 4" firms to a group made up of either nine or ten unidentified "independent" firms. Although not specified, it would appear that all production for the firms covered is included, and not simply that for part of their plants. If this is so, the comparison of factory costs is a comparison of costs in about 18 "Big 4" plants having an average size equal to about 4 per cent of national capacity, with about 9 or 10 independent plants having an average size probably between 1.5 and 2 per cent of national capacity.

Any conclusions based on this comparison are extremely precarious in view of the substantial dispersion of plant sizes within each group. For whatever it is worth, however, this comparison for November 1941 for a 6:00–16 natural-rubber replacement tire of "100-level" quality shows:

(a) No significant difference in factory overhead and net waste costs as between the large-plant and small-plant groups;

(b) A disadvantage to small-plant firms of from 25 to 30 per cent in direct materials and labor cost, resulting in a net disadvantage of about 5 per cent in the total unit factory cost of a tire (in absolute terms, the labor cost disadvantage is about three fifths of the total disadvantage);

(c) That the materials-cost disadvantage is centered almost entirely in the plants of 4 independent firms with high selling expense, although the reason for this is not evident. Labor-cost disadvantages are about the same as between subgroups of independents.

Comparisons of warehouse, transportation, and selling and administrative expenses between "Big 4" and independent firms seem idle here in view of unascertained but evidently systematic differences in the degree of distributive integration and in the net price yield from sales.

The same data show about a 5.5 per cent factory-cost disadvantage to

---

[20] From capacity data in an unpublished manuscript by Professor Richard B. Heflebower. The larger independents are General and Armstrong.

[21] See Office of Temporary Controls, *O.P.A. Economic Data Series No. 10*, 1947, and also the unpublished manuscript by Heflebower, which provides further detail from the same basic data.

the small-plant firms in 6:00–16 six-ply truck tires and about an 8 per cent disadvantage in 7:00–20 ten-ply truck tires (again mainly in labor and materials), but no significant disadvantage in 7:50–20 ten-ply truck tires.

Since the percentage differences in total unit cost are relatively small, and since the material cost disadvantage may be unrelated to plant scale, the preceding findings should probably not be asked to bear much weight in an analysis of plant scale economies. So far as they are given any attention, they would tend to substantiate the notion that some slight added economies are attained as plant size is extended from about 1.5 per cent of national capacity (our low estimate of optimal plant size) and to 2.75 or 3 per cent (our high estimate) and even perhaps to 4 or 5 per cent. On the other hand, one independent estimate [22] places a reasonably efficient plant scale as low as 0.3 per cent of national capacity, and points to the Ford plant built in 1937 at 4,000 tires per day or 1.1 per cent as supposedly having optimal efficiency.

Perhaps the best net guess we can make is that costs will become reasonably low at a scale of from 4,000 to 5,000 tires per day (or, perhaps, between 1 and 1.5 per cent of national capacity), may decline by a very small proportion if this scale is doubled or trebled, but will be appreciably higher at scales much smaller than 4,000 per day.

12. *Gypsum products.* Estimates in questionnaire replies placed the optimal scale of a gypsum products plant at from 2 to 3 per cent of national capacity, or 8 to 12 per cent of the capacity supplying the largest submarkets. The corresponding absolute figures at the lower limit would be 100 million square feet of plaster board and 50,000 tons of plaster products annually. No specific information was received on the shape of the plant scale curve at smaller scales.

The only added source of evidence is found in statistics on the numbers and sizes of actual plants in the industry. The principal relevant findings here are:

(a) With about 40 end-product plants in the United States (exclusive of mines and simple calcining plants), the first 34 plants contributed 2.6 per cent apiece of the value added of gypsum products (wallboard and plaster) in 1947.

(b) The second largest firm in the industry (National) is said by *Moody's Industrials* to have nine wallboard plants with capacities ranging from 225,000 to 475,000 square feet *daily* capacity. On the basis of a 300-day operation, this would be from 2/3 to 1 1/3 of a hundred million square feet annually, or very roughly 1.5 to 3 per cent of national wallboard capacity.

[22] James W. McKie, "Bilateral Oligopoly in Industrial Product Markets" (unpublished doctoral dissertation, Harvard University).

(c) The average plant of the largest 4 firms in 1937 produced 3.7 per cent of the plasterboard and lath produced nationally, 3.9 per cent of the wallboard, 5.4 per cent of the industrial plaster, and 4.2 per cent of the calcined plaster.[23]

(d) The 26 plants of the 3 largest firms produced 3.3 per cent apiece of total gypsum board output in 1946; the 7 plants of 7 smaller firms produced 1.9 per cent apiece.[24]

All available evidence shows that, with gypsum products heavy in weight and low in intrinsic value, freight costs and the location of gypsum rock deposits relative to markets are strategic determinants of the effective optimum in plant scale.

13. *Rayon.* Estimates developed from questionnaire data placed optimal plant capacity at from roughly 4 to 6 per cent of total national capacity; they also suggested that costs would be up about 8 per cent at half-optimal capacity and 25 per cent at quarter-optimal capacity. In physical terms, the optimal plant would be able to produce from 50 to 75 million pounds annually of yarn and fiber combined; for a plant producing yarn alone, the figure might be somewhat smaller.

We are fortunate in having available as another source of data an excellent industry study, Jesse W. Markham's *Competition in the Rayon Industry.*[25] In this volume Markham does not commit himself to a firm estimate of optimal plant size, but he cites the facts [26] that (1) industry sources typically see *some* economies of large plant for any conceivable extension of size; (2) multiplant firms have typically duplicated plants with capacities of 40 to 60 million pounds of yarn per year; (3) the strictly technical economies of making plants much bigger than that are evidently outweighed by "advantages of new locations" or of geographical dispersion of plant facilities. (Outshipment freight is evidently not the primary consideration here.)

At a later point,[27] Markham reproduces a plant scale curve prepared by the industrial engineering and accounting staffs of an unidentified firm. This graph (evidently referring to yarn production alone) expresses both capacity and costs in relatives, with the absolute optimal scale not being specified. If the optimal plant capacity is assumed to be 5 per cent of the national total, the Markham scale curve would appear about as follows (as read from a diagram):

[23] *T.N.E.C. Monograph No. 27*, pp. 455–456.
[24] Smaller War Plants Corporation, *Economic Concentration and World War II*, p. 289.
[25] Cambridge, 1952.
[26] Markham, pp. 42 ff.
[27] Markham, p. 150.

Plant capacity as a percentage of the national total	Relative unit cost
5	100
4	102
3	105
2	112
1	137
0.5	180

This is closely consistent with our questionnaire findings at the available check points, but of course much more detailed. The plant scale curve is shown to be fairly flat back to three-fifths of the optimal scale, but thereafter to rise quite rapidly as scale is further reduced.

In 1947, the Census shows that the largest 13 plants provided 4.9 per cent apiece of the national value added in synthetic fibres, that the next 9 plants contributed 3.3 per cent apiece, the next three 1.3 per cent apiece, and the remaining six 0.6 per cent apiece. Markham [28] shows the rated capacities of the 23 of 24 plants of the 6 multiplant firms in the industry in 1949, and also of all plants in the industry. These include both textile-yarn and tire-yarn capacity, but it is not clear whether they include staple fibre. For these plants (which account for about 96 per cent of industry capacity as measured) the following alternative size distributions are evident:

Plant capacity in millions of lbs. of yarn (and fibre) annually	Number of plants	
	Multiplant firms	All firms
Above 60	2	
51 – 60	3	8
41 – 50	3	
31 – 40	3	4
21 – 30	6	6
11 – 20	4	6
1 – 10	2	7

If these capacities include staple fibre, then a 30-million-pound plant represents about 2.5 per cent of industry over-all capacity and 12 out of 31 plants are this large or larger; if the capacities refer to yarn only, the corresponding percentage of yarn capacity alone is about 3.3 per cent. The occurrence of a rather large number of plants in the 21–30 million pound range, including some newly constructed plants, suggests that operation at from 2 to 3 per cent of total industry capacity — or half the estimated optima — may not confer substantial disadvantages. This may in turn suggest either that our 4-to-6-per-cent estimate of the opti-

[28] Markham, pp. 43, 150.

mum may be slightly long, or that the rise of the scale curve back to half of optimal scale may be slightly exaggerated.

14. *Soap.* Estimates from questionnaire data placed the optimal scale of a soap plant at from 4 to 6 per cent of national capacity, and indicated that unit costs would be up 3 per cent at half-optimal capacity and 5 per cent at quarter-optimal capacity. The absolute quantities produced at the optimum would thus range from 150 to 225 million pounds per annum of soap and household detergents combined.

The additional evidence here concerns entirely averages of actual plant sizes from the *Census of Manufactures*. In 1947, the 5 largest soap plants averaged 7.6 per cent apiece of national value added in soap, the next 10 plants 3.0 per cent, the next 13, 1.6 per cent, and the next 15, 0.3 per cent. Comparison of market shares attributed to Procter & Gamble, Colgate-Palmolive-Peet, and Lever Bros. with the number of their plants as listed by *Moody's* suggests an average plant size for these firms equal to from 3.5 to 5 per cent of the national capacity.

15. *Cigarettes.* Estimates developed from questionnaire data placed optimal plant scale in cigarettes at around 5 to 6 per cent of national capacity (18 to 23 billion cigarettes per annum) and showed a *very* flat plant scale curve back to at least 1 per cent of national capacity. Some additional data are available from O.P.A. records, and from qualitative appraisals of the plant economies issue in three separate industry studies.

Reavis Cox, in his *Competition in the American Tobacco Industry, 1911–1932* [29] states that a "medium-sized" plant should be as efficient as a "large" one in cigarette production, and that some existing plants are larger than need be for efficiency simply because production is concentrated on sites near tobacco supplies. Richard Tennant, in *The American Cigarette Industry* [30] analyzes the character of processes and equipment and concludes that "maximum" plant efficiency could be reached with a production equal (very roughly) to from 0.25 per cent to 2 per cent of 1949 national production, or 0.5 to 4 per cent of 1939 production. Warren Baum, in "Workable Competition in the Tobacco Industry," [31] concludes that "moderately large" plants such as those of the Lorillard, Brown-Williamson, and Phillip Morris firms (with 5, 6, and 9 per cent respectively of 1949 cigarette production) should realize all available economies of large-scale production. So far as is ascertainable, none of these estimates takes account of freight and shipping costs, in which large firms appear to have a slight but systematic advantage.

[29] New York, 1933, pp. 108 ff.
[30] New Haven, 1950, pp. 231 ff.
[31] Unpublished doctoral dissertation, Harvard University, pp. 348 ff.

In general, Baum's estimate is in agreement with that previously developed, and Tennant and perhaps Cox tend to place optimal scale below our 5 to 6 per cent of the market. Since our previous estimates had costs up only 2 per cent at a capacity equal to one per cent of the national total, however, no very significant disagreement is involved.

The O.P.A. data in question, as conveniently summarized by Tennant,[32] actually compare firms, but the comparisons of factory costs (exclusive of leaf, freight and shipping, and selling and administrative costs) of "standard brand" and "economy brand" firms implicitly involve a comparison of two groups of plants of distinctly different average size. Six standard brand firms are compared as a group with 5 economy-brand firms for both 1941 and 1942. The economy-brand firms averaged from 2.6 to 3.3 billion cigarettes per annum each, which on the assumption that they are one-plant firms would have given them roughly from 0.7 to 0.8 per cent apiece of the national market. The standard-brand firms, on the other hand, produced most of their outputs from plants evidently ranging between 2 and 10 per cent apiece (or more) of national output. The factory-cost comparison (covering casing, wrapping, labor, and factory overhead) give the economy brands a unit-cost disadvantage of about 2/3 of 1 per cent in 1941 and of about 10 per cent in 1942. Tennant finds that the differences are not significant in terms of the fit of individual-firm observations to a linear regression line, but he is unable to show individual-firm data and evidently has not tried the less demanding tests for the significance of cruder sorts of association of cost to size. In any event, the maximum factory-cost advantage revealed for the larger plants is only about 3 cents per thousand cigarettes — an insignificant fraction of total production costs inclusive of tobacco-leaf and excise taxes. These data seem to bear out the notion of a plant-scale curve which is very flat indeed back to about 1 per cent of the national market.

Statistics relative to plant size show that in 1947 the 9 largest plants in the industry supplied on the average 9.6 per cent apiece of the national value of cigarettes, and that the next 15 plants supplied on the average about 0.7 per cent. American Tobacco, with 31.3 per cent of the national market in 1949, is said by *Moody's* to have 4 plants; Liggett & Myers, with 20.2 per cent, is said to have 3; Reynolds, with 26.3 per cent, apparently has a sort of multiple plant on a single site; Lorillard, with 5 per cent and shrinking, apparently had 2 plants.

16. *Automobiles.* Estimates from questionnaire data place the optimal scale of one automobile plant ("plant" being used in the sense of a related complex of facilities for manufacturing components normally "integrated" by the assembler and then assembling them), at from 5 to 10 per

[32] Pp. 264 ff.

cent of national output. Estimates relative to shares of specific submarkets
(Table V) do not asume that there will be a coupling by the firm of low-
price-line and medium-price-line production to take advantage of economies of large-scale production of interchangeable components; if they
did, submarket percentage might be somewhat reduced. In general,
300,000 units per annum is a low estimate of what is needed for productive efficiency in any one line; there are probable added advantages to
600,000 units.

These estimates refer to production costs alone and not to advantages
of large-scale sales promotion and distributive systems (which are related
to firm size rather than plant size *per se*). As regards the shape of the
plant scale curve at smaller outputs, the trend of the estimates is that
costs would be "moderately" higher at 150,000 units, or 5 per cent of the
low-priced field, substantially higher at 60,000 units, and uneconomical
at smaller scales. But it has been impossible to obtain quantitative estimates of what a "moderate" cost disadvantage is; the firms of the automobile industry seem generally uninterested in publicizing their plant
and firm scale curves.

The critical stage in plant economies is evidently found in the production of components and not in assembly. In assembly alone, from 60,000 to
180,000 units per annum is considered optimal, with advantages to a
multiplant decentralized development as the critical figure is passed.
There are some components which are typically either integrated by the
assembler or otherwise manufactured to special designs so as not to be
generally interchangeable with those used by other firms, however, and
economies of large plant in the production of these are such as to require,
for best over-all efficiency, a larger integrated plant complex than required for efficient assembly alone. The most important components of
this sort under traditional automobile-industry practice (as oriented to
securing distinctiveness of product) are bodies and engines, which together make up enough of the cost of an automobile to dominate the
scale-economy picture. Economies in specialized component manufacture
impose the strategic limits on the efficient size of the plant complex used
by any one firm.[33]

Evidence corroborating this finding is scattered and largely circum-
stantial, but some of it is probably worth reviewing. Plant counts for the
Big 3 firms, from data in *Moody's* and in company releases suggest the
following:

(1) Assembly is generally conducted on a multiplant basis by the

[33] This suggests that an "enforced" interchangeability of major components among
different assembling firms might reduce the importance of economies of large plant
complexes in the hands of individual assemblers. We speak here, however, of the
status quo.

Big 3. General Motors lists 10 assembly plants for Chevrolet alone that average a little above 2 per cent apiece of national passenger car output, and also apparently 10 Buick-Oldsmobile-Pontiac assembly plants (of which three are evidently specialized to one make apiece), that average about 1.66 per cent apiece of national passenger car output. Ford lists 17 assembly plants (including River Rouge), which placed them in 1951 at about 1.3 per cent apiece of national passenger car output.[34] Each of two independents — Studebaker and Nash, with roughly 2.5 to 4 per cent apiece of national output in 1951 — had either two or three separate assembly plants.

(2) For engines — normally specialized in design to the individual firm and integrated — the typical pattern appears to involve only one engine plant per brand or "make" of car. Individual engine plants apparently produce from 5 to 15 per cent apiece of total industry engine output for the large-selling brands of the Big 3, and from 2 to 3 per cent for their lesser makes. Independent automobile firms (having 1 to 4 per cent apiece of the total market) normally have one engine plant apiece.

(3) For bodies, which are generally specialized in design to the firm and usually integrated (General Motors and Ford have traditionally been integrated, Chrysler not officially so until very recently), it appears that the Big 3 have made maximum efforts to concentrate all possible body production (at least function by function or part by part) in single plants. First evidence of this is that, according to *Consumer Reports*,[35] Ford and Mercury have used common body shells, to reach about 20 per cent of national passenger car volume in any given body style; Chevrolet and Pontiac did the same to get about 30 per cent of national volume in a single line of bodies; Chrysler and De Soto bodies were interchanged to reach 5 per cent, although Dodge and Plymouth used separate sedan shells; the Buick "Special" and the Oldsmobile interchanged to reach 6 to 8 per cent of national volume; independents used body interchange between adjacent price lines to a maximum extent.

Data on the extent of centralization of production of single body lines in single plants are rather sketchy, but the following appears generally from published information. Ford apparently has or approaches one-plant centralization of major body components. General Motors — for its total operation in all makes, which encompasses over two-fifths of national passenger-car output — lists in addition to assembly plants: (a) one plant for steel blanking operations; (b) three plants for metal stampings; (c) three plants for auto body hardware; (d) four plants for metal fabrication and trim fabrication; (e) one plant for station-wagon bodies.

All of this makes it appear that plant economies in body production

[34] Chrysler Corporation data as released do not reveal very much here.
[35] May 1953.

are probably fairly important up to 5 or 10 per cent of national volume. Non-interchangeability of bodies among firms, moreover, makes these plant economies effective in determining the efficient size of the individual firm.

(4) For the production of many other components, there are evidently very important economies of large plants, but here inter-firm interchangeability may mean that they are not effective in determining the efficient scale of a single firm. This would apply potentially in general to the manufacture of such components as electrical and ignition systems, car heaters, radios, rubber and plastic accessories such as steering wheels, hydraulic brakes, bearings, oil pumps, automatic and other transmissions, hubcaps, carburetors, fuel pumps, water pumps, wheels, steering gear parts, batteries, spark plugs, gauges, radiators, thermostats, forgings, springs, and so forth. There is a very high plant concentration industry-wide in many of these components, but the convention of inter-firm interchangeability (not generally observed in engines and bodies) potentially permits the smaller assembler to take advantage of economies of big-plant production without using all or most of the output of any components plant.

The preceding information permits no conclusions on the quantitative cost advantages of large-scale plants, but it is consistent with the judgments: (1) that the critical stage in automobile manufacture from the standpoint of plant economies is in engine- and body-making, at least as long as engine and body designs are specialized to the firm; and (2) that optimal plant operations for engines and bodies together probably require at least 5 or 10 per cent of national passenger car output to be made within the plant complex of a single firm. We simply lack information on the quantitative effect on the total unit cost of an automobile of variations in plant-complex capacity between 2.5 and 20 per cent of the national total.

17. *Fountain pens.* Estimates from questionnaire data place the size of an optimal plant in fountain pen manufacture at from 5 to 10 per cent of national capacity, these figures being based on the assumption that the plant would specialize either in quality pens, in low-priced conventional pens, or in ballpoints. The "quality pen" plant might produce from 3 to 3.5 million pens annually, or from a quarter to a third of recent quality-pen outputs; the low-priced-pen plant or the ballpoint plant might produce from 6 to 8 million pens per year, or very roughly from a 10 to 15 per cent of total pen output outside the "quality" class. No estimates were obtained of the shape of the plant scale curve at smaller outputs.

The 1947 Census shows that for pens and mechanical pencils (the former being the dominant item in value), the largest 5 plants averaged

11.5 per cent apiece of the national value added, the next 6, 2.2 per cent, the next 14, about 1 per cent, and the next 16, 0.4 per cent. About 90 per cent of total value added was supplied by the first 40 plants, but over 40 per cent came from plants supplying 2.25 per cent or less apiece of national output. This does not suggest a very steep plant scale curve back to perhaps a quarter of the estimated optimal scale.

18. *Copper.* Questionnaire estimates place the plant scale of an optimal electrolytic copper refining operation, typically integrated, at about 10 per cent of the United States total. In this estimate, electrolytic refining alone was a sufficient critical stage in imposing the 10 per cent requirement, though parallel economies of large plants might be found at earlier stages also. No definite estimate was made of the shape of the plant scale curve.

Our principal further source of information on copper is Frederick T. Moore's "Industry Organization in Non-Ferrous Metals." [36] Pointing to the practical necessity for integration by a refiner back to and including a copper ore supply — a point on which industry sources are in apparent agreement — Moore distinguishes scale economies in mining, ore milling, smelting, and electrolytic refining. He finds little actual cost data except for milling (crushing and grinding ore), where very substantial operating-cost economies are indicated for milling plants sufficiently large to process 10 or more per cent of United States ore production. The over-all effect of these economies on the final cost of pure copper cannot be appraised from available data. Considerable economies of large scale are held to be "probable" in both smelting and refining.

That there are probably substantial economies of large plants at least in the primary processing stages of the copper industry are revealed by the following: [37]

(a) Thirteen smelter plants controlled by the largest 5 firms in the industry accounted for 96.6 per cent of national smelting capacity in 1947. This is an average of about 7.5 per cent apiece, although if we eliminate the huge Anaconda smelter (19.8 per cent of U. S. capacity alone), we get about 6.4 apiece on the average for the remaining twelve.

(b) Electrolytic refining capacity is about 92 per cent of total United States copper refining capacity. It is all contained in 7 refineries.

In mining ore, open-cut mining is evidently much more economical than either "caving" or underground mining, and our principal open-cut mines are very large, with nine mines supplying about 82 per cent of our total national copper production. Whether the last reflects economies of

---

[36] Unpublished doctoral dissertation, University of California. See also Federal Trade Commission, *The Copper Industry* (1949).

[37] *The Copper Industry.*

large plants or the fortunes of finding copper deposits is not evident. The small number and large size of individual open-cut mines predispose toward a similar phenomenon in smelters, which are closely tied either to mines or to tidewater, but they do not explain high plant concentration at the refinery level. In general, the estimate of a large minimum-optimal plant scale for an integrated operation is sustained, but we have little information on the shape of the plant scale curve.

19. *Tractors.* Estimates from questionnaire data place the optimal scale of a tractor plant at from 10 to 15 per cent of national capacity, with costs only slightly higher at half of the minimum optimal scale and only "moderately" higher at a fifth or even a tenth of it. In terms of recent postwar demands, this assumes production by the optimal plant at a rate of from 200 to 300 tractors per day, or at the outside perhaps 90,000 per year.

The 1947 Census shows that the largest 10 tractor plants averaged 7.6 per cent apiece of the national value added in tractors, the next six 2.1 per cent, the next three 0.9 per cent and the next seven 0.7 per cent. Production at much less than one per cent of the market per plant seems rare, and actual plant concentration is relatively high.

20. *Typewriters.* Estimates from questionnaire data placed optimal plant size in typewriters at from 10 to 30 per cent of national capacity, or roughly from 150,000 to 450,000 units capacity per year. It is also stated that costs would be *substantially* higher if capacity dropped to 5 or 7.5 per cent of the national total. Census data for 1947 list 28 typewriter plants, but show the first 3 plants averaging 20.1 per cent of national value added apiece, the next 6 averaging 5.1 per cent, and the next 6 after that averaging 1.2 per cent. This accounts for 98 per cent of the value added of typewriter output. From data in *Moody's* it appears that Underwood, with about 20 per cent of the market, has 2 typewriter plants, that L. C. Smith with about 10 per cent also has 2, that Royal with about 20 per cent has 1 plant. (Plant data on Remington are not available.) Individual plant sizes are not known, but it is known that typewriter factories in some cases also manufacture other machines. The general picture here sustains the notion of important economies to very large-scale plants.

APPENDIX C

Economies of Large Firms: Supplementary Data

Although much supplementary evidence has some bearing on the economies of the large firm, its significance is sometimes ambiguous. This is particularly true of data on the existing sizes of actual firms, and on the profit rates of firms of different sizes. Actual firm sizes cannot be considered a generally reliable index to the most economical sizes, even in the roughest sense. As to profit rates, relative "profitability" potentially reflects not only relative efficiency, but also relative advantages in product differentiation and in absolute cost, and these advantages are not of necessity systematically linked to the size of firm. Also, accounting profit rates (normally rates on equity) are affected by numerous aberrations of accounting measurement, and in addition there is the possibility of a systematic lack of proportionality between relative profit rates and relative unit costs. It thus seems desirable not to ask profit-rate data to bear very much weight in the analysis of the relation of firm size to efficiency, or to bear any weight at all except where product differentiation and absolute cost advantages as they appear among established firms seem relatively unimportant.

Let us now turn to the supplementary data in question, referring in turn to industries in which, according to replies to questionnaires, (a) there were no economies to multiplant firms (Group 1 in Table IX); (b) such economies were held to exist and their extent was specified (Group 3); and (c) there were no reasonably definite estimates of the extent of the economies of multiplant firms (Group 2).

Group 1: Industries in which economies of multiplant firms were held to be negligible or absent.

The 6 industries in this group include canned fruits and vegetables, petroleum refining, meat packing, fountain pens, copper, and typewriters.

In *canned goods*, an optimal plant was held to supply from 0.25 to 0.5 per cent of the national market, or 2.5/to 5 per cent of the largest product line. Census data for 1947 show 22.7 per cent of national output (as measured by value) supplied by 4 firms, or over 5 per cent apiece, although this degree of concentration is evidently influenced somewhat by the relatively high concentration in such specialties as cranberry sauce, infant vegetables, grape juice, spaghetti, applesauce, tomato sauce, baked beans, orange juice, and so forth.[1] No economies of the multiplant firm are suggested by questionnaire estimates.

Professor Leonard A. Doyle states, on the basis of extensive investigations, that there are no significant economies of multiplant operation in this industry, excluding possible advantages of large-scale sales promotion of a multiproduct or full line of canned goods. He holds that any apparent profit advantage of the largest firms is due mainly to the inclusion in the product mix of branded specialties with a product differentiation advantage — e.g., soup, ketchup, and pineapple. Small firms are held to do as well as large ones in the common fruit and vegetable products. There are possible monopsony advantages to large firms in buying cans and cartons, but these are unevaluated.

In *petroleum refining*, where the size of the optimal plant (coastal refining) was put at 1.75 per cent of national capacity or 4.3 per cent of capacity in the largest submarket, economies of multiplant firms are generally denied in estimates. The 4 largest firms have a distinct multiplant development and together supplied about 37 per cent of refinery output in 1947.

In the *meat-packing industry*, the size of an optimal plant was given as 2 to 2.5 per cent of national capacity in diversified packing, and as well under 0.5 per cent in fresh packing. No case is made for significant multiplant economies in the questionnaire estimates, although the 4 largest firms are of a multiplant type and together account for about 40 per cent of non-farm meat slaughter.

With both product differentiation and absolute cost advantages seeming relatively unimportant, it may be pertinent to mention profit data here. A comparison of meat packing profits for different-sized firms is found in W. E. Hoadley, E. Baughman, and W. P. Mors, *A Financial and Economic Survey of the Meat Packing Industry*.[2] In this study firms are divided into the 4 or 5 largest ones, accounting roughly for from 5 to 15 per cent apiece of non-farm slaughter, a group of medium-sized firms accounting for from 1 to 2 per cent apiece of the same quantity, and a group of small firms accounting for less than 1 per cent apiece of the total market.[3] The largest firms are full-line, multiplant organizations with national distribution; as firms become smaller than this they tend to specialize (progressively with decline in size) by regions or by product

---

[1] *T.N.E.C. Monograph No. 27*, pp. 420–421.
[2] Federal Reserve Bank of Chicago, 1946. These data are corroborated by data drawn from the Securities and Exchange Commission's *Survey of Listed Corporations*.
[3] Data presented on "very small" firms seem inconclusive and will not be discussed here.

lines or both. It is quite clear from the Hoadley study that the medium-sized firms as a group had persistently higher rates of profit on equity than the large firms from 1930 until the end of the last war, and data from *Moody's* for 1947 to 1951 indicate that this tendency has persisted. (The medium-sized firms also generally outscore the small ones in profit rates.) The size of the advantage is generally in the neighborhood of two or three out of ten percentage points in the profit rate on equity.

Although a profit rate on equity is not a direct index to efficiency or level of cost, these rates are not inconsistent with the finding that multi-plant economies are not found beyond the stage where a firm in diversified packing supplies 1 or 2 per cent of the national market in meat, or perhaps two or three times this percentage of some regional market. Hoadley's explanations of the profit-rate superiority of the middle-sized firms are interesting in this regard; he lists (a) better locations relative to the source of supply; (b) faster inventory turnover; (c) more emphasis on pork products; and (d) a product mix requiring a smaller ratio of capital investment to sales. Large multiplant firms seem to encounter virtual disadvantages in cost at least sufficient to offset the virtual advantages which have been so frequently emphasized.

In the *fountain-pen industry*, where optimal plant size is set at 5 to 10 per cent of the physical volume in the national market, and at more for product submarkets, the existence of multiplant economies seemed doubtful, and no supplementary data are available.

The situation is similar in the *typewriter industry*, although here a claim was made in estimates of some unspecified advantages to the multiplant firm in manufacturing and distribution costs. The situation in both industries seems effectively to be that total industry output is small enough or plant economies great enough that even with high concentration by firms multiplant development has not proceeded far.

In the *copper industry*, where the optimal scale of integrated plant is set at 10 per cent of the market, the indication in estimates was for a lack of multiplant economies. Here again, multiplant development has not proceeded far, although two of the large firms have 2 and 3 electrolytic refineries respectively, and 3 of these firms have from 2 to 4 smelters apiece. Supplementary data are not available, and profit-rate comparisons are not germane in view of the incomplete integration, small plant size, and resource disadvantages of firms outside the largest 4 or 5.

In general, our previous findings for industries in Group 1 are not altered by supplementary evidence, but in 4 of 6 cases they are not reinforced.

Group 3: Industries in which economies of multiplant firm were held to be present, though ordinarily slight in magnitude.

The 6 industries in this group include shoes, cement, steel, gypsum products, soap, and cigarettes.

In the *shoe industry*, where the first four firms in 1947 supplied about 28 per cent of national output, questionnaire estimates indicated advantages to a firm with from 3 to 5 plants supplying in all from 0.5 to 2.5 per cent of total shoe output or from 2 to 6 per cent of output in the largest product line, specialization of the firm to a line being assumed.

Corroborative data are scanty. Mr. Bruce Cheek has indicated that an advantage of multiplant development in the production of shoes is that it permits the firm to become large enough to undertake integrated wholesaling or retailing of its shoes, thus avoiding the market channels open to smaller shoe firms, such as sales to jobbers or to retailers at "shows," sales to retail shoe chains, or sales through the distributive outlets of large competitors. The advantages which such integrated distribution confers are apparently (a) longer runs in production and a lowered seasonality of output, resulting from a secure access to the market, and (b) escape from the monopsony pressure of large buyers. Cheek does not estimate the extent of such economies, but indicates that the largest 10 or 15 firms, with market shares ranging from 9 per cent to 0.5 per cent or less of the national total, have integrated wholesaling and in some cases integrated retailing also. Data from *Moody's* generally corroborate this finding.

In the *cement industry*, optimal plant size was placed at 0.8 to 1 per cent of national capacity or 4 to 5 per cent of capacity in the largest regional market, and savings of from 2 to 4 per cent in unit cost were claimed for a multiplant firm with from 3 to 10 plants.

The only available primary check on these conclusions is found in some unit cost data for the year 1929 and in profit-rate data, from *T.N.E.C. Monograph No. 13.*[4] The cost data, which include imputed interest but not outward freight, refer to four groups of firms:

(a) 3 large firms, with capacity from about 9 to about 18 per cent apiece of the national total, and with from 9 to 13 plants apiece.

(b) 4 middle-sized firms, with capacity from about 4 to about 6 per cent apiece of the national total, and with from 6 to 8 plants apiece.

(c) 6 small firms, with capacity roughly from 1 to 2 per cent apiece of the national total, or either 1 or 2 plants apiece.

(d) 32 very small firms, with less than 1 per cent apiece of national capacity and evidently 1 plant apiece.

[4] P. 23. These are reproduced in Kaplan, *Small Business: Its Place and Problems*, p. 84.

Group	Weighted average unit cost per bbl. of cement	Range of individual-company unit costs
Large firms	$ 1.23	$ 1.18 – $ 1.32
Middle-sized firms	1.23	1.14 – 1.41
Small firms	1.21	0.99 – 1.34
Very small firms	1.37	0.91 – 2.17

Evidently (1) there is no significant difference among the recorded unit costs of the first three groups of firms, and (2) very small firms show average unit costs which are probably higher than those of the other groups by a statistically significant amount. (A significance test was not made in the original study and has not been made here.) As this finding bears on the issue of economies of scale, it would be consistent with the finding that either one or two optimal-scale plants per firm will result in costs as low as can be obtained with multiplant firms, and that supernormal costs result mainly from operating plants of suboptimal scale. This would seem in the main to challenge the claims for multiplant economies entered in our estimates, although the present finding has only the slender support of accounting cost data for one year about twenty-five years ago.

The same source compares the average rates of profit on equity for 3 large firms, 4 middle-sized firms, 5 small firms, and 5 very small firms (same classification) for the period 1917 to 1936.[5] The general picture here is (1) that Western firms, including some very small ones, were generally more profitable than other firms; and (2) that, the Western bias aside, there is apparently no significant difference in profit rates as among the first three groups of firms, but that very small firms probably do a little worse than the others in profit rates. The last observation, however, is a bit shaky, since 2 very small firms out of 5 are high-profit Western concerns, and since we are not in a position to assess the extent to which the general demand-supply and competitive situation in the West was more favorable to profits during the period in question. The general tendency of the supplementary findings is to question the estimates that significant multiplant economies exist, but to support the estimates concerning optimal plant scales.

In the *steel industry,* the optimal scale of plant for a fully integrated operation was set at from 1 to 2.5 per cent of national capacity (2.5 to 6.25 per cent for the largest regional submarket), with a small cost advantage claimed by some estimators for up to an 8-plant firm, although multiplant economies were denied by other estimators. Corroborative data are distressingly lacking, and about all we can point out, from *S.E.C.* and *Moody's* data, is that for the period 1936–40 and the period 1947–51, there

[5] Single-year comparisons for 1935 and 1936 are also presented.

was apparently no significant relation of profit rate on equity to size of firm among the 15 largest steel firms in the United States, although these firms ranged in size from U. S. Steel, with about 19 steel mills, down to single-plant firms. Although these profit-rate data are not conclusive, they are consistent with the hypothesis that economies did not result from expansion beyond a single integrated plant with from 1 to 2½ million ingot tons capacity.

In the *gypsum products industry*, estimated optimal plant size is 2 to 3 per cent of national capacity or 8 to 12 per cent of the capacity supplying the largest submarket; small cost advantages are claimed for multiplant operations running up to eleven plants. The largest two firms in 1939 controlled 55 per cent and 23 per cent respectively of national plasterboard sales east of the Rockies.[6] Unfortunately, no corroborative data are available; even profit figures are so scanty as to be useless in this connection.

In the *soap industry*, 4 to 6 per cent of national capacity was attributed to an optimal plant, and slight advantages — primarily in distribution costs — were claimed for a two- to three-plant firm. Four firms supplied 79 per cent of the value product in soap in 1947. Corroborative data, including available profit data, are insufficient to permit any evaluation of these estimates.

In the *cigarette industry*, the size of an optimal plant was set at from 5 to 6 per cent of national capacity, and 3 or 4 plants per firm were held to confer small additional cost advantages. There was some corroboration in O.P.A. cost data of the claims for relatively slight economies of large plant.

As to economies of the large firm, Tennant[7] holds that there are no economies of large-scale buying of tobacco leaf and other materials but that for large firms (with 20 to 30 per cent of the market apiece) there may be *small* advantages in the costs of distribution and selling. Baum[8] also holds that there are no economies of large-scale materials purchases, and feels that all other economies would be exploited with a 5 to 10 per cent market share. Cox[9] cites, but does not specify the amount of, possible economies in capital and administrative costs of the multiplant firm.

The O.P.A. data[10] show an advantage in distribution and selling costs (ex advertising) to 6 "standard" brands of cigarettes over 5 "economy" brands in 1941 and 1942. The average volume per standard brand was about 15 per cent of the total market, while that per economy

[6] *U.S. vs. United States Gypsum Co.*, 333 U.S. 364 (68 Sup. Ct. 525. 1948).
[7] *The American Cigarette Industry.*
[8] "Workable Competition in the Tobacco Industry."
[9] *Competition in the American Tobacco Industry, 1911–1933.*
[10] See Tennant, pp. 258 ff.

brand was under 2 per cent. The advantage in distribution and selling costs enjoyed by standard brands amounted to from 2½ to 5½ cents per 1,000 cigarettes, or $\frac{1}{20}$ to $\frac{1}{10}$ cent per package, although the statistical significance of the indicated cost differences is in question. In addition, standard brands enjoyed a ½-cent-per-1,000 (or $\frac{1}{100}$-cent-per package) advantage in freight and shipping costs. A maximum total advantage of 6 cents per 1,000 or about 0.12 cents per package to standard brands would amount to about 4 per cent of total unit costs ex taxes and to less than 2 per cent if federal taxes are included in costs. In general, this finding is consistent with the claim for slight economies (excepting advertising) to a multiplant operation in cigarettes, although Tennant questions the statistical significance of his findings on the ground that there is not a significant fit of observations to a linear regression.

For the 6 Group 3 industries, it appears: (1) that in two industries — gypsum products and soap — germane corroborative data are substantially unavailable; (2) that in two others — steel and cement — fragmentary data from other sources generally tend to question the claimed existence of multiplant economies, though these data are certainly insufficient to establish anything very strongly; and (3) that for the remaining two industries — cigarettes and shoes — there is some slight corroboration of the claims for small advantages to multiplant operation. Perhaps the only change positively suggested in our previous conclusions would be accomplished by placing a question mark next to the classification of the steel and cement industries under the "possessing-multiplant-economies" category. The suggested change would not be very important from the standpoint of over-all economies of scale, since the suggested multiplant developments would not necessarily increase the percentage supplied of any one regional submarket.

Group 2. Industries unclassified with respect to the existence of economies of the multiplant firm.

The 8 industries in this category produce flour, liquor, metal containers, tires and tubes, rayon, farm machinery and tractors (dealt with together here), and automobiles. For a number of these there are fortunately some supplementary data which may help resolve the existing indecision as to classification.

In the *flour-milling industry*, multiplant development is common among the larger firms. According to the Federal Trade Commission,[11] General Mills had at the time of a recent study 25 listed mill locations, Pillsbury 9, International 13, Colorado Milling and Elevator 20, Com-

---

[11] *Report on Growth and Concentration in the Flour Milling Industry* (1947), pp. 2 ff.

mander-Larrabie 6, and Standard Milling 3. With the estimated optimal size of a plant lying between 0.1 and 0.5 per cent of the national capacity (or 0.3 to 1.5 per cent of that of the largest regional market), most of the plants of these firms were within or beyond the optimal range. The largest 4 flour firms in 1947 supplied 29 per cent of the value of flour output.

The only added source of data of any consequence is *T.N.E.C. Monograph No. 13*,[12] which compares costs for different sizes of flour-milling firms, the major limitation being that the data refer only to 1922. These data show that, omitting the costs of wheat and of in-freight thereon, 3 large firms with probably 7 to 10 per cent apiece of the national market had total manufacturing costs 20 per cent or more below those of smaller firms, which generally did not exceed 1 per cent apiece of the national market. Although the delivered-at-mill wheat costs of the big firms were much higher, it is not evident whether or not these were offset by proximity to selling markets and consequent reduction in outshipment freight. It is difficult to draw any conclusion from this fragment of old data, and the picture is further muddied by the fact that the same *T.N.E.C. Monograph No. 13*,[13] shows no significant net profit-rate advantage to the largest firms in the period 1919–22.

For the *liquor industry*, which has extensive multiplant development on the part of the Big 4, no significant supplementary data are available, and profit-rate data can hardly be adduced in connection with efficiency because of the dominant importance of product differentiation.

In the *metal container industry*, optimal plant size was set at 0.3 to 2 per cent of the national market or 2 to 12 per cent of the largest packers'-can submarket, but there was no estimate on multiplant economies. Data for 1944 [14] suggest that American Can, the largest firm, had about 18 packers'-can plants and 14 general-line-can plants in the United States, and that Continental Can had about 11 and 7 plants respectively in the two categories — the two companies together making nearly 85 per cent of all can sales.

Hession [15] cites a number of economies or closely related advantages of large firms in the packers'-can field. These are:

(1) Discounts on raw materials, especially steel, amounting to 7 to 8 per cent of material cost or 4 or more per cent of total cost — allegedly obtained at least by American Can. But industry sources hold that since the passage of the Robinson-Patman Act (1936) any such buying-price advantages have been eliminated.

[12] Pp. 65–67.
[13] Pp. 85 ff.
[14] C. H. Hession, *Competition in the Metal Food Container Industry*, pp. 67 ff.
[15] Chs. 4, 5, and 7.

(2) Advantages in an amount unspecified of large-scale research for the development of new products and techniques. But industry sources hold that the large-scale research activities of the big firms result in a virtual disadvantage financially, since smaller firms can and do copy many of the big firms' expensive developments without paying for them.

(3) Advantages of offering field services to buyers, leasing closing machines to buyers, and so on — an area in which the big companies excel. This might seem to be a sales-promotional rather than a cost advantage; in any event its extent is not assessed by Hession.

(4) Advantages of an improved load factor on the facilities of a multiplant organization, resulting from being able to meet peak seasonal demands in specific regions with the slack capacity of plants in other regions with different seasonal peaks. This observation is unsupported by Hession; its extent is not estimated, nor is the extent of offsetting disadvantages in freight costs.

(5) Advantages of spreading central-office overheads, to an extent not evaluated. Industry sources concur that there are virtual advantages of this order, but hold that they are offset by virtual disadvantages.

Available profit data are too sketchy to permit the drawing of any firm inferences. The net conclusion is that no convincing case for economies of multiplant firms (aside from posssible sales-promotion advantages) has been established, provided that the enforcement of the Robinson-Patman Act has eliminated buying-price advantages in steel for the large can firms.

In the *tire and tube industry*, the size of an optimal plant was placed at from 1.37 to 2.75 per cent of the national capacity. No definite estimates of the extent of multiplant economies was received, and the tire and tube industry was thus unclassified in this regard. One questionnaire reply, however, did refer to advantages (extent unspecified) in material prices, in spreading overhead, and in research and development in large firms.

There is a distinct multiplant development among the Big 4 of the tire industry, which together supply from 70 to 75 per cent of total tire and tube capacity and output. *Moody's* shows Goodyear with 5 plants, Firestone with 3, U. S. Rubber with 5, and Goodrich with 5, with a pattern of regional decentralization running throughout. The average size of the plants of the Big 4 runs around 4 per cent apiece of national capacity.

Data previously presented showed that the Big 4 firms appeared in the immediate prewar and early-war period to have about a 5 per cent advantage in manufacturing costs over a group of smaller firms. The advantage was almost entirely in raw-material and direct-labor costs, and not significantly in factory overheads. Since the average size of Big 4 plants was apparently around 4 per cent of the national market, whereas that of the smaller firms was probably around 1.5 per cent, this cost advantage was tentatively ascribed to plant size. It is conceivable, at least for that two-fifths of the advantage connected with raw-material costs, that the advantage is attributable to firm size. This is quite uncertain, however, since some but not all of the small firms suffered the raw-material-cost disadvantage.[16] In our present state of knowledge, about all we can do is to raise the question of whether the apparent cost advantages to larger firms require only moderately large plants (e.g. plants supplying 3 or 4 per cent of national output), or require multiplant firms with 3, 4, or 5 good-sized plants apiece. We are similarly uncertain whether or to what extent the economies in question are strictly pecuniary or real.

Further data on distributive costs and on the relation of net price realization to cost (from O.P.A. data and from Heflebower) are so presented that it is impossible to distinguish economies in production and distribution from product-differentiation and sales-promotion advantages. Profit-rate data are not illuminating for the same reason. It is notable, however, that in the period 1936–40, 5 smaller firms (General, Lee, Seiberling, Dayton, and Phares) all had significantly higher profit rates on equity than the average of the Big 4,[17] and that in 1947–51 the three smaller firms listed in *Moody's* did almost as well as the Big 4.

In the *rayon industry*, optimal plant size was placed at from 4 to 6 per cent of national capacity, but no estimates of multiplant economies were received. The largest 6 rayon firms had from 3 to 5 yarn plants apiece in 1949.[18] Supplementary data bearing on multiplant economies are lacking, and profit-rate data reveal nothing of immediate relevance. Average profit rates on equity for 1933–41 [19] for the largest seven firms exhibit a very large variance as among firms, but are uniformly well above rates for four small companies. The latter, however, have plants well below the estimated optimal size, and it seems fair to attribute their relatively poor earning records to undersized plants rather than to a lack of multiplant organization.

The *farm machinery industry* (excluding tractors) and the *tractor industry* may be treated together here, since although there is frequently plant specialization as between the two categories, the combination of tractors and farm implements in a single firm is common among the larger companies. For farm machinery "other than tractors," the size of an optimal plant was estimated (very roughly) to be sufficient to supply 1 to 1.5 per cent of the value of "large, complicated" (usually tractor-drawn field) machinery, or 4 to 6 per cent of any of 4 major product

---

[16] See p. 239 above.
[17] S. E. C., *Survey of Listed Corporations.*
[18] Markham, *Competition in The Rayon Industry,* p. 43.
[19] Markham, p. 54.

categories. For tractors, the plant optimum was set at 10 to 15 per cent of national capacity, although it was indicated that the plant scale curve might be moderately flat back to a substantially smaller capacity. There were no definite estimates on multiplant economies, although questionnaire respondents in general saw "some" savings in management, purchased-material, or financing costs of a multiplant, "long-line" operation. (A "long-line" organization refers to one which produces a variety of major "complicated" farm implements in all or most of the major categories, and probably also tractors.)

Most respondents also saw some advantage in integrated regional distribution plants, which were held to be feasible only with "long-line" production, although again the extent of advantages were not evaluated. Against this, however, it was stated in questionnaire replies that small "short-line"·companies can do as well as larger, long-line firms by selling in restricted areas and designing a product or products to meet specialized local needs. In view of all of this, it seemed safest on the basis of questionnaire replies to enter farm machinery and tractors as "unclassified" with respect to multiplant economies.

If the tentative suggestion made in the questionnaire estimates were accepted as fact, the general effect would be to establish that a long-line company would need at the most perhaps one optimal plant in each major implement category — supplying 4 to 6 per cent of national output in each — plus tractor output. Thus the percentage of all major farm implement output required for efficiency would be increased by the long-line requirement, but the percentage of output in any major category would not. The possible exception to this is tractor output, where more than 5 per cent of national output might be required. But most information suggests that integrated tractor production would not occasion an increase in the market percentage of an efficient long-line firm.

The Federal Trade Commission [20] emphasizes quite strongly the advantages of long-line production by the firm, and of the connected development of integrated "branch houses" for wholesale distribution. The Commission is not clear, however, as to just what is the crucial overall market percentage needed for effective long-line distribution. In addition, of course, there is the unanswered question as to what extent long-line advantages are respectively cost-saving and sales-promotional in character. We are disposed to classify such advantages — ultimately reflected in the relationships of factory net-back prices to retail prices — as of a cost-saving character, though realizing that this decision is in some degree arbitrary.

The principal other sources of supplementary data are an unpublished doctoral dissertation by Michael Conant, and some Congressional hear-

[20] *Report on the Manufacture and Distribution of Farm Implements* (1948).

ings.[21] They show in general that reasonably long-line distribution, including tractors, was attained in 1936 and 1940 by all of the first seven or eight firms in the industry, and also that:

(a) The *second* 3 firms (Case, Oliver, Minneapolis-Moline) had roughly from 3.5 to 5.5 per cent apiece of major farm-implement sales, and the *next* 2 (Massey-Harris, Avery) had from 1 to 2 per cent of the same market.

(b) These 5 firms *outside the biggest 3* (i.e. other than International Harvester, Deere, and Allis Chalmers) had the following percentages of the national market in eight large implements (excluding tractors):

Case	– 4.6,	5.5,	6.3,	4.9,	6.3,	3.8,	4.7,	19.7
Oliver	– 0.0,	6.4,	6.1,	0.0,	6.6,	4.9,	3.9,	14.8
Minneapolis-Moline	– 0.0,	0.2,	1.2,	0.0,	2.8,	9.1,	2.5,	3.2
Massey-Harris	– 2.2,	2.1,	2.4,	6.0,	0.8,	1.0,	2.4,	0.0
Avery	– 0.4,	1.8,	2.8,	0.0,	0.1,	0.4,	0.4,	0.0

The implements referred to are binders, mowers, rakes, corn binders, tractor-drawn cultivators, combines, corn planters, and grain threshers. In general, all or most of these firms had tractor production roughly in balance with their other outputs.

From this it might appear that something like long-line production and distribution may be secured with from 1 or 2 to 6 per cent of the total market, and do not require market shares like that of International Harvester (35 to 40 per cent of the total market) or Deere (18 to 20 per cent).

Profit data are of course not completely reliable on the point at issue, since they reflect product-differentiation advantages as well as economies of scale. What they show is that from 1936 through 1940, the Big 2 (I-H and Deere) had a profit rate on equity substantially above that of all smaller companies,[22] but that in 1947–51 the smaller companies on the average did at least as well in profit rate as the Big 2. In the interval between the two periods referred to, of course, two or three mergers among smaller firms took place. Evidence on the financial welfare of the really short-line firms smaller than the first 7, 8 or 10 companies is substantially lacking. About all that we can safely conclude is that:

(1) A firm with from 2 to 6 per cent of the market in each of several major categories of implements and in tractors may well be more efficient than short-line firms specializing in one line or a few implements.

[21] See Michael Conant, "Aspects of Monopoly and Price Policies, in the Farm Machinery Industry" (unpublished doctoral dissertation, University of Chicago, 1949) — relying for the statistics quoted here on *T. N. E. C. Monograph No. 36*, pp. 241 ff.; and *Hearings*, Subcommittee No. 3, Committee on Judiciary, House of Representatives, 79th, 1st, on HR 2357, Serial No. 8 (1945, pp. 145 ff.).

[22] S.E.C., *Survey of Listed Corporations.*

(2) The extent of economies attributable to a further growth of the firm is undecided.

The recognition of economies of a multiplant firm here does not suggest that the proportion of any one product submarket required for efficiency is larger than that required for efficiency of individual plants.

In the *automobile industry*, plant economies, including those of integrated component production, were estimated to require a capacity to supply 5 to 10 per cent of the national market, 10 to 20, per cent of the low-priced market alone, or 30 to 60 per cent of the upper-middle-priced market alone. The individual submarket percentages might be reduced if there were component production interchangeable between adjacent price lines in a single firm. As to multiplant economies, no reasonably definite opinions or estimates were received, except as embraced in the preceding statement.

Such supplementary data as are available must be interpreted in the light of the apparent fact that production economies *per se* are pretty well accounted for in the estimates of integrated plant economies; economies of large-scale distribution are the possibility to be explored in connection with economies of the multiplant firm. It seems probable, in view of evidences from many sources, that multiplant firms (producing some multiple of 5 to 10 per cent of national output in several related price lines) do enjoy distributional advantages. It also seems likely, however, that these are primarily advantages of large-scale sales promotion rather than advantages in production and distribution cost. We have therefore treated the distributional and related advantages of the large automobile firm in Chapter 4.

For the eight Group 2 industries, it appears: (1) that for 4 industries — flour, liquor, metal containers, and rayon — there are no adequate data to permit reevaluation of any previous classification in terms of scale economies; (2) that in the rubber tire industry there is some possibility of slight economies to multiplant firms (sales promotion advantages aside) but that the evidence is too inconclusive to justify reclassification; and (3) that in the farm machinery and tractor industry and in the auto industry, economies of multiplant development oriented to the production of a diversified product line are indicated as possible or probable, but that in neither case does the multiplant scale requirement necessarily require an increase in the percentage of individual product submarkets previously predicted as necessary for efficiency of the plant. Thus, no reclassification of industries in Group 2 is clearly suggested by these supplementary findings.

APPENDIX D

Product-Differentiation Barriers to Entry in Individual Industries

Since the summary treatment of product-differentiation barriers to entry in Chapter 4 is highly synoptic, we will discuss here the character of findings for each industry. This may serve to supply some previously omitted information and to give the source and character of the data underlying the tables in that chapter. For purposes of this discussion, industries may be grouped into four categories: those with (1) slight, (2) moderate, and (3) great product-differentiation barriers to entry; plus (4) "mixed" industries within which the product-differentiation barriers to entry differ in height as among different product lines.

1. Industries with negligible or slight product-differentiation barriers to entry.

The members of this category, excluding segments of "mixed" industries, were listed in Table XI as copper, rayon, cement, steel, gypsum products, and meat packing. Since the findings here are essentially negative in character, corroborating evidence is often brief in compass, and estimates are often confined to simple flat statements, though both tend to be rather convincing.

(a) *The copper industry* presents a picture of the basic minimum in importance for product differentiation. The end products of the industry are primary refined copper (dominantly so-called virgin copper) or scrap copper (usually furnished in the form of ingots of reclaimed brass, bronze, etc.). Primary copper is supplied to buyers from the industry both in relatively unfinished pure form as ingots, ingot bars, cakes, cathodes, and wire bars, and in more finished pure form as wire, sheet, and so forth, or in alloyed form, as in brass. Although there are thus several important product categories, outputs within any category are effectively standardized and graded, so that substantial homogeneity of the products of different sellers in any category is found. Price relationships among categories appear to be based roughly on relative copper content and on differences in processing cost, although available price data bearing on this matter are inadequate.[1]

[1] For a discussion of the product structure of the copper industry see F. T. Moore,

Branding of basic copper products is of negligible importance, and as might be expected advertising expenditures by the major smelting and refining firms generally amount to a small fraction of one per cent of sales revenues. Provision to buyers of services such as technical consultation seems generally unimportant. Estimates submitted in response to questionnaires indicate that (1) no established seller is able to command a perceptible price premium over another for a given product by reason of product preferences, and (2) an entrant would be without advantage or disadvantage in this respect as compared to established sellers, except possibly in slight degree at first while he demonstrated his ability to deliver up-to-standard production. Disadvantages in profit-making power such as small established firms or entrants do or would enjoy are evidently attributable mainly to the inferiority of their resource positions (and possibly to diseconomies of small scale), rather than to any product-differentiation disadvantage.

(b) *The cement industry* presents a similar, though even simpler picture. We find an essentially one-product industry, with Portland cement constituting about 95 per cent of the value product, and special cements (produced in conjunction with Portland) the remainder.[2] Branding and advertising are unimportant. Industry people state that among established firms there are slight buyer attachments based on long association and service, but that these are insufficient to permit one seller to command a perceptibly higher price than another. Small firms are apparently at no disadvantage as compared to large by reason of product differentiation. Industry estimates also suggest that a new seller would suffer no price or sales-promotional disadvantage, except perhaps in slight degree for a short break-in period.

(c) *The rayon industry* has a relatively simple product structure, with three primary types of rayon — viscose (about 70 per cent of the total), acetate (29 per cent), and cuprammonium (1 per cent).[3] Essentially an industrial raw material for use in fabric manufacture (woven cloth, knit goods, tire fabric, rugs), rayon is now generally supplied either as yarn or as staple fibre. Within any one product category, there is a substantial homogeneity of the outputs of different sellers; in addition, there is close substitution in use between principal product categories, as for example between viscose and acetate yarn, or between yarn and staple fibre. There is a smaller number of sellers for individual product categories than for the industry as a whole; for example, Markham finds only four firms

"Industry Organization in Non-Ferrous Metals," unpublished doctoral dissertation, University of California; also, Federal Trade Commission, *The Copper Industry*, Part I, Chs. 2 and 3.

[2] See *Federal Trade Commission vs. Cement Institute, Respondent's Brief, Appendix A,* for general data on the industry.

[3] Markham, *Competition in the Rayon Industry*, Ch. 3.

producing staple fibre at the date of his writing, and only five making tire yarn. But there is effective homogeneity within categories. Advertising costs generally run under 1 per cent of sales revenue.

Replies to questionnaires indicate that there are no significant attachments of buyers to sellers, no significant product patents still in effect, and no ability of one seller to command a higher price than another. Any difficulty in entering the industry would be attributable not to product differentiation, but to absolute-cost considerations involving access to production know-how and to a long shakedown period in obtaining quality production.

The rayon industry until a very few years ago was the dominant and almost unopposed synthetic fibres entity, and it is this industry which we study here. Recent developments involving the introduction of a variety of new synthetic fibres, each generally under monopolistic patent protection, promise to create a new and broader synthetic fibre industry in which patent-protected product differentiation will be a factor for some time.

(d) *The steel industry* has as its end products a substantial variety of so-called finished steel products, principal among which are sheets, bars, pipes and tubes, plates and tinplate, heavy structural shapes, wire and nails, strip, and rails. Direct ingot sales constitute a very small proportion of total industry sales.[4] So far as physical properties of products are concerned, there is effectively no differentiation among the outputs of competing sellers. Products are either standardized or produced to specifications in various product lines. Advertising costs are a fraction of 1 per cent of sales of the industry. Although one or two steel firms have entered into programs of direct-to-the-final-consumer advertising, the general opinion of their non-advertising competitors is that such advertising has little effect on steel buyers. The testimony is that no established seller can consistently command appreciable price premia as compared to his competitors.

There is nevertheless a sort of product differentiation in the industry. Personal sales representation is important, and in addition steel firms seek to obtain or hold customers by offering a variety of services, including technical consultation on the development of steel specifications and on the use of the steel, market analysis services, etc. In addition, some differentiation results from offering customers special treatment in the matter of delivery dates. Various steel firms more or less match each other's efforts in this regard, but some degree of customer allegiance to particular sellers (though perhaps not "worth" 1 per cent in steel prices) develops as a result.

[4] See American Iron and Steel Institute, *Iron and Steel Works Directory for the United States and Canada,* recent annual issues.

As to the potential entrant, industry replies to questionnaires suggest that (1) "it would be a matter of urgency" for an entrant to match the sales-promotional activities of the established firms, but (2) the entrant could effectively accomplish this matching within a short period of time. There seems to be agreement among respondents that in order to break into the market an entrant would have to spend about $2 per ton (2 per cent of price) more on sales promotion than established firms for one or two years — or make equivalent price concessions — while establishing a reputation for quality of product and service. Some entry barrier is thus imposed by product differentiation, but we rate it as "slight." The existence of economies of large-scale sales promotion for sales beyond that of an optimal plant is not evident.

(e) *The gypsum products industry* makes a number of products from a common basic raw material, gypsum rock. About a quarter of the volume of gypsum rock quarried goes to use "uncalcined," but only 5 per cent of the sales revenue of the industry comes from this use. The remainder goes to building materials uses, and here the principal fabricated products are wallboard and lath (with gypsum block, tile, metal-edged gypsum plank, etc. occupying a very minor position), while calcined gypsum plaster is the principal bulk material supplied to the building industry. Plaster accounts for from a fifth to a quarter of sales revenue, and the fabricated products for upwards of two-thirds.[5]

Uncalcined gypsum and calcined gypsum plaster have long been un-patented products, and there has apparently been no significant product differentiation in these lines. In the wallboard and related fabricated lines, the situation was otherwise until the court decree in 1951 resulting from the *U.S. vs. United States Gypsum Co.* antitrust suit. The United States Gypsum Co. had enjoyed a long-sustained control of strategic gypsum board patents, amounting to a product-patent monopoly on an overwhelmingly superior line of fabricated products. After the expiration of its basic "Utzman" patent in 1929, it still held the strategic "starch" and "bubble-board" patents, together with many other patents of lesser importance. These were so essential to the competitive production of gypsum wallboard and related products that U. S. Gypsum was able to establish a restrictive licensing plan for the entire industry, and also apparently able to control the selling prices and customer selection of its licensees.[6]

[5] See *U. S. vs. United States Gypsum Co. 333 U. S. 364* (68 Sup. Ct. 525; 1948); also, *Minerals Yearbook*. (Gypsum-product firms also produce related building-materials lines, such as paint, paper, insulation board, and roofing, although the heavier products are ordinarily not made at gypsum-product plants. We neglect this participation in other industries here. Data from O.P.A. records suggest that the largest five or six firms in the industry derive about 70 per cent of their sales revenue from gypsum products.)

[6] *U. S. vs. United States Gypsum Co.*, cited at note 5.

Although the patent royalties charged to licensees were evidently moderate (ranging from 3.5 per cent of sales at the outset down to 1 per cent after 1941), it appears that the patent-protected product differentiation of United States Gypsum enabled it (1) to reserve to itself a dominant and protected market share (about 55 per cent); (2) to restrict the number and size of its rivals; (3) to foreclose absolutely further entry to the production of the preferred fabricated products; and (4) to discourage entry of inferior products while earning an appreciable excess profit return on its protected lines. As to restrictions on the number of rivals, there were apparently only five licensees. As to the foreclosure of entry, new names appeared in the field only through the acquisition of licensed going concerns, and various unlicensed wallboard companies were acquired by licensees. Celotex entered the industry in 1939 by acquiring the assets and licenses of American Gypsum Co. As to acquisitions by established firms, U. S. Gypsum acquired Niagara Gypsum in 1929; National Gypsum (number two company in the industry) acquired Universal Gypsum in 1935 and Atlanta Gypsum in 1936; Certainteed acquired Beaver Products and Beaver Board Co. in 1928; Newark acquired Kelley Plasterboard Co. in 1937. Thus it appears that until the 1951 decree a product-differentiation advantage resting on patents placed a high barrier in the way of entry to the fabricated-products sector of the gypsum industry, although there was no such barrier to entering the production of plain building plaster.

With the 1951 decree, the situation changed, since U. S. Gypsum was required to offer non-discriminatory and non-exclusive licensing of all gypsum board patents then held or acquired in the next five years, to all applicants at reasonable royalty rates (about 1 per cent of sales price).[7] Moreover, the last bubble-board patent was to expire in 1954. In this altered situation it appears that the product-differentiation barrier to entry has become slight, and industry testimony confirms this. The potential entrant's disadvantage, if any, should not exceed that imposed by the 1 per cent royalty rate.

The remaining question is whether company brand names and reputations create a significant degree of product differentiation or appreciably affect entry. There is some advertising in the industry — though traceable advertising ran well under 1 per cent of sales in 1950, in 1940 total advertising expense equal to 1.6 per cent of sales was reported.[8] Industry respondents to questionnaires, however, assert that brand names are actually unimportant in the industry, and that no individual seller can command price premia on the basis of brand or of product difference. Nonetheless,

[7] *U. S. vs. United States Gypsum Co.*, Final Amended Decree (CCH. Trade Cases 1950–51, par. 62578).

[8] Federal Trade Commission, *Distribution Methods and Costs*, Part V (1944) p. 7.

the reputations of established firms are held to confer some holding power over customers. As to the potential entrant, it is held that entry would entail "extra promotional costs" to gain a trade position, but neither the amount of the excess nor the time period over which it would have to be spent is estimated. On the basis of this rather sketchy evidence, we very tentatively have classified the present product-differentiation barrier to entry to the gypsum products industry as slight. It may be higher.

This classification, however, refers to the period from 1951 on. A different classification — probably as having great product-differentiation barriers — is evidently in order when we are discussing the behavior of the industry in the 1930's and 1940's.

(f) *The meat-packing industry* produces primarily fresh meat, from the three principal species of meat animals and from fowl, and processed meats, including smoked and cured meats and various canned meats. The larger companies frequently offer a full line of both fresh and processed meats, whereas smaller firms often specialize, particularly in the fresh meat field.[9] Branding is clearly in evidence in processed meats, and present though much less evident in fresh meats. The products in general are subject to grading by quality, and various qualities or grades of the different products are present in the market. Particular qualities are to some extent identified with particular sellers or groups of sellers, but any seller is rather easily able to match the quality of another. Physical product differences which can be protected or maintained are then not significant in the industry; the primary issue concerns the importance of branding.

In this connection, advertising costs are not large. Total advertising costs in 1940 were reported for 30 firms at under 0.5 per cent of sales,[10] whereas 1950 traceable advertising for the Big 4 firms runs consistently under 0.5 per cent. Relative expenditure on the advertisement of fresh and of processed meats are not distinguished in available data, but it is apparent that processed meats receive the bulk of attention in advertising by meat packers.

The testimony of several industry respondents on the importance of product differentiation in the industry reveals a high degree of agreement on most essential matters. First, it seems agreed that brand attachments in fresh meats, either at the consumer level or as reflected in the disposition of retailers to buy for stock, are very slight. Such price differences as result among brands are held to rest not on brand *per se* but on a

[9] For general information on the industry see Hoffman, "Large Scale Organization in the Food Industries" (unpublished doctoral dissertation, Harvard University, 1939), Ch. 3; American Meat Institute, *Reference Book on Meat*, 1950; Lewis Corey, *Meat and Man*, 1950.

[10] Federal Trade Commission, *Distribution Methods and Costs, Part I*, pp. 187 ff.; *Part V*, pp. 8, 27.

measurable quality associated with a brand (coupled with reputation for quality maintenance). Protracted price differences among brands of similar quality in a given fresh meat line are not maintained. In processed meats, the importance of brand is held to be slightly greater, although again physical quality and quality maintenance seem to be the keys to any price advantage in a market where the end buyers are unusually well equipped to evaluate quality for themselves. Nevertheless, consumers show some inertia in shifting from accepted and familiar brands to others in the processed meat field, and this is reflected in a reluctance of retailers to stock unfamiliar brands, since they fear slow turnover. Among established brands, the largest sellers (e.g. the Big 4) do not appear to enjoy a perceptible product-differentiation advantage over medium-sized and small firms; the latter have consistently done as well profit-wise for many years.

The product-differentiation disadvantage of an entrant to the fresh meat field is held to be negligible. The corresponding disadvantage in entering the processed meat field (as reflected in promotional costs) is variously evaluated: 2 to 6 per cent of price in extra promotional costs for about a year to break into the market, generally very small, very large for several years. The bulk of the testimony appears to sustain the notion that the effective barrier is rather slight.

2. Industries with moderate product-differentiation barriers to entry.

The members of this category, excluding segments of mixed industries, were listed in Table XI as metal containers, rubber tires and tubes, petroleum refining, and soap. Since there are numerous difficulties in classifying industries in this range, the following comments should be viewed as essentially qualifying the findings in Table XI.

(a) *The metal container industry* offers an output classified under four main headings: "packers' cans" for food products, "general line cans" for a variety of uses, beer cans, and terneplate cans for lubricating oil. The shares of the industry value-product in these four categories in 1943 were roughly 55, 35, 5, and 5 per cent. Can purchasers are of course packagers such as food canners, brewers, refiners making lubricants, etc. It is worthy of note that the can is useful to the purchaser only as used jointly with specialized machinery for closing or sealing cans, and that not only acquisition of the use of such machinery but training or assistance in its use is essential to the can purchaser.[11]

Although over 80 per cent of all can sales have generally been accounted for by the first two firms in the industry — American and Continental — branding *per se* does not appear to be very important, and ad-

[11] For general information on the industry see Hession, *Competition in the Metal Food Container Industry,* Ch. 2 and 3.

vertising costs are small (0.6 per cent of sales for 9 firms in 1940).[12] The sources of product differentiation in the industry seem in general to have been found in the services provided by can makers to their customers, in the sellers' abilities to supply can-closing machinery for lease to buyers, and in certain patents.

To take these matters in reverse order, two general types of patents are of potential importance in the industry — product patents (which may be equivalent to patents on can-making machinery), and patents on can-closing machinery. Either sort of patent may enable a can seller to differentiate his product significantly.

With respect to basic or "prior arts" patents, it seems agreed that they have practically all long since expired and offer no present deterrent to entry. This is the testimony of industry informants, and also of Hession,[13] who cites the experience of a 1936 entrant to the industry (Crown Can), which found a more or less free and open market for purchasing both can-making and can-closing machines. The effective patents in the industry today are apparently in the main "improvement" and special-product patents. They cover machinery developments designed to allow, for example, speedier production or closing of cans, and new product-process combinations such as for high-speed vacuum packing of coffee and linings for beer cans. Writing in 1948, Hession reports very little cross-licensing of patents in the industry, and quotes industry sources as attributing this to the fact that "competitors" have their own patents and do not need to apply for cross licenses. But Hession is unwilling to conclude that these patents are unimportant in competition or in their effect on entry; he concludes merely that patents "do not constitute an insuperable obstacle to entry." [14]

No quantitative evaluation of the impact of such patents on intra-industry competition or on entry is available. It appears, however (1) that the smaller firms (i.e., those other than American and Continental, which are the principal developers and holders of patents) are at an appreciable though not very large disadvantage in consequence of the patent-protected process-product superiority of the Big 2 in numerous lines; and (2) that any entrant would be at a corresponding if not greater disadvantage.

The second source of product differentiation may inhere in the differential ability of sellers to provide buyers with can-closing machinery on lease. This service has been customarily provided by the Big 2, and also by several smaller firms supplying much smaller fractions of the market.[15] Since the basic patents on such machinery have expired and

[12] Federal Trade Commission, *Distribution Methods and Costs*, Part V, p. 6.
[13] Pp. 167 ff.
[14] Hession, pp. 167–171.
[15] Hession, p. 174.

since any can company could apparently acquire machines for lease to customers without much difficulty, no barrier to entry or competition other than that inhering in improvement patents might seem to result from the leasing practices in question. It does appear, however, that there are probably appreciable advantages to scale in this machine-leasing business, and that the Big 2 gain a corresponding advantage over small competitors and over entrants of the one-plant size. If an entrant could overcome this disadvantage through entry at a substantial scale, he might encounter counterbalancing impediments to entry due to the large scale of his entry.

All this can hardly be considered apart from the provision of field service to customers who lease machines from the can suppliers. As Hession points out,[16] field service of leased can-closing machines, together with the provision of various sorts of technical advice and assistance, are extremely important to purchasers of cans. In the provision of these services, the Big 2 appear to enjoy appreciable advantages of scale over smaller firms, since the field-service organization is most economically organized by the very large firm; and the purchaser who acquires his own closing machines from independent sources is without benefit of the essential services to large can makers are able to provide.

The extent of the resultant barrier to entry (product differentiation and advantages of large-scale sales promotion being taken into account) cannot be appraised quantitatively, although certain scraps of evidence are available. Hession points out [17] that, in order to obtain business, National Can (without about 3 per cent of the market in 1939) has consistently shaded Big 2 prices, by about 2 per cent in the period from 1936 to 1946. Similarly, Crown Can shaded Big 2 prices by around 2 per cent, and Pacific Can by about 6 per cent. These price disadvantages may of course be offset in some degree by lower promotional costs. Industry sources are in general agreement on the point, stating that "preferred sellers get preferred prices" and that a new entrant would have to accept lower prices at least for a time. These price disadvantages suggest either (1) that patents are significant, or (2) that smaller firms, faced with diseconomies of small-scale sales promotion, provide less service at a lower price rather than incurring promotional costs sufficient to put their service on a parity with that of the Big 2.

The maximum extent of the competitive leverage possessed by the Big 2 is suggested by the allegations made in parallel antitrust suits against them, brought in 1946.[18] Here it was alleged in the main that the Big 2 had (1) leased their can-closing machinery on three- to five-year

[16] Hession, pp. 178 ff. and 273 ff.
[17] Hession, pp. 203–205.
[18] U. S. vs. American Can Co. 87 F.Supp. 18 (N.D. Cal. 1946); Civil Action No. 26345H; and U. S. vs. Continental Can Co. (summarized, not reported; N.D. Cal. 1946); Civil Action No. 26346R.

tying contracts generally requiring that the lessees purchase their total requirements of cans from the lessor,[19] and (2) that they had otherwise entered into long-term total-requirement contracts with purchasers for periods such as 5 years. Their ability to do this would seem to reflect in some degree the competitive advantages just referred to. In addition, the existence of a large number of such tying and/or total-requirement contracts would impose a serious immediate deterrent to entry. (At least 2 or 3 of the principal smaller can firms had apparently also employed such contracts.)

The outcome of the antitrust suits in question was a decree handed down in 1950 and aimed at reducing the competitive advantages of the Big 2 and the corresponding barriers to entry. In the main it imposed (1) injunctions against all tying contracts in the leasing and sale of can-closing machinery by the defendants, plus the requirement that machines be leased or sold on equal terms and conditions to all applicants; (2) injunctions against total-requirement contracts of more than one-year duration, plus the requirement that any single contract must be written only for an individual plant of a buyer; and (3) requirements that existing can-closing machinery patents be leased royalty-free to all applicants, and that future patents be similarly leased at reasonable royalty rates.

Enforcement of this decree would tend of course to reduce at least somewhat the product-differentiation barriers to entry to the can-making industry. We have at present no information on its possible consequences. In the light of the complex nature of the product-differentiation advantages of the large established firms, however — involving special product and process patents of various sorts as well as evident advantages of large-scale sales promotion through service organizations — our guess is that product-differentiation barriers to entry would not be entirely eliminated by the maximum practical enforcement of the decree, and that present classification of the can-making industry as having moderate product-differentiation barriers to entry is still in order. Prior to 1951, however, a great product-differentiation barrier to entry probably existed.

The preceding refers in the main to the entrant of single-efficient-plant scale. It has been recognized in our estimates that extensive multiplant development would probably confer advantages in sales promotion of the sort enjoyed by the Big 2, which in general have multiplant developments not only nationally but within regional markets. The general rule seems to apply, however, that as far as product-differentiation barriers were lowered through large-scale multiplant entry, barriers dependent on the scale of the entrant firm would in some offsetting degree be raised. Available data do not permit any very close judgment in this regard.

[19] See Hession, pp. 172 ff., for a further discussion of this matter.

A word may be added about the competition of cans with other types of containers, and the effect of this on entry to the markets occupied primarily by can manufacturers. In these markets — including those for food containers and numerous general-line containers — the can industry has been subject to the competition of glass containers, fibre containers for dry products, and frozen-food containers. As yet, the tin can still generally dominates as the low-priced packaging medium, and thus "extra-industry" competition has not visibly affected can prices. Nevertheless it has encouraged rivalry in sales promotion, and faces the can industry with added "threats of entry" which would become actual in greater degree if can prices were substantially raised.

The other side of the coin is that cans have invaded fields primarily supplied by other containers — notably beer, coffee, and lubricating oil containers. Here the substitutability between cans and other containers (with the going price ratios) is generally close, and the threat of entry or expanded competition by makers of the other packaging media seems strong enough so that the effective "barrier to entry" is probably quite low. Data are lacking, however, to permit any quantitative judgments on this matter.

(b) *The rubber tire and tube industry* of course supplies tires and inner tubes for all sorts of vehicles, from small passenger cars to heavy trucks and busses and from bicycles to airplanes. Passenger-car tires and truck tires are the dominant items, and these are sold principally to the "original equipment" market of vehicle manufacturers, and the "replacement" market of vehicle users. Generally, original equipment sales will account for from 30 to 40 per cent of automotive tire and tube volume, and replacement sales for the remainder. The composition of replacement sales in 1947 has been estimated as about 52 per cent through independent dealers handling factory brands, 23 per cent through service-station chains of petroleum refining companies, 16 per cent through other chain and mail-order houses, 6 per cent through the tire-makers' integrated retail stores, and 3 per cent miscellaneous. In other terms, about 40 per cent of replacement tire volume moved through so-called mass distributors, and three-fourths of the mass-distributor volume (or about 30 per cent of the total) was sold under the "private" brands of the distributors as distinct from the "factory" brands of the tire makers.[20]

As to the importance of product differentiation, generally it seems quite significant in the replacement market as far as ultimate sales to users go, but it is not so significant in the intermediate market which involves mass distributors as buyers from tire makers. It is significant again in the original equipment market, insofar as auto makers wish to attach

[20] General information on the industry is drawn largely from R. B. Heflebower's unpublished manuscript on the rubber tire industry.

"prestige" brands of tires to their products, but here the monopsonistic power of the auto makers somewhat modifies the significance of the differentiation.

The primary basis of product differentiation in tires does not seem to be found in differences of physical design and quality. Designs are easily imitated and qualities easily duplicated, and the product is not complex enough to give much range to distinctiveness in design. Product innovations have been made periodically since the early days of the industry (the tubeless tire is the latest one of prominence), but in general appear to have conferred only transitory advantages on the innovators, who are quickly copied once the saleability of the new product is established. The primary bases of differentiation lie in (a) long-established product reputations, developed and sustained by moderately heavy advertising; (b) control over or continued affiliation with systems of well-established retail dealers; and (c) provision of service to customers through these dealer systems, especially in such matters as guarantee adjustments and repairs. As far as the replacement market is concerned, the Big 4 companies obtain a considerable sales promotional advantage by dominating the original equipment market, so that new cars nearly always carry their brands, although they pay for this by selling original equipment tires at very low prices.

Advertising costs, exclusive of other selling expenses, appear to have run from 1 to 2 per cent of tire and tube sales at the beginning of the 1940's. The Big 4 had advertising costs equal to 2.1 per cent of sales in 1942, or 2.4 per cent on replacement sales alone; the corresponding figures for 13 small sellers were around 1.2 per cent.[21] (To these are added other expenses classified as "selling," to the amount of 8 to 10 per cent of sales, but the detailed composition of these expenses is not known.)

The Big 4 and one or two of the strongest independents distribute their products dominantly. or entirely under their own brands and through chains of retail dealers who are supplied by factory-owned branch wholesale outlets. Less than a fifth of this volume moves through factory-owned retail outlets, but there are generally long-standing contractual or "franchise" affiliations of systems of independent dealers with given tire makers. The smaller independents, on the other hand, are in substantial degree dependent on the market of the mass distributors (primarily a private-brand market), although factory-brand sales are also made via independent wholesalers to independent dealers. In general, there is a rather distinct differentiation between the Big 4 products as one group and the products of most of the independents as another (reflected as we shall see in differences in actual price realizations at both factory and

---

[21] From O.P.A. data in Office of Temporary Controls, *Economic Data Series No. 10*, and Heflebower.

retail levels), with the one or two of the strongest independents occupying some sort of middle position.

The extent of the net advantage thus conferred on the large sellers, or of the resultant barrier to entry, is not readily established from the questionnaire replies received. These replies recognize that preferred sellers have and exercise the ability to obtain preferred prices, though at the expense of higher costs of sales promotion and customer service. They recognize some difficulty for an entrant in entering either the factory-brand or the mass-distributor market, but do not estimate the extent and duration of the entrant's disadvantage. This may be connected with the fact that the tire industry — engaged in working off serious excess capacity since 1930 and with apparently severe intra-industry competition — has been substantially without new entry for a long time.

In consequence, we must rely primarily on records of the relative performances of large and small firms in the industry as bases for estimating the probable impact of product differentiation on entry. Fortunately, such records are available from the O.P.A. in relative profusion,[22] although their showings are not necessarily conclusive on the points at issue. With reference primarily to a month in 1941 (taken as the last prewar year), two things stand out in these records.

First, the brands of the Big 4, as sold in the replacement market, appeared to command on the average both a higher actual retail price and a higher net wholesale price realization to the manufacturer than the brands of their smaller competitors. For 1941, for example, the following comparison of net retail prices (after trade-ins) received by independent dealers for first-grade 6:00–16 tires is found:

Brands	Retail list price	Net retail price after trade-in
Big 4 brands	$14.75	$13.77
Brands of 22 small companies, including 8 associated with the Big 4	14.77	12.77
Brands of 5 small companies with "high" list prices, including 1 associated with the Big 4	16.82	13.61

A substantial net price advantage to the Big 4 (Goodyear, Goodrich, Firestone, U. S. Rubber) as compared to independents in general is noted, although a few stronger independents are at no very great retail price disadvantage. When the focus shifts to the wholesale net-back of the tire manufacturer (same tire size, November 1941) the cleavage between the Big 4 and others becomes more distinct:

---

[22] See Heflebower for an extensive presentation and analysis of the O.P.A. data, including the tabular material presented on the next several pages.

Brands	Retail list price	Wholesale price to small dealers	Wholesale price at maximum announced discount
Big 4 brands	$14.75	$10.18	$8.16
Brands of 22 small companies, as above	14.77	9.15	6.84
Brands of 5 small companies with "high" list prices, as above	16.82	9.71	7.42
Brands of 4 small independents with "high" selling expenses	15.68	9.87	7.18
Brands of 5 small independents with "low" selling expenses	15.84	9.81	6.70
Brands of all small companies	—	9.70	7.15

A rather distinct advantage to the Big 4 in the small dealer's wholesale price, and an even more distinct one in the "maximum-announced-discount" wholesale price, are apparent. Data are not available to reveal the proportions of volume passing at various net wholesale prices. It may be emphasized also that the small-firm prices evidently refer to factory-brand output sold through dealer channels and not to private-brand sales direct to mass distributors.

Set off against the price advantage of the Big 4 is some virtual disadvantage in the expense of distribution and selling — attributable partly to more intensive sales promotion, but also seemingly to a higher degree of distributive integration on the part of the Big 4. The second finding is that, *if the prices at maximum announced discount are taken as representative of the comparative average realizations*, the net realization to the manufacturer after deducting all commercial expenses still favors the Big 4. Thus we find for three groups of companies the following, again for 6:00–16 regular tires in November, 1941:

Brands	Price at maximum announced discount	Total commercial expense	Net realization after commercial expense
Big 4 brands	$8.16	$2.08	$6.08
Brands of 4 small independents with "high" selling expenses	7.18	1.53	5.65
Brands of 5 small independents with "low" selling expenses	6.70	0.81	5.89

Using maximum-announced-discount prices as representative of comparative realizations, the Big 4 maintain a clear though reduced advantage after deducting all distributive and selling expense. If list wholesale prices to small dealers were used, however, the Big 4 would appear at some disadvantage in net realizations. Lacking data on actual average wholesale prices, some cross-check on the reliability of the findings just tabulated is desirable. This may be done by deducting the corresponding factory costs from the net realizations above, computing hypothetical percentages of profit on sales, and then comparing these percentages with the over-all percentages of profit on sales for the same groups as reported by O.P.A. The reported factory costs in 1941 for the 6:00–16 tires in question were $5.04 for the Big 4, $5.46 for the four small firms with high selling expense, and $5.17 for the five small firms with low selling expense. After deducting these factory costs from the previous net realizations, we find profit margins on sales of about 13, 2.5, and 11 per cent for the three groups on 6:00–16 tires. On *all* replacement tire sales for the same groups in 1941, on the other hand, O.P.A. data show profit rates of 11.1 per cent for the Big 4, 6.2 per cent for the four high-selling-expense independents, and 5.1 per cent for the five low-selling-expense independents. This generally sustains the notion that the Big 4 held an appreciable net advantage in the replacement tire field, but suggests that the maximum-discount price data for 6:00–16 tires may tend to understate the position of some of the independents.

Looking at the available data as a whole, it appears that in the replacement tire field, the Big 4 had two advantages over the independents as a group — one of perhaps 2.5 to 5 per cent in average net price realization after commercial expenses, and one of perhaps 2 to 5 per cent in factory costs. A very few independents probably had a smaller aggregate disadvantage than the average, and many others a somewhat greater one. In consequence of this combined advantage of the Big 4, it would appear that they might be able to reduce independent competition to a point of zero profit while earning 5 or more per cent on replacement sales (before deduction of interest on investment), and that about half this advantage might be attributable to a product differentiation in their favor.

Before turning to the possible implications of the existing intra-industry competitive situation for the welfare of a potential entrant, we must consider the original-equipment sales of the Big 4. In general they dominate this market and their independent competition has been unable to penetrate it. On the other hand, they supply the market at lower net price realizations and lower profit rates on sales (given their system of allocating expenses) than they earn in the replacement market, at rates varying from a fifth to two-thirds as great, according to O.P.A. data. This leads to a poorer over-all profit showing, and lessens but does not erase their superiority over the independents in terms of over-all profits on sales. It should be noted, however, that the fact that the Big 4 apparently practice the indicated price discrimination between the replacement and original-equipment market, and thus reduce their over-all profit percentages, does not necessarily detract from the fact that they enjoy a clear product-differentiation advantage, price superiority, and extra profit in the replacement market — at least as compared to the bulk of their independent competition. Unless we view the price concessions made to original-equipment purchasers a concealed promotional cost, the product-differentiation advantage in the replacement market is not taken away through original-equipment sales.[23]

Let us now turn to the matter of potential entry. The statement in Table XI that the potential entrant of efficient one-plant scale would incur "up to 5 per cent price or promotion-cost disadvantage for a prolonged period, partly offset by lack of original-equipment business," has been based upon two principal speculations. First, we have supposed that such an entrant would tend to have at least as much price or promotional disadvantage in the factory-brand replacement market as long-established independent brands, and more than that of the top one or two independents. Thus the barrier to entry is tentatively measured as the same or greater than the product-differentiation disadvantage of small established firms, so far as reference to the factory-brand replacement market is concerned. Second, we have presumed that such an entrant could not tap the original equipment market at all, but that as a result his over-all profit showing would not be damaged by carrying this low-price business. This does not detract from the ability of the Big 4 to elevate replacement-tire prices significantly above minimal costs while forestalling entry, but it does detract from their ability to earn superior over-all profits while doing so.

So far as the possibility of large-scale entry is concerned, it is conceivable that with entry at a scale comparable to the smallest of the Big 4 (supplying 12 or 13 per cent of the total tire market) the new firm could overcome the product-differentiation disadvantage in large part, though with high initial promotional expenses for advertising and development of dealer systems. If it could do so, however, the impediments to entry consequent upon its scale would tend to counterbalance the lessening of the product-differentiation disadvantage. Thus we are left with the tentative conclusion that the product-differentiation barrier to entry to the tire

---

[23] That the net advantage of the Big 4 is not transitory or limited to a single year is indicated by the following figures on profit rates on all tire sales (replacement plus original equipment) for the Big 4 and for 10 small tire firms from 1936 to 1941 (from Heflebower):

| Year | Profits as a percentage of all tire sales | |
	Big 4	Small 10
1936	6.9	3.3
1937	4.7	2.8
1938	3.9	6.0
1939	6.5	9.1
1940	7.5	3.8
1941	12.4	9.4

Aside from exceptionally depressed years, some net advantage in rates on sales seems persistent.

industry, all things considered, probably falls in the "moderate" range. But the conclusion rests on relatively unsatisfactory and inconclusive data.

(c) *The petroleum refining industry* has as its principal product gasoline, which accounts for the largest single share of physical volume of output and a dominant share of sales revenue to the refiner. Lubricants are of course distributed jointly with gasoline for motor vehicle use, whereas gas oil and heavy fuel oil move predominantly through other channels and to other than vehicle uses.[24] By and large there is little product differentiation in the "by-product" outputs such as the fuel oils, which are customarily purchased in bulk and to specification. Even in home deliveries of furnace oil to consumers, brand names appear to have slight importance. Product differentiation is found primarily in gasoline (and in the adjunct, lubricants). But, since petroleum refining necessarily involves the joint production of gasoline with the lower-valued and heavier products, and since the bulk of the revenue of the typical refiner must come from gasoline, product differentiation in gasoline affects the condition of entry to the production of every refined product. Thus we are justified in emphasizing gasoline product differentiation as the phase of product differentiation which is crucial to the refinery industry in general.[25]

It seems fair to say that (1) there is a distinct product differentiation in gasoline, in some degree among major-firm brands and in greater degree between major-firm and "independent" brands; (2) the differentiation rests in minor part only on actual physical product differences; and (3) it rests in major part on brand allegiances developed through advertising and through the maintenance by refiners of chains of exclusive-dealing service stations, the latter fostering differentiation through their in-built advertising values and through offering customer service. Such differentiation appears important in the two-thirds to three-fourths of gasoline volume moving through service stations to individual consumers; for the remainder which moves to commercial buyers, it is less important.

The basis of the product differentiation is not readily apparent from 1950 traceable advertising data, which indicate advertising as a small fraction of 1 per cent of total petroleum-product sales, although various casual industry estimates place total advertising of gasoline somewhere between 1 and 2 per cent of gasoline sales. In any event, its major basis is evidently found in the exclusive-dealing service-station chains sponsored and maintained by refiners — sometimes through actual ownership and

---

[24] See J. S. Bain, *Economies of the Pacific Coast Petroleum Industry, Part 1* (Berkeley, 1944), for general descriptive material on the petroleum refining industry.

[25] Exception to this generalization may be made for a relatively few refinery operations specializing in the processing of very heavy crude oils to obtain asphalt and related products, with gasoline essentially as a by-product.

operation of the retail facilities, but more typically through a variety of contractual arrangements involving concessions by the refiners to the operators, made to secure continued representation in the retail market. Such arrangements, encouraging the use of relatively high-valued land for service-station sites, usually mean that the refiner assumes a part of the cost of land rent and service-station plant and equipment, so that implicitly the refiners subsidize retail distribution to an appreciable extent. The subsidies may be viewed as sales-promotional expenses, although they can of course also be stated as direct price concessions in the tank-wagon wholesale market.

Aside from the accumulation of direct and indirect sales-promotion expenses, the incidence of product differentiation in intra-industry competition is principally apparent in the relative positions of the large or major refiners and their smaller independent competitors. In general, the major seller is unable or unwilling to try to command actual price premia over his major rivals in any sustained fashion — a balance frequently struck in industries with relatively simple products and a heavy sales promotional emphasis. But there has been an appreciable price cleavage between major and independent refiner brands, amounting to from 5 to 10 per cent of the retail price (excluding taxes) and apparently to corresponding percentages at the tankwagon wholesale level. This disadvantage of the independents is apparently offset in some part by the lower promotional costs, but not entirely. They have in general fared less well in profit rates unless heavily assisted by the imputed profits of integrated crude oil holdings. This refers, however, to refiner-brand independent sales made through the tankwagon market to service stations. In some areas (e.g. the Pacific Coast), such would be practically the only available outlet for independent gasoline. In other areas (e.g. the Midwest), there is a developed group of independent gasoline jobbers who buy direct from refiners and undertake subsequent distribution, usually under their own brands. In selling to them, independent refiners can obtain almost as good a price (within 1 or 1.5 per cent, at any rate) as can the larger refiners. It is not indicated whether this realization is as good as the larger refiner gets through the tankwagon market, but the evidence generally is that it is usually inferior, though the disadvantage is smaller than would be incurred if the independent distributed his own brand direct to service stations. The existence of a real independent jobber market in a region may thus improve somewhat the competitive position of the small refiner, although it will probably not give him equality of position with the majors.

For an appraisal of the impact of product differentiation on the condition of entry, we turn to the estimates of various respondents to questionnaires. The estimate of the barrier, presented in Table XI, Chapter 4, is a sort of compromise among somewhat divergent views, the divergences evidently reflecting among other things differences among the respondents as to the regions in which their firms operate. The range of opinions is roughly as follows. For entry to the tankwagon market, with sales of refiner-brand gasoline to service stations, one estimate (apparently referred primarily to the East Coast and the South) is that the entrant would, as compared to large established sellers, incur extra promotional costs and/or price concessions of from 1 to 2 cents per gallon for 3 to 5 years. This is more or less backed by other estimates to the effect that such an entrant would incur a fairly prolonged period of disadvantage in costs of advertising and subsidizing dealers, or alternatively extra price concessions of around 1 cent per gallon for a substantial time interval. For entry to the so-called refinery wholesale market — involving sales to jobbers, probably of unbranded gasoline — the general consensus of respondents is that the disadvantage of the entrant would be either zero or quite small. Not indicated, however, is what the net disadvantage of the entrant supplying the jobber market would be, relative to the major who supplies (as he does primarily) the tankwagon market. This is presumably not a negligible disadvantage, although it would appear that in those areas with large independent-jobber markets the product-differentiation disadvantage of the entrant would be less than elsewhere.

The estimates in question seem generally appropriate to the entrant penetrating a regional market at or near the scale of a single maximum-efficient refinery. Since this refinery scale is quite large in absolute terms, advantages of large-scale distribution seem likely to be subject to fairly adequate exploitation without the firm becoming larger in any region than this indicated scale. Data on this point, however, are far from adequate. One final point deserves emphasis. Suppose in fact that an entrant of the scale indicated incurred a price or promotional cost disadvantage of from 1 to 2 cents per gallon for three to five years, and that prices in the industry were set so that established firms made no excess profits. Then the entrant might anticipate losses ranging from 5 to 20 million at a minimum up to 35 to over 100 million at a maximum — depending on the version of optimal scale chosen as appropriate to the regional market in question — as a price for breaking into the market and ultimately obtaining a position without net disadvantage. This would substantially increase the capital requirements for entry at efficient scale; correspondingly, the importance of discovering oil in order to meet the early capital requirements of entry would be emphasized.

(d) *The soap industry* has been classified as having only moderate product-differentiation barriers to entry, but it is evidently on the borderline between the "moderate" and "great" barrier categories, and could readily be put in the latter.

The principal products are household soaps, including laundry and related soaps, toilet soaps, and various liquid and cream soaps, shampoos, etc., in order of importance. Of lesser importance are other cleaning and polishing preparations and various industrial soap products, but the major market is for household soaps. These fall in recent years into (a) the traditional fatty-acid soaps, and (b) the detergents ("non-soap" chemical compounds with detergent qualities). By 1952, detergents had almost the same physical volume of output as fatty-acid soaps and were still gaining. In the same year, the Big 3 of the industry (Procter & Gamble, Colgate, and Lever Bros.) were estimated to supply about 75 per cent of fatty-acid soaps and 95 per cent of detergents; [26] much of the remainder was supplied by 6 lesser soap makers (four of them meat packers); a more extensive fringe (perhaps 20 in laundry soaps and an unspecified number in toilet soaps) of "small soapers" accounted for the balance of industry output. The principal firms have come to offer full lines of both fatty-acid and detergent soaps, and also of both laundry and toilet products.

It is no secret to the owner of a radio or television set, mailbox, or newspaper subscription that there are continual vigorous efforts in the industry to establish product differentiation. Even so, the advertising costs of the industry seem astonishingly high, and are probably the highest (as a percentage of sales) of any major consumer-good industry. The Federal Trade Commission reported advertising costs for 20 soap firms as 10.9 per cent of sales revenue in 1940 (plus 8.9 per cent other selling and delivery costs).[27] Traceable advertising in 1950 was 5.8 per cent of sales for one of the Big 3, 10 per cent for another, and comparably high for several smaller firms. The first 3 firms spent together about 59 million dollars on traceable advertising. Advertising is centered around attempting to develop consumer allegiances to particular brands, of which each major seller has one or more in the several product divisions of the industry.[28] Product differentiation evidently rests in minor degree on differences in the physical properties of competing products and in major degree on persuasive advertising *per se*.

How great is this differentiation among products of established firms? It may seem paradoxical that the bulk of industry opinion is to the effect that customer allegiances to particular established brands are in fact not very strong in the soap industry, and certainly not strong enough to permit one seller to command a perceptible price premium as compared to others. This observation presumably applies mainly to customer prefer-

[26] See *Business Week*, Dec. 20, 1952, p. 54.
[27] *Distribution Methods and Costs*, Part V, p. 7.
[28] Such divisions would include, for example, light-duty detergents, heavy-duty detergents, detergent powders, soap shreds and powder, liquid dishwashing compounds, dishwashing detergents, bar toilet soap, shaving creams, etc., etc.

ences among the numerous brands of the Big 3 plus a handful of the stronger smaller brands in any line. Thus as among the brands accounting for the great bulk of industry output, the relatively large expenditures on advertising seem to have been largely self-cancelling, at least to the extent that no one seller has built up a following of customers loyal enough to pay a premium price for soap in the name of their allegiances.

Industry comments in this regard are revealing. Brand attachments are characterized as "ephemeral" in toilet soaps, "very slight" and very temporary in standard laundry soaps, "somewhat stronger" in the fine-fabric soaps. A continual shifting of customers among brands is noted, which is encouraged by recurring promotional price concessions involving "special" prices and "couponing," and by non-price promotional tactics such as varying grocery-store display designs. Such attachments as exist are held to survive only if continually nourished by heavy advertising. The buyers (typically women shoppers) are characterized as acutely price-conscious and quality-conscious, so much so that no principal seller can maintain even a ½ cent or 1 cent retail price differential above his competitors and hold his volume.

The relative positions of large and small firms are a bit obscure. Apparently very small firms in general do not hold a parity in consumer preferences in the bulk markets for laundry soap chips and powders and low-priced toilet-soap bars, although a few firms outside the Big 3, such as meat packers, have very successfully penetrated these markets and attained something like competitive parity in one or several lines. However, there are fairly numerous instances of success by small sellers who gain a good market position through product innovations, as in the case of *Glim* (a liquid detergent), *Spic and Span* (wall and woodwork cleaner), and *All, Electrosol,* and *Calgonite* (automatic dishwater soaps). In addition, a few smaller firms have successfully tapped regional markets, as in the case of the *White King* soap powder of the L. A. Soap Co. on the Pacific Coast.

This brings us to the question of the height of the barrier to entry imposed by product-differentiation advantages of established as compared to entrant firms. The weight of industry opinion here is that established brands as a group have substantial advantages over new brands (whether of a new entrant or of an established firm), but that entry may be substantially eased by product innovations, the latter being most feasible in various "specialty" lines. The following paraphrases of questionnaire responses characterize this general opinion. Any firm would have to spend more on promotion to establish a new brand than it would have to spend to maintain the position of an established brand. Two or three years or longer of plowing back profits into promotion would be necessary for an entrant brand. To do even this well, the entrant would have to be one already distributing other products to the typical retail outlets — e.g., a meat packer who could promote a laundry soap through his established grocery-store connections. Otherwise, the entrant would have an extra disadvantage. Many years of higher advertising and other promotional expenses than established firms need would be required for an entrant to establish a market, unless he could enter on a true product innovation. In the latter case, exceptionally heavy advertising for a few years might do the trick. Established firms have an advertising advantage from their long-held radio and TV programs, which actually give them lower advertising costs "per message delivered" than a new entrant could attain at the outset.

In these responses, several things stand out: (1) there is an appreciable product-differentiation barrier to entry even for the most favored category of entrant; (2) the most favored category of potential entrants would be firms already distributing non-soap products through grocery and drug stores; (3) established firms can make a more economical use of radio and TV media than entrants could, because of the developed popularity of their programs; (4) a successful product innovation essentially provides a sort of cut-rate ticket to entry, and product innovations have proved feasible in numerous cases.

The last point is worth pondering in general as well as in the particular case of soap. It would appear that, in spite of product differentiation based on intensive sales promotion, that industry in which tangible product innovations are readily developed and can be made by small outsiders without access to the resources for research of the largest established companies will be an industry with easier entry than one in which the product is not significantly variable in any tangible sense. Hence, the soap industry can probably be distinguished, for example, from the cigarette and liquor industries.

Because of the apparent impact of product innovations in easing entry — plus the existence of a rather well-equipped set of potential entrants with established grocery-store or drug-store connections in distributing other products — we have hesitated between classifying the soap industry as having "moderate" or "high" product-differentiation barriers to entry. In the present state of information, perhaps the decision can best be made by flipping a coin. On the whole, it seems very probable that the product-differentiation barrier to entry in the soap industry is somewhat lower than in the cigarette, liquor, automobile, and "quality" fountain-pen industries.

The estimates in question are apparently applicable to entry at a scale not in excess of that of a single optimal plant, which would supply around 5 per cent of national industry output. The estimators apparently do not conceive of an entrant obtaining a significantly larger size, and certainly the successful entrants of recent decades have not. As to possible advantages of large-scale sales promotion involving multiplant scales, it would appear that the Big 3 established firms have reaped some virtual advantages of this character. Ability to saturate the media while holding advertising costs within a specified percentage of sales probably leads to a greater promotional effectiveness of the average advertising dollar. Whether big-budget advertising by an entrant would produce a similarly favorable relationship of advertising costs to sales for an entrant is unknown, and perhaps questionable. The risk that it would not may deter experiments along this line, or in any event make the effective capital requirements for entry more oppressive. If such advantages are available to entrants, however, any reduction of product-differentiation barriers to entry through very large-scale promotion would be roughly offset by increased barriers due to the scale of entry.

3. Industries with great product-differentiation barriers to entry.

The members of this category, excluding segments of "mixed" industries, were presented in Table XI as typewriters, cigarettes, liquor, and automobiles. In addition, there is the tractor industry, but although it is identified as a separate industry in the Census, it may best be dealt with in conjunction with the farm machinery industry. We turn, therefore, to the first four industries.

(a) *The typewriter industry* has a simple product mix — mechanical office typewriters, portables, and electrics. The Big 4 — Remington, Royal, Underwood, and L. C. Smith — account for about 80 per cent of the dollar sales in the industry, and International Business Machines (specializing in the expensive electrics) probably about 10 per cent.[29]

The rival products are differentiated, though not primarily in basic design. Industry sources indicate that all the basic product patents have expired, and that differentiation in design is largely confined to new and special "selling features" protected by patents. (This may not be true in the relatively new electrics field.) The primary basis of differentiation seems to lie in product reputations and particularly in customer service (involving repair, maintenance, inspection, etc.) built around established chains of dealers. The customer has allegiance to the reputation of the product and to the dealer, and is evidently influenced by the character and adequacy of the service provided. Advertising *per se* is of relatively minor importance compared to these things.

The importance of sales promotion along these lines is suggested both by various qualitative appraisals of the industry and by relevant statistics. Standard financial services characterize the industry as having "a merchandising rather than a production emphasis." The Federal Trade Com-

---

[29] Data on the typewriter industry are scanty. Much of the routine information here is drawn either from *Moody's* or from Federal Trade Commission, *Business Machine and Typewriter Manufacturing Corporations* (1941).

mission found for 1939 that for 10 business machine corporations, cost of goods sold was only 48 per cent of total sales, *and selling, general, and administrative expenses were 40 per cent of sales.* A further breakdown showed advertising as 2.6 per cent and "other selling expenses" as 26.2 per cent of sales.[30] Some supplementary data suggest that the percentages may be a bit lower for typewriters alone (excluding other business machines) but they are certainly still quite high.

Industry opinion received is to the effect that brand attachments of customers are not such as to permit premium prices to any major seller in comparison with others, but that at comparable prices the ties to brands and their dealers are quite strong. Comparative profit data suggest that in the last decade Remington and Royal have done substantially better than Underwood and L. C. Smith, but profit rates are influenced by so much more than product differentiation that it is hazardous to conclude much from this showing.

As to the disadvantage of prospective entrants, we have only rather broad general estimates to the effect that an entrant would have a "considerable" disadvantage in advertising costs for 5 or 10 years, and a similarly prolonged disadvantage in attempting to match the repair and maintenance services of the established firms. On a guess, we place the industry in the category of great product-differentiation barriers to entry. Certainly there has been no significant entry for a long time, except for that of IBM to the electrics field and a dribble of imported European portables.

Since the scale of an efficient typewriter plant is so large, possible economies of large-scale promotion involving multiplant development are generally unexplored and unknown.

(b) *The cigarette industry* is a simple, single-product industry. Differentiation in terms of physical properties is relatively unimportant. The product has been made short and long, with premium, regular, or cheap tobacco, with various sorts of tips and filters, and with somewhat different tobacco blends. But almost any variation a seller may undertake can be readily and quickly imitated by his rivals; moreover, product competition has in general led toward substantial identity, rather than variety, in the physical properties of the brands accounting for a preponderant share of cigarette sales. Thus 4 sellers with 4 principal brands and 4 or 5 secondary brands of consequence accounted for about 87 per cent of cigarette sales in 1949, substantially all with identical or closely similar blends and qualities; and perhaps half of the rest of the market went to brands without appreciable physical product differentiation. The remainder went largely to the cheap-tobacco economy brands, specialties, and premium grades.[31]

---

[30] *Business Machine and Typewriter Manufacturing Corporations,* p. 16.
[31] For general information on the industry, see Richard B. Tennant, *The American Cigarette Industry,* 1950.

Nevertheless, there is a very substantial product differentiation — evidenced in consumer allegiances to particular brands and in preferences for known over unknown brands — which has been built by heavy advertising over long periods. Advertising costs for the major brands (in periods when fully recorded rather than estimated from "traceable" figures) have amounted to around 5 per cent of sales inclusive of federal excise taxes, or 10 per cent of sales exclusive of these taxes. Thus O.P.A. records show that on the average from 1936 through 1941, advertising for 4 standard brands was 5.4 per cent of sales inclusive of excises, and that it was 12.1 per cent of sales exclusive of excises for 6 standard brands in 1941. Other sources generally verify these showings. When, before the second world war, the so-called economy brands — generally retailing at 2 or more cents below the standard brands — were a factor in the market, their absolute advertising costs per 1,000 cigarettes were lower. But their percentages of advertising to sales were slightly higher than for standard brands when sales were measured inclusive of excises, and much higher when sales were measured exclusive of excises (the excise being at a flat rate regardless of the grade or price of the cigarette). In general, cigarette advertising costs are in the high but not the maximum range for major consumer-good industries.

As to consumer allegiances to brands, it is apparent, and is also borne out by industry sources, that none of the sellers of the standard brands feels it can command a price premium over its successful rivals. Sales of all cigarettes priced higher than the standard brands have traditionally been very small until the recent wave of "filter-tips," which at this writing constitute a higher price line and command an increasing percentage of the market. (It appears that at the moment the market is in a state of flux, and will probably reach a new stable resting place within a few years.) Otherwise, the principal price differential in the industry has been that between the standard brands as a group and the "economy" brands as a group. The latter held a significant share of the market in the 1930's and were recognized as representing a lower level of quality sold at a different level of price.

On the other hand, loyalties of consumers to brands sold at identical prices seem surprisingly strong. Tennant [32] cites a commercial survey showing that, of the smokers sampled, 75 per cent had used a single brand for three or more years, and 31 per cent had used a single brand for eight or more years. Loyalties of consumers to the old standard brands as a group seem to have been seriously shaken only twice in recent times — by the economy brands via price concessions in the low-income 1930's, and by filter-tip brands following the development of the lung-cancer scare in connection with cigarettes.

[32] P. 135.

The relative positions of large and small firms established within the industry cannot be thoroughly appraised from available data. The several published works and doctoral theses written on the cigarette industry in the postwar years have given great emphasis to the relative positions of the economy brands *vis-à-vis* the standard brands in the last prewar decade. This is perhaps in part because the available O.P.A. records produced voluminous data comparing the two groups, but offered little else in the way of interfirm comparisons, and also because the rise and fall of the economy brands reflected the only significant emergence of price rivalry in the industry in a very long time and were the subject of attention in the antitrust litigation of the 1940's. Actually, all the data are more pertinent to assessment of the marketing possibilities of cut-rate cigarettes than to appraisal of the relative advantages of large and small firms *per se*. The data show that a group of about 10 economy brands were able to penetrate the market seriously with price differentials of three or more cents per pack at retail when consumer incomes were at low levels in the early and middle 1930's, and that they could not hold the market in the face of a narrowing of the price differential by the standard brands and the improvement of consumer incomes. Their success even in the favorable climate of depression is attributed to errors in judgment by the standard-brand manufacturers in permitting a wide rather than a narrower price differential to be sustained for some time. In our terms, there apparently was a substantial product-differentiation barrier to the entry of the economy brands, but the established firms set their prices so high at one time that the economy brands could make successful entry in spite of it.

Though changing income conditions somewhat complicate the picture, this is more or less substantiated by price, cost, and profit comparisons of standard-brand with economy-brand groups in the later 1930's and the beginning of the 1940's. The economy brands competed at the lower price by using substantially cheaper tobacco, allowing smaller absolute distributive margins, and incurring smaller absolute advertising costs. However, the fact that they paid the same flat excise tax rate as the standard brands meant that their advertising and distributive costs were higher percentages of net sales (after deducting excise taxes) than the standard brands incurred, and their tobacco-leaf cost percentage on the same basis was only very slightly lower. In consequence, the 1936–41 average profit on net worth (before deducting income tax) was about 21.6 per cent for standard brands as compared to 12.6 per cent for economy brands, whereas the corresponding percentages of profits to sales (inclusive of excise taxes) were 11.9 and 4.9. By 1941 and 1942 the percentage-on-sales comparison was that of 10 or 11 per cent to 1 or 2 per cent, and the gap appears much wider if sales after deducting excise taxes are used as a base of calculating percentages.[33]

From these data it would appear that, as of the immediate prewar period, the established standard-brand firms could make substantial excess profits while the economy brands made much smaller ones (dwindling toward minimal interest returns or less by the end of the war and after). Some rough calculations from the data cited suggest that, considering the necessary price differential to keep the economy brands seriously in the market (probably 3 cents per pack at retail [34]), the standard brands should have been able for the five or six years before the war to exclude or eliminate economy-brand competition from the market while charging prices sufficiently above costs to permit a return on net worth (after income taxes) of 12 to 14 per cent. (Postwar developments are not inconsistent with this estimate.) This corresponds roughly to an indicated *persistent* superiority in price minus advertising costs of 6 to 8 percentage points in ratio of profits to sales (including excises) — even against economy brands which had initially gained a fair foothold in the market. The initial break-in disadvantage of a new economy brand would presumably be greater, although large consumer-income variations might affect the height of the indicated barrier to entry.

The available data do not cast much light on the possible existence of advantages of large-scale sales promotion. Comparisons of promotional costs for different standard brands lead to no definite conclusion. For 10 standard brands in 1938 and 1939, no systematic association of traceable advertising costs to volume of sales is in evidence, and about all that can be concluded is that the four biggest selling brands maintained their volume without doing worse in per-unit advertising outlays than the smaller standard brands.[35] If advantages of very large-scale advertising are present in the industry (as distinct from simple consumer preferences favoring one brand over another), this is not confirmed by available data. If they are encountered, the increase in the scale-economy effect on entry would tend to counterbalance the decrease in the product-differentiation disadvantage. On the other hand, it is quite possible that less-favored brands (or entrants) might encounter serious disadvantages of very large-scale advertising if they tried to match the performance of the biggest three or four firms.

Let us turn now directly to the question of the condition of entry. We have already suggested that entry at the economy-brand level faces a high product-differentiation barrier, sufficient perhaps to permit established standard brands to earn an accounting profit before taxes equal to 6 or 8

[33] Cf. Tennant, Chs. 9, 10; and Office of Temporary Controls, *Economic Data Series No. 21.*

[34] Cf. Tennant, p. 160.

[35] Cf. Tennant, p. 167.

per cent of sales (inclusive of excises) while holding the economy brands
to a zero return as calculated on the same basis. In general, there is no
reason to suppose that entry to the economy-brand field would be any
easier than to the standard-brand field. Addressing themselves primarily
to the latter sort of entry, industry sources appraise the product-differentiation barrier as rather high. The highest estimate received placed the
advertising costs per unit of an entrant at ten to twenty times that of
established brands for seven years, in order to gain a market position comparable to that of the largest sellers. This would imply advertising costs
running up to several cents per package over a long break-in period, and
break-in losses of 100 or 200 million dollars or more in the current market.
This estimate might well be discounted if entry at a more modest scale
were contemplated.

Other respondents suggest that "much higher" advertising costs for a
long period of years would be required to establish a new brand, citing
the experience of American Tobacco's *Pall Mall*. Also cited are recurring
episodes of attempts to establish new brands, at great expense for advertising, which failed more or less completely. Against this, we have the
successful introduction of *Philip Morris*, which rose from a fraction of 1
per cent of the market in 1930 to over 9 per cent in 1949,[36] while maintaining earnings on net worth at at least as good as the Big 3 from early
in the period.

It would appear from the record that although it is not impossible to
enter the cigarette market successfully through a fortuitously designed
promotional campaign, the risks of failure in attempted entry are high
and the stakes large. Any reasoned appraisal of the condition of entry
must take account not only of the probable price or promotional disadvantage while entry is attempted, but also of the relative probability
of failure — the losses of which are assignable as a risk cost against any
prospective entry. Any specific numbers assigned to measure the disadvantage of a prospective entrant are extremely conjectural, but there
seems little doubt that the product-differentiation barriers to entry are
great enough to permit established firms to earn substantial excess profits
without a significant probability of inducing successful entry.

(c) *The liquor industry* is defined as producing distilled alcoholic
liquors in general. Of these whiskey is of overwhelming importance,
domestic whiskey accounting for nearly 90 per cent of distilled liquor
sales, imported whiskey for 3 per cent. Gin (or vodka) is the only other
product of consequence — about 7.5 per cent — and the rums, brandies,
and cordials follow with negligible market shares.[37] For all practical pur-

[36] Cf. Tennant, p. 94.

[37] 1947 data for 17 "license" states as prepared by the Wholesale Liquor Distributors' Association of Northern California.

poses, everything except the market for whiskey may be neglected in appraising the broad character and impact of product differentiation in the industry.

The trade classification of whiskies recognizes in general: (a) "bonds": 100-proof straight whiskies aged at least 4 years in bonded warehouses; (b) "straights": aged straight whiskies (single-variety or mixed together) generally bottled at less than 100 proof, and (c) "blends": mixtures of aged straight whiskies with neutral spirits (the latter also sometimes aged a bit) in proportions typically in the neighborhood of 20 to 40 per cent straight whiskies and 80 to 60 per cent neutral spirits. Blends are further classified into "A" blends and "B" blends, the distinction running primarily in terms of price but also in terms of the proportion of straight whiskey in the blend and the quality of all ingredients. Moreover, there are "Canadian" whiskies, representing distinctive blends of ingredients, and imported Scotch whiskies. Others, of very slight importance, may be neglected.

The composition of the market as among whiskey types has been strongly influenced by the youth of the new industry (revived, after a Rip-Van-Winkle slumber, with "repeal" in the 1930's), and by the fluctuating supplies of aged whiskey. Such supplies were of course short at the time of repeal, and again dwindled seriously as alcohol production was diverted to munitions in World War II. Straight whiskies (of improving age and quality) were dominant in the prewar period; blends took over almost the whole market during the war as distillers stretched their supplies of aged whiskey through blending. In spite of the establishment of habits in favor of blends and strong backing of blends through advertising, straight whiskey sales went up after the war as soon as aged whiskey became plentiful again. By 1951, the market was approximately 72 per cent blended whiskies, 21 per cent straights, and 7 per cent bonds, and since then straights have gained steadily at the expense of the other two categories.

There are recognizable physical differences in taste, potency, and so forth among the different classes of whiskey and also among individual brands within a class, although from the standpoint of chemical analysis inter-brand differences within classes are slight. Consumers apparently recognize these differences, and also develop habits and preferences in favor of particular classes and brands. Such preferences also survive for a considerable period of time; for instance, the rather mild-tasting blends, consumed during the war largely because of a lack of alternatives, gained a dominant popularity which the more traditional straights and bonds have been able to overcome since the war only rather slowly. Nevertheless the general impression remains that, as far as physical qualities of whiskey are concerned, consumers do change their tastes over time, and that all the major classes of whiskey are fairly close substitutes, or would be if prices were comparable.

The major basis of product differentiation, however, in general and especially within any broad class of whiskey, is branding as backed by heavy advertising. The Big 4 (National, Schenley, Seagram, Walker) supply about 75 per cent of the market, and 5 larger independents (Publicker, Glenmore, Brown-Forman, Park & Tilford, American Distilling) another 15 per cent. Branding is generally multiple, with each major seller having several or many brands which are strongly promoted, and frequently two or three in a single whiskey class. Seagram's, for example, had six brands of blended whiskey among the 25 top-selling brands of whiskey in 1951, and the others of the Big 4 had two or three blend brands apiece on the same list. And the number of actively promoted brands per seller appears greater as we go beyond the "top 25" list. Over time, brands have been moved rather flexibly among whiskey classes; for example, many "straight" brands of the prewar period were applied to blends during the war and have remained there; in recent postwar years, established blend and bond brands have both been shifted into the straight field. The importance attached to the drawing power of the long-known and heavily promoted brand is evident. Also, the major sellers have developed some degree of specialization, at least as a matter of emphasis, according to the whiskey classes that they sell. Thus, Seagram's has traditionally offered only blends, Schenley is relatively stronger in straights than the others, Walker is not really entered in the "bond" markets.

The hold of established brands on the market is revealed by the degree of "brand concentration" of whiskey sales. In 1951, for example, the top 25 brands accounted for over 75 per cent of all whiskey sales.[38] Of these, 20 brands belonged to the Big 4 and 1 each to 5 principal independents. Nineteen were blends (including 2 Canadians) and 6 were straights. Concentration in the "blends" field alone was higher, the Big 4 controlling 80 per cent of blend sales with 13 brands (excluding Canadians) and 4 independent blends adding another 8 per cent. Brand concentration in straights was substantially less; the first 5 straight brands had only about 35 per cent of the straight market, as against about 55 per cent of the blend market for the first 5 blends.

Over any short period of years, there appears to be relatively minor turnover in the population of the top 20 or 25 whiskey brands, although movements in position on the list are common. Persistent consumer attachments to a limited group of established and heavily promoted brands are thus indicated. As far as can be ascertained, these attachments depend on the persuasive effects of advertising, the "conspicuous consumption" motives of consumers to serve and be seen consuming known brands, de-

[38] *Business Week*, February 26, 1952.

pendence on the reputation of established brands for uniformity of content and quality over time, and attachments to the particular physical qualities of given branded whiskies.

As to the volume of advertising, O.P.A. records for 1940 for 17 distilled liquor manufacturing corporations show advertising expense as 5.2 per cent of sales revenue (inclusive of excise taxes), and "selling" expense as another 5.4 per cent. These percentages are roughly doubled in that year if excise taxes are excluded in the measurement of sales. Other estimates for the prewar period are generally in accord with this one. Traceable advertising figures are apparently under-inclusive to a serious degree. For 1950 they show a typical advertising cost for the Big 4 at or slightly under 2 per cent of sales, though "traceables" are from 3 to 4.5 per cent of sales for 3 of the 4 principal independents reported. In general, it appears that the liquor industry falls in the "very heavy advertising" category.

As we will note below, there does not appear to be any systematic relationship of unit advertising cost to volume of sales for the top-selling 25 brands. There is, however, a generally higher advertising cost per unit for the independent brands among the top 25 than for Big 4 brands in the same group. That this difference is systematically attributable to differences in brand sales volume is not evident from the data; it might be attributable to differences in firm size (leading to differential opportunities for multiple brand promotion), or simply to a generally stronger position in consumer preferences of the principal Big 4 brands.

What are the consequences of the observed product differentiation for intra-industry competition? One measure of the impact of brand preferences is the ability of certain brands to command premium prices as compared to others of comparable class and quality, or to obtain the same price with a lower unit promotional cost. The usual opinion expressed by members of the industry is that there are significant differential advantages among brands, although the magnitude of the differentials varies among classes of whiskey. In general, brand preferences are most important in the "quality" or high-priced bonded whiskey field, very important in the "A" blends, and perhaps less so in the "B" blends and in the "straight" whiskey field (possibly including the "inexpensive bonds" which fall in the same price class).

In the market for "quality" bonded whiskies, it is noted that six brands are dominant, and that three of these have generally commanded a top premium price. For example, in March of 1953, the three top bonds — Old Granddad, Taylor, and Harper — were priced at $7.20 retail in California; the next three of the Big 6 — Forrester, Kentucky Tavern, and Fitzgerald — listed at $6.45; other high-quality bonds such as Old Crow, Pepper, and Yellowstone retailed at or below $5.95. (Below this level were generally found inexpensive and generally lower quality bonds selling competitively with straights.) Evidently the six "premium" and "super-premium" brands were able to dominate the quality bond market while they simultaneously enjoyed a price advantage over competitors. Traceable advertising costs appeared very high on the six brands, averaging about $1.40 per case in 1951; but any disadvantage in unit advertising costs is held to be significantly less than the advantage in price. It is worth noting that the three second-level bonds were. produced by smaller distillers rather than by the Big 4, while the three super-premium brands belonged to two Big 4 firms. The quality bond market in general is held to be "brand-conscious" much more than it is "price-conscious."

The "A" blend market (identified in 1953 in California, for example, as in a $4.30 retail price class, compared to $3.90 to $4.00 for "B" blends) is also characterized as a "brand-conscious" market. Six brands, produced by 3 of the Big 4, dominated this market, and only 2 smaller distillers even had listed entries in this area. The extent of the price advantage here is indirectly reflected in the fact that smaller distillers in general "cannot make" an "A" blend — that is, any blend they produce can be marketed in volume only in the "B" blend price class. Among the "A" blends, the top seller (Seagram's 7 Crown) shows substantially lower unit costs of traceable advertising than the others, while 2 others among the top 25 brands are substantially above the average in this respect (Hunter, also a Seagram product, and Sunnybrook, made by National).

In the "B" blend market, there were 4 entries to the top 25 brands by independents in 1951, and 6 by the Big 4. Though retail prices were similar, advertising costs were not. Traceable advertising costs per case in 1950 and 1951 for these brands were as follows:

Brand	Company	Traceable advertising per case [39]	
		1950	1951
Guckenheimer	American	$0.07	$0.29
Corby's Reserve	Walker	0.33	0.42
Imperial	Walker	0.37	0.33
Cream of Kentucky	Schenley	0.38	0.41
Paul Jones	Seagrams'	0.47	0.55
Carstairs	Seagrams'	0.51	0.58
P.M.	National	0.62	0.92
Fleischmann	Fleischmann	0.70	0.77
Park & Tilford	Park & Tilford	0.73	0.99
Old Thompson	Glenmore	0.99	0.93

These data, even if they should be an accurate measure of relative advertising costs, do not tell the whole story, since price concessions to whole-

[39] Computed from reports on brand sales (*Business Week*, February 26, 1952) and from traceable advertising data.

salers and dealers apparently play a significant role in this area. An industry source characterizes the "B" blend field as primarily a "price" field in
this sense, holding that a few cents' price differential is frequently sufficient to switch a bar from one "B" blend to another as its "bar whiskey,"
or to induce package stores similarly to switch mass displays and promotional emphasis. It is held further that the "B" blend volume fluctuates
rapidly from one brand to another. Evidently, more would have to be
known of net price realizations to distillers on various "B" blends in order
to appraise fully their relative advantages.

In the "straights" field (which as a price class has come increasingly
to include inexpensive bonds and premium-priced straight-whiskey versions of brands previously applied only to "quality" bonds), a good deal
of the market is supplied by brands sold "on a price basis" (in the neighborhood of $4.35, California 1953 retail). Among the leaders selling at the
basic price (e.g., Old Stagg and Echo Springs, both by Schenley) there
is no notable difference in traceable advertising costs. Several things,
however, stand out. One independent straight (Early Times, by Brown-
Forman) has commanded a retail price differential of about 40 cents per
fifth while attaining first position in the straight whiskey field. In 1950
and 1951, at least, its traceable advertising costs per unit were not significantly different from those of its principal lower-priced competitors.
Opinion is that if actual total advertising costs are higher, they do not eat
up all of the price advantage. More recently, the entry of "quality bond"
brands in the straight whiskey field (Old Crow, Taylor) has enabled
members of the Big 4 to obtain great or greater price premia, thus joining
the established Walker brand in a category of premium-priced straights.
Unit advertising costs cannot be computed, but the net advantage to these
brands is apparently appreciable. In general, a rather wide range of
differential advantages among established brands is apparent in all the
major classes of the whiskey market.

The next question concerns the differential advantages of large and
small firms. Available data reveal only that the larger independent firms
as a group have a distinct advertising-cost disadvantage in the "B" blend
field as compared to the Big 4, although one of them has been able to
attain a very favorable premium-price position in the "straights" field.
Their indicated disadvantage in traceable advertising costs for "B's" might
run in the neighborhood of from 1 to 3 per cent of the distiller's price of
whiskey. Industry opinion is to the effect that the smaller firms in general,
and especially those below the first 4 or 5 largest independents, have
appreciable disadvantages in net price realization in any line. Price concessions to wholesalers, dealers, or bars must be made in order to obtain
volume against Big 4 competition, and result in a lower net realization
than the Big 4 get on brands of similar retail price. For smaller firms

generally, unit sales promotion costs are held to be higher, or "bordering on excessive." Whether this is due to product-differentiation disadvantages, or to diseconomies of small-scale sales promotion, is not clear.

Now let us turn to the relative position of the prospective entrant. Industry sources in general characterize this as worse than that of the smaller established firms. Entry on a relatively small scale — e.g. at that of the average of the 5 firms next to the Big 4 or smaller — would encounter overwhelming disadvantages. For entry to the quality bond market, it is estimated that the entrant would incur a disadvantage equal to perhaps 20 per cent of the distiller's price (exclusive of excise taxes) in price or selling cost or both, for a long period. It is felt that a new firm simply "could not enter" the "A" blend market effectively — i.e. selling costs or their equivalent needed to gain an appreciable volume in this retail price class for blends would be prohibitive if not astronomical. The "B" blend field could probably be entered more easily, but at a disadvantage of around 15 per cent of distiller's price per case, either in promotional costs or price concessions, for an indefinitely prolonged period. The only lightening of this grim prospect is that, when entering on a moderately large scale, a firm *might* be able to lessen its disadvantage somewhat by purchasing some known brand names (if available) and using them instead of trying to develop new ones. But it may be noted that (a) mere change in the ownership of going concerns would not constitute entry as we understand it here; and (b) the extent of the market in "known brands for sale" has not been appraised.

Large-scale entry is not viewed as conceivable to the industry sources consulted, which cite among other things the unavailability of distributors and distributive capital to handle the output of a very large entrant. The extent of economies of large-scale sales promotion available to an entrant in moving from a "large independent" scale to the scale of one of the Big 4 is, as previously suggested, not apparent from available data. If the entrant's price and promotional-cost disadvantage were lessened by large-scale entry, the effect of the increased scale on the condition of entry would evidently in some degree counterbalance this.

(d) *The automobile industry* (passenger cars) would appear to present at least as high a product-differentiation barrier to entry as any industry studied here. The extent of seller concentration and the product structure are well known. Three firms dominate the industry, and until recently there were 6 independent fringe companies (the number is now three). In 1951, General Motors controlled about 43 per cent, and Ford and Chrysler about 22 per cent apiece, of the physical volume of passenger-car sales, for a total of about 87 per cent of the market. The remainder was shared by Studebaker, Nash, Kaiser, Hudson, Willys, and

Packard, in fractions ranging from about 4 per cent to a little over 1 per cent of the market. This picture, except for the addition of Kaiser, was more or less typical of the industry since the later 1930's. Since 1951, the Studebaker-Packard, Nash-Hudson, and Kaiser-Willys mergers have halved the number of independents, though not of independent brands. Since then also, Chrysler has lost out considerably and Ford has gained more or less correspondingly, while the aggregate share of the independents has sunk drastically. But these are possibly transitory phenomena.

The product is differentiated visibly in terms of "price classes," with a generally corresponding differentiation in such gross product specifications as power, length, and weight. The generally recognized price classes are "low," "low-middle," "high-middle," and "high"; in 1951 there was on the average a $300 to $400 per unit retail price gap between adjacent price classes. The respective sales in the 4 classes were roughly 54, 28, 13, and 5 per cent of the total physical volume. (Imports, neglected here, accounted for less than 0.5 per cent of total volume.) Brands of the Big 3 are dominant in each price class, but relatively more so in the low-priced and high-priced lines; the independents account for much of their volume in the two middle-priced classes. Thus in 1951, the 6 independents accounted for 4 per cent of physical volume in the low-priced class, about 18 per cent in the low-middle-priced class, about 21 per cent in the high-middle-priced class, and about 8 per cent in the high-priced class. Independents have persistently failed to penetrate the low-priced class to any appreciable degree.

The modern automobile is a large and complex piece of machinery, offering maximum opportunity for physical product differentiation in design, mechanical features, and styling, and there is a notable degree of such differentiation among competing brands. Nevertheless, there is a general similarity of gross specifications of products of the Big 3 in any price class. Thus in 1951, the low-priced class could be defined in general as having 105 to 120 horsepower, 200 to 240 cubic inches piston displacement, and 2,750 to 3,400 pounds weight; the low-middle-priced class in general had 120 to 145 horsepower, 240 to 270 cubic inches displacement, 3,400 to 3,700 pounds; the high-middle-priced class had 145 to 170 horsepower, 275 to 330 cubic inches displacement, 3,500 to 3,900 pounds; the high-priced class generally rated still larger in all three respects. It is interesting that in most cases the independents (excepting the Hudson Hornet and the Packard Clipper, in the high-middle-priced class) entered a given price class with smaller gross specifications than the Big 3: lower power, lighter weight, etc.; and evidently secured customers through special features of design, quality, style, or performance which would appeal to some minor fraction of the market. Thus the Studebaker Commander,

Hudson Wasp, and Kaiser 6 were priced in the low-middle range while offering gross specifications comparable to the low-priced products of the Big 3; the Nash Ambassador offered low-middle-priced gross specifications at a high-middle price; the Hudson Jet, Studebaker Champion, Willys, Nash Rambler and Statesman, and Henry J offered lower power and lighter weight than the Big 3 low-priced cars although selling at about the same prices. This has been a persistent and developing pattern since 1946, although it may of course be subject to reversal.

Within the price class, there is an appreciable degree of physical product differentiation featuring specialty in such matters as appearance of the automobile body, engine design, and design of transmissions, running gear, etc. Protective imitation is a strong motif in product policies, however, so that similarities of competing products are perhaps more striking than their differences. The recent rapid adaptation of the entire industry to high-powered V-8 engines, low and wide bodies, and identity of "extra" accessories or features is illustrative of this tendency.

Coupled with the pattern of physical product differentiation is one of frequent product variation over time, involving periodic revisions in body style and in mechanical design. The "annual model change" has been a pattern for the entire industry ever since Ford succumbed to it in the early 1930's, having found apparently that the economies of spreading tooling costs over a number of years on a single model failed to offset the disadvantages in demand in competing with the annually changed products of the rest of the industry. In a market for a durable good such as this, readily susceptible of progressive variations in design, bought with conspicuous consumption motives clearly in play, with a used-product market offering a clear alternative to the lower-income or more frugal buyers, and with the new-product market dominantly a replacement market, demand is kept alive from year to year by successive product variations by all sellers. In general, the usual though not invariant pattern in the industry now involves a thoroughgoing redesign and corresponding major retooling every third year, with two "faceliftings" (perhaps one minor, one major) in the intervening years. (The faceliftings involve superficial styling changes and minor changes in design and do not require major retooling costs for such things as body shells and engines.) Protective imitation again operates in product variation policies, so that physical product differentiation does not tend to increase over time.

In this connection, it is notable that the smaller firms tend to be at a disadvantage in holding a parity in the product-differentiation struggle as models are varied at regular intervals. Retooling costs for a major model change (the triennial one, for example) are very high. Recent press reports, for example, put the cost of the 1955 model change for Chevrolet at about $100,000,000. A large though not definitely specified share of such costs is fixed, or invariant with the variation of production volumes from very small up to the level where most major tools would have to be duplicated (perhaps 10 or more per cent of the total national market). In consequence, there are substantial economies of scale attributable to the spreading of fixed retooling overhead over larger output volumes — economies which are greatly accentuated by the fact that competition has brought all sellers into the practice of frequent product variation. Faced with this fact, the smaller sellers encounter significant diseconomies in retooling costs per unit if they attempt to match the performance of the large sellers in varying models. On the other hand, they may choose (or be forced by lack of sufficient liquid funds) to "trim corners" in their product variation policies, by making less sweeping changes in their products at given model-change intervals, or by making important changes less frequently. This seems to have been a tendency among the independents of the industry in the postwar period. As it proceeds, the physical product differentiation between Big 3 and independent products tends to become more distinct in the average year, though the independent may more or less "catch up" in product design every five or six years. In consequence the independents are forced more and more to depend on "special corners" of the market: demands of small minority groups of buyers not satisfied by the relatively uniform products of the Big 3. At any rate, there has been a drift in this direction, with the introduction of light, low-powered "economy" cars by Nash, Willys, Hudson, Studebaker, and Kaiser representing the major instance to date.

In general, patent protection of product designs does not appear to play an important role in sustaining physical product differentiation or in giving one seller an advantage over another. Relatively unrestricted cross-licensing of patents has been the practice within the industry for many years. In addition, parts-making divisions of the Big 3, and especially General Motors, supply patent-protected parts to independent competitors in a more or less unrestricted fashion. This practice in recent years has been important primarily with respect to improvement and accessory patents covering such things as automatic transmissions and power steering. Basic patents covering the principles of engine design, power transmission systems, and numerous related things are long expired. If any member of the Big 3 gains an advantage over independent competitors through control of improvement and accessory patents, it is generally gained not by excluding competitors from the use of new designs, but by selling them parts at a price which includes a substantial excess profit, while the Big 3 member can of course supply itself at cost inclusive of a normal profit, whatever the interdepartmental bookkeeping technicalities.

That this happens to a certain degree is suggested by industry opinion from several sources.

So much for physical product differentiation among the products of established sellers — differentiation evidently sufficient to create substantial and moderately durable buyer allegiances to particular brands. Such allegiances are developed and maintained in part by advertising. Traceable advertising in 1950 ran around 1 per cent for most sellers, although General Motors' traceable advertising of 44 million dollars amounted to only 0.5 per cent of its sales. Total advertising and sales-promotion costs of auto manufacturers were reported by the Federal Trade Commission for 1937 as 2.2 per cent of sales for Chrysler, 4.2 per cent for Hudson, 1.7 per cent for Nash, and 4.0 per cent for Packard.[40]

The most important basis of product differentiation aside from physical design, however, is probably not found in advertising *per se*. Three other considerations loom large. First, product reputation counts for a great deal with the typical automobile buyer. The passenger car is a large and complex mechanism, so complex that the average buyer (though he may not admit this) is quite unequipped to evaluate its mechanical design and its general level of quality. Moreover, the product is very expensive per unit, and is purchased so infrequently that the buyer has a limited opportunity to experiment with different makes and also is unwilling to risk experiment. He therefore depends on the "reputation" of the product. This gives an advantage to the long-established brands, and as we will see is very unfavorable to the new entrant. In addition, buyers have the evident tendency to attribute "better repute" to the brands with large sales, thus making a strong market position (once attained) self-perpetuating in a degree, and placing the smaller-selling brands at a distinct disadvantage in their ability to expand their market shares.

Second, strong "conspicuous-consumption" motives evidently operate in the purchase of automobiles, motives tending to perpetuate allegiances to the more popular brands and work against the independents. The anecdote circulated in 1953 that the residents of some wealthy California suburbs had generally removed the "Ike for President" stickers from their Cadillacs, so that no one would know that they had last year's models, dramatizes the importance of conspicuous consumption by automobile users.

Third and most important, the dealer systems of the established sellers are important in maintaining the product preferences of buyers. All sellers attempt nationwide distribution; all generally use exclusive franchise policies to restrict the dealer to a brand or brands of a single manufacturer. A huge amount of capital, generally invested by independent

[40] *Distribution Methods and Costs, Part IV*, pp. 6–11 and pp. 91 ff.

dealers holding franchises, is tied up in land, building, equipment, parts inventories, and so forth. The function of the dealer is of course primarily to promote sales, but equally important is his function of providing specialized maintenance, repair service, and easy access to replacement parts for the users of the dealer's brand of automobile. In general, the number and geographical density of dealer-service representatives of a given manufacturing concern are directly related to its volume of sales, if only because a certain minimal sales volume is necessary to maintain a solvent dealer. In the matter of density of outlets, therefore, the independents stand in general at a substantial disadvantage as compared to the Big 3.

The importance of dealer systems in maintaining product preferences is generally twofold. First, there is considerable allegiance of buyers to individual dealers, based on their reputations for fair dealing and for provision of satisfactory service, and on the relative probability of their remaining solvent and in business while the car being purchased is in use. Second, there is an observed tendency for buyers to consider it an advantage to purchase a brand of auto offered nationally by a relatively large group of dealers with a high density of locations, regionally or nationally. This is because access to service from specialized mechanics and to replacement parts becomes easier, especially "out of town," as the dealer system becomes larger and geographically denser.

The Big 3 generally or on the average have significant advantages over the independents in both respects. On one hand, their larger volume permits them to obtain a substantially greater density of dealer outlets across the country. This density is attractive *per se* to the buyer who contemplates the relative convenience of obtaining service on his car; also it permits somewhat more intensive sales promotion in large cities, and representation in small towns where most or all of the independents have none. Ford and General Motors are able to obtain this density while generally restricting dealers to the distribution of a single brand — especially in the case of the Ford car and the Chevrolet. Chrysler has more or less equalled their performance in the case of the Plymouth by having that brand carried by the dealers in each of the larger cars made by the firm: Dodge, deSoto, and Chrysler. In addition, the Big 3 have been able over time to develop a "stronger" and perhaps more effective group of dealers than the average of the independents. This ability is apparently attributable mainly to two things. First, with large national sales volumes, the Big 3 can on the average offer dealers the prospect of larger annual volumes than they could get with independent brands, and at the same time maintain a relatively high density of outlets. In consequence, there is a larger and perhaps better selection of "bidders" for Big 3 dealer fran-

chises, and the Big 3 have been in general able to select and hold financially stronger dealers who are likely to stay in business and build their
local reputations for longer periods of time. The better financial status
(and higher profits) of the Big 3 dealers in turn tends to be reflected in
better locations and more attractive and ample sales and service facilities.
Second, in critical times the financial resources of the Big 3 have better
enabled them to maintain adequate dealer systems, either because of the
initial greater financial strength of their dealers or through assistance or
subsidy to dealers. The last dramatic change in the structure of the industry came with the great depression of the early 1930's. In 1929, independents supplied about 28 per cent of all passenger cars sold; by 1933, they
were down to about 12.5 per cent, and by 1937 down to about 11.5 per
cent — a position they have not systematically bettered since, and are not
even attaining at the moment. Though the Chrysler acquisition of Dodge
played a strong role in this increasing concentration, it was also evidently
attributable in good part to the fact that the members of the Big 3 dealer
systems survived bankruptcy on the average much better than the dealers
of the independents.[41]

The objective evidences of intra-industry product differentiation are
not found primarily in price differences as among the Big 3 products in
any price class. Products are of course sufficiently non-uniform so that
exact price identity among competing makes is not required or obtained,
but close similarity of prices (within 1 or 2 per cent of each other in any
price class) is generally found. We have already noted, however, that the
independents as a group have tended actually to charge higher list prices
than the Big 3 for autos of similar gross specifications, though they compensate for this through various special features — e.g., engines built for
exceptional gasoline mileage instead of high horsepower. In this connection, it is interesting to note some plausible speculations which have been
advanced concerning the elasticity of demand in response to price changes
for independent makes. In his unpublished doctoral dissertation, writing
with primary reference to the Kaiser-Frazer experience after entry, David
K. Smith [42] suggested that the demand for the Kaiser (and probably for
other independents) was rather inelastic or unresponsive to price changes,

[41] An aside on sales-promotional costs in automobile distribution is in order. Although advertising costs directly incurred by the manufacturers do not loom very large
in percentage-of-sales terms, promotional costs incurred by dealers (largely for personal
sales representation) are much more substantial — generally above 5 per cent of retail
sales of new automobiles. Incursion of these promotional costs is in turn tacitly encouraged by the spread between dealer-wholesale and retail prices established by the
manufacturers, ranging generally from a fifth to more than a quarter of announced
retail price.

[42] "The Problems of a New Firm in an Oligopolistic Industry: Kaiser-Frazer's Experience in the Automobile Industry," Harvard doctoral dissertation, 1950.

even though the prices of the Big 3 might remain unchanged. This observation was based in part on Kaiser's lack of success, with an initially "overpriced" car, in stimulating sales through price reductions. It was supported by industry opinion that two out of three auto owners buying a new car purchase the same make of car as their present ones. The general tendency of established independents to price over rather than under or equal to Big 3 competition is at least consistent with the notion that they generally believe that they can attract a fairly small fraction of buyers at any of an appreciable range of prices, but will not expand this share much by feasible reductions in their relative prices or diminish it much by significant price increases.

If this is the case, we find in the automobile industry a much more substantial evidence of the force of product differentiation than is found in such product-differentiated industries as those producing soap, cigarettes, and gasoline — in which sellers appear to feel that individual demands for any separate product would be very elastic indeed if its price were raised above or below a level common to all products. It is quite possible, however, that competitive Big 3 automobile brands face considerably more elastic demands than the independents in response to changes in their relative prices.

The effects of product differentiation on intra-industry competition are of course seen first in the differentials among market shares attracted by different firms and brands. Without going into detail on this matter, it is perhaps sufficient to reiterate that General Motors (with 5 brands) has long held a leading position (40 to 45 per cent of the total market); that the next 2 firms combined (with 3 and 4 brands each) have done about as well as General Motors; and that the 5 or 6 independents as a group have either held even or declined with very small individual market shares (1 to 4 per cent of the market) and have shown no consistent ability to enlarge their shares in spite of numerous ingenious stratagems in design and sales promotion over the past twenty years.

Evidence of product differentiation is seen also in the differential rates at which the sales values of used cars of different makes decline as they become older. An apparently typical pattern in this regard is revealed in the computation of the decline in the retail values of various makes of cars from their new retail prices in 1950 to their reported "retail values used" in October, 1952.[43] For the northeastern quarter of the

---

[43] From *Red Book National Used Car Market Report* (October 1, 1952) *Region A*. (Region A is roughly the northeastern quarter of the United States.) Prices used in computing depreciation of used cars are, for standard four-door sedans only, (1) the factory retail delivered prices for 1950 models as of their introduction, and (2) the Region A retail used-car prices in October, 1952 for the same 1950 models, as reported in the *Red Book*. Other reporting services for this and for other postwar years show generally similar comparative depreciations among different makes.

United States, the picture was as follows for standard four-door sedans, without extras:

	Depreciation, from new-car retail (factory delivery) in 1950 to used-car retail, October 1952		
	In dollars	As a percentage of new-car retail	Firm
(1) Low-priced class:			
Chevrolet Styleline	$ 70	4.8	General Motors
Ford V-8 De luxe	180	11.6	Ford
Plymouth De luxe	201	12.9	Chrysler
Studebaker Champion	322	20.2	Studebaker
(2) Low-medium-priced class:			
Pontiac Chieftan	183	9.6	General Motors
Oldsmobile 88 De luxe	231	11.3	" "
Buick Special	289	15.2	" "
De Soto De luxe	391	19.7	Chrysler
Dodge Coronet	382	19.8	"
Mercury	412	20.3	Ford
Nash Statesman	403	23.2	Nash
Studebaker Commander	463	24.3	Studebaker
Hudson Pacemaker	483	25.0	Hudson
(3) High-medium-priced class:			
Buick Super	324	15.2	General Motors
Chrysler Windsor	454	19.5	Chrysler
Olds 98 De luxe	518	21.7	General Motors
Lincoln V-8	626	24.4	Ford
Nash Ambassador	594	28.7	Nash
Hudson Commodore 6	657	28.7	Hudson
Packard 8	674	29.9	Packard
Kaiser 6	720	36.1	Kaiser-Frazer
(4) High-priced class:			
Cadillac 62	284	8.8	General Motors
Buick Roadmaster	683	26.0	" "
Chrysler New Yorker	718	26.0	Chrysler
Lincoln Cosmopolitan	1,065	32.9	Ford
Packard 8 Super De luxe	1,084	37.1	Packard

Several generalities stand out from all relevant data. First, General Motors brands usually occupy a preferred position in used-car and "trade-in" value relative to those of the other 2 big firms in every price class, this advantage ranging from 3 to 8 percentage points in 2-year depreciation as expressed in terms of original new-car price. Its advantage over Chrysler and Ford, as over independents, is smallest in the high-medium-priced class. Second, the established independents are in general at a disadvantage in trade-in values as compared to Ford and Chrysler products, this disadvantage ranging from 4 or 5 up to 10 or more percentage points in 2-year depreciation. The fact that in many cases the independent products have lower gross specifications than the Big 3 products in the same price class may have something to do with this. Third, the only recent-entrant product — Kaiser — was at an overwhelming disadvantage in trade-in values. For example, the buyer of a Kaiser Special sedan at $1995 at the factory would have sustained a $720 depreciation in two years, about 36 per cent of new price, whereas the buyer of a Buick Super sedan at $2139 would have suffered a $324 depreciation, or about 15 per cent of new price, in two years. Finally, of course, the depreciation percentage rises systematically with the price class — Cadillac excepted.

The implications of these findings are a little more difficult to determine. One hypothesis is that the used-car buyers accord greater preference to General Motors as compared to Ford and Chrysler products, and greater preference to Big 3 products as compared to independent products, than do new-car buyers. This hypothesis would presuppose that new-car purchasers of the less-favored makes actually pay the same proportion of the retail list price as the buyers of the more-favored makes do (that they do not get larger discounts or longer trade-in allowances), and that therefore their preference scales are on the average distinctly different from those of used-car buyers. If this were true, the "cost of owning" an independent car as compared to a Big 3 car, or a Chrysler or Ford car as compared to a General Motors product, would be greater to the new-car purchaser as repeated trade-ins and purchases were contemplated. This could go some way toward explaining the division of market shares among different automobile manufacturers.

An alternative hypothesis is that buyers in general, of new cars as well as used cars, undervalue the Ford and Chrysler products as compared to General Motors, and the independent cars as compared to the Big 3 cars, and on the average purchase the inferior alternatives only if the net selling price is appropriately reduced by the retail dealers through longer trade-in allowances or larger cash discounts. This implies that the manipulation by retail dealers of trade-in allowances and discounts results on the average in some relative reduction of the net prices of the less preferred brands of autos, so that price differentials not apparent in "factory-list" quotations exist at the new-car as well as at the used-car level. It also implies that either (a) dealers in the more preferred brands will in general have more profitable operations and be financially stronger, with the result that the manufacturers of the preferred makes will be able to maintain larger and stronger dealer organizations; or (b) that the manufacturers of the preferred makes will be able to maintain dealers while allowing them smaller distributive markups, and thus reaping larger factory-net-wholesale prices. Evidence available suggests that the former rather than the latter tendency in manufacturers' price policies is the rule. It also suggests that the existing balance in market shares is in fact maintained by net price reductions in less-favored brands through "long trading" or cash discounts at the retail level, so that new-car buyers of the less-favored makes do not in fact sustain so much of a disadvantage in "cost-of-owning" the cars they buy as a comparison of used-car resale values would suggest. On the other hand, the manufacturers of the less-favored brands — particularly the independents — are then able to sustain only weaker and thinner dealer organizations, since the dealers rather than the ultimate buyers absorb much of the virtual price disadvantage of the independent makes.

It is impossible to tell from available data the extent to which advantages of large-scale sales promotion are strategic to the preferred positions of the larger sellers. The attainment of their large volumes may simply be a result of an over-all absolute brand preference in their favor, regardless of scale, so that less-favored makes could not attain a comparably favorable relation of price, selling cost, and volume through expanded promotional activity. The fact that the biggest sellers do the best, that is, does not necessarily imply that the smaller sellers could do as well in reaching that size; the costs of doing it, for them, might be staggering and prohibitive.

About all that we have on this point is an assortment of industry opinions. Such opinion is apparently unanimous on the point that a volume sufficient to permit the maintenance of nationwide system of dealerships and servicing facilities is crucial to the survival of a firm in the industry; if such a volume is not attained, the general acceptability of the product is more or less fatally impaired. The minimum "sufficient" volume in this regard is placed at 2 to 3 per cent of national industry sales, or perhaps 100,000 to 150,000 units per year in reasonably good times. The fact that independents in general have either gone broke, headed toward bankruptcy, or fled into mergers when their volumes ran significantly below 2.5 or 3 per cent for very long is consistent with this, although production diseconomies of small-scale manufacturing are a concurrent consideration here. Whether and to what extent the effectiveness of sales promotion increases with further expansion of the firm is not so much a matter of agreement, although tentative indications are that systematic added benefits of some magnitude accrue as the firm expands up to 10 or more per cent of the market. If such advantages are present, they tend to reinforce the production-economy advantages of the large firm up to around the 10-per-cent-of-the-market level, but do not necessarily increase the optimal scale of the firm.

Even if we accept tentatively the notion that there are systematic advantages to large-scale sales promotion, however, it would have to be insisted that there are also absolute product differentiation advantages to the principal firms such that the independent or new-entrant firm would have some net disadvantage as compared to the Big 3 at any scale it reached. This inheres in part in the fact that effective national dealership organizations are not bought or built at a standard price, and that the cost of creating or greatly expanding one now would place the entrant or independent firm at a substantial disadvantage as compared to its major competitors.

We turn now to the prospective product-differentiation disadvantage of a new entrant to the automobile industry. The extent of such disadvantage is to a certain degree speculative, although certain inferences may be drawn from the now apparently abortive attempt of Kaiser-Frazer to enter the industry in the postwar period.[44] (In spite of entry in the most favorable imaginable market situation — that involving the immediate postwar shortage of new automobiles — and with impressive financial backing and management personnel, the Kaiser auto enterprise has by now run up a staggering series of deficits, has failed to establish an effective nation-wide dealership organization, and has seen sales dwindle to the vanishing point.)

From the record and from speculations based on it, we can gather that:

(1) The entrant is at the outset likely to have a crushing disadvantage in the trade-in or resale value of his products when used. As soon as this is generally established, sales can be built and maintained only either by concessions in list prices or by exceptionally long trading by dealers. Since an effective dealership system can hardly be built and maintained with candidates who are becoming insolvent through long trading, the entrant manufacturer will have to absorb much of the loss in both cases. This net price disadvantage to the entrant — as compared to the Big 3 established firms — is likely to average at least 5 per cent of factory price over the first 5 or 10 years. It would seem likely to be incurred to gain only 3 or 4 per cent of market volume at the end of 5 or 10 years; the cost of gaining larger volumes might be higher. The price disadvantage would be reflected in losses, or reductions of profits, of from 50 to 100 million dollars over the first decade — all invested in the face of a substantial risk of ultimate failure. The disadvantage in question would seem to result primarily from (a) difficulty in establishing consumer acceptance for a new product, and (b) time and expense required to establish an effective new dealer organization.

(2) Added to this disadvantage is the fact that a volume of even 3 or 4 per cent of the market could under ordinary conditions be built only slowly over a period of perhaps a decade. During the break-in period, therefore, the entrant would have on the average low-volume operations and would incur correspondingly elevated costs per unit for retooling for

---

[44] See Smith; also, "Kaiser-Frazer — The Roughest Thing We Ever Tackled," *Fortune*, July 1951, pp. 7ff.

model changes. Yet at least keeping pace in product variations and improvements would be essential to ultimate success. One estimate is that the entrant would have a virtual loss or reduction of profit of about 150 million dollars in the first 10 years because of the high per-unit burden of retooling costs during this period — this in addition to the price disadvantage already mentioned, and similarly incurred with a substantial risk of ultimate failure.

In sum, an entrant might expect, in order to secure 3 or 4 per cent of the market at the end of a decade, to incur virtual break-in losses of $200 million or more. Apportioned over the probable output of the first 10 years, this might mean a price and cost disadvantage of $200 per automobile (over 10 per cent of price); certainly not less than a $100 per unit disadvantage would have to be contemplated. If established firms follow pricing policies permitting themselves perhaps 2 per cent of excess profits on sales during such a period, a 10-year accounting deficit of at least 100 million dollars (plus the loss of interest on shareholders' investment) might be contemplated by the entrant. Such losses would be invested in the face of a substantial risk of failure. In this setting, how far above their costs can large established firms elevate price without making it probable that new entry will be attracted?

Established independents who would expand their outputs apparently face comparable though probably lesser disadvantages as compared to the Big 3. The relative unsuccess of independents in numerous tentative forays into the low-priced field, for example, suggests that the deterrents to revision of the existing industry structure are almost as strong as those to new entry.

4. Industries with "mixed" product-differentiation barriers to entry.

The industries in this category are all ones in which there is some segmentation of the industry market either by product lines or by marketing channels, and in which the product-differentiation barrier to entry differs significantly among different market segments. The category includes flour, canned fruits and vegetables, shoes, and fountain pens, and a complex including two industries previously identified separately — farm machinery and tractors.

(a) *The flour industry* produces dominantly a simple and relatively standardized product — wheat flour — the physical differentiation of which into regular flour for bread, cake flour, biscuit and cake mixes, etc., is substantially reducible to standardized groups. Physical product differentiation is evidently a minor factor in the industry. The segmentation of the market occurs primarily between buying groups; about two-thirds of the flour is sold by millers to industrial or non-consumer users such as bakers, and the remainder to consumers via regular wholesale and retail channels. The consumer-market flour is divisible generally into that sold under the miller's brand and that sold to mass distributors such as grocery chains for the affixing of the "private labels" of the distributors. So far as the importance of product differentiation goes, the private-label consumer market may generally be grouped with the industrial market, leaving the miller's-brand consumer market, with 25 to 30 per cent of total volume, as the second distinct category.

In the industrial and private-label markets, industry sources hold that product differentiation and allegiance to particular millers are of negligible importance. "The loyalty of industrial users to a particular supplier does not exceed five cents per hundredweight" is a typical comment. Such evidence as has been obtained is consistent with the notion that product differentiation is of negligible importance either as an influence on intra-industry competition or as a barrier to entry in the flour markets in question.

The case is otherwise in miller's-brand consumer sales of flour and flour products. For the industry as a whole, the Federal Trade Commission placed advertising at from 3 to 4.5 per cent *of all sales* in the prewar period.[45] In 1950, traceable advertising for General Mills (with about 9.5 per cent of industry capacity) was about 4 per cent of all sales; for Pillsbury (with about 6 per cent of industry capacity), the corresponding percentage was about 3.5. The indicated advertising expenditures are influenced of course by a considerable emphasis on specialties; on the other hand, the fact that the stated percentages apply to all sales of these firms suggests that the ratio of advertising to the sales of brands actually being promoted is substantially higher than just indicated. And in addition to straight advertising, the largest firms also promote their brands through offering various services to consumers.

In consequence of their promotional activities, the largest millers obtain a price advantage over private labels in the neighborhood of 5 to 7 per cent of price on regular flour; in addition, they have more or less preëmpted such specialty lines as cake flours. Their *net* advantage over non-advertising suppliers of the private-label market is in doubt, however, since their promotional costs evidently eat up a considerable part of their gross price advantage. Similarly, net advantages of large-scale sales promotion are in doubt, though they may conceivably exist.

As far as new entry is concerned, it would appear that entry to the miller's-brand market, now dominated by General Mills and Pillsbury, would be difficult enough to constitute an inferior alternative to entering the private-label market if consumer sales were contemplated. In entering the miller's-brand market, the entrant would presumably be at about a 5 to 7 per cent price disadvantage for some time, given comparable unit

[45] *Distribution Methods and Costs, Part I*, pp. 70ff.; *Part V*, pp. 7–8.

promotion costs. The fact that entry to the miller's-brand market is thus at least moderately difficult, however, does not mean that entry to the consumer flour market in general (private-label sales considered) is equally difficult. In fact, the pressure of threatened entry on consumer flour prices generally may be quite strong.

(b) *The canned fruit and vegetable industry* has a bewildering variety in its product mix, running from peaches through cranberries in eight principal domestic fruits, from peas through spinach in a comparable number of vegetables, from canned soup through spaghetti in specialties, from orange juice through ketchup in juices and sauces. There is a high degree of specialization by plants in individual lines and products, and also by firms except for a handful of multiplant, "full-line" firms at the top of the industry.

As in the case of flour, the consumer market is divided between canner's-brand and private-label sales, although the division is different in different product categories: only in certain specialty lines such as canned soups and pineapple do the large canners' brands enjoy a dominant position with strong product preferences in their favor. Accordingly, the importance of product differentiation should be treated separately for such specialties and for the mill-run of canned fruits and vegetables.

For the latter category, product differentiation seems generally of slight importance. To be sure, there is fairly heavy promotion of a few major brands of multi-product firms; traceable advertising in 1950 ran generally from 1 to 2.5 per cent of sales for such large diversified firms as Calpak, Heinz, Hunt, and Libby, and a bit higher for such more specialized firms as Gerber (baby foods) and Green Giant. This advertising has contributed to the establishment of small price advantages in favor of the nationally advertised brands. On the other hand, expert opinion runs to the effect that the price advantage in question is largely offset by higher promotional costs, and O.P.A. data more or less confirm the lower unit promotional costs of smaller sellers.[46] Thus non-advertising sellers supplying chain stores and wholesale grocers with canned goods for private labelling may do about as well on the average in profits as their large, nationally advertising competitors.

In certain specialties, on the other hand, a few major brands enjoy a superior position, price advantage and promotional cost both being considered. Profit data tend to confirm this, and we have the expert opinion that the superior profit positions of some large, diversified firms are attributable mainly to their profits of certain specialty lines which they produce, and not so much to profits on the bulk of their total output.

The position of the potential entrant needs to be evaluated correspondingly. To enter the bulk of the market, certain specialties aside, a new

[46] Office of Temporary Controls, *Economic Data Series, No. 24.*

firm would incur slight and transitory disadvantages in price. To enter the canner's-brand market, "introductory discounts" plus heavy promotional support would be necessary for several years, placing the entrant at some net disadvantage. Entry to the private-label market is probably easier, and is an alternative providing almost equally effective competition to established firms. For selected specialties, like soup and pineapple, the picture is probably different: appreciable extra promotional expenses or price concessions for at least several years would be prerequisite to successful entry to such lines. Unfortunately, we are not in a position to make a more precise or quantitative appraisal of the product-differentiation barriers to entry to such specialty lines.

(c) *The shoe industry* has an output readily divisible into several main classes; the principal ones are men's dress, men's work, women's, youths' and boys', misses' and children's, babies' and infants', athletic, and slippers. Some of these categories (e.g. men's shoes) are in turn significantly subdivided into price classes. Women's shoes account for around 45 per cent of all physical volume in shoes, and men's dress shoes for about 20 per cent. Our remarks here on product differentiation must refer primarily to these categories, since we lack specific information on the others. The general tendencies observed in these categories, however, are thought to be reflected in the other major divisions of the industry.

In the shoe industry generally the primary means of product differentiation by the manufacturer are branding, control of retail distributive outlets, and "style." A large majority of the first 10 or 15 firms sell either part or all of their outputs through either integrated or affiliated retail stores. On the other hand, there is an adequate alternative channel for the smaller manufacturers through non-manufacturing shoe-store chains and other mass retailers and through independent retailers. Manufacturers' brands are generally pushed by the large firms, and supported by national advertising on a modest scale. The heaviest advertisers in the industry in 1950 had traceable advertising costs a bit above 1 per cent of sales; others had much less. There is also brand identification of various chain-store lines, but these brands are usually those of the buyers and not of the shoe manufacturers. In general, it appears that brand allegiances are fairly strong in higher-priced men's dress shoes, have less importance in lower-priced men's dress shoes, and have still less importance in women's shoes in general.

The element of "style" — design, appearance, and changes therein over time — is also important in shoes, as in any article of outer wearing apparel. It is of principal significance, however, in women's shoes, which are bought generally with a heavy emphasis on appearance, and in which frequent style variations and innovations are quite important. In the bulk of women's shoe sales, style would appear substantially to outweigh brand *per se* as a force in product differentiation, whereas the reverse is probably true for higher-priced men's dress shoes.

The effects of product differentiation on intra-industry competition vary accordingly among lines. In higher-priced men's shoes, there appear to be relatively stable preferences in favor of certain long-established brands (Florsheim, Nunn-Bush, etc.) sufficient to permit them to obtain significant price premia over their competitors. In lower-priced men's shoes, such advantages to leading brands are characterized as negligible, and competition in terms of price is much stronger. In women's shoes, there is very active style competition; but with a premium placed on the year-to-year ingenuity of the producer in developing style, and with no monopoly of certain firms over such ingenuity, the product differentiation which develops is not such as to give certain brands a persistent advantage over time. The phenomenon of frequent product variation in a setting where there are not great advantages to scale, long experience, or large financial resources in developing innovations, actually tends to lessen the importance of product differentiation as a source of stable structuring of consumer preferences as among brands and firms. In this respect, the women's shoe industry is probably more like the women's dress industry than like the men's shoe industry. It also has certain essential similarities to some sectors of the farm machinery industry, to which we will turn shortly.

The effect of product differentiation on entry also varies among lines. In women's shoes, the burden of opinion is that product-differentiation barriers to entry are generally slight, because of the relative ease with which an entrant can break into the market on a style innovation and because of the relatively slight importance of branding *per se*. Small extra promotional costs for a few years might be the only disadvantage to the entrant. In low-priced men's dress shoes, the barriers are similarly low, though style is a less important consideration. Estimates that an entrant firm (probably selling to independent and mass distributors) might incur extra selling costs of 1 to 3 per cent of sales for 5 years are typical here. In high-priced men's dress shoes, the product differentiation barrier is probably substantially greater, but it is difficult to obtain quantitative appraisals. At least a moderate price disadvantage over a long period seems in store for the entrant to this field.

What the situation is in other shoe lines — children's, athletic, etc. — is a matter for speculation until further data are accumulated. With the exception of specialties like athletic shoes, corrective children's shoes, and the like, however, it appears from scattered evidence that most would fall in a general category with lower-priced men's dress shoes.

(d) *The farm machinery and tractor industries*, separately identified in the Census, are grouped together here, although this grouping is a little forced. The majority of tractors are evidently produced as farm machines, but tractors and tractor-driven devices also are made for other purposes, such as earth-moving, and some tractor firms (e.g. Caterpillar) more or less specialize in non-farm designs. Aside from this, however, it is convenient to view tractors as a significant division of farm machinery, and generally an essential part of the balanced farm-machinery line of a manufacturer.

The product mix of the farm machinery industry is one of astonishing variety; over twenty types of specialized implements of importance may be listed in addition to tractors. These range from very large and complicated machines such as grain combines, through large tractor-drawn equipment such as binders, threshers, and planters, and down to relatively simple-implements such as horse-drawn plows and harrows and ensilage cutters and cream separators. Seller concentration generally declines as we move into the smaller and simpler implements, and it is at or close to the maximum in tractors *per se*. A good many of the larger implements as well as some smaller ones are essentially complementary products to tractors, the implement designed for coupling to the tractor, and vice versa.[47]

The larger six or eight firms in the industry generally produce a diversified range of farm machinery, including tractors and either all or many of the major farm implements. These are generally referred to as "long-line" firms, and accordingly they generally feature, either entirely or as a matter of emphasis, distribution through integrated branch wholesale houses and thence through exclusive or quasi-exclusive dealers who feature all locally saleable items of the manufacturer's long line and do not carry items competitive to the long line. The smaller firms generally produce one or a few items or a "short line"; they are more likely to distribute through independent wholesalers and thence through various dealers, either by placing non-competitive specialties with dealers carrying the long lines of other firms, or through independent dealers.

Matters of physical product differentiation, product reputation, and branding aside, there is thus a source of product differentiation found in the differentiation in distributive channels. The Federal Trade Commission has made much of the alleged advantages in sales promotion, as in distributive costs, of the long-line, branch-house distribution of the larger farm-machinery firms. Industry opinion generally holds that there are probably some cost savings through this type of distribution, although no one seems to know how much. As to an advantage in selling price

---

[47] For general information on the industry, see Michael Conant, "Monopoly and Price Policies in the Farm Machinery Industry" (unpublished doctoral dissertation, University of Chicago); also Federal Trade Commission, *Report on the Manufacture and Distribution of Farm Implements* (1948).

resulting from customer attachments to established dealer systems, there is some difference of opinion, but the general consensus would seem to be that whereas such attachments are important in determining and maintaining an apportionment of business among firms, they are not the basis for certain firms obtaining price premia as compared to others. Although the industry in terms of product and distributive techniques has many superficial similarities to the automobile industry, the general opinion seems to be that because the farmer is a sufficiently better-informed and more price-conscious buyer than the automobile purchaser, the relative hold of the large firms is somewhat less in farm machinery.

If there is at least some advantage to the long-line, branch-house firms as such, it is evidently in part an advantage of large-scale sales promotion. How big does a firm need to be to exploit these advantages? From all relevant indications available, and especially from comparative profit rates prewar and postwar, it would appear that 3 or 4 firms below the Big 3 (International Harvester, Deere, and Allis-Chalmers), each controlling with long-line production 4 to 6 per cent of the total market, fare about as well as the Big 3 do; for example, Case, Oliver, and Minneapolis-Moline are apparently big enough to match the performance of the Big 3. Exploitation of the advantages of large-scale sales promotion probably does not require a larger scale as measured in terms of proportion of the market in any one implement line than production-distribution advantages of multi-product firms do.

The product-differentiation advantage which goes to the larger, long-line firms may differ among specific categories of products. One aspect of the general picture here is that the introduction of product innovations by small or new-entrant firms may tend to break down the brand and related advantages of large established firms, and to forestall the perpetuation of persistent advantages in their favor. In this respect, the farm-machinery industry is like the shoe industry, discussed above, and unlike the automobile industry. It seems relatively easy for the small or new firm to use its ingenuity to advantage in developing products which will secure a market position in the face of established product reputations — perhaps in this case because of the existence of a well-informed buying market and of numerous specialized needs in specific localities. Thus the successful introductions in recent times of the Baldwin gleaner, the New Holland Baler, the Farm Hand front-end loader, and various New Idea products are cited as examples of the instability of the product-preference pattern through time — an instability that does not work in the favor of larger companies. To this may be added the fact that Allis-Chalmers became a major factor in the industry after 1928, with the introduction of a revolutionary tractor design, and enhanced its position with the introduction of a small harvester combine in 1935; that the Ford-Ferguson tractor, with hydraulic controls, captured 30 per cent of the low-horse-power tractor market after its introduction in 1939, and so forth. The importance of product variation, coupled with the ability of small or new firms to make such variations, has thus tended to reduce the importance of stable product-differentiation advantages in favor of certain firms, and to ease the condition of entry.

By and large, however, in considering the advantages of established distributive systems, it appears (a) that the competitive position of the small or new firm is likely to be better in the production of local and other specialties, specifically promoted for specific needs; and (b) that their position is not as favorable generally in the production of the tractors and the heavy, complex machinery which constitute the heart of the "long lines" of the larger companies. The leverage provided by innovations is likely to be most effective outside the tractor and heavy-machinery categories, in part perhaps because of the greater range for independent ingenuity in design in local and other specialties. To this area of comparative advantage for smaller firms may be added that of small or simple implements, such as, for example, horse-drawn plows or ensilage cutters. In general, small firms can obtain distribution of these, as well as of local and other specialties, more effectively than they could in the case of tractors and heavy machinery.

The advantage of the larger, long-line companies in the tractor and heavy machinery sector does not, according to industry testimony, inhere primarily in differentiation of physical designs or in patent protection thereof, although there are exceptions to this rule. Long-line distribution plus product reputations are apparently the strategic factors. Patents and exclusiveness of design seem important primarily in the sector where small firms thrive through product innovation.

The situation with respect to the condition of entry appears in general parallel to that concerning intra-industry competition. That is, entry encounters no significant product-differentiation barriers in the case of simple implements, and in the case of local and other specialties the entrant is assisted sufficiently by the opportunities for innovation that he is not much hurt by the long-line advantages of the large established firms. In tractors and heavy implements, on the other hand, established product reputations plus the advantages of established long-line distributive systems place the entrant in a more difficult position. Here, the product differentiation barrier to entry must be considered great (though probably not as great as in some other industries), and the entrant would sustain a substantial net disadvantage were he to attempt establishment of a long-line, large-scale operation. In this respect, at least, the farm machinery industry is similar to the automobile industry.

(e) *The fountain pen industry* is of course relatively tiny — industry sales are generally under $150 million a year (including mechanical pencils), and in 1951 the net worth of shareholders' equities in the Big 3 of the industry, which together accounted for about 70 per cent of industry sales revenue, ranged only from 12.5 to 16 million dollars per firm. Nonetheless, product differentiation is extremely important in one of the two major sectors of industry.

The product of the industry (overlooking the relatively minor value-output of mechanical pencils) is primarily divisible into two sectors: (1) high-priced, "quality" pens, and (2) utility pens and ballpoints in the lower-priced category. In the latter class, there is in addition a wide range of qualities and prices. Generally only 3 firms — Parker, Eversharp, and Sheaffer — are able to obtain a significant volume in the "quality" field, although Waterman is nominally in this market. These 4 plus 10 or 15 others sell in the "middle-price" range of better utility pens and in the higher-priced ballpoints, whereas 20 or more small firms dominate the cheap pen market.[48]

In the "quality" pen field (which would currently find its lower price limit at around $10, retail) product differentiation is very important. Superficial evidence of this is found in advertising costs, with traceable advertising in ratio to sales in 1950 running at 5.7 per cent for Sheaffer, 4.7 per cent for Parker, and 8.4 per cent for Eversharp — advertising ratios in the highest range. The basis for strong brand attachments and for the 3-firm domination of the field are not in the main found, in industry opinion, in exclusiveness of design or in product patents protecting design. There are many "new feature" patents in existence, but there would be no great difficulty in designing another quality fountain pen without running into patent conflicts. Industry opinion is that production is clearly inferior to advertising and marketing, and that the brand name of a principal firm is likely to have a greater value than all its tangible assets. Why is this so?

The major consideration would appear to be that the quality fountain pen is bought either (a) very infrequently, for use by the buyer, so that product reputation is a major consideration; or (b) for use as a gift, in which case the buyer will generally be heavily concerned with the "prestige value" of the gift (with "conspicuous consumption in giving") and thus be disposed toward the brands which have developed prestige through long-term advertising policies. Consumer appraisals of the physical qualities of what they purchase is likely to be relatively unimportant in a market of this sort, and this of course places both small competitors and new entrants at a great disadvantage.

The effect of the system of product preferences thus established and

[48] For details on the product and price structure of the industry as of a somewhat earlier time, see *O.P.A., MPR 564, Doc. 40224,* 1944.

sustained would appear to be such as to make it very difficult if not impossible for either a new firm or a firm now supplying the lower-priced pen market to enter the "quality" field. Industry opinion characterizes the selling-cost disadvantage of either sort of entrant to the quality field as huge and probably prohibitive. "Successful freaks" have gained some market for a limited time period (see the Reynolds ballpoint) but even these have not established a real foothold in the quality market. It may be added that, in industry opinion, the markets and prices for lower-priced and "quality" fountain pens are substantially independent.

In the lower-priced field, pens are generally bought for use by the buyer and more frequently. Physical qualities are relatively more important, and brand reputations less so. The force of product differentiation in the lowest-priced pens (under $1.00 retail) seems negligible, as affecting either intra-industry competition or entry. This very-low-priced field has become increasingly that of the inexpensive ballpoint. In the medium-priced range, there is evidently some net advantage to the established brands of the top 4 or 5 firms, although the use of the high-quality ballpoint as a competitor to the medium-priced conventional fountain pen has tended to reduce this advantage. Some firms specializing in utility pens — e.g. Esterbrook — apparently have a net price advantage in this field. In the absence of any very conclusive data, we tentatively classify the product-differentiation barrier to entry in this field (as well as in the very-low-priced field) as slight rather than moderate, although this matter may deserve further study.

WORKS CITED

Publications of the United States Government

Bureau of the Census, *Census of Manufactures*, 1947.

Bureau of Mines, Information Circular 7646.

—— *Minerals Yearbook*, 1946.

Congress, House of Representatives. *Hearings*, Subcommittee on Study of Monopoly Power, Committee on Judiciary, 81st Cong., 1st Sess., Serial No. 14, Part 2-B, 4-A, 4-B, 1947.

—— *Hearings* on H. R. 2357, Subcommittee No. 3, Committee on Judiciary, 79th Cong., 1st Sess., 1945. See also Serial No. 8.

Congress, Temporary National Economic Committee. *Hearings*, 76th Cong., 2nd Sess., pursuant to Public Resolution No. 113 (75th Cong.), 1940. Part 15 (Petroleum industry)

—— *Monograph* No. 13, "Relative Efficiency of Large, Medium-sized, and Small Business."

—— *Monograph* No. 27, "The Structure of Industry."

Federal Trade Commission. *Business Machine and Typewriter Manufacturing Corporations* (1941).

—— *The Copper Industry* (1947).

—— *Distribution Methods and Costs.*
    Part I. "Important Food Products." 1943.
    Part IV. "Petroleum products, Automobiles, Rubber Tires and Tubes, Electrical Household Appliances, and Agricultural Implements." 1944.
    Part V. "Advertising as a Factor in Distribution." 1944.

—— *The Divergence Between Plant and Company Concentration* (1947).

—— *Report on Growth and Concentration in the Flour Milling Industry* (1947).

—— *Report on the Manufacture and Distribution of Farm Implements* (1948).

Federal Trade Commission vs. Cement Institute, Respondent's Brief, Appendix A, Vol. I.

Office of Price Administration, *MPR 564, Doc. 40224*, 1944.

Office of Temporary Controls, *Office of Price Administration Economic Data Series*, Nos. 10, 21, 24 (1947).

Securities and Exchange Commission, *Survey of Listed Corporations*, 1936–1951.

Smaller War Plants Corporation, *Economic Concentration and World War II* (1946).

U. S. vs. American Can Co., 87 F. Supp. 18 (N.D. Cal. 1946); Civil Action No. 26345 H.

U. S. vs. Continental Can Co. (summarized, not reported; N.D. Cal. 1946); Civil Action No. 26346 R.

U. S. vs. United States Gypsum Co., 333 U.S. 364 (68 Sup. Ct. 525; 1948).

U. S. vs. United States Gypsum Co., Final Amended Decree, CCH Trade Cases 1950–51, par. 62578 (Commerce Clearing House, Trade Regulation Reports, No. 217, July 21, 1951).

Books and Articles

Bain, J. S., "Conditions of Entry and the Emergence of Monopoly," *Monopoly and Competition and Their Regulation*, edited by E. H. Chamberlin. (Papers and Proceedings of a Conference Held by the International Economic Association, London, 1954.)

—— *Economics of the Pacific Coast Petroleum Industry*, Part I (Berkeley, California, 1944).

—— "Relation of Profit Rate to Industry Concentration," *Quarterly Journal of Economics*, August 1951.

Burns, A. R., *The Decline of Competition* (New York, 1936).

Chamberlin, E. H., *Theory of Monopolistic Competition*, 1st edition (Cambridge, Mass., 1933).

Corey, Lewis, *Meat and Man* (New York, 1950).

Cox, Reavis, *Competition in the American Tobacco Industry, 1911–1933* (New York, 1933).

Florence, P. Sargent, *The Logic of Industrial Organisation* (London, 1933).

Hession, C. H., *Competition in the Metal Food Container Industry* (Brooklyn, 1948).

Hoadley, W. E., E. Baughman, and W. P. Mors, *A Financial and Economic Survey of the Meat Packing Industry* (Federal Reserve Bank of Chicago, 1946).

Kaplan, A. D. H., *Small Business: Its Place and Problems* (New York, 1948).

Markham, Jesse W., *Competition in the Rayon Industry* (Cambridge, 1952).

Robinson, E. A. G., *The Structure of Competitive Industry* (New York, 1932).

Steindl, J., *Small and Big Business — Economic Problems of the Size of Firms* (Oxford, 1945).

Stigler, George J., "Monopoly and Oligopoly by Merger," *American Economic Review*, May 1950.

Tennant, Richard B., *The American Cigarette Industry* (New Haven, 1950).

Wolbert, George S., Jr., *American Pipe Lines* (Norman, Okla., 1952).

Trade Journals and Other Periodicals

American Iron and Steel Institute, *Iron and Steel Works Directory for the United States and Canada,* recent annual issues.

American Meat Institute, *Reference Book on Meat,* 1950.

American Newspaper Publishers Association. Bureau of Advertising. *National Advertising in Newspapers,* 1950.

Business Week, Feb. 26, 1952, Dec. 20, 1952.

Consumer Reports, May, 1953.

Fortune, July, 1951.

Iron Age, *Official Steel Industry Capacities,* 1952.

Moody's Industrials, 1936–1952.

Publisher's Information Bureau. Reports on periodical, radio, and TV advertising. Various. 1950.

Red Book National Used Car Market Report (Oct. 1, 1952) *Region A.*

Unpublished Manuscripts and Doctoral Dissertations

Baum, Warren, "Workable Competition in the Tobacco Industry" (unpublished doctoral dissertation, Harvard University).

Conant, Michael, "Aspects of Monopoly and Price Policies in the Farm Machinery Industry" (unpublished doctoral dissertation, University of Chicago).

Heflebower, Richard B., unpublished mss. on rubber tire industry.

Hoffman, A. C., "Large Scale Organization in the Food Industries" (unpublished doctoral dissertation, Harvard University).

McKie, James W., "Bilateral Oligopoly in Industrial Product Markets" (unpublished doctoral dissertation, Harvard University).

Moore, Frederick T., "Industry Organization in Non-Ferrous Metals" (unpublished doctoral dissertation, University of California).

Smith, David K., "The Problem of a New Firm in an Oligopolistic Industry: Kaiser-Frazer's Experience in the Automobile Industry" (unpublished doctoral dissertation, Harvard University).

Vatter, H. G., "The Problem of Small Enterprise as Seen in Four Selected Industries" (unpublished doctoral dissertation, University of California, Berkeley).

Index

Absolute capital requirement effect: and entry, 156ff.; nature of, 55, 145

Absolute cost advantages: and public policy, 214ff.; cause of, 14; circumstances supporting, 15ff., 144ff.; definition of, 12; estimates concerning, 147ff.

Advertising: and public policy, 217; associated with product differentiation, 115; in individual industries, 263ff.; prediction of, 179ff.; related to condition of entry, 201ff.; related to efficiency, 203n; traceable, 121n

Allis-Chalmers, 193, 261, 314

Alpha Portland, 194

American Can, 193, 237, 257, 269ff.

American Distilling, 292

American Gypsum, 267

American Rolling Mill, 236

American Smelting & Refining, 193

American Tobacco, 192, 244, 290

Anaconda Copper, 193

Armour, 194

Assembly, automobile, 245ff.

Atlanta Gypsum, 267

Atomistic markets: behavior in, 30ff.; definition of, 26ff.

Automobile industry: absolute cost advantages in, 149, 150–151; advantages of large-scale sales promotion in, 137, 138; aggregate scale economies in, 140f.; assembly, 245ff.; capital requirements in, 158, 162, 165; characteristics of, 45; multiplant economies in, 86, 262; optimal plant size in, 72, 76, 244–247; over-all entry barriers in, 169, 170; passenger-car depreciation, 304; passenger-car specifications, 297f.; plant-scale curve in, 78, 244–247; predicted performance in, 179f.; product-differentiation barriers in, 129, 296–308; product differentiation in, 124, 296–308; profit rates in, 192, 195; sizes of firms in, 84

Avery, 261

Bain, J. S., 5n, 19n, 47n, 175n, 191n, 195n, 206n, 279n

Baldwin, 314

Barriers to entry. *See* Condition of entry

Baugham, E., 251

Baum, W., 243, 255

Beaver Board Co., 267

Bethlehem, 193, 236

Blair, J., 231n

Break-in losses, 117, 156

Brown-Forman, 292

Brown Shoe, 194

Brown-Williamson, 243

Bubble board, 266

Burns, A. R., 60n

Business machines. *See* Typewriter industry

Cal-Pak, 193, 310

Can-closing machinery, 271

Canned fruits and vegetables. *See* Canned goods industry

Canned goods industry: absolute cost advantages in, 149; advantages of large-scale sales promotion in, 137, 138; aggregate scale economies in, 140f.; capital requirements in, 159, 163, 165; characteristics of, 45; multiplant economies in, 86, 250; optimal plant size in, 72, 76, 230; over-all entry barriers in, 169, 170; plant-scale curve in, 78, 230; predicted performance in, 179f.; product-differentiation barriers in, 127, 310–311; product differentiation in, 123, 310–311; profit rates in, 193, 195; sizes of firms in, 84

Capital requirements, 55, 145, 158ff.; discussed, 55, 145; estimates of, 158ff.

Case, J. I., 193, 261, 314

Celanese, 194

Celotex, 267

Cement industry: absolute cost advantages in, 151; advantages of large-scale sales promotion in, 137, 138; aggregate scale economies in, 140f.; capital requirements in, 158, 164–165; characteristics of, 45; costs and size in, 254; excess capacity in, 190; multiplant economies in, 86, 253–254; optimal plant size in, 72, 76,

230–232; over-all entry barriers in, 169, 170; plant-scale curve in, 80, 230–232; predicted performance in, 180f.; product-differentiation barriers in, 127, 264; product differentiation in, 123, 264; profit rates in, 194, 195; questionnaire, 225f.; sizes of firms in, 84
Certainteed, 267
Chamberlin, E. H., 40, 64n, 114
Cheek, B., 49, 129n, 230
Chrysler, 192, 246, 296, 301, 304
Cigarette industry: absolute cost advantages in, 149; advantages of large-scale sales promotion in, 137, 138; aggregate scale economies in, 140f.; capital requirements in, 158, 163ff.; characteristics of, 45; multiplant economies in, 86, 255–256; optimal plant size in, 72, 243–244, over-all entry barriers in, 169, 170; plant-scale curve in, 80, 243–244; predicted performance in, 179f.; product-differentiation barriers in, 129, 286–290; product differentiation in, 124, 286–290; profit rates in, 192, 195; sizes of firms in, 84
Classification of industries: by importance of aggregate entry barriers, 169f.; by importance of economies of large scale, 140f.; by importance of firm economies, 86; by importance of plant economies, 81f.; by importance of product differentiation, 123f.; by importance of production economies, 90ff., 103ff.; by importance of sales-promotion economies, 137ff.; by plant sizes, 70, 73, 77; by predicted performance, 179f.; by size of capital requirements, 158f.; by size of product-differentiation barriers, 127ff.
Clayton Act, 219
Collective action: consequences of, 33ff.; definition of, 26ff.
Colorado Milling and Elevator, 256
Competitive level of prices: definition 6ff.
Colgate, 193, 282
Commander-Larabee, 229n, 257
Conant, M., 261n, 313n
Concentration of sellers: and public policy, 217f.; in 20 industries, 45; rationale of existing, 110ff.; related to profits, 197; theoretical importance of, 25ff.
Condition of entry: and workability of competition, 203ff.; definition of, 3, 4ff.; determinants of, 11ff.; effects of, 19ff.; effects of absolute cost barriers

on, 147ff.; effects of product differentiation on, 125ff.; effects of scale economies on, 93ff.; general, 9, 21ff.; immediate, 9; lags affecting, 11; related to profits, 198f.; stability of, 18; types of, 21ff., 25, 173ff.; usual treatment of, 1–3; value of, 20
Conjectures concerning entry, 97ff.
Continental Can, 193, 257, 269
Copper industry: absolute cost advantages in, 154; advantages of large-scale sales promotion in, 137, 138; aggregate scale economies in, 140f.; capital requirements in, 159, 162; characteristics of, 45; multiplant economies in, 86, 252; optimal plant size in, 72, 248–249; over-all entry barriers in, 169, 170; plant-scale curve in, 79, 248–249; predicted performance in, 179f.; product-differentiation barriers in, 127, 263–264; product differentiation in, 123, 263–264; profit rates in, 193, 195; sizes of firms in, 84
Corey, L., 268n
Cox, R., 243, 255
Crown Can, 237, 270f.
Crude oil. See Petroleum refining industry; Pipeline costs
Cudahy, 194

Dayton Tire, 259
Deere & Co., 193, 261, 314
Detergents, 282
Diseconomies of large scale, 20, 61f., 118, 135
Distilled liquor industry. See Liquor industry
Distributive integration. See Integration
Diversification, 215
Doyle, L., 49, 129n, 230

Easy entry, 3, 11ff., 21
Economies of large scale: aggregate, 140f.; and public policy, 211ff.; as a rationale for concentration, 110ff.; as barriers to entry, 13, 15ff.; conflicting views on, 59ff.; definition of, 53; effect of fluctuations on, 62ff.; effects on condition of entry, 93ff.; estimates for firms, 83ff.; estimates for plants, 71ff.; sales promotion, 63ff., 117ff., 133ff.; significance of, 13, 29, 35, 53ff.; theory concerning, 56ff., 93ff.
Efficiency: of firm sizes, 187ff.; of plant sizes, 110ff., 184ff.
Endicott-Johnson, 194

Entry: anticipation of, 4; blockaded, 22, 25, 173ff.; definition of, 5ff.; easy or free, 3, 11ff., 21; effectively impeded, 22, 25, 173ff.; effects of absolute cost barriers on, 147ff.; effects of product differentiation on, 125ff.; effects of scale economies on, 93ff.; ineffectively impeded, 22, 25, 173ff.; lags in, 11, 174

Entry, condition of. *See* Condition of entry

Esterbrook, 317

Eversharp, 316

Excess capacity, 189ff.

Farm machine industry: absolute cost advantages in, 149, 150; advantages of large-scale sales promotion in, 137, 138; aggregate scale economies in, 140f.; capital requirements in, 159, 162; characteristics of, 45; long-line distribution in, 261f.; multiplant economies in, 86, 259–262; optimal plant size in, 72, 76, 232–233; over-all entry barriers in, 169, 170; plant-scale curve in, 78, 232–233; predicted performance in, 179f.; product-differentiation barriers in, 127ff., 312–315; product differentiation in, 123, 312–315; profit rates in, 193, 194, 195; sizes of firms in, 84

Fetter, F., 60

Firestone, 194, 238, 258, 275

Firms, multiplant. *See* Multiplant firm economies

Fischer, E., 238

Florence, P. Sargent, 59n

Florsheim, 193, 312

Flour milling industry: absolute cost advantages in, 149; advantages of large-scale sales promotion in, 137, 138; aggregate scale economies in, 140f.; capital requirements in, 159, 163, 165; characteristics of, 45; excess capacity in, 190; multiplant economies in, 86, 256–257, 262; optimal plant size in, 72, 76, 228–229; over-all entry barriers in, 169, 170; plant-scale curve in, 79, 228–229; predicted performance in, 179f.; product-differentiation barriers in, 127f., 308–310; product differentiation in, 124, 315–317; profit rates in, 194, 195; sizes of firms in, 84

Ford, 246, 296, 298, 301, 304

Fountain-pen industry: absolute cost advantages in, 149; advantages of large-scale sales promotion in, 137,

138; aggregate scale economies in, 140f.; capital requirements in, 159, 162, 165; characteristics of, 45; multiplant economies in, 86, 252; optimal plant size in, 72, 76, 247–248; over-all entry barriers in, 169, 170; plant-scale curve in, 78, 247–248; predicted performance in, 180f.; product-differentiation barriers in, 127ff., 315–317; product differentiation in, 124, 315–317; profit rates in, 193, 194, 195; sizes of firms in, 84

Gasoline. *See* Petroleum refining industry

General condition of entry, 9

General Mills, 194, 229n, 256, 309

General Motors, 192, 246, 296, 299ff., 303, 304

General Shoe, 194

General Tire, 238, 259

Gerber, 310

Glenmore, 292

Goodrich, 194, 239, 258, 275

Goodyear, 194, 238, 258, 275

Green Giant, 310

Gypsum products industry: absolute cost advantages in, 152–153; advantages of large-scale sales promotion in, 137, 138; aggregate scale economies in, 140f.; capital requirements in, 159, 163, 165; characteristics of, 45; multiplant economies in, 86, 255; optimal plant size in, 72, 76, 240–241; over-all entry barriers in, 169, 170; plant-scale curve in, 79, 240–241; predicted performance in, 180f.; product-differentiation barriers in, 127, 266–268; product differentiation in, 123, 266–268; profit rates in, 193, 194, 195; sizes of firms in, 84

Heflebower, R., 49, 129n, 239n, 259, 273n, 275n

Heinz, 310

Hession, C., 129n, 237, 257, 269n, 270n, 271n, 272n

Hoadley, W., 251

Hoffman, A., 268n

Hudson, 296, 299f., 304

Hunt, 193, 310

Immediate condition of entry, 9

Independent action: consequences of, 30ff.; definition of, 26ff.

Industries: list of those studied, 45; seg-

mentation of, 74f.; theoretical definition of, 47n
Inefficient fringe, 185ff.
Inland Steel, 236
Integration: and absolute cost disadvantage, 145f., 149ff.; and public policy, 212ff.; and sales promotion, 115
International Business Machines, 285
International Harvester, 193, 261, 314
International Shoe, 194

Jones & Laughlin, 193, 236

Kaiser-Frazer, 296, 299, 302n, 304, 307
Kaplan, A., 231, 253n
Kelley Plasterboard, 267
Kennecott, 193
Knight, F. H., 60
Know-how, 148f.

L. A. Soap Co., 283
Lags in entry, 11, 174
Large scale: and sales promotion, 63ff., 117ff., 133ff.; diseconomies of, 20, 61f., 118, 135; economies of, 13, 15ff., 29, 35, 53ff., 71ff., 83ff., 140f., 211ff.
Lee Tire, 259
Lehigh Portland, 194
Lever Bros., 282
Libby, 193, 310
Liggett & Myers, 192
Liquor industry: absolute cost advantages in, 149–150; advantages of large-scale sales promotion in, 137, 138; aggregate scale economies in, 140f.; capital requirements in, 158, 164, 165; characteristics of, 45; multiplant economies in, 86, 257, 262; optimal plant size in, 72, 232; over-all entry barriers in, 169, 170; plant-scale curve in, 80, 232; predicted performance in, 179f.; product-differentiation barriers in, 129, 290–296; product differentiation in, 123, 290–296; profit rates in, 192, 195; sizes of firms, 84
Lone Star, 194
Long-line distribution, 261f.
Lorillard, 243

Management personnel, 148
Market structure: atomistic, 26, 30; instability of, 31; oligopolistic, 26, 33ff.
Markham, J., 155n, 241, 259n, 264n
Massey-Harris, 261
McKie, J., 240n
Meat packing industry: absolute cost advantages in, 149; advantages of large-scale sales promotion in, 137, 138; aggregate scale economies in, 140f.; capital requirements in, 158, 164; characteristics of, 45; multiplant economies in, 86, 251–252, 262; optimal plant size in, 72, 76; over-all entry barriers in, 169, 170; plant-scale curve in, 78; product-differentiation barriers in, 127, 268–269; product differentiation in, 123, 268–269; profit rates in, 194, 195; sizes of firms in, 84
Metal container industry: absolute cost advantages in, 151; advantages of large-scale sales promotion in, 137, 138; aggregate scale economies in, 140f.; capital requirements in, 159, 162–163, 165; characteristics of, 45; multiplant economies in, 86, 257–258; optimal plant size in, 72, 76, 237–238; over-all entry barriers in, 169, 170; plant-scale curve in, 79, 237–238; predicted performance in, 179f.; product-differentiation barriers in, 128, 269–273; product differentiation in, 123, 269–273; profit rates in, 193, 194, 195; sizes of firms in, 84
Milling. See Flour milling industry
Minneapolis-Moline, 261, 314
Moore, F., 49, 248n, 263n
Mors, W., 251
Most favored firms, 8
Multiplant firm economies: and efficiency, 110ff.; estimates concerning, 83ff.; in sales promotion, 133ff.; theory concerning, 57ff.

Nash, 246, 296, 299f., 304
National Can, 271
National Gypsum, 193, 267
National Steel, 236
New Idea, 314
Niagara Gypsum, 267
North American Rayon, 194
Nunn-Bush, 193, 312

Oligopolistic markets: behavior in, 33ff., 93ff.; definition of, 26
Oliver, 261, 314
Optimal scales: definition of, 54; estimates of actual, 71ff., 86; extent to which attained, 110ff., 184ff., 187ff.; revisions of estimates of, 133ff., 140f., 146
Organization of study, 43

Pacific Can, 271

Packard, 296, 300, 304

Park & Tilford, 292

Parker, 193, 316

Passenger cars: new-car depreciation, 304; specifications, 297f.

Patents, 144, 148f., 151, 152, 266ff.

Penn Dixie, 194

Percentage effect, 55

Petroleum refining industry: absolute cost advantages in, 152; advantages of large-scale sales promotion in, 137, 138; aggregate scale economies in, 140f.; capital requirements in, 158, 162, 165; characteristics of, 45; multiplant economies in, 86, 251; optimal plant size in, 72, 76, 233–235; over-all entry barriers in, 169, 170; plant-scale curve in, 80, 233–235; predicted performance in, 179f.; product-differentiation barriers in, 128, 279–281; product differentiation in, 124, 279–281; profit rates in, 194, 195; refinery capacities, 235; sizes of firms in, 84

Phares, 259

Phelps-Dodge, 193

Philip Morris, 192, 243, 290

Pillsbury, 194, 229n, 256, 309

Pipeline costs, 234n

Plant economies: and efficiency, 110ff.; and sales promotion, 134; Census data concerning, 68ff.; estimates concerning, 71ff.; theory concerning, 56ff.

Plant sizes: Census data on, 68ff.; efficiency of, 110ff.; estimates of optimal, 71ff.; in individual industries, 227ff.

Price-to-minimal-cost gap, 20ff.

Procter & Gamble, 193, 282

Product differentiation: classification of industries according to, 123f.; consequences of, 114ff.; sources of, 114, 123f.

Product-differentiation advantages: and public policy, 216ff.; and scale economies, 117ff.; cause of, 14; character of, 116f.; circumstances supporting, 16; definition of, 12; estimates concerning, 125ff.; relative importance, 142ff.

Profits: of individual firms, 192f.; of industries, 195; predictions concerning, 175ff., 190ff.; related to concentration, 197; related to condition of entry, 198ff.

Publicker, 292

Public policy: existing, 218ff.; proposals, 206ff.

Questionnaires: description of, 49ff.; examples of, 223ff.

Rayon industry: absolute cost advantages in, 155; advantages of large-scale sales promotion in, 137, 138; aggregate scale economies in, 140f.; capital requirements in, 158, 162, 165; characteristics of, 45; multiplant economies in, 86, 259, 262; optimal plant size in, 72, 241–243; over-all entry barriers in, 169, 170; plant-scale curve in, 80, 241–242; plants in, 242; predicted performance in, 180f.; product-differentiation barriers in, 127, 264–265; product differentiation in, 123, 264–265; profit rates in, 194, 195; size of firms in, 84

Recognized interdependence, 4

Reduction of entry barriers, 208ff.

Refiners, 235

Remington-Rand, 192, 249, 285

Republic, 193, 236

Resource control, 145, 148, 151ff.

Reynolds Pen, 317

Reynolds Tobacco, 192

Robinson, E. A. G., 59n

Robinson-Patman Act, 148, 251

Royal Typewriter, 192, 249, 285

Rubber tires. See Tire and tube industry

Sales promotion: and product differentiation, 115; diseconomies of large scale in, 118; effect on distributional economies, 141n; large-scale economies in, 63ff., 117ff.

Sample of industries, 44ff.

Scale curves: and sales promotion, 139, 140f.; classification of, 100f., 103ff.; data concerning shape of, 78ff., 83ff.; theory concerning shape of, 58ff.

Scale of plant and firm. See Economies of large scale; Multiplant firm economies; Plant economies; Plant sizes; Scale curves

Schenley, 192, 292

Seagrams, 192, 292, 294

Segmentation of markets, 74f.

Seiberling, 259

Seller concentration. See Concentration of sellers

Selling costs. See Advertising; Integration

Sheaffer, 193, 316

Sherman Act, 205ff., 218ff.

Shoe industry: absolute cost advantages in, 149; advantages of large-scale sales promotion in, 137, 138; aggregate scale economies in, 140f.; capital requirements in, 159, 164, 165; characteristics of, 45; excess capacity in, 190; multiplant economies in, 86, 253; optimal plant size in, 72, 76, 230; over-all entry barriers in, 169, 170; plant-scale curve in, 78, 230; predicted performance in, 179f.; product-differentiation barriers in, 128, 311–312; product differentiation in, 123, 311–312; profit rates in, 193, 194, 195; sizes of firms in, 84

Simons, H., 60

Smith, D. K., 129n, 302

Smith, L. C., 192, 249, 285

Soap industry: absolute cost advantages in, 149; advantages of large-scale sales promotion in, 137, 138; aggregate scale economies in, 140f.; capital requirements in, 158, 164, 165; characteristics of, 45; multiplant economies in, 86, 255; optimal plant size in, 72, 243; over-all entry barriers in, 169, 170; plant-scale curve in, 80, 243; predicted performance in, 179f.; product-differentiation barriers in, 128, 281–285; product differentiation in, 124, 281–285; profit rates in, 193, 195; sizes of firms in, 84

Socony-Vacuum, 193

Standard Milling, 229n, 257

Standard Oil (Ind.), 193

Standard Oil (N. J.), 193

Standard Oil of California, 193

Stokely-Van Camp, 193

Steel industry: absolute cost advantages in, 153–154; advantages of large-scale sales promotion in, 137, 138; aggregate scale economies in, 140f.; capital requirements in, 158, 163, 165; characteristics of, 45; mills, 236; multiplant economies in, 86, 254–255; optimal plant size in, 72, 76, 236–237; over-all entry barriers in, 169, 170; plant-scale curve in, 78, 236–237; predicted performance in, 179f.; product-differentiation barriers in, 127, 265–266; product differentiation in, 123, 265–266; profit rates in, 193, 195; sizes of firms in, 84

Steindl, J., 59n

Stigler, G., 60n

Studebaker, 246, 296, 299, 304

Swift, 194

Synthetic fibre industry. *See* Rayon industry

Tennant, R., 129n, 255, 286n, 289n, 290n

Tin cans. *See* Metal container industry

Tire and tube industry: absolute cost advantages in, 151–152; advantages of large-scale sales promotion in, 137, 138; aggregate scale economies in, 140f.; capital requirements in, 158, 164, 165; characteristics of, 45; multiplant economies in, 86, 258–259, 262; optimal plant size in, 72, 238–240; over-all entry barriers in, 169, 170; plant-scale curve in, 80, 238–240; product-differentiation barriers in, 128, 273–279; product differentiation in, 123, 273–279; profit rates in, 194, 195; questionnaire, 223ff.; sizes of firms in, 84

Traceable advertising costs: source, 121n

Tractor industry: absolute cost advantages in, 149; advantages of large-scale sales promotion in, 137, 138; aggregate scale economies in, 140f.; capital requirements in, 158, 162, 165; characteristics of, 45; multiplant economies in, 86, 259–262; optimal plant size in, 72, 249; over-all entry barriers in, 169, 170; plant-scale curve in, 78, 249; predicted performance in, 179f.; product-differentiation barriers in, 129, 312–315; product differentiation in, 123, 312–315; profit rates in, 193, 194, 195; sizes of firms in, 84

Typewriter industry: absolute cost advantages in, 149; advantages of large-scale sales promotion in, 137, 138; aggregate scale economies in, 140f.; capital requirements in, 159, 162; characteristics of, 45; multiplant economies in, 86, 252; optimal plant size in, 72, 249; over-all entry barriers in, 169, 170; plant-scale curve in, 78, 249; predicted performance in, 179f.; product-differentiation barriers in, 129, 285–286; product differentiation in, 123, 285–286; profit rates in, 192, 195; sizes of firms in, 84

Underwood, 192, 249, 285

Universal Gypsum, 267

U. S. Gypsum, 153, 193, 266f.

U. S. Rubber, 194, 239, 258, 275

U. S. Steel, 193, 236

Vatter, H., 229n

Walker, Hiram, 192, 292, 294

Wallboard. *See* Gypsum products industry

Waterman, 316

Whiskey, 290ff. *See also* Liquor industry
Willys, 296, 299
Wilson, 194

Wolbert, G., 234n

Youngstown, 236

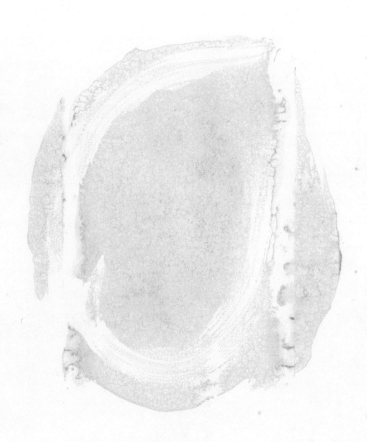